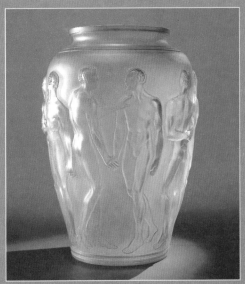
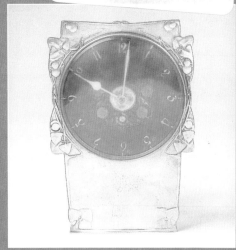

art nouveau
& art deco

art nouveau
& art deco

ERIC KNOWLES CONSULTANT

MILLER'S ART NOUVEAU & ART DECO BUYER'S GUIDE

Compiled and designed by
Miller's Publications Ltd
The Cellars, High Street
Tenterden, Kent TN30 6BN
Tel: 01580 766411
Fax: 01580 766100

Contributing Editor: Eric Knowles
Project Editor: Jo Wood
Editorial Assistants: Caroline Bugeja, Rosemary Cooke,
Carol Gillings, Lalage Johnstone, Carol Woodcock
Production Assistants: Elaine Burrell, Gillian Charles
Advertising Executive: Jill Jackson
Advertising Assistants: Jo Hill, Melinda Williams
Index compiled by: DD Editorial Services, Beccles
Design: Philip Hannath, Kari Reeves
Additional photography: Ian Booth, Robin Saker

First published in Great Britain in 1995.
This edition published in 2001 by
Miller's, a division of Mitchell Beazley,
imprints of Octopus Publishing Group Ltd,
2–4 Heron Quays, London E14 4JP

©1995, 2001 Octopus Publishing Group Ltd
Reprinted 2002

A CIP catalogue record for this book is
available from the British Library

ISBN 1-84000-375-8

Whilst every care has been exercised
in the compilation of this guide,
neither the authors, editors nor publishers accept any
liability for any financial or other loss incurred
by reliance placed on the information contained in
Miller's Art Nouveau & Art Deco Buyer's Guide.
Some images have appeared in previous editions of
Miller's Antiques Price Guide.

Bromide output by Perfect Image, Hurst Green, East Sussex
Illustrations by G. H. Graphics, St. Leonard's-on-Sea, East Sussex
Colour origination by Scantrans, Singapore
Printed and bound by Toppan Printing Co (HK) Ltd, China
Film output CK Litho, Whitstable, Kent

Miller's is a registered trademark of
Octopus Publishing Group Ltd

ACKNOWLEDGEMENTS

Miller's Publications would like to acknowledge the great assistance given by our consultants:

GENERAL INTRODUCTION

Eric Knowles, our Contributing Editor, is a director of Bonhams & Brooks, a major London auction house. A leading authority on 19th and 20th Century Decorative Arts, he appears regularly on the BBC's *Antiques Roadshow* and is the resident antiques expert on *Crimewatch UK* and on BBC Radio 2's *Jimmy Young Show*. He has also contributed to a number of publications including *Miller's Understanding Antiques, Victoriana to Art Deco,* and *Miller's Checklists, Victorian, Art Nouveau* and *Art Deco.*
Bonhams & Brooks, Montpelier Street, London SW7 1HH

BRONZE & IVORY FIGURES

Audrey Sternshine began dealing in antiquarian books in 1973, concentrating on Victorian children's books and art reference. She runs a large gallery in Manchester with a comprehensive stock of Decorative Arts items, with special emphasis on Art Nouveau and Art Deco sculpture. She has appeared in antiques programmes on television, contributed many articles on bronze and ivory for various publications, including *The British Art and Antiques Yearbook,* and has been a consultant on Decorative Arts for other Miller's Publications titles.
AS Antique Galleries, 26 Broad Street, Pendleton, Salford, Manchester M6 5BY

DECORATIVE GLASS

Joy McCall, after graduating with a Masters in British Art History and Critical Theory from the University of Sussex, began employment with Bonhams auctioneers in 1996. Within six months she joined the Decorative Arts Department, where she remains, specializing primarily in applied arts from 1860–1950, with a particular emphasis on Art Nouveau and Art Deco.
Bonhams & Brooks, 65–69 Lots Road, Chelsea, London SW10 0RN

Patrick and Susan Gould started collecting glass in the early 1970s. By 1973 their passion for collecting focused on Studio Ceramics and Art Nouveau and Art Deco glass, and they opened their first stall in the Portobello Road arcades. When Gray's Mews opened in 1978 they moved their shop there where they remained until the late 1990s.

DOULTON

Mark Oliver started his career at Phillips (London) in 1981. After working in the saleroom he became a Doulton specialist in 1989. Mark has lectured on Doulton in the US and has contributed several articles for collector's club magazines. In 1991 and 1992 he was responsible for two very successful Doulton exhibitions and auctions at Phillips in New York.
Phillips, 101 New Bond Street, London W1S 1SR

FURNITURE

Chris Parker started his career as a general valuer with Sotheby's, before progressing into their 20th Century Decorative Arts Department predominantly specializing in objects from the British Arts and Crafts Movement onwards.
Sotheby's, 34–35 New Bond Street, London W1A 2AA

Fiona Baker graduated from Cambridge and joined Phillips Art Nouveau and Decorative Arts Department in 1979 cataloguing a wide field of late 19th and 20th century objects, concentrating latterly on furniture and furnishings. She is currently a freelance valuer and writer, co-authoring *Twentieth Century Furniture* with her husband Keith.

JEWELLERY, SILVER & METALWARE

Cathy Turner has been a passionate collector since her student days and has had an antiques centre in Stamford, Lincolnshire since 1990. She opened a specialist shop in Camden Passage, London in 1997.
Art Nouveau Originals, 4/5 Pierrepoint Row Arcade, Camden Passage, London N1 8EF

Keith Baker is an independent consultant, valuer and dealer, concentrating on all aspects of late 19th and 20th century Decorative Arts. He is currently a consultant for auctioneers Dreweatt Neate in Newbury, having headed the Art Nouveau and Decorative Arts Department at Phillips in London for 23 years. He is a regular member of the BBC's *Antiques Roadshow*, contributing to their books, *How to Spot a Fake* and *A-Z of Twentieth Century Antiques* and, with his wife Fiona, has co-authored *Twentieth Century Furniture*.
e-mail: krbaker47@yahoo.co.uk

LOUIS COMFORT TIFFANY & TIFFANY STUDIOS

Marybeth McCaffrey is an associate of J. Alastair Duncan Ltd, in New York and has been with the firm for ten years. She has travelled extensively in the Far East and Europe to appraise collections of art, and has assisted in the research and preparation of fourteen books on the Decorative Arts, as well as numerous catalogues and exhibitions, both in the United States and Japan.
J. Alastair Duncan Ltd, 1435 Lexington Avenue, New York, NY 10128, USA

POTTERY & PORCELAIN

Mark Wilkinson joined Christie's South Kensington as a sales clerk in 1978.
Since then he has worked in a variety of collectors departments including Motoring Art, Toys and Dolls. In 1989, Mark took over the 20th Century Decorative Arts Department and is credited with the expansion of specialist sales in this field. Christie's South Kensington now hosts more 20th Century Decorative Arts sales than any other auction house. He has initiated many specialist sale categories at Christie's South Kensington, including Clarice Cliff, Moorcroft, 20th Century Bronzes and Sculpture, Modern Design and Studio Pottery.
Christie's South Kensington, 85 Old Brompton Road, London SW7 3LD

INDEX TO ADVERTISERS

CONTENTS

KEY TO ILLUSTRATIONS

Each illustration and descriptive caption is accompanied by a letter code. By referring to the following list of contributors, auctioneers (denoted by *) and dealers (•), the source of any item may be immediately determined. In no way does this constitute or imply a contract or binding offer on the part of any of our contributors to supply or sell the goods illustrated, or similar articles, at the prices stated. Advertisers are denoted by †.

A   *   Aldridges, Newark House, Cheltenham Street, Bath, Somerset BA2 3EX Tel: 01225 462830

AA   No longer trading

AAA   No longer trading

ABS   •   Abstract, 58–60 Kensington Church Street, London W8 4DB Tel: 020 7376 2652

ADC   •   Art Deco Ceramics, The Stratford Antique Centre, Ely Street, Stratford-upon-Avon, Warwickshire CV37 6LN Tel: 01789 297496/299524

AG   *   Anderson & Garland (Auctioneers), Marlborough House, Marlborough Crescent, Newcastle-upon-Tyne NE1 4EE Tel: 0191 232 6278

AGr   *   Andrew Grant, St Mark's House, St Mark's Close, Worcester WR5 3DJ Tel: 01905 357547

AH   *   Andrew Hartley, Victoria Hall Salerooms, Little Lane, Ilkley, Yorkshire LS29 8EA Tel: 01943 816363

AJ   No longer trading

AOS   No longer trading

APO   •   Apollo Antiques Ltd, The Saltisford, Birmingham Road, Warwick CV34 4TD Tel: 01926 494746

ARE   •   Arenski, 185 Westbourne Grove, London W11 2SB Tel: 020 7727 8599

ARF   •   Art Furniture, 158 Camden Street, London NW1 9PA Tel: 020 7267 4324

ASA   † • A. S. Antiques, 26 Broad Street, Pendleton, Salford, Greater Manchester M6 5BY Tel: 0161 737 5938

AW   No longer trading

BA   No longer trading

Bea   *   Bearnes, Avenue Road, Torquay, Devon TQ2 5TG Tel: 01803 296277

BEC   No longer trading

BEV   † • Beverley, 30 Church Street, Marylebone, London NW8 8EP Tel: 020 7262 1576

BKK   † • Bona Art Deco Store, The Hart Shopping Centre, Fleet, Hampshire GU13 8AZ Tel: 01252 616666

BLO   (See NCA)

Bon   *   Bonhams, Montpelier Street, Knightsbridge, London SW7 1HH Tel: 020 7393 3900

BRI   •   Britannia, Grays Antique Market, Stand 101, 58 Davies Street, London W1Y 1AR Tel: 020 7629 6772

BWe   *   Biddle & Webb Ltd, Ladywood, Middleway, Birmingham, West Midlands B16 0PP Tel: 0121 455 8042

C   † * Christies, 8 King Street St James's, London SW1Y 6QT Tel: 020 7839 9060

C(Am) *   Christie's Amsterdam, Cornelis Schuystraat 57, Amsterdam 107150 Tel: 00 31 20 57 55 255

CA   •   Crafers Antiques, The Hill, Wickham Market, Suffolk IP13 0QS Tel: 01728 747347

CAG   *   Canterbury Auction Galleries, 40 Station Road West, Canterbury, Kent CT2 8AN Tel: 01227 763337

CAR   •   Carlton Gallery, 60 Burnston Road, Hull, Humberside HU5 4JY Tel: 01482 443954

CDC   *   Capes Dunn & Co, The Auction Galleries, 38 Charles Street, Off Princess Street, Greater Manchester M1 7DB Tel: 0161 273 6060/1911

CEd   *   Christie's Scotland Ltd, 164–166 Bath St, Glasgow, Scotland G2 4TB Tel: 0141 332 8134

CG   *   Christie's (International) SA, 8 Place de la Taconnerie, Geneva, Switzerland 1204 Tel: 00 41 22 319 17 66

CH   *   Chancellors, R. Elliott, 32 High Street, Ascot, Berkshire SL5 7HG Tel: 01344 872588

CHa   No longer trading

CIR   No longer trading

CNY   *   Christies International Inc, 502 Park Avenue, (including Christie's East), New York NY 10022 USA Tel: 00 1 212 546 1000

CS   No longer trading

CSK   *   Christie's South Kensington Ltd, 85 Old Brompton Rd, London SW7 3LD Tel: 020 7581 7611

DEC   No longer trading

DID   •   Didier Antiques, 58–60 Kensington Church Street, London W8 4DB Tel: 020 7938 2537/07836 232634

DM   •   Diamond Mills & Co, 17 Hamilton Road, Felixstowe, Suffolk IP11 7BL Tel: 01394 282281

DN   *   Dreweatt Neate, Donnington Priory, Donnington, Newbury, Berkshire RG13 2JE Tel: 01635 553553

DSA   No longer trading

DSH   (See AH)

DWB   (See DN)

E   *   Ewbank, Burnt Common Auction Rooms, London Road, Send, Woking, Surrey GU23 7LN Tel: 01483 223101

EG   No longer trading

EH * Edgar Horn Fine Art Auctioneers, 46–50 South Street, Eastbourne, East Sussex BN21 4XB Tel: 01323 410419

F No longer trading

FA No longer trading

FHF * Frank H. Fellows & Sons, 19 Augusta Street, Hockley, Birmingham, West Midlands B18 6JA Tel: 0121 212 2131

G (See PSG)

GAK * G. A. Key, Aylsham Salerooms, 8 Market Place, Aylsham, Norfolk NR11 6EH Tel: 01263 733195

GC No longer trading

GCA • Gerald Clark, 1 High Street, Mill Hill Village, London NW7 1QY 7 Tel: 020 8906 0342

GIL * Gildings, 64 Roman Way, Market Harborough, Leics LE16 7PQ Tel: 01858 410414

GSP * Graves, Son & Pilcher, Hove Auction Rooms, Hove Street, Hove, East Sussex BN3 2GL Tel: 01273 735266

HAE No longer trading

HAM * Hamptons International, Baverstock House, 93 High Street, Godalming, Surrey GU7 1AL Tel: 01483 423567

HAR * William Hardie Ltd, 15a Blythswood Square, Glasgow, Scotland G2 4EW Tel: 0141 221 6780

HCH * The Cotswold Auction Company Ltd, The Coach House, Swan Yard, 9–13 Market Place, Cirencester, Glos GL7 2NH Tel: 01285 642420

HER No longer trading

HEW †• Muir Hewitt, Halifax Antiques Centre, Queens Road, Gibbet Street, Halifax, Yorkshire HX1 4LR Tel: 01422 347377

HM No longer trading

HO/ HOD Clevedon Salerooms, Herbert Road, Clevedon, Somerset BS21 7ND Tel: 01275 876699

HOW • Howards Antiques, 10 Alexandra Road, Aberystwyth, Dyfed, Wales SY23 1LE Tel: 01970 624973

HP * Hobbs Parker, Romney House, Ashford Market, Elwick Road, Ashford, Kent TN23 1PG Tel: 01233 622222

HSS * Phillips, 20 The Square, Retford, Nottinghamshire DN22 6BX Tel: 01777 708633

IM * Ibbett Mosely, 125 High Street, Sevenoaks, Kent TN13 1UT Tel: 01732 452246/456731

IS • Ian Sharp Antiques, 23 Front Street, Tynemouth, Tyne & Wear NE30 4DX Tel: 0191 296 0656

JES • John Jesse, 160 Kensington Church Street, London W8 4BN Tel: 020 7229 0312

JG No longer trading

KNG No longer trading

Ksh No longer trading

JJIL (See JES)

L * Lawrence Fine Art Auctioneers, South Street, Crewkerne, Somerset TA18 8AB Tel: 01460 73041

L&E * BBG Locke & England, 18 Guy Street, Leamington Spa, Warks CV32 4RT Tel: 01926 889100

LAN * Bonhams & Langlois, Westaway Chambers, 39 Don Street, St Helier, Jersey JE2 4TR Tel: 01534 22441

LB • Linda Bee, Art Deco Stand L18–21, Grays Antique Market, 1–7 Davies Mews, London W1Y 1AR Tel: 020 7629 5921

LBP No longer trading

LE (See L&E)

LEX No longer trading

LF * Lambert & Foster, 102 High Street, Tenterden, Kent TN30 6HT Tel: 01580 763233

LRG * Lots Road Galleries, 71–73 Lots Road, Chelsea, London SW10 0RN Tel: 020 7351 7771

LT * Louis Taylor Auctioneers & Valuers, Britannia House, 10 Town Road, Hanley, Stoke-on-Trent, Staffordshire ST1 2QG Tel: 01782 214111

M * Morphets of Harrogate, 6 Albert St, Harrogate, Yorkshire HG1 1JL Tel: 01423 530030

McC * McCartneys, Ox Pasture, Overture Road, Ludlow, Shropshire SY8 4AA Tel: 01584 872251

MA No longer trading

MAT No longer trading

MGM * Bonhams West Country, Dowell Street, Honiton, Devon EX14 8LX Tel: 01404 41872

MJB * Michael J Bowman, 6 Haccombe House, Netherton, Newton Abbot, Devon TQ12 4SJ Tel: 01626 872890

MN No longer trading

MSh • Manfred Schotten, The Crypt Antiques, 109 High Street, Burford, Oxfordshire OX18 4RG Tel: 01993 822302

MSL No longer trading

MT No longer trading

N * Neales, 192–194 Mansfield Road, Nottingham NG1 3HU Tel: 0115 962 4141

NCA • New Century, 69 Kensington Church Street, London W8 4BG Tel: 020 7376 2810/020 7937 2410

OCA • The Old Cinema, 160 Chiswick High Road, London W4 1PR Tel: 020 8995 4166

OD • Offa's Dyke Antique Centre, 4 High St, Knighton, Powys, Wales LD7 1AT Tel: 01547 528635/528940

OL * Outhwaite & Litherland, Kingsway Galleries, Fontenoy Street, Liverpool, Merseyside L3 2BE Tel: 0151 236 6561

OO • Pieter Oosthuizen, Unit 4 Bourbon Hanby Antiques Centre, 151 Sydney Street, London SW3 6NT Tel: 020 7460 3078

OT No longer trading
P †*Phillips, Blenstock House, 101 New Bond Street, London W1Y 0AS Tel: 020 7629 6602/7468 8233
P(CW)* Phillips, Baffins Hall, Baffins Lane, Chichester, West Sussex PO19 1UA Tel: 01243 787548
P(M)* Phillips, 114 Washway Road, Sale, Greater Manchester M33 7RF Tel: 0161 962 9237
P(Re) (See P(M))
P(S)* Phillips (Scotland), The Beacon, 176 St Vincent Street, Glasgow, Scotland G2 5SG Tel: 0141 223 8866
PAR • Park House Antiques, Park Street, Stow-on-the-Wold, Gloucestershire GL54 1AQ Tel: 01451 830159
PB * Phillips, 39 Park End Street, Oxford OX1 1JD Tel: 01865 723524
PBJ * Phillips, 1 Old King Street, Bath, Somerset BA1 2JT Tel: 01225 310609
PC Private collection
PCh * Peter Cheney, Western Road Auction Rooms, Western Rd, Littlehampton, West Sussex BN17 5NP Tel: 01903 722264/713418
Pea * Phillips of Winchester, The Red House, Hyde Street, Winchester, Hampshire SO23 7DX Tel: 01962 862515
PGA • Paul Gibbs Antiques, 25 Castle Street, Conwy, Gwynedd, Wales LL32 8AY Tel: 01492 593429
Ph • Robert Phelps Ltd, 133–135 St Margaret's Road, East Twickenham, Middlesex TW1 1RG Tel: 020 8892 1778/7129
POW† •Sylvia Powell Decorative Arts, 18 The Mall, Camden Passage, London N1 0PD Tel: 020 7354 2977
PSG • Patrick & Susan Gould, Stand L17 Gray's Mews Antique Market, Davies Mews, Davies St, London W1Y 1AR Tel: 020 8993 5879
PWC* Phillips, 49 London Road, Sevenoaks, Kent TN13 1AR Tel: 01732 740310
RAG No longer trading
Re (See P(M))
RG * Gorringes Auction Galleries, 15 North Street, Lewes, East Sussex BN7 2PD Tel: 01273 472503
RIC † •Rich Designs, Unit 1, Grove Farm, Bromyard Road, Worcester WR2 5UG Tel: 01905 748214
RID * Riddetts of Bournemouth, 177 Holden Hurst Road, Bournemouth, Dorset BH8 8DQ Tel: 01202 555686
RO No longer trading
ROW No longer trading
RP • Robert Pugh Tel: 01225 314713
RUM • Rumours, 4 The Mall, Upper Street, Camden Passage, Islington, London N1 0PD Tel: 020 7704 6549/07836 277274/ 07831 103748
S(C) No longer trading

S(NY)* Sotheby's, 1334 York Avenue, New York NY 10021 USA Tel: 00 1 212 606 7000
S(S) * Sotheby's Sussex, Summers Place, Billingshurst, West Sussex RH14 9AD Tel: 01403 833500
SAI No longer trading
SBA No longer trading
SBe (See Bea)
SC No longer trading
SH No longer trading
SN No longer trading
ST No longer trading
STU No longer trading
SV • Sutton Valence Antiques, Unit 4 Haslemere, Parkwood Estate, Maidstone, Kent ME15 9NL Tel: 01622 675332
SWO* G. E. Sworder, incorporating Andrew Pickford, The Hertford Saleroom, 42 St Andrew Street, Hertford SG14 1JA Tel: 01992 583508/501421
TA No longer trading
THA No longer trading
TP † The Collector, Tom Power, 4 Queens Parade Close, Friern Barnet, London N11 3FY Tel: 020 8361 7787/020 8361 6111
TRU • The Trumpet, West End, Minchinhampton, Gloucestershire GL6 9JA Tel: 01453 883027
TVA • Teme Valley Antiques, 1 The Bull Ring, Ludlow, Shropshire SY8 1AD Tel: 01584 874686
TW * Thomas Watson & Son, Northumberland Street, Darlington, Co Durham DL3 7HJ Tel: 01325 462559/463485
VAS No longer trading
VH • Valerie Howard, 4 Campden Street, London W8 7EP Tel: 020 7792 9702
VIN No longer trading
W • Walter's, No 1 Mint Lane, Lincoln LN1 1UD Tel: 01522 525454
Wai • Peter Wain, Glynde Cottage, Longford, Market Drayton, Shropshire TF9 3PW Tel: 01630 638358
WHB* William H Brown, Ashford House, Saxmundham, Suffolk IP17 1AB Tel: 01728 603232
WHL* W. H. Lane & Son, Jubilee House, Queen Street, Penzance, Cornwall TR18 2DF Tel: 01736 361447
WIL * Peter Wilson, Victoria Gallery, Market Street, Nantwich, Cheshire CW5 5DG Tel: 01270 623878
Wor (See CAG)
WW * Woolley & Wallis, Salisbury Salerooms, 51-61 Castle Street, Salisbury, Wiltshire SP1 3SU Tel: 01722 424500
ZEI • Zeitgeist Antiques, 58 Kensington Church Street, London W8 4DB Tel: 020 7938 4817

INTRODUCTION

Before I began my career in the world of fine art and antique auctioneering, I was a regular visitor to my local junk shops and second-hand shops. What to buy was never a problem: the shops appeared crammed full, with new stock arriving almost daily – in fact, the biggest problem was what to leave behind after spending my budget. In later years some of the shops I had known took on a grander status by replacing the work 'junk' in their name with 'antique'. The stock itself remained much the same: a collection of Victoriana and pre-WWII items.

My personal interest at this time was focused on antique pottery and porcelain, which was starting to become more difficult to find. In contrast, pre-war pieces in the Art Deco style were relatively plentiful. Unfortunately, these items simply failed to excite me, and consequently I tended to ignore much of what I saw – until I decided to take a trip to my local museum in nearby Burnley.

Purely by chance my visit occurred at a time when the museum was hosting a travelling exhibition of Art Deco, organized by the Victoria and Albert Museum. This was definitely not the type of Art Deco ware I had become accustomed to seeing in the local shops: both the design and the quality of the craftsmanship were breathtaking. The exhibits featured were credited with the names of their makers and designers, many of which were unfamiliar and relatively exotic. It was here that I discovered the work of Maurice Marinot, Jean Despret, Ferdinand Preiss, Marcel Goupy and René Lalique.

That chance visit had a magical effect, and subsequently I was stimulated to achieve a better understanding not only of Art Deco, but of 20th-century decorative and applied arts in general.

My understanding and appreciation of Art Nouveau began many years prior to my exposure to the best of Art Deco. Once again, it was a nearby museum that was to play an important role in educating my untutored eye. However surprising it may sound, the town of Accrington in Lancashire can boast probably the finest public collection of Tiffany glass outside the United States. The collection was assembled, and eventually bequested, by Joseph Briggs – a local lad made good. Briggs had travelled to New York in the 1890s, whereupon he found employment with Tiffany Studios working initially in the mosaic department. Over almost 40 years, Briggs rose to a top management position and became one of Louis Comfort Tiffany's most valued employees. It was Briggs who, prior to Tiffany's death in 1936, was responsible for winding up the company's affairs at the founder's instigation.

The collection is housed in the Haworth Art Gallery and Museum in Accrington, and on my first visit I remember being totally spellbound by the strange, often fluid, shapes, complemented by mesmerising iridescent decoration. My schoolboy imagination concluded that I must be witnessing the achievements of a transatlantic sorcerer. At the time I first saw it, the collection was spread throughout the numerous rooms of the Edwardian mansion with most pieces being unceremoniously positioned upon mantel-shelves and sideboards, and readily available for hand-held inspection. Today the pieces are displayed behind toughened plate glass and protected by a regularly updated security system. The need to rethink the presentation was a response to the escalation in values, evident from prices paid for similar pieces in auction rooms in London and New York.

Since those early formative years, the demand for good examples of both Art Nouveau and Art Deco has continued to grow, and the prices paid today would have been considered unthinkable all those years ago. In recent years the market has proved to be just as fickle as those for the more traditional collecting areas. Japanese interest in French art glass, especially the work of Gallé, Daum and Lalique, resulted in prices spiralling throughout the late 1980s, only to end up 30 per cent and, in certain instances, 50 per cent down by as early as 1992. Today the market appears to be stabilizing, with Daum glass in particular gaining in demand from Japanese, European and North American buyers.

The popularity of the Art Nouveau/Art Deco market was further enhanced by the knowledge that both styles found favour among those within the world of music and show business. The sales of collections assembled by Elton John and Barbra Streisand both achieved record prices and worldwide attention of the type normally associated with the sale of Impressionist or Old Master paintings.

Since this Buyer's Guide was first published in 1995, the whole spectrum of the fine art and antiques trade has continued to embrace the benefits of the worldwide web. The growth of the internet auction has now added an extra dimension by offering a truly global marketplace. It will be interesting to monitor how such auctions fare in the ensuing years.

Today Art Nouveau and Art Deco are both well-established collecting fields that continue to attract new collectors eager for both historical information and a sound knowledge of prices and trends. *Miller's Art Nouveau & Art Deco Buyer's Guide* sets out to equip both the new and the established collector with reports on the state of the market, what to look out for when buying and warnings of possible pitfalls. With information provided by a team of highly respected specialists, this comprehensive guide combines expert and practical advice, making it an invaluable companion for anyone interested in Art Nouveau and Art Deco. **Eric Knowles**

FEATURED DESIGNERS & MANUFACTURERS

Aalto, Alvar (1898–1976) Finnish Modernist architect and furniture designer. Director of Finmar and founder of Artek (1931), furnishing companies.

Argy-Rousseau, Gabriel (1885–1953 French designer of pâte-de-cristal glass objects.

Artificers' Guild (1901–1942) London-based metalworking firm founded by Nelson Dawson.

Ashbee, Charles R. (1863–1942) English architect and designer associated with the Arts and Crafts movement. In 1888, founded the Guild of Handicraft in order to perpetuate the ideals of medieval craft guilds. Ashbee and Guild marks are stamped.

Barnsley, Sydney (1865–1926) and Ernest (1863–1926) Furniture designers and co-founders of the Bath Cabinet Makers Co. Ltd. Pieces unmarked.

Bauhaus (1919–1933) German design school. Founded by the architect Walter Gropius, it included architects, engineers, designers, sculptors and painters, who sought to relate form to function and aesthtic qualities to the demands of machine production.

Bayes, Gilbert (1872–1953) English sculptor working in a style that combined Art Nouveau and medieval influences.

Bevan Charles (active 1860s) English designer and manufacturer of furniture, specializing in Gothic-revival style.

Bouraine, Marcel (dates unknown) French sculptor, best known for his Amazon figures in bronze. Mark: 'M.M.A. Bouraine'.

Brandt, Edgar-William (1880–1960) French designer and metalworker, best known for his fine wrought iron work, sometimes burnished or painted a silver colour.

Brannam, Charles (1855–1937) English art potter. Pieces are often signed and dated.

Breuer, Marcel (1902–81) Hungarian-born architect and furniture designer; studied interior design at the Bauhaus. Used wood and tubular steel in his designs. Moved from England to the United States in 1937. Unmarked, but his designs for Thonet and DIM have makers' labels and PEL and Standard-Mobel catalogues note some of his steel chairs.

Bugatti, Carlo (1855–1940) Italian furniture designer and craftsman.

Carlton Ware (est. 1897) Brand name used by Wiltshaw & Robinson, a pottery founded in 1897 in Stoke-on-Trent. Marks: 'W&R/STOKE ON TRENT' forming a circle which encloses a swallow, topped by a crown; 'Carlton ware' hand painted over name and address of firm.

Cartier (est. 1897) Paris jewellers. Opened in London (1903), New York (1912).

Century Guild (est. c1882) English Arts and Crafts society of designers, artists, architects and metalworkers, founded by Arthur Mackmurdo to restore responsibility for the decorative crafts to the artist from the tradesman. Marks: on metalwork, hammered; on textiles, printed initials.

Cheuret, Albert (dates unknown) French sculptor, working in Art Nouveau and Art Deco styles, producing functional work, featuring naturalist motifs. Mark: ALBERT CHEURET, incise cast.

Chiparus, Demêtre (Dimitri) (dates unknown) Rumanian-born sculptor who worked in Paris in the 1920s.

Christofle, Orfevèrie (1829) Metalworkers, founded in Paris.

Cliff, Clarice (1899–1972) English potter, designer and decorator. Art director at Wilkinson's Royal Staffordshire Pottery and its subsidiary, Newport Pottery. Cliff also decorated wares designed by other artists. Mark: black printed pottery mark, name of design and facsimile signature.

Colinet, Jeanne Robert (dates unknown) French sculptor. Mark: 'J.R. Colinet'

Cooper, Susie (b1902) English potter. Designed for A. E. Gray & Co. (c.1925), especially bright geometrical forms. Formed her own company in 1932.

Cotswold School Association of English furniture designers, led by Ernest Gimson and the Barnsley brothers.

Couper, James & Sons (dates unknown) Scottish glassmaking firm best known for 'Clutha' glass.

Crane, Walter (1845–1915) English painter, graphic artist and designer associated with the Arts and Crafts movement. Designed pottery and tiles for Wedgwood, Minton, Pilkington and Maw & Co. Painted monogram. Designed textiles for Morris and Co.

Daum Frères (1875–present) Nancy glassworks founded by brothers, Auguste (1853–1909) and Antonin (1864–1930); made fine vases and lamps. Marks: relief cut, etched or painted.

Décorchement, François-Emile (1880–1971) French glassmaker, exponent of pâte-de-verre and pâte-de-cristal.

de Morgan, William (1839–1917) English ceramic designer connected with the Arts and Crafts Movement. Founded the William de Morgan Pottery (1872) and other works. Marks: impressed.

Doulton & Co. (1815–present) Lambeth-based producer of commercial and industrial stoneware and porcelain figures, including saltglazeware. Marks: printed, impressed or painted. Doulton Lambeth Potteries, their art department, were pottery manufacturers founded by Henry Doulton and John Sparkes, head of the Lambeth School of Art.

Dresser, Christopher (1834–1904) Scottish-born botanist, designer and writer. Most famous for silver and metalwork designs for various firms, including Elkington, Coalbrookdale and Benham and Froud. Marks: on glass – etched; on metalwork – stamped.

Dufrêne, Maurice (1876–1955) French designer of furniture, ceramics, metal, glass and carpets. Later work included Modernist designs using tubular steel. Had a shop in Galeries Lafayette.

Elkington & Co. (c1830–present) English silversmith founded by George Elkington, who, with his cousin Henry, patented their electroplating process in 1840. Marks: stamped.

Ellis, Harvey (1852–1904) English-born architect and designer associated with Gustav Stickley.

Elton, Sir Edmund (1846–1920) English baronet and self-taught potter. Produced art pottery on his Somerset estate, first as the name Elton Ware. Mark: painted.

Farhner, Theodor (1868–1928) German jeweller: mass-produced fine jewellery in an abstract Art Nouveau style.

Finmar (est. 1934/5) Finnish furniture manufacturers headed by Alvar Aalto, producing items in laminated wood. Unmarked, although the Decorative Arts Journal shows the full range of their wares, and pieces made by Aalto in Finland are marked 'Aalto Möbler, Svensk Kvalitet Sprodurt'.

Foley (later Shelley) (1892–1925) Staffordshire pottery and producer of decorative earthenwares and bone china.

Follot, Paul (1877–1941) French interior decorator and designer and early exponent of Art Deco. Pieces unmarked, but some have characteristic 'Follot rose'.

Fouquet, Georges (1862–1957) Innovative French jewelry designer. Jointed his father's Paris firm in 1891 and took over in 1895, on his father's retirement.

Gaillard, Eugène (active 1895–1911) French furniture designer and associate of the Paris School.

Galliard, Lucien (b1861) French jeweller and silversmith, famous for fine hand-made work in unusual materials.

Gallé, Emile (1846–1904) French designer and glassworker; considered the greatest of glass craftsmen. Marks: on glass – large variety of etched marks; on furniture – signature in marquetry.

Goldscheider, Marcel (1855-1953) Viennese ceramics manufacturer; mass-produced Art Nouveau vases and later Art Deco pieces.

Gropius, Walter (1883–1969) German architect, founder of the Bauhaus and director until 1928. Exponent of Modernism. His multi-combination modular furniture (1927) was highly influential.

Guild of Handicraft (1888–1908) British silverworking guild famous for exquisitve silverware.

Gurschner, Gustav (b1873) Bavarian sculptor and metalworker.

Hagenauer (established 1898) Austrian foundry based in Vienna, known for its face masks and figures inspired by Negro art.

Heal, Sir Ambrose (1872–1959) English cabinet-maker and director of family firm, Heal & Son. He used many woods in his designs and, eventually, steel and aluminium. Mark: stamped or labelled company name.

Hoffman, Josef (1870–1956) Architect, designer, founder member of the Vienna Secession.

Hunebelle, André (active 1920s) French glass artist inspired by Lalique. Mark: 'A Hunebelle', impressed.

Hunt & Roskill (est. 1843) Formerly Storr & Mortimer. Important silversmith headed by Storr's nephew, the silversmith, John Samuel Hunt.

Hutton, William & Sons (1800–1923) English producer of silver, pewter and Britannia metal.

Jensen, Georg (1866–1935) Danish silversmith specialising in high-quality silverware and jewellery. Mark: stamped.

Knox, Archibald (1864–1933) Manx metalwork designer, notably of Liberty's Cymric range.

La Faguays, Pierre (dates unknown) French sculptor.

Lalique René (1860–1945) French master jeweller and glass maker, famous for his scent bottles. The Lalique works also made glass screens, lamps, innovative car mascots, fountains and lights. Marks: 'R Lalique' during Lalique's lifetime, the 'R' being dropped after his death.

Larche, Raoul-François (1860–1912) French sculptor known for gilt-bronze female figures.

Legrain, Pierre (1889–1929) Leading French Art Deco furniture designer, often showing an African influence. Used expensive and unusual materials.

Legras (1864–present) French glassmaking firm; produced cameo wares and commercial glass similar to Daum and Müller Frères.

Léonard, Agathon (b1841) French ceramist and sculptor. Made Art Nouveau-style biscuit figures and gilt-bronze statuettes.

Liberty & Co. (1875–present) English retail firm established by Arthuyr Lasenby to sell fine British-made goods and Oriental art and fabrics, later expanding to include ceramics, metalwork and furniture.

Lorenzl, Josef (dates unknown) Austrian sculptor.

Mackintosh, Charles Rennie (1868–1928) Scottish architect, designer. Formed the 'Glasgow Four' with Margaret Mackintosh, Frances Macdonald and J.H. McNair.

Mackmurdo, Arthur Heygate (1851–1942) English architect and founder of the Century Guild. Marks: hammered initials.

Massier, Clement (1845–1917) French ceramicist and producer of earthenware with iridescent or lustre decoration.

Mies van der Rohe, Ludwig (1886–1969) German Modernist architect and an innovative and influential furniture designer. Vice-president of Deutscher Werkbund, 1926; 1930–33 director of the Bauhaus; 1937 moved to America. Pieces unmarked.

Minton & Co. (1793–present, from 1873, Mintons Ltd) Staffordshire pottery; produced earthenware, art pottery and porcelain. Marks: printed.

Moorcroft, William (1872–1945) Head of Art Pottery Department of MacIntyre & Co. Best known for Florian ware vases. Mark: signature or monogram.

Morris, William (1834–96) English poet, writer, socialist and designer. Founded Marshall, Faulkner and Co. in 1861 (became Morris and Co.) to execute his designs for furniture, textiles and wallpapers.

Moser, Koloman (1868–1918) Austrian artist and designer for furniture, ceramics and glass; founder member of the Vienna Secession and co-founder of the Wiener Werkstätte.

Müller Frères (active c1900–36) French glassmaking firm run by Henri and Désirée Müller. Marks: etched or relief cut.

Murrle Bennett & Co. (1884–present) Anglo-German mass-producer of jewelry. Marks: stamped.

Nancy School A group of artists and designers inspired by the work of Gallé and Majorelle in Nancy towards the end of the 19thC.

Navarre, Henri (1885–1970) French glass artist. His sculptural, textured vases and bowls were influenced by Marinot. Mark: 'Henri Navarre'.

Olbrich, Josef Maria (1867–1908) Architect, designer and founder member of the Vienna Secession.

Orrefors (est. 1898) Swedish glassworks. From 1915 produced decorative glasswares designed by Edvard Hald and Simon Gate, amongst others.

Pèche, Dagobert (1887–1923) Austrian artist and designer of ceramics and metalwork, and co-director of the Wiener Werkstätte.

Poole Pottery (est. 1873) Originally Carter, Stabler & Adams. Partnership formed 1921 at Poole, Dorset. Traded as Poole Pottery Ltd from 1963.

Powell, James & Sons (c.1830–1980) Innovative London glasshouse, influential in the late 19thC. Acquired Whitefriars Glassworks in 1883. Designers included Philip Webb and Joseph Leicester. Marks: stamped.

Preiss, Ferdinand (1882–1943) German sculptor. Opened foundry in 1906. Mark: 'F Preiss'; foundry mark 'PK'.

Prutscher, Otto (1880–1949) Designer for the Wiener Werkstätte of distinctive glass, jewellery and silver. Wares unsigned.

Pugin, Augustus Welby Northmore (1812–52) English furniture designer whose work epitomises the Gothic revival in Britain. Produced solid and utilitarian furniture, usually of oak.

Quezal (1901–25) American glassmaking firm inspired by Tiffany.

Riessner, Stellmacher and Kessel (R.S.K.) (est. 1892) Bohemian ceramics firm; main contribution to Art Nouveau was the 'Amphora' range.

Rietveld, Gerrit T. (1888–1964) Dutch architect and furniture designer. Joined the de Stijl, the Dutch artists' association, in 1919; the geometric forms, primary colours and revealed construction of his furniture epitomize the work of the group.

Rohlfs, Charles (1853–1936) American actor, stove maker and designer of furniture, particularly in oak. Mark: burned initials.

Rörstrand (est. 1726) Prominent Swedish pottery: producer of bold designs under the influence of French Art Nouveau.

Rosenthal, Philip (d1937) German potter and founder of the Rosenthal factory, producer of high-quality tablewares in the Art Nouveau style. Marks: printed.

Royal Dux (1860–mid 20thC) Bohemian ceramicists known for their classically-inspired figures.

Rozenburg (1883–1916) Pottery whose 'eggshell' porcelain is considered foremost Dutch contribution to Art Nouveau.

Ruhlmann, Jacques-Émille (1879–1933) French painter, master-cabinet-maker from 1925. Mark: branded signature.

Sabino, Marius Ernest (active 1920s and '30s) French glass architect inspired by Lalique. Mark: 'Sabino, France'.

Shelley Potteries (1872–1966) The name from 1925 of Foley, pottery firm established 1860 in Staffordshire, England.

Steuben Glass Works (1903–present) New York-based glassworks founded by Howkes family and Frederick Carder.

Stickley Brothers, L. and J.G. (1891–1910) George and Albert, brothers of Gustav, made oak furniture in a style popularized by Gustav, but of inferior quality.

Stickley, Gustav (1847–1942) American furniture designer; produced pieces with an Arts and Crafts feel, notably his range of 'Craftsman furniture'.

Stoor, Paul (active early 19thC) Most famous 19thC English silversmith. Best known for Neo-classical pieces in silver gilt.

Thompson, Robert 'Mouseman' (d1955) British cabinet maker who followed the principles of the Cotswold School. Work mainly in oak and largely undecorated. The figure of a mouse, usually in relief, but sometimes carved into a niche, became his trademark.

Thonet Brothers (Gebrüder Thonet, Thonet Frères) (est. 1853) Furniture manufacturers. Designed and manufactured bentwood furniture. Largely for export.

Tiffany & Co. (1837–present) American jeweller and retailer founded by Charles Louis Tiffany (1812–1902) and John B. Mill Young. Now established in Geneva, Paris, New York and London. Marks: stamped.

Tiffany, Louis Comfort (1848–1933) Founder of Louis C. Tiffany in the United States. Initially designed interiors but is now better known for glasswares, particularly lamps.

Toft, Albert (1862–1949) English sculptor of bronze figural pieces, mainly of ethereal, cloaked female subjects.

Van de Velde, Henri (1863–1957) Belgian architect and designer; worked with Samuel Bing and at Meissen.

Van Erp, Dirk (1860–1933/53) Dutch-born metalworker.

Vever (1821–1982) Leading French Art Nouveau retailer and jewellers.

Villeroy and Boch (1836–present) German producer of stoneware art pottery.

Voysey, Charles A (1847–1941) English architect. Designed interiors, wallpapers, textiles and furniture.

Wahliss, Ernst (1863–1930) Bohemian potter influenced by Michael Powolny.

Walton George (1867–1933) Scottish designer of interiors and furniture.

Walter Alméric (1859–1942) French Art Nouveau and Art Deco glass artist; worked primarily in pâte-de-verre.

Wiener Werkstätte (Vienna Workshops) (1903–32) Series of Austrian craft workshops founded by Koloman Moser and Josef Hoffmann, which sought to combine utility and aesthetic qualities in furniture, metalwork and building designs.

Wilkinson, A. J. Ltd. (est. 1896) English pottery company. Factories included Royal Staffordshire Pottery. Clarice Cliff was art director, although the company also produced the designs of other artists – for example, Vanessa Bell and Duncan Grant.

Wright, Frank Lloyd (1867–1959) American architect and designer, father of the Prairie School of architecture. Used pure forms, modern materials and modern techniques. Pieces are unsigned but usually well-documented.

Zach, Bruno (dates unknown) Austrian sculptor, best known for his erotic figures. Mark: 'Zach'.

Württembergischer Metallwarenfabrik (W.M.F.) (1880–present) Austrian metalwork foundry; produced decorative and domestic metalwork. Marks: stamped.

Zsolnay (est. 1862) Hungarian ceramics firm; helped the development of Art Nouveau in eastern Europe.

POTTERY & PORCELAIN

Over the last two decades there has been a positive surge in all categories of collecting, with new areas and specialist sales appearing every year. One of the biggest growth areas has been in Art Nouveau and Art Deco pottery and porcelain.

Many factors have contributed to this onslaught of change. For instance, no longer are ceramic collectables secretly hidden away in dusty cabinets, they are now being incorporated into the interior design of lounges and other rooms in the home. Collectors of Art Nouveau and Art Deco pottery and porcelain once had to hunt through antiques shops and auction sales packed with many other collecting fields to find what they were looking for. Today there are specialist fairs, shops and auctions which cater exclusively to Art Nouveau and Art Deco collectors. In fact, there is now an Art Deco fair somewhere in Britain every week and there are auctions entirely devoted to Clarice Cliff pottery, Moorcroft pottery, Carlton Ware and Studio pottery.

As a result, the auction houses have seen enormous changes in the last ten years. No longer are the London auction rooms the sole domain of dealers, the rich and the famous; rather, they are now viewed by a growing variety of people as a new and enjoyable way of purchasing art. Catalogues are now illustrated in colour, many have condition reports enabling clients to bid by telephone or in writing, rather than having to attend a sale personally. Once or twice a year collectors are now presented with a whole catalogue of Clarice Cliff ceramics, for instance, which one can choose to bid for.

Another reason for the dramatic growth in the popularity of pottery and porcelain is the rising number of publications that provide interested readers with valuable information and visual references. It can be difficult understanding pottery and porcelain if you cannot see the entire range produced – for instance, to an untrained eye a Clarice Cliff 5in (12.5cm) high conical sugar sifter (which can be worth as much as £5,000) hardly looks interesting when in a cabinet full of Doulton stoneware, but when seen reproduced in a book with twenty other sifters, all with different patterns to compare it to, its appeal can be appreciated.

Shrewd collectors now try to predict the next popular theme and stock-pile items in the hope there will be an exhibition or a book published on the subject which will help push up the price, as was recently experienced with Troika and Poole Pottery. It is generally at this point that auctioneers take an interest and in some cases organize a specialist sale.

Many of the new collecting fields now have special clubs with web sites (these were seldom found a few years ago) that publish newsletters and may arrange outings and conferences. The better known ones cater for collectors of Clarice Cliff, Carlton Ware, Shelley, Wade and Moorcroft.

Most Art Nouveau and Art Deco items collected in the UK are ceramic, unlike in France where they are glass (such as Lalique and Gallé). If you visit a British Art Nouveau and Art Deco fair, 70% of the items for sale will be ceramic and there always seems to be a 'newly discovered' factory to learn about. Some of the up and coming factories include Royal Winton, Troika, 1960s and 1970s Poole Pottery, Burleigh Ware and Rye Pottery.

Why are more people than ever investing in Art Nouveau and Art Deco ceramics? Perhaps this is a result of the currently low Building Society rates and the uncertainty of shares. When one considers how long a Building Society investment of £100 would take to double, one can appreciate why so many people are turning to alternative investments.

Examples of good buys can be identified in retrospect by looking through old auction catalogues. For instance, Clarice Cliff plates worth £600 today made £80 ten years ago. Not everything you buy will be a bargain, but if you do purchase an object you like you also have something to view an enjoy, and not just a bank statement or share certificate.

Most collectors find their bad buys more than compensated for by their good ones and as one learns more about a subject so the good buys increase. The secret is to amass as much information as possible about a chosen category, using books, exhibitions, booklets, websites and old auction catalogues, as well as visiting as many museums, collections, antique fairs and auctions as possible. Do not be afraid to talk to dealers or auctioneers about a particular field as it is in their interest to encourage new disciples to the fold. As this is one of the fastest changing and most exciting art markets, there is always something new to be learnt.

Finally, take the plunge and experience how infectious collecting can be once you start.

Mark Wilkinson

A Clarice Cliff Bizarre 'Crocus' pattern individual tea set, with 7 pieces, 1935.
£700–800   *GC*

A Newport Pottery Clarice Cliff plaque, painted and moulded with stylised flowers, 13in (33cm) diam.
£350–400   *Re*

A Clarice Cliff Bizarre 'Crocus' pattern vase.
£400–500   *HAR*

A Clarice Cliff 'Age of Jazz' two-sided plaque, modelled as 2 girls, one in an apple green ball gown, the other dressed in orange, dancing the tango with their respective escorts, facsimile signature 'Bizarre' and factory marks, 7in (17.5cm) high.
£12,000–13,500   *P*

A Clarice Cliff Bizarre shallow dish, with everted rim, 16½in (42cm) diam.
£300–350   *Bea*

A Clarice Cliff wall mask, printed marks, 7in (17.5cm) high.
£200–250   *CSK*

l. A Clarice Cliff breakfast set.
£250–300   *JAD*

A Clarice Cliff pottery tête-à-tête.
£500–600   *CDC*

Production Dates of Major Designs and Ranges

Design	
Original Bizarre	1928–30
Crocus	1928–39
Latona Range	1929–32
Inspiration	1929–32
Melon	1930–32
Trees and House	1930–32
Delecia Range	1930–33
Applique Range	1930–33
Autumn	1931–33
Summerhouse	1931–33
House and Bridge	1931–32
Gibraltar	1931–32
Chintz	1932–33
Secrets	1933–36
Coral Firs	1933–38
My Garden	1934–39
Rhodanthe	1934–38
Forest Glen	1935–37

A Clarice Cliff wall mask, printed marks, 7in (17.5cm) high.
£200–250   *CSK*

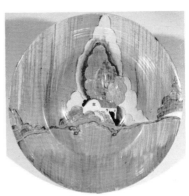

A Wilkinson Bizarre charger, by Clarice Cliff, with a dished centre, 18in (46cm) diam.
£2,500–3,000   *DSH*

A Clarice Cliff Bizarre Lotus jug, decorated in the Dahlia pattern, in black, green, pink, blue and yellow on a matt ground, rubber stamp mark, painted 'Latona', 12in (30.5cm) high.
£2,000–2,500 *CSK*

A Clarice Cliff Bizarre seven-piece cabaret set, with yellow and green geometric decoration on a cream ground, printed marks 'Bizarre by Clarice Cliff, Wilkinson Ltd, England', c1930.
£600–700 *C*

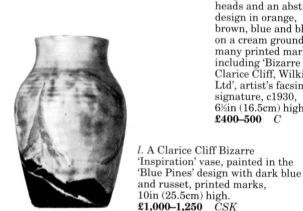

l. A Clarice Cliff Bizarre 'Inspiration' vase, painted in the 'Blue Pines' design with dark blue and russet, printed marks, 10in (25.5cm) high.
£1,000–1,250 *CSK*

A Clarice Cliff mug, designed by Laura Knight, with female heads and an abstract design in orange, brown, blue and black on a cream ground, many printed marks including 'Bizarre by Clarice Cliff, Wilkinson Ltd', artist's facsimile signature, c1930, 6½in (16.5cm) high.
£400–500 *C*

A Clarice Cliff Bizarre Lotus twin-handled vase, painted in orange, black rust-red and mauve, printed factory marks, 'Newport Pottery', 12in (30.5cm) high.
£800–1,000 *P*

A Clarice Cliff Bizarre Lotus vase, with a geometric band between wide yellow and iron-red bands, printed and impressed marks and 'Newport', late 1930s, 12in (30.5cm) high.
£1,000–1,200 *SS*

A Clarice Cliff Bizarre ewer and basin wash set, painted in strong bright colours, detailed with black, printed marks, ewer 10in (25.5cm) high, basin 15in (38cm) diam.
£3,500–4,250 *CSK*

A Clarice Cliff jar and cover, painted in blue, purple, yellow, pink, grey and black, with a vorticist pattern, black printed marks and facsimile signature, 1930s, 10in (25.5cm) high.
£3,000–3,750 *SS*

A Newport Pottery Clarice Cliff 'Applique' teapot and cover, 6in (15cm) high.
£2,500–3,000 *Re*

A Newport Pottery Clarice Cliff Bizarre 'Sunray' pattern confiture and cover of plain cylindrical form, printed mark in black, 3in (7.5cm) high.
£700–850 *HSS*

A Clarice Cliff breakfast set for one, painted in the 'Pansy Delecia' design with blue, pink and lilac flowerheads above a yellow, green and brown running glaze, printed marks, c1931, teapot 4½in (11.5cm) high.
£1,500–1,800 C

A Clarice Cliff tea-for-two set, painted with the 'Canterbury Bell' design, with a spray of orange flowers before green foliage with coloured rim borders, printed marks, c1930, teapot 4½in (11.5cm) high.
£1,000–1,200 C

A Clarice Cliff 'Sunshine' tea-for-two, painted with hollyhocks on a cream ground, yellow and russet borders, c1934, teapot 5in (12.5cm) high.
£600–700 C

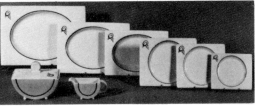

A Clarice Cliff 'Biarritz' 24-piece dinner service, decorated in 'Modern' design with black printed stylized scroll and painted silver borders, printed marks, 1932.
£1,000–1,200 C

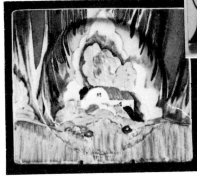

A 'Biarritz' plate, painted with a cottage in stylized garden and with tall trees before a streaked amber, grey and brown sky, printed marks, c1933, 9in (23cm) wide.
£500–600 C

A Bizarre 'Biarritz' pottery plate, by Clarice Cliff, painted in the 'Autumn' pattern, printed marks, 9in (23cm) wide.
£750–900 CSK

A Clarice Cliff Bizarre 'Biarritz' pottery plate, printed marks, 9in (23cm) wide.
£750–900 CSK

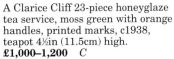

A Clarice Cliff 23-piece honeyglaze tea service, moss green with orange handles, printed marks, c1938, teapot 4½in (11.5cm) high.
£1,000–1,200 C

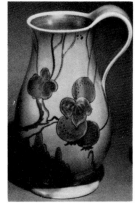

A Clarice Cliff oviform ewer, painted in the 'Oriental' design on a turquoise ground, printed marks, star crack, 11in (28cm) high.
£80–100 C

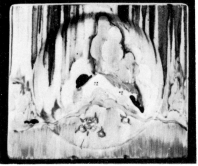

A 'Biarritz' plate, painted with a cottage in stylized garden before a streaked amber, grey and brown sky, printed marks, c1933, 9in (23cm) wide.
£500–600 C

'Biarritz' refers to the rectangular shaped design.

A Clarice Cliff coffee service for 6, painted with striped borders of yellow, russet and black, 1933, coffee pot 7½in (19cm) high.
£600–700 C

A Clarice Cliff Bizarre vase, Wilkinson's Shape No. 370, with hand-painted coloured design, 6in (15cm) high.
£600–750 *CDC*

A Newport Pottery Clarice Cliff Bizarre 'Patina' vase, 10in (25.5cm) high.
£1,000–1,200 *CDC*

A Clarice Cliff Bizarre vase, painted with orange fruit and purple, blue and green leaves between orange rim and foot borders, printed marks, moulded '370' 6in (15cm) high.
£2,000–2,500 *L*

A Clarice Cliff globular vase, painted with the 'Summerhouse' design, 6in (15cm) high.
£2,000–2,500 *Bea*

r. A Clarice Cliff Bizarre 'Fantasque' Lotus vase, painted with red, orange and yellow leaves in a coloured landscape, printed marks, 12in (30.5cm) high.
£4,000–5,000 *CSK*

l. A Clarice Cliff jam pot, decorated with pine trees.
£250–300 *BEV*

A Clarice Cliff 'Fantasque' coffee set, with the 'Orange Trees and House' pattern in orange, black and green, against a cream ground, printed factory marks and facsimile signature.
£2,000–2,500 *P*

A Clarice Cliff Bizarre one-person tea service, painted in green and black, with sponged green handles, comprising: teapot and cover, milk jug, sugar bowl, teacup and saucer, all with printed marks.
£250–300 *CSK*

l. A Clarice Cliff Lotus vase, painted in bright colours, with the 'Summerhouse' pattern, printed facsimile signature and 'Bizarre Newport' marks, 9½in (24cm) high.
£2,000–2,500 *P*

r. A Clarice Cliff Bizarre jug, hand-painted with 'Crocus' pattern, 3½in (9cm) high.
£100–120 *HM*

l. A Clarice Cliff Bizarre jug and bowl, hand-painted with 'Crocus' pattern, 3in (7.5cm) diam.
£250–300 *HM*

A Clarice Cliff Fantasque plate, painted in black, orange, yellow, red and green, stamped marks, 1931, 9in (23cm) diam.
£400–500 *C*

A Clarice Cliff Fantasque ginger jar and cover, painted with cottages, printed marks 1932, 8in (20.5cm) high.
£2,500–3,000 *C*

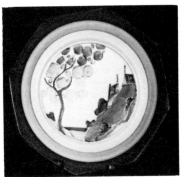

Four Clarice Cliff Fantasque octagonal plates, painted in the 'Secrets' pattern with cottages on a hillside, in a coastal landscape, printed marks, 1931.
£500–600 *C*

A Fantasque conical bowl, on 4 flange feet, painted in pure colours with 'Windbells' pattern, with stylized trees and harebells, printed marks, hair crack to rim, 1933, 9in (23cm) diam.
£600–700 *C*

A Clarice Cliff plate, painted with trees and flowerheads, printed marks, 9in (23cm) wide.
£300–350 *C*

A Clarice Cliff Bizarre Fantasque Viking Longboat centrepiece, painted with 'Gibraltar' pattern in pink, blue, green, yellow and purple, with separate flower holder, printed marks, 15½in (39.5cm) long.
£1,600–2,000 *CSK*

A Clarice Cliff coffee set, in orange, yellow, green brown and blue comprising: coffee pot, cream jug, sugar bowl and 6 cups and saucers, printed marks, 1936.
£1,000–1,200 *CSK*

A Clarice Cliff 'Sungleam' handled pitcher, decorated with yellow and orange 'Crocus' pattern, shape No. 634, 7in (17.5cm) high.
£300–350 *RIC*

A Clarice Cliff Bizarre Fantasque Lotus vase, painted in red, yellow, green and black, the neck painted orange, printed marks, 11½in (29.5cm) high.
£4,000–5000 *CSK*

Two Clarice Cliff 'Crayon' plates, painted in pastel colours, printed marks, 1934, 9½in (24cm) diam.
£200–250 *C*

A Clarice Cliff coffee service for 6, on a tray, painted in orange, yellow and brown, printed marks, chips to one saucer, 1935, teapot 7½in (19cm) high.
£1,000–1,200 *C*

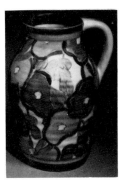

A Clarice Cliff Fantasque single handled Isis vase, painted with coloured foliage, printed marks, 1932, 9½in (24cm) high.
£1,000–1,200 *C*

A Clarice Cliff Lotus jug, with 'Alpine' pattern, c1932, 12in (30.5cm) high.
£3,000–3,500 *AOS*

A Clarice Cliff cylindrical vase, decorated in geometrical pattern, 6in (15cm) high.
£400–480 *RIC*

A Clarice Cliff 'Dover' shape jardinière, with 'Canterbury Bells' pattern, 8in (20.5cm) high.
£380–430 *RIC*

A Clarice Cliff ribbed vase, decorated in 'Poplar' pattern, 7in (17.5cm) high.
£1,000–1,200 *RIC*

A Clarice Cliff vase, decorated with 'Alpine' pattern, c1932, 7in (18cm) high.
£400–480 *AOS*

A Clarice Cliff Inspiration floral vase, decorated with flowers in typical underglaze shades of blue, pink and buff heightened in orange and green enamel, printed mark, c1931, 6in (15cm) high.
£1,500–1,800 *S(S)*

A Clarice Cliff 'Tulips' vase, No. 583, 5½in (14cm) high.
£500–600 *ADC*

A Clarice Cliff Bizarre jug, decorated in 'Cottage' pattern, 6½in (16.5cm) high.
£400–480 *PC*

A Clarice Cliff Fantasque two-handled vase, 11½in (29.5cm) high.
£2,000–2,400 *Bea*

A Clarice Cliff fish group, 10in (25.5cm) wide.
£300–350 *ADC*

l. A Clarice Cliff Lotus vase, Patina design, painted in green, brown, orange and yellow, against a random slip textured ground of pink and honey, printed title, facsimile signature, 'Newport' and 'Provisional Patent No. 23385', 10in (25.5cm) high.
£800–1,000 *P*

A Clarice Cliff pottery vase, 16½in (42cm) high.
£350–400 *Bea*

A Clarice Cliff posy bowl, 8in (20.5cm) diam.
£90–120 *BEV*

A Clarice Cliff part coffee service, painted in orange, grey and black enamels, one saucer missing.
£4,000–4,800 *Bea*

A Clarice Cliff Crocus pattern 22-piece matched part tea service. **£1,500–1,800** *SWO*

A Clarice Cliff Fantasque bowl, painted with orange, red, black, green and yellow, Farmhouse design, No. 441, printed 'F.B.F.S.N.P.' marks, c1930, 8in (20.5cm) diam.
£750–900 *MN*

A Clarice Cliff Bizarre muffineer set, decorated to a design by Dame Laura Knight, of stylized head and scroll motifs, painted in pink, brown, orange, turquoise and black, comprising: a salt and pepper shaker, and a mustard pot and cover, slight firing crack to salt, printed marks and facsimile signature.
£600–700 *CSK*

A Clarice Cliff Bizarre part dinner service, with 'Kew' pattern of a red-roofed pagoda in parkland scenery, comprising: 3 tureens and 2 covers, 3 sauceboats and stand, 6 grapefruit dishes and 8 stands, 5 meat dishes, 12 dinner plates, 8 dessert plates, and 7 small plates, some damage.
£1,000–1,200 *Bea*

A Clarice Cliff Bizarre sugar sifter, painted with trees and houses on a mottled brown ground, 5½in (14.5cm) high.
£600–720 *Bea*

r. A Clarice Cliff jam pot.
£200–250 *BEV*

A Clarice Cliff breakfast set,
decorated with 'Secrets' pattern.
£1,500–1,800 *JAD*

A Clarice Cliff vase,
shape No. 464,
8in (20.5cm) high.
£600–720 *JAD*

A Clarice Cliff Fantasque coffee service,
painted in 'Summerhouse' pattern in red,
yellow, green, black and blue,
comprising: a coffee pot and cover, milk
jug, sugar bowl and 6 cups and saucers,
minor chips stamped marks 'Fantasque
Bizarre by Clarice Cliff, Newport Pottery,
England', coffee pot 8in (20.5cm) high.
£2,000–2,400 *C*

A Clarice Cliff Bizarre tea service,
painted with concentric light and dark
brown rings on a cream ground, and a
'Crocus' pattern preserve jar and cover,
some damage.
£300–360 *Bea*

A Clarice Cliff Bizarre Latona vase,
boldly painted in blue with stylized
pink, purple, blue and green flowers
in panels, 12in (30.5cm) high.
£2,500–3,000 *OT*

A Clarice Cliff Bizarre pottery
coffee service, each piece boldly
painted in colours.
£600–720 *Bea*

A Clarice Cliff Fantasque vase,
7½in (19cm) high.
£1,500–1,800 *Bea*

A pair of Clarice Cliff bookends,
decorated with 'Crocus' pattern,
6⅓in (16cm) high.
£600–720 *Bea*

A Clarice Cliff Bizarre
Lotus jug, painted in
bright enamel colours,
11in (28.5cm) high.
£600–720 *Bea*

A Clarice Cliff Fantasque Lotus
jug, boldly painted in bright
enamel colours, 11⅓in (29cm) high.
£2,000–2,400 *Bea*

A Clarice Cliff Delecia jug.
£1,000–1,200 *HP*

l. A Clarice Cliff wall pocket,
in the form of 2 budgerigars,
painted in green, blue and yellow,
9in (23cm) high.
£150–200 *OT*

A Clarice Cliff Bizarre biscuit
barrel, boldly painted in yellow
and green against a blue and
orange ground, with a wicker
handle, 6½in (16.5cm) high.
£400–500 *OT*

A Clarice Cliff 'Blue Autumn' pattern coffee pot, with sinuous tree painted in blue, green and yellow above red grass, a cottage half hidden by purple trees on the reverse, printed 'Fantasque, Bizarre, Clarice Cliff', 7½in (19cm) high.
£400–480 *Bon*

A complete set of Clarice Cliff Midwinter limited edition reproductions, comprising: 6 conical sugar sifters in 'Pastel Autumn', 'Pastel Melon', 'Crocus', 'Rudyard', 'House and Bridge' and 'Red Roof Cottage' patterns, a 'Summerhouse' wall plaque, an Umbrellas and Rain conical bowl and a Honolulu baluster vase, all in original boxes, printed factory masks.
£2,500–3,000 *CSK*

r. A Newport Pottery Clarice Cliff Bizarre pattern bowl, decorated with geometric shapes in shades of blue, green and mauve enclosing 2 leafy branches, printed mark in black, 9½in (24cm) diam.
£300–360 *HSS*

l. A Clarice Cliff Bizarre vase, painted in Rhodanthe design, oviform on ribbed foot, printed marks, 8in (20.5cm) high.
£500–600 *Bon*

r. An Applique Bizarre baluster vase, in the 'Blue Lugano' pattern, painted in colours, printed and painted marks, 12in (30.5cm) high.
£8,000–9,000 *CSK*

l. A Clarice Cliff Isis vase, decorated in 'Limberlost' pattern, with red and white floral clusters with brown and green bushes nearby, under a canopy of red flowering trees, factory marks and facsimile signature to base, 10in (25.5cm) high.
£800–1,200 *P*

Three Clarice Cliff coasters, 'Delecia Pansy', 'Cabbage Flower', and 'Orange Roof Cottage' patterns, and 2 ashtrays in 'Rhodanthe' and 'Aurea' patterns, painted in colours, printed factory marks.
£350–400   *CSK*

A Clarice Cliff Bizarre 'Age of Jazz' figural group, modelled as a two-dimensional dancing couple, he in black tie and she in a bright green gown with red, yellow and black decoration, raised on a stepped rectangular base, factory marks and facsimile signature to base, 7in (17.5cm) high.
£8,000–9,500   *P*

'Age of Jazz' figures such as this dancing couple are much sought after. They have a two-dimensional effect but are, in fact, freestanding plaques.

A Clarice Cliff Applique Bizarre plate, Eden design, painted in colours with yellow, red and black banding, lithograph mark, 9in (23cm) diam.
£2,700–3,200   *CSK*

This pattern is previously unrecorded in the Applique range.

A Clarice Cliff Bizarre cat, depicted with a cheerful countenance, painted orange with black spots and sporting a green bow tie, printed factory mark and facsimile signature, 6in (15cm) high.
£500–600   *P*

A Clarice Cliff 'Geometric' pattern comport, painted with a central star motif supporting 4 segmented triangles, in blue, yellow, red, green and purple on a cream ground, printed marks, 7in (17.5cm) diam.
£250–300   *Bon*

A Clarice Cliff Lotus 'Geometric' pattern jug, the ribbed tapering cylindrical body painted with a band of orange, blue and yellow triangular motifs, between orange and green bands, gilt printed mark, 11½in (29cm) high.
£800–950   *Bon*

l. A Newport Pottery Clarice Cliff Bizarre Stamford shape part tea service, each piece painted with a small rectangular panel enclosing cottage with orange roof, yellow door and window among rolling hills with poplars beyond, on a cream ground within a wide green band, comprising: teapot and cover, tea plate, sugar basin, milk jug and conical tea cup with solid triangular handle, printed mark in black, inscribed '5954' in brown, damaged.
£500–600   *HSS*

A Clarice Cliff Lotus jug, decorated with 'Geometric' pattern with green, blue and orange triangular motifs, between orange and green bands, black printed factory mark, 11½in (29cm) high.
£800–950   *Bon*

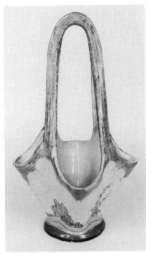

A Clarice Cliff basket, decorated with 'Fragrance' pattern, 13in (33cm) high.
£350–420 *AOS*

A Clarice Cliff cup and saucer, decorated in 'Football' pattern, c1929.
£400–500 *AOS*

A Clarice Cliff Melon bowl, 8in (20.5cm) diam.
£330–400 *AOS*

l. Two Clarice Daffodil shape Cliff grapefruit dishes, 6½in (17cm) wide.
£65–75 each *ADC*

A Clarice Cliff plate, decorated with 'Rudyard' pattern, 9in (23cm) diam.
£325–375 *RIC*

A Clarice Cliff 'Chloris' bowl, 9in (23cm) diam.
£125–150 *AOS*

A Clarice Cliff octagonal bowl, decorated with 'Woodland' pattern, 9in (23cm) diam.
£250–300 *ADC*

l. A Clarice Cliff plate, decorated in the 'Honolulu' p attern, painted in colours with green and black striped rim, printed factory marks, 9in (23cm) diam.
£425–500 *CSK*

r. A Clarice Cliff Bizarre plate, painted with 'Rudyard' pattern in pastel colours with striped rim, printed factory marks, 9in (23cm) diam.
£400–500 *CSK*

A Newport Pottery Clarice Cliff Bizarre globular shaped vase, decorated with 'Alton' pattern, impressed 'No. 370', 6in (15cm) diam.
£1,600–2,000　*L&E*

A Clarice Cliff Bizarre Café au Lait vase, the brown speckled ground decorated with 'Red Roofs' pattern, shape No. 358, printed marks, c1931, 8in (20.5cm) high.
£800–950　*S(S)*

A Clarice Cliff 'Umbrellas and Rain' vase, shape No. 342, 8in (20.5cm) high.
£1,250–1,500　*ADC*

A Newport Pottery Clarice Cliff Latona vase, the globular body with a graduated ringed neck, painted with blue, pink, green, yellow and black flowers above a yellow band, black printed factory mark, c1930, 8in (20.5cm) high.
£700–850　*S(S)*

A Clarice Cliff vase, shape No. 342, decorated with 'Flora' pattern, 7½in (19cm) high.
£1,000–1,200　*AOS*

A Clarice Cliff two-handled Lotus vase, painted with Geometric' with a band of shapes within rectangular panels, in purple, orange, brown and yellow between orange bands, black printed factory mark, c1930, 11in (28cm) high.
£800–950　*S(S)*

A Clarice Cliff 'Geometric' pattern vase, shape No. 355, 8in (20.5cm) high.
£750–900　*AOS*

A Newport Pottery Clarice Cliff Latona candlestick, painted with stylized blue, pink, green, yellow and black flowers, with a yellow band below, black printed factory mark, remains of paper label, c1930, 8in (20.5cm) high.
£300–360　*S(S)*

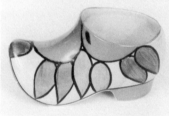

A Clarice Cliff sabot, decorated with 'Oranges' pattern, c1932.
£300–350　*AOS*

A Clarice Cliff Bizarre bowl, hand-painted with 'Crocus' pattern, 9in (23cm) diam.
£80–100　*ADC*

A pair of Clarice Cliff vases, decorated in the 'Oranges and Lemons' pattern on a white ground, shape No. 451, 8in (20.5cm) high.
£1,500–1,800   *P*

l. A Clarice Cliff Bizarre plate, painted with the 'Delecia Pansy' pattern, 9in (23cm) diam.
£300–360   *Bea*

A Clarice Cliff Bizarre single handled jug, painted with 'Lightning' pattern in black, blue and purple, red, orange and yellow, printed factory marks and facsimile signature to base, 10in (25.5cm) high.
£3,000–3,500   *P*

A Newport Pottery Clarice Cliff 'Berries' pattern part coffee service, painted with orange and red berries with blue and purple foliage, comprising: coffee pot and cover, 6 coffee mugs, 5 saucers, milk jug and sugar bowl, minor surface scratching, printed mark 'Fantasque', hand-painted, c1930, pot 6½in (16.5cm) high.
£3,000–3,500   *S(C)*

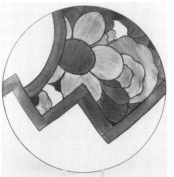

A Clarice Cliff Bizarre Fantasque part tea set, decorated in the 'Pastel Autumn' pattern, painted in colours, comprising: milk jug, 5 cups and 6 saucers, 6 tea plates, and a sandwich plate, slight damage, lithograph marks.
£1,700–2,000   *CSK*

l. A Latona Bizarre wall plaque, decorated in the 'Dahlia' pattern, printed and painted marks, 13in (33cm) diam.
£1,700–2,000   *CSK*

A Clarice Cliff Fantasque sandwich set, decorated in the 'Geometric Flowers' pattern, painted in colours, some damage, gilt rubber stamp marks, oblong plate 11½in (29cm) wide.
£1,700–2,000   *CSK*

A plate, designed by Ernest Proctor for Clarice Cliff, with a bride and groom on horseback, in pale green with silver lustre, 9in (23cm) diam.
£175–200   *BEV*

A Clarice Cliff Fantasque charger, decorated with 'Broth' pattern, with coloured star-like motifs on a bubble ground within an orange border, 17in (43cm) diam.
£1,500–1,800   *GSP*

A Clarice Cliff single-handled Isis jug, painted with the 'Forest Glen' pattern, in bright, warm enamel colours, 10in (25.5cm) high.
£1,500–1,800   *Bea*

l. A Clarice Cliff Fantasque sandwich plate, decorated in the seven-colour version of the 'Trees and House' pattern, in orange, yellow, blue, purple, green, rust and brown, minor wear, rubber stamp mark, 11½in (29cm) wide.
£450–500   *CSK*

l. A charger, decorated to a design by Sir Frank Brangwyn, printed and painted in colours with a procession of figures of various nationalities in a tropical garden, hand painted inscription, 17in (43cm) diam.
£1,600–2,000   *CSK*

This was adapted from the Empire panels originally intended for the Palace of Westminster, but was eventually erected within the now Brangwyn Halls, Swansea, South Wales.

A Clarice Cliff Bizarre Fantasque two-handled Lotus jug, decorated with 'Football' pattern, in shades orange, yellow, blue, purple, green and black, printed mark, 11½in (29cm) high.
£4,000–5,000   *HSS*

A pair of Clarice Cliff candlesticks, 3½in (9cm) high.
£250–300   *SAI*

A Fantasque Bizarre bonbon set, shape No. 471, decorated in the 'Windbells' pattern of blue foliate trees in a stylized garden, painted in green, orange, yellow and blue, comprising: oval dish with overhead handle and 6 triangular dishes, minor wear, lithograph mark.
£1,250–1,500   *CSK*

A Clarice Cliff cruet set, decorated in 'Orange Chintz' pattern, 3½in (9cm) high.
£200–220   *BEC*

A Clarice Cliff Bizarre jug and basin set, painted in bright red, green and blue stylized flowering plants, outlined in black and with yellow, blue and red banding, factory marks, 8in (20.5cm) high.
£1,250–1,500   *P*

A Clarice Cliff Bizarre single handled Lotus vase, decorated with 'Limberlost' pattern, printed marks, 12in (30.5cm) high.
£675–800   *CSK*

r. A Clarice Cliff Bizarre part tea service, with blue, orange and yellow flowers with green leaves, comprising a D-shaped teapot and cover, a cream jug and a sugar bowl, all with printed marks.
£1,000–1,200   *CSK*

A Clarice Cliff Original Bizarre jardinière, painted with a band of yellow and mauve diamond shapes outlined in green on a blue ground, printed marks, 9½in (24cm) high.
£550–650   *CSK*

A Clarice Cliff Bizarre Fantasque tea service, painted in 'Summerhouse' pattern in red, black and yellow, comprising: a teapot, milk jug, sugar caster, slop bowl, biscuit barrel, cake plate, 6 tea cups and saucers, 6 side plates, all with printed marks.
£3,300–4,000   *CSK*

A Clarice Cliff Bizarre Inspiration two-handled vase, painted in the 'Persian' pattern in turquoise, blue and pink, printed marks, 11⅛in (29cm) high.
£2,500–3,000   *CSK*

A Clarice Cliff Fantasque pottery jardinière, painted with the 'Melon' pattern, the lower body orange, 8in (20.5cm) diam.
£1,000–1,200   *P*

A Clarice Cliff Bizarre sgraffito vase, painted in black, royal blue, silver and pale blue, printed mark 'Newport', painted '5995 Sgraffito', 9in (23cm) high.
£450–500   *P*

A Clarice Cliff vase, decorated with 'Persian' pattern in reds, blues, green and brown disected by a central foliate band, signed 'Persian by Clarice Cliff Newport Pottery Burslem', 8in (20.5cm) high.
£300–360   *P*

A Clarice Cliff plate, by Graham
Sutherland, impressed mark,
1934, 9in (23cm) diam.
£125–150   *AOS*

A Clarice Cliff Athens shape
jug, with 'Sliced Fruit' pattern,
8in (20.5cm) high.
£425–500   *RIC*

A Clarice Cliff plate, with Laura
Knight design, from the Artists in
Industry range, 9in (23cm) diam.
£850–1,000   *RIC*

A Clarice Cliff jug, in 'Gibraltar'
pattern, 4in (10cm) high.
£500–550   *ADC*

A Newport Pottery Clarice Cliff
Bizarre Inspiration 'Persian' pattern
charger, decorated with a quatrefoil
flowerhead within a border of scrolls
in mottled blue, green, apricot and
lilac glazes, inscribed in brown,
13in (33cm) diam.
£600–700   *HSS*

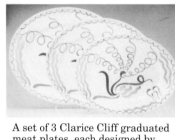

A set of 3 Clarice Cliff graduated
meat plates, each designed by
Ernest Proctor and painted in
pink, green, black and blue with
abstract waves and coils, printed
and impressed marks, 1934,
largest 18½in (47cm) wide.
£600–700   *S(S)*

A Newport Pottery Clarice Cliff
Fantasque Lotus jug, decorated
with 'Melon' pattern, printed
mark and facsimile signature
in black, 11½in (29cm) high.
£1,650–2,000   *HSS*

A Clarice Cliff Athens shape
'Umbrellas and Rain' teapot,
7in (17.5cm) high.
£425–475   *RIC*

A Clarice Cliff Oceanic jug, with
'Windbells' pattern, 6in (15cm) high.
£225–275   *RIC*

A Clarice Cliff Athens shape teapot,
decorated with 'Berries' pattern,
4½in (11cm) high.
£300–350   *ADC*

A Clarice Cliff Lotus shape
jug, decorated with 'Goldstone'
pattern, 6½in (16cm) high.
£200–250   *GAK*

A Newport Pottery Clarice Cliff
teapot, in the form of a teepee,
by Betty Silvester, moulded with
moss and leaves, the spout in the
form of a Red Indian, the handle
as a totem pole, inscribed under
the base 'Greetings from Canada',
7in (17.5cm) high.
£700–850   *Bea*

l. A Clarice Cliff Fantasque Lotus jug, in orange, purple, green and blue, gilt printed on base 'Lawley's Norfolk Pottery Stoke', and 'Fantasque by Clarice Cliff', 11½in (29cm) high.
£500–600 *Bon*

A Clarice Cliff Bizarre oviform jug, painted in yellow and black, printed marks, 7in (17.5cm) high.
£850–1,000 *CSK*

A Clarice Cliff Bizarre Inspiration two-handled Isis vase, painted with bands of yellow, blue and turquoise stylized foliage outlined in brown on a turquoise ground, printed marks, 10in (25.5cm) high.
£3,000–3,500 *CSK*

A Clarice Cliff Bizarre part dinner service, comprising: 2 tureens and covers, a gravy boat, a pair or graduated oval dishes and 6 plates.
£250–300 *Bea*

r. A Clarice Cliff Fantasque Isis single handled vase, decorated with 'Gardenia' pattern, printed marks, 9½in (24cm) high.
£900–1,100 *L*

A Clarice Cliff Bizarre ginger jar and cover, painted with bright colours, signed with factory marks on base, 8in (20.5cm) high.
£2,000–2,500 *P*

A Clarice Cliff Lotus shape jug, painted in bright colours on a cream ground with coloured banded borders, printed facsimile signature, factory marks, Newport, 11½in (29cm) high.
£2,000–2,500 *P*

A Clarice Cliff Fantasque baluster-shaped vase, painted with bands of yellow, blue, orange and green, outlined in black between horizontal bands of orange, black, blue and green, printed marks, 16in (41cm) high.
£3,300–4,000 *CSK*

A Clarice Cliff Bizarre Crocus pattern tea service, comprising: teapot, milk jug, sugar basin, 2 bread and butter plates, 10 cups, 12 saucers and 12 side plates.
£1,600–2,000 *Bea*

l. Clarice Cliff Lotus shape jug, painted in bright colours, reserved against a cream ground with orange borders, printed facsimile signature and factory marks, Newport, 11½in (29cm) high.
£3,000–3,600 *P*

A Clarice Cliff Inspiration plate, painted with pink lilies, with black stems and black lily pads, on a green ground, black printed factory mark, 'Hand Painted, Bizarre, by Clarice Cliff, Wilkinson Ltd, England', 1931, 10in (25.5cm) diam.
£300–360 *S(C)*

A Clarice Cliff Inspiration vase, 'Persian' pattern, vibrant azure blue with spiral and ogee motif in turquoise, lavender and amber, signed 'Persian', printed Bizarre marks, 10in (25.5cm) high.
£1,000–1,200 *CNY*

A Clarice Cliff Fantasque plate, decorated in 'Melons' pattern, with a band of fruits in yellow and orange, with blue sections and green dots, minor damage, printed mark, 'Hand Painted, Fantasque, by Clarice Cliff, Wilkinson Ltd, England', 10in (25.5cm) diam.
£300–360 *S(C)*

A pair of Clarice Cliff 'Cottage' bookends, decorated in red on a green ground with a blue sky, one cracked, one chipped, black printed mark 'Clarice Cliff, Wilkinson Pottery', retailer's mark, 'Lawley's, Regent Street', late 1930s, 5½in (14cm) high.
£500–600 *S(C)*

A Clarice Cliff Bizarre single handled Isis jug, painted in 'Sliced Circle' pattern with bright colours, printed factory marks and facsimile signature, 10in (25.5cm) high.
£2,000–2,400 *P*

A Clarice Cliff pierced floral wall plaque, moulded in low relief with flowers, printed factory mark, 'Hand Painted, Bizarre, Newport Pottery, England, the property of Threlfalls Brewery', signed 'Clarice Cliff', c1930, 13in (33cm) diam.
£200–240 *S(C)*

A Clarice Cliff Apples Isis vase, painted with apples and grapes, in pink, orange, black, yellow and green, fitted as a lamp base, with electric fittings and shade, black printed factory mark, 'Fantasque, Hand Painted, Bizarre, by Clarice Cliff, Newport Pottery, England', c1932, 10in (25.5cm) high.
£1,250–1,500 *S(C)*

A Clarice Cliff Isis vase, boldly painted with trees in Latona glazes, 10in (25.5cm) high.
£600–720 *Bea*

A Clarice Cliff Conical sugar sifter, decorated with pink pearls, 3in (7.5cm) high.
£200–250 *RIC*

A Clarice Cliff Tankard shape coffee set, decorated in 'Gay Day' pattern.
£1,000–1,200 *RIC*

A Clarice Cliff 'Solitude' pattern sugar sifter, 5½in (14cm) high.
£1,500–2,000 *RIC*

A pair of Clarice Cliff 'Autumn' design vases, 8½in (21.5cm) high.
£2,500–3,000 *HEW*

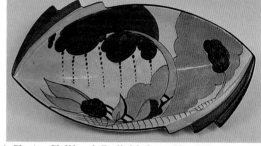

A Clarice Cliff bowl, Daffodil shape No. 475, decorated in 'Devon' pattern, 13in (33cm) long.
£1,000–1,200 *ADC*

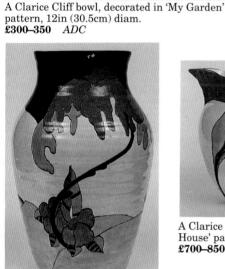

A Clarice Cliff bowl, decorated in 'My Garden' pattern, 12in (30.5cm) diam.
£300–350 *ADC*

A Clarice Cliff jug, decorated in 'Orange House' pattern, 5in (12.5cm) high.
£700–850 *RIC*

A Clarice Cliff baluster shaped vase, in 'Sliced Fruit' pattern, 15in (38cm) high.
£2,500–3,000 *RIC*

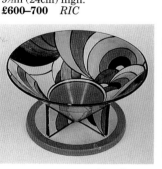

A Clarice Cliff Isis vase, decorated in 'Woodland' design, 9½in (24cm) high.
£600–700 *RIC*

A Clarice Cliff footed bowl, c1930, 9in (23cm) diam.
£2,000–2,200 *HEW*

A Clarice Cliff Latona Red Rose stepped vase, 6in (15cm) high.
£1,200–1,500 *RIC*

A Clarice Cliff Athens shape teapot, decorated in 'Diamonds' pattern.
£650–800 *ADC*

A Clarice Cliff plate, decorated
with 'Gibraltar' pattern,
9in (23cm) diam.
£650–800   *BEV*

A Clarice Cliff plate, painted
with 'House and Tree' pattern,
9in (23cm) diam.
£550–700   *BEV*

A Clarice Cliff plate,
painted with 'Idyll' pattern,
9in (23cm) diam.
£400–500   *BEV*

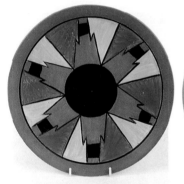

A Clarice Cliff plate, painted
in 'Geometric' pattern, c1925,
10½in (26cm) diam.
£450–550   *BEV*

A Clarice Cliff plate,
painted in 'Gardenia' pattern,
9½in (24cm) diam.
£450–550   *BEV*

A Clarice Cliff blue and
yellow unnamed plate,
9in (23cm) diam.
£350–450   *BEV*

A Clarice Cliff plate, painted
with 'Orange Roof Cottage'
pattern, 9in (23cm) diam.
£650–800   *BEV*

A Clarice Cliff plate, in 'Geometric'
pattern, 7in (17.5cm) diam.
£350–400   *BEV*

A Clarice Cliff plate, painted
in 'Autumn' pattern,
9in (23cm) diam.
£450–550   *BEV*

A Clarice Cliff plate, painted with
'Moonlight' pattern, 9in (23cm) diam.
£450–550   *BEV*

Collecting Clarice Cliff Pottery

- Check condition carefully. Restoration is not always
  easy to detect.
- Look particularly at spouts and handles, check rims
  and bases for chipping or repainting.
- Look out for any slight variation in the colour where
  the pattern may have been touched up.
- Genuine Clarice Cliff reproductions do exist, but are
  clearly dated.
- On flatware, three circles or stilt marks around the
  signature where the pot stood in the kiln are signs
  of authenticity.

MUIR HEWITT
ART DECO
ORIGINALS

A WIDE SELECTION OF
ORIGINAL 1920/30'S
CERAMICS BY
CLARICE CLIFF
AND OTHERS, PLUS
FURNITURE, MIRRORS
AND LIGHTING.

OPEN: Tuesday to Saturday 10.00am to 5.00pm

CLOSED: Sunday & Monday

Tel/Fax: 01422 347377
www.muir-hewitt.com/hewitt

Posters also available
Halifax Antiques Centre, Queens Road Mills,
Queens Road/Gibbet Street, Halifax,
West Yorkshire, HX1 4LR, England.

A Clarice Cliff Nuage bowl, shape No. 33,
13in (33cm) wide.
£450–550   *ADC*

A Clarice Cliff
Bizarre vase, c1930.
£1,500–2,000   *HEW*

Clarice Cliff Pottery Marks

Hand-painted marks were used from July to October 1928, when they were replaced by the first stamped marks. The names of designs were sometimes hand-painted above a stamped mark from 1929 to 1931, but from 1931 to 1934 lithograph marks were mostly used.

A Clarice Cliff Bizarre conical vase,
decorated in 'Inspiration' pattern,
restored, 7in (17.5cm) high.
£1,200–1,500   *HEW*

A Clarice Cliff Nuage
Stamford shape biscuit barrel.
£1,200–1,500   *RIC*

A pair of Clarice Cliff
'Geometric' patten vases,
7in (17.5cm) wide.
£1,000–1,200   *HEW*

A Clarice Cliff vase,
decorated in 'Inspiration'
pattern, 10in (25.5cm) high.
£2,500–3,000   *HEW*

A Clarice Cliff vase,
in 'Orange Roof
Cottage' pattern,
7in (17.5cm) high.
£2,500–3,000   *HEW*

A Clarice Cliff
umbrella stand.
£4,500–6,000   *RIC*

A Clarice Cliff mask,
7in (17.5cm) wide.
£450–500   *HEW*

A Clarice Cliff coffee service, decorated in 'Sunburst'
pattern, coffee pot 7in (17.5cm) high.
£3,500–4,000   *HEW*

A Clarice Cliff basket vase, decorated in
'Bridgewater' design, 13in (33cm) wide.
£1,200–1,500   *HEW*

A Clarice Cliff Lynton coffee cup and saucer, in 'Orange Hydrangea' pattern, cup 2in (5cm) high.
£120–150 *RIC*

A Clarice Cliff Original Bizarre plate, 6in (15cm) diam.
£200–250 *RIC*

A Clarice Cliff Latona vase, Shape No. 370, decorated with 'Knight Errant' pattern, 6in (15cm) high.
£2,500–3,000 *BKK*

A Clarice Cliff vase, Shape No. 119, 9½in (24cm) high.
£400–500 *RIC*

A Clarice Cliff vase, decorated with 'Aurea' pattern, c1935, 8in (20.5cm) high.
£350–450 *RIC*

A Clarice Cliff Odilon four-footed bowl, decorated with 'Berries' pattern, 7½in (19cm) diam.
£450–550 *RIC*

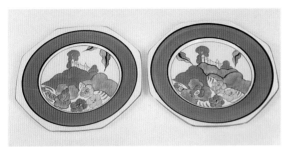

A pair of Clarice Cliff Bizarre Fantasque plates, decorated with 'Orange Alton' pattern, 9in (23cm) diam.
£400–500 each   *BKK*

A Clarice Cliff Inspiration vase, Shape No. 451, decorated in 'Marigold' pattern, 8in (20.5cm) high.
£1,000–1,200   *BKK*

A Clarice Cliff Meiping vase, in 'Blue W' pattern, c1929, 9in (23cm) high.
£2,500–3,000   *BKK*

A Clarice Cliff charger, decorated in 'May Avenue' pattern, c1932, 13in (33cm) diam.
£7,500–9,000   *BKK*

A Clarice Cliff Stamford tea-for-two, decorated in 'Applique Idyll' pattern, c1932, plate 6in (15cm) diam.
£4,500–6,000   *PC*

Clarice Cliff (1899–1972)

Clarice Cliff was born in January 1899 in Tunstall, Staffordshire. She became interested in making clay models at school, and often visited her aunt who was in charge of the decorating shop at Alfred Meakin's factory in Tunstall. Clarice joined the firm of Hollinshead & Kirkham in 1915 as an apprentice in lithography, and after only a year she joined A. J. Wilkinson's Royal Staffordshire Pottery in Burslem. She then dominated the British pottery scene during the late 1920s and '30s. There she learned all aspects of pottery-making including modelling and firing and, in 1927, recognizing her talent and enthusiasm, the firm set her up in a studio in their nearby Newport Pottery with a team of paintresses.

Clarice Cliff designed all her own earthenwares, which were then hand-painted, sometimes by several people in production-line fashion. The early geometric patterns are regular in design, and use wide bands of colour. Later patterns are more abstract and use finer banding, sometimes to provide a textured background to floral or landscape motifs. Glazing was not rigidly controlled, and enamels were usually laid on so thickly that the brush strokes are visible. Clarice Cliff's pieces are mainly collected by pattern or object, rather than in sets. Crocus, the earliest floral design, was very popular at the time and was produced in large quantities. More popular are designs produced on rarer shapes including geometric At Deco forms with unusual rims or flanges. Collectors also prefer the strong geometric patterns, while floral moulded pieces and flower vases in water lily form are less sought after.

A Clarice Cliff Lotus jug, in the 'Blue W' pattern, 12in (30.5cm) high.
£4,500–5,500 *F*

A charger, painted by Clarice Cliff from one of the Brangwyn panels (No. 7), designed for the House of Lords, 1925, first exhibited at Olympia 1933, 17½in (44cm) diam.
£2,000–2,500 *ARE*

A Clarice Cliff pottery biscuit barrel and cover.
£450–550 *HCH*

A Doulton figure of a sealyham terrier, HN1030, 9in (23cm) wide.
£75–90 *PCh*

An Art Nouveau Gouda pottery vase, decorated in Chryso design, from Regina factory, c1920, 11½in (29cm) high.
£300–350 *OO*

A Doulton Burslem vase, by Fred Sutton, a portrait artist, c1900, 11½in (29cm) high.
£1,000–1,200 *HER*

A Clarice Cliff Lotus jug, in 'Applique Orange Lucerne' pattern, printed marks.
£6,500–8,000 *Bon*

A Doulton Lambeth vase, designed by Hannah Barlow and Eliza Simmance, c1891, 20in (51cm) high.
£1,500–2,000 *POW*

A Clarice Cliff caster, 'Passion Fruit' pattern, 5in (13cm) high.
£250–300 *PCh*

A Clarice Cliff wall plate, decorated in 'Applique Idyll' pattern, c1932, 10in (25.5cm) diam.
£1,800–2,200   *PC*

A Clarice Cliff candlestick, decorated in 'Applique Lugano' pattern, c1930, 8in (20.5cm) high.
£2,000–2,200   *PC*

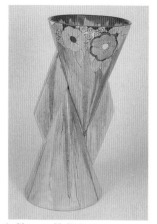

A Clarice Cliff Yo Yo vase, decorated with 'Delecia Lydiat' pattern, 18in (45.5cm) high.
£2,500–3,500   *PC*

A Clarice Cliff Sign of the Zodiac, 'Aquarius', 6in (15cm) wide.
£350–450   *RIC*

A Clarice Cliff Conical jug, decorated with 'Applique Lugano' pattern, c1930, 7in (17.5cm) high.
£2,500–3,000   *PC*

A Clarice Cliff vase, Shape 358, decorated with 'Applique Avignon' pattern, c1930, 8in (20.5cm) high.
£6,000–7,000   *PC*

A Clarice Cliff Athens jug, decorated with 'Applique Palermo' pattern, c1930, 7in (17.5cm) high.
£2,500–3,000   *PC*

A Clarice Cliff vase, Shape 341, decorated with 'Applique Blossom' pattern, c1932, 5½in (14cm) high.
£3,500–4,500   *PC*

A Clarice Cliff Lotus jug, decorated with 'Diamonds' pattern, 12in (30.5cm) high.
£3,500–4,000   *RIC*

A Clarice Cliff plate, decorated with 'Tulip' pattern, 9in (23cm) diam.
£350–450   *RIC*

A Clarice Cliff vase, Shape 264, 'Applique Caravan' pattern, c1930, 8in (20.5cm) high.
£5,500–6,500   *PC*

A fifteen-piece ceramic coffee set, painted mark by Clarice Cliff, coffee pot 6½in (16.5cm) high.
£1,800–2,000 *C*

A selection of Clarice Cliff pottery.
£600–8,000 each *P*

A Clarice Cliff Bizarre charger, factory marks, 16½in (42cm) diam.
£2,500–3,500 *P*

A Clarice Cliff Fantasque Farmhouse vase printed 'F.B.', 'F.S', and 'N.P.' marks, c1930, 16½in (42cm) high.
£6,500–7,500 *MN*

l. A Clarice Cliff Bizarre jardinière, Applique pattern, printed in Newport Pottery, marked, 7½in (19cm) high.
£4,000–4,500 *MN*

A vase, by Carter Stabler Adams, 14in (35.5cm) high.
£250–300 *AW*

A sugar bowl, designed by Susie Cooper, by A. E. Gray & Co Ltd, marked.
£100–120 *AW*

A Moorcroft flambé squat vase, 'Leaf and Berry' design, c1932, 6in (15cm) high.
£750–900 *LIO*

A Moorcroft vase, 'Baraware' design, made for Liberty, restored, c1908, 3½in (9cm) high.
£600–750 *LIO*

A Moorcroft 'Anemone' design lustre vase, made for Liberty, c1909, 8in (20.5cm) high.
£1,500–2,000 *LIO*

A Walter Moorcroft vase, yellow 'Hibiscus' design, c1960, 6in (15cm) high.
£250–300 *LIO*

A Moorcroft MacIntyre vase, with salmon and green 'Carnation' design, c1898, 12in (30.5cm) high.
£1,200–1,500 *LIO*

A Moorcroft flambé vase, 'Waratah' design, 1939, 17in (43cm) high.
£8,000–12,000 *LIO*

A Moorcroft saltglaze vase, 'Fish' design, dated '1931', 14in (36cm) high.
£2,500–3,000 *LIO*

A Moorcroft vase, matt glaze ochre 'Leaf and Berry' design, c1936, 4in (10cm) high.
£350–450 *LIO*

A Minton stick stand, 23in (58cm) high.
£600–750 *CAR*

A Moorcroft MacIntyre vase, Florian Ware 'Blue Tree' design, c1902.
£2,500–3,000 *LIO*

A Moorcroft MacIntyre vase, 'Pansy' design, restored, c1912, 10½in (26cm) high.
£650–750 *LIO*

A pair of floral skittle vases, inscribed 'W. Moorcroft MacIntyre Burslem', 12in (30.5cm) high.
£1,500–2,000 W

A Moorcroft oviform jardinière, with inverted rim, decorated with bands of peacock feathes, restored, signed in green, 8in (20.5cm) high.
£750–900 CSK

A Moorcroft flambé vase, signed, 10in (25.5cm) high.
£1,000–1,200 CSK

A Moorcroft vase, impressed and signed.
£350–400 CSK

A Moorcroft twin-handled pedestal fruit bowl, the interior decorated with pansies, restored, signed, 8in (20.5cm) diam.
£550–650 CSK

A William Moorcroft vase, banded 'Pomegranate' design, c1928, 17in (43cm) high.
£3,500–4,000 RUM

A Moorcroft jardinière, decorated with a band of foliage, damaged, signed, 8in (20.5cm) diam.
£400–500 CSK

A Moorcroft vase, decorated in 'Moonlit Blue' pattern, signed in blue, impressed factory mark, 10in (25.5cm) high.
£1,000–1,200 CSK

A Moorcroft bowl, on a Tudric pewter foot, the interior decorated with pansies, the exterior with buds and foliage, stamped marks, 8in (20.5cm) diam.
£400–500 CSK

A Moorcroft bowl, in 'Claremont' pattern, Liberty mark, signed, 10in (25.5cm) diam.
£1,000–1,500 CSK

A Walter Moorcroft vase, decorated with 'African Lily' design, c1955, 12in (30.5cm) high.
£1,000–1,200 RUM

A Moorcroft vase, restored, marked, 12in (30.5cm) high.
£2,500–3,000 CSK

A Walter Moorcroft vase, 'Clematis' design, c1955, 5in (12.5cm) high.
£350–400 RUM

A pair of Moorcroft vases, 'Pomegranate' pattern signed, factory mark, 10½in (26cm) high.
£1,000–1,500 CSK

A Moorcroft MacIntyre jardinière, marked.
£1,500–2,000 CSK

r. A Moorcroft bowl, decorated inside and outside, factory mark, signed, 8in (20.5cm) diam.
£350–400 CSK

A Moorcroft vase, with everted rim, impressed factory mark, signed in blue, 10in (25.5cm) high.
£500–600 CSK

A Foley Intarsio bowl, decorated with a Shakespeare scene, c1900, 11½in (29cm) diam.
£500–600 *AJ*

A Clarice Cliff bowl, decorated with 'Kandina' pattern, 8in (20.5cm) diam.
£450–550 *BEV*

A Shelley lustre bowl, signed by Walter Slater, c1920, 7in (17.5cm) high.
£150–200 *AJ*

A Bernard Moore bowl, initialled by Cicely Jackson, 9in (23cm) diam.
£250–300 *BLO*

An Austrian amphora, 9in (23cm) high.
£180–200 *BLO*

An Ault Grotesque jug, 7in (17.5cm) high.
£350–400 *BLO*

A Clarice Cliff Lotus jug, with 'Inspiration Caprice' pattern, rim cracked, 12in (30.5cm).
£1,500–2,000 *SWO*

l. A Foley Intarsio jardinière on stand, by Frederick Rhead.
£2,000–2,500 *PC*

A porcelain Limousine water jug, 8in (20.5cm) high.
£80–100 *BLO*

A Foley Intarsio jardinière, decorated in the 'Goose' pattern, c1900, 4⅓in (11cm) high.
£300–400 *AJ*

A Clarice Cliff stepped jardinière, 3½in (8.5cm) high.
£400–500 *BEV*

A pair of Liberty & Co stoneware jardinières, designed by Archibald Knox, 16in (40.5cm) high.
£2,500–3,000 *C*

An eartheware charger, by John Bennett, signed, 1878, 14½in (37cm) diam.
£3,000–3,500 *CNY*

A Minton blank, painted by an amateur artist, exhibited in 1883, 10in (25.5cm) diam.
£250–300 *BLO*

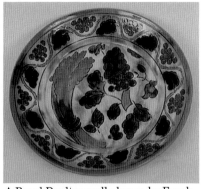

A Royal Doulton wall plaque, by Frank Brangwyn, in 'Harvest' pattern, decorated by hand, 13in (33cm) diam.
£350–450 *ADC*

A Martin Brothers salt-glazed porcelain Love Birds group, 1902.
£6,500–7,500 *S(NY)*

A Royal Dux two-handled vase, 16in (40.5cm) high.
£350–450 *PCh*

A Gray's Pottery Art Deco eight-piece coffee set, in yellow and black geometric pattern.
£550–700 *PCh*

A Susie Cooper charger, signed and dated '1934'.
£700–850 *CAR*

A Martin Brothers bird and cover, c1913.
£3,500–4,500 *S*

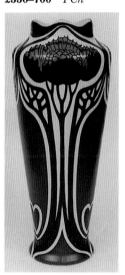

A pair of Mettlach vases, 1904, 14½in (37cm) high.
£700–800 *POW*

A pair of Burmantofts vases, by V. Kremer, 11in (28cm) high.
£1,500–2,000 *NCA*

A figure of Bat Girl, 8½in (21cm) high.
£350–450 *ASA*

A Bursley Ware tray, No. TL43, designed by Charlotte Rhead, in shades of blue on grey, 9in (23cm) wide.
£100–120 *ADC*

A Charlotte Rhead vase, 7in (17.5cm) high.
£100–120 *HEW*

A Royal Doulton vase, by Frank Butler, c1906, 19in (48cm) high.
£2,500–3,000 *POW*

A Charlotte Rhead 'Rhodian' patternbowl, 10in (25.5cm) diam.
£100–120 *HEW*

An Art Deco group, by Lobel Riche, c1925, 14in (35.5cm) high.
£600–700 *POW*

A Charlotte Rhead posy bowl, 6in (15cm) diam.
£100–120 *HEW*

An Austrian porcelain figure of a girl, by Ernst Wahliss, c1910, 17½in (44cm) high.
£1,200–1,500 *HOW*

A Goldscheider ceramic figure, c1930, 14in (35.5cm) high.
£650–800 *ASA*

A pair of Katshütte figures of skiers, 11½in (29cm) high.
£1,000–1,200 *ASA*

A Royal Dux porcelain female figure, Bohemian, c1910, 15½in (39cm) high.
£1,200–1,500 *HOW*

A Royal Doulton figure, 'The Hornpipe', HN2161, 10in (25.5cm) high.
£350–400 *PCh*

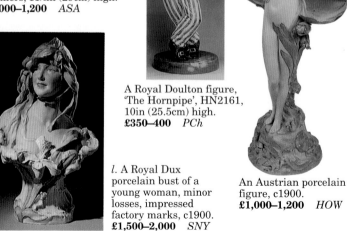

l. A Royal Dux porcelain bust of a young woman, minor losses, impressed factory marks, c1900.
£1,500–2,000 *SNY*

An Austrian porcelain figure, c1900.
£1,000–1,200 *HOW*

A Rosenthal porcelain figure, depicting a snake charmer, c1920.
£400–500 *ASA*

A William de Morgan plate, 'Panthers' design, decorated on reverse, 9½in (24cm) diam.
£1,200–1,600 *BLO*

A Foley Intarsio tea caddy, c1900, 6in (15cm) high.
£300–400 *AJ*

An Art Deco Shelley 21-piece tea service, decorated in blue, black and silver block pattern, c1931.
£1,000–1,200 *AJ*

A Clarice Cliff 50-piece painted dinner service.
£2,000–2,500 *Bea*

A Shelley Art Deco 21-piece tea service, 'Orange J' pattern, teapot missing, c1931.
£450–600 *AJ*

An Art Deco Quimper cup and saucer, signed, saucer 7½in (19cm) diam.
£25–30 *VH*

A Clarice Cliff tea set, 'Patina' design, comprising: milk jug, sugar bowl, cup, saucer and plate, teapot 5in (13cm) high.
£1,400–1,800 *BEV*

A pair of Dutch Villeroy & Boch vases, c1900.
£350–450 *BEV*

A pair of Villeroy & Boch jars, c1900, 7in (17.5cm) high.
£300–350 *BEV*

A Minton vase, with Aesthetic influence, c1886, 12in (30.5cm) high.
£550–650 *BLO*

A Foley Intarsio vase, designed by Frederick Rhead, 9in (23cm) high.
£650–750 *PC*

r. A Moorcroft vase, 9½in (24cm) high.
£450–500 *SBA*

r. A swan design vase by Frederick Rhead, 12½in (32cm) high.
£850–950 *BEV*

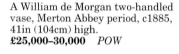

A William de Morgan two-handled vase, Merton Abbey period, c1885, 41in (104cm) high.
£25,000–30,000 *POW*

A Carlton Ware spill vase, decorated with an exotic bird in gilt lustre on a blue ground, 6in (15cm) high.
350–450 *PCh*

A Foley Intarsio vase, designed by Frederick Rhead, c1900, 11in (28cm) high.
£700–850 *AJ*

A Shelley Intarsio vase, designed by Walter Slater, c1912, 10in (25.5cm) high.
£350–400 *AJ*

An Art Nouveau vase, Rozenburg factory, The Hague, c1897, 7in (17cm) high.
£650–750 *OO*

A pair of Art Nouveau Florian Ware tapered vases, signed, early 20thC, 8in (20.5cm) high.
£1,400–1,800 *PCh*

A Dutch pottery jug, Arnhem factory, c1926, 10⅛in (26cm) high.
£200–250 *OO*

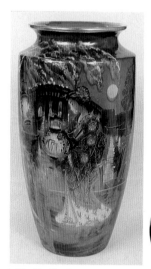

A Shelley lustre vase, signed 'Walter Slater', c1920, 15in (38cm) high.
£500–600 *AJ*

A Foley faïence trio, designed by Frederick Rhead, centrepiece 8in (20.5cm) high.
£550–650 *AJ*

l. A Rozenburg vase, 'Julianna' pattern, The Hague, c1910, 13½in (34cm) high.
£500–550 *OO*

An iridescent glazed ceramic figural jardinière, signed 'Zsolnay-Pecs' and 'Made in Hungary', 7in (17cm) high.
£3,000–3,500 *S(NY)*

A Clarice Cliff Bizarre batchelor tea set, painted in greens, orange and yellow, printed marks. **£3,000–3,500** *CSK*

A Clarice Cliff Bizarre Lotus vase, painted with the 'Honolulu' pattern, striped green and black trees with orange, red and yellow foliage, printed marks, 11½in (29cm) high. **£3,300–4,000** *CSK*

A Clarice Cliff Bizarre Isis vase, painted in 'Applique Lucerne' design, in orange, yellow, green and black, with a deep blue sky above, printed and painted marks, impressed 'Isis', 9½in (24cm) high. **£5,000–6,000** *CSK*

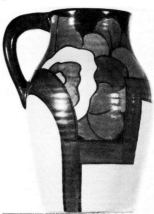

A Clarice Cliff Bizarre Lotus vase, 'Clouvre Tulip', the mottled matt lilac and blue ground painted in vermilion, lime green and yellow, painted and printed marks, 11½in (29cm) high. **£4,300–5,000** *CSK*

A Clarice Cliff Bizarre two-handled Lotus vase, painted in pink, green, yellow and blue, printed marks, 11½in (29cm) high. **£2,000–2,500** *CSK*

A Clarice Cliff Bizarre Lotus Latona vase, printed marks, 11½in (29cm) high. **£2,500–3,000** *CSK*

A Clarice Cliff Fantasque Bizarre tea-for-two, painted in the 'SummerHouse' design, printed marks. **£3,300–4,000** *CSK*

A Clarice Cliff Bizarre coffee set, in orange, yellow, green, brown and grey, comprising: a coffee pot, 7 cups, 6 saucers, cream jug and sugar bowl, printed marks. **£750–900** *CSK*

A Clarice Cliff Bizarre twin-handled Lotus vase, painted in a rich chestnut, blue, purple and green, printed marks, 11½in (29cm) high. **£1,000–1,200** *CSK*

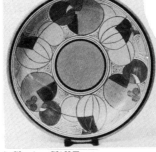

A Clarice Cliff Bizarre green, orange and red, 'Golly' pencil holder, in printed marks, 5½in (14cm) high. **£850–1,000** *CSK*

A Clarice Cliff Fantasque 'Melon' pattern wall plate, painted in vivid oranges, yellow, blue, red and green, factory marks and facsimile signature, 16½in (42cm) diam. **£1,000–1,200** *P*

r. A Clarice Cliff Fantasque Isis vase, painted in orange, green, brown and black between wide orange and yellow borders, printed marks, 9½in (23cm) high. **£750–900** *CSK*

Original artwork for a Clarice Cliff advertisement, depicting several young ladies drinking coffee from a Tankard coffee set, gouache on paper, 22 x 28in (56 x 71cm).
£850–950 *CSK*

Two Clarice Cliff Circus plates, designed by Laura Knight, one centred with a horse and trainer performing in the ring, enclosed by an audience and clown border, in mauve, yellow, brown, black and green, another with a girl astride a horse, in same colours, with factory marks and facsimile signatures to base, both 9in (23cm) diam.
£750–900 each *P*

A Clarice Cliff Inspiration 'Persian' pattern vase, shape No. 342, painted with abstract shapes in vertical and horizontal bands in turquoise, blue, orange and brown, factory marks and facsimile signature with 'Persian' to base, 8in (20.5cm) high.
£1,000–1,200 *P*

A Clarice Cliff Bizarre vase, with horizontally ribbed neck, decorated with 'Orange Secrets' pattern in vivid colours with cottages on a rolling hillside, factory marks and facsimile signature to base, 8in (20.5cm) high.
£1,000–1,200 *P*

A Clarice Cliff Bizarre 'Honolulu' patterned Lotus jug, Fantasque, hand-painted by Newport Pottery, 11½in (29cm) high.
£3,000–3,600 *GAK*

A Clarice Cliff Conical coffee set, in the 'Rising Sun' design, painted in orange, mauve and yellow blooms with blue grapes against an orange and white sunburst ground, comprising: a coffee pot and lid, 6 cups and saucers, a milk jug and sugar bowl, factory marks and facsimile signature to base, coffee pot 7in (17.5cm) high.
£2,000–2,400 *P*

A Clarice Cliff Isis Lotus vase decorated in Green Japan design with a summerhouse by a lake, an exotic orange and green leaved tree nearby with purple and black foliage, beneath a yellow sky, factory marks and facsimile signature to base, 11½in (29cm) high.
£1,500–1,800 *P*

l. A Clarice Cliff Bizarre cup and saucer and plate, in the 'Broth' pattern, painted in colours with orange banding, rubber stamp mark.
£250–300 *CSK*

A Clarice Cliff tea service for 4, painted in the
'Crocus' pattern, some pieces marked, c1935.
£450–550 *C*

A Clarice Cliff Biarritz dinner service,
the cream ground painted in green, black
and orange, comprising: 5 meat plates,
12 dinner plates, 12 side plates, 12 dessert
plates, 6 soup plates, 2 tureens and covers,
and a sauceboat.
£550–700 *SS*

A Clarice Cliff Isis vase,
painted with 'Gayday' pattern,
with a border of colourful daisies
between a yellow rim and brown
and green foot borders, printed
marks, painted marks, 1936,
10in (25.5cm) high.
£300–400 *C*

A Clarice Cliff Bizarre
Fantasque vase, painted in
red, blue, yellow and green
against a cream ground,
printed factory marks,
10in (25.5cm) high.
£900–1,100 *SBe*

A Clarice Cliff vase,
painted with 'Honey
Glaze' pattern,
8in (20.5cm) high.
£250–350 *ASA*

A Newport Pottery Bizarre
candlestick, painted with a
formalized landscape in shades of
yellow, blue and green, printed
marks, c1930, 5½in (14cm) high.
£750–900 *S*

A Newport Pottery
Clarice Cliff vase,
7in (17.5cm) high.
£350–450 *CSK*

A Newport Pottery Clarice
Cliff Bizarre vase, printed
factory and designer's marks,
c1930, 6in (15cm) diam.
£1,000–1,200 *SB*

A Clarice Cliff inspiration charger,
decorated with 'The Knight Errant',
reserved against a green and
turquoise ground, printed factory
marks and facsimile signature,
18in (45.5cm) diam.
£3,500–4,000 *P*

A Clarice Cliff Bizarre vase,
10in (25.5cm) high.
£2,000–2,500 *Bea*

A Newport Pottery Clarice Cliff
Bizarre earthenware wall plaque,
painted in bright orange, yellow
and red, c1930, 13in (33cm) diam.
£200–250 *SB*

STARTING A DOULTON COLLECTION

The serious collector of Doulton faces a choice; to concentrate on building up a representative collection from the different types of ceramics produced (stoneware, figurines, character jugs, series ware, to name a few), or simply to focus on one area. Once that choice has been made, the next difficulty is finding good quality items.

Over the past few years, growing interest in Doulton has resulted in a decreasing supply of such items. Specialist magazines have nurtured a greater interest in Doulton not only in Britain but all over the world, and there are established collectors' clubs in the USA, Canada, Australia and New Zealand. Often there is demand for Doulton that has links with a collector's own country; for example, Hannah Barlow pieces decorated with kangaroos are nearly all exported to Australia.

Prices – most areas are governed by the simple laws of supply and demand. People who began acquiring pieces ten years ago are now concentrating on finding the rarer or missing items for their collections and hence creating more competition for these pieces. The recession caused people to be more selective in what they buy – many would rather save to buy one expensive object than choose several lesser pieces at whim. When a private Doulton collection does come onto the market, prices can be very high as collectors like to see 'fresh' pieces for which they are willing to pay a premium. Other collectors who have been priced out of certain areas (for example, artist stoneware), have been shown greater interest in the more affordable and mass produced stonewares such as Slaters Patent Ware and 'Natural foliage' ware.

Certain pieces have acquired great value because they are unique or have been produced in very short numbers. The 'Village Blacksmith' character jug, for example, surfaced at auction a few years ago. Dating from the 1950s, it was produced by the factory as a trial piece but was then discarded and literally thrown out. An employee who rescued it from a dustbin kept it at home for many years before placing it in a specialist Doulton sale where it realized £6,000 despite being badly damaged by a large crack.

The prices of figurines are also influenced by scarcity value. 'Top o' the Hill', Doulton's most popular figurine (in production since the 1930s) can be bought for under £100, while rarely seen figures at the beginning of the HN series (Doulton assigned letters and numbers to their figurines) can command prices in the £2,000–4,000 bracket. The Art Deco figurines, such as the 'Butterfly Girl' and 'Sunshine Girl' which exude the frivolous mood of the 1920s, continue to rise in popularity. The character jug market, on the other hand, has now levelled out from a rather over-inflated position in the mid-1980s.

Doulton collectors can be fascinated by colour and model variations, particularly in the figurine and character jug field. The price of a 'Cavalier' character jug, for example, might be £100 whereas the same jug with a small goatee beard would cost closer to £1,500, just because it was in production for only one year. Also, an item that did not sell well in its day may be very sought after today. 'The Bookworm' plate from the 'Professionals' series might set you back £200, while all the other plates in the series might cost only £60 each.

With the series ware, those pieces decorated with historical, literary or nursery rhyme subjects are very desirable, although sporting subjects (especially golf) are the most popular. Stoneware is collected by artist name, with the Barlows, George Tinworth and Eliza Simmance being the most sought after. Collectors will pay a premium for particular work by these artists, for example the Tinworth Mouse groups.

The golden rule when buying Doulton is to check condition carefully. Obvious damage such as cracks or chips will affect the value, as will restoration which can be more difficult to spot. Figurines may have had their heads knocked off and then have been restored around the neck, vases may have chips filled in or handles replaced. Do not forget that many of these items will have been around for over 100 years, so always make sure the auction house or dealer can confirm whether restoration does or does not exist – it might be so well done that you might still wish to acquire the piece but at a price level that takes this into account. For the more common item, damage or restoration might halve or even quarter its value, but collectors are much more tolerant of the faults to rarer pieces. One or two small chips on a Tinworth clock would hardly affect the value.

There is of course a wide variety of Doulton marks used throughout the long history of the company and collectors should familiarize themselves with these as they will help date a piece. Figurines often have a number to the top right of the lion and crown mark and if this is added to the year 1927 it will give a date of production for the figurine – hence a number five will mean it was produced in 1932.

All Doulton products have a degree of hand crafting to them. Most involve the initial use of a mould and then a process of several stages of glazing and hand-crafting down to the most intricate floral embellishment. Many of Doulton's greatest designers, such as Peggy Davies or Mary Nicoll, managed to create facial expressions of great character and all their studies have a sense of time, place and movement. At the very top of the range the 'Prestige studies' such as 'Princess Badoura' are produced to order and reveal a wealth of historical detail and flamboyant glazing through the intricate hand-crafting they have commanded. The retail price reflects this – some £14,000!   **Mark Oliver**

A Royal Doulton musical character jug, 'Toby Weller', designed by L. Harradine and H. Fenton, D5888, printed marks, 6in (15cm) high.
£350–400 *CSK*

A Royal Doulton character jug, 'Old Charley', printed marks, 7in (17.5cm) high.
£700–800 *CSK*

A Royal Doulton character jug, known as 'Toothless Granny', designed by H. Fenton and M. Henk, D5521, printed marks, 7in (17.5cm) high.
£350–400 *CSK*

A Royal Doulton character jug, 'Paddy', designed by H. Fenton, D5887, printed marks, 6in (15cm) high.
£400–500 *CSK*

l. A Royal Doulton figure, 'Sunshine Girl', designed by L. Harradine, HN1344, printed and painted marks, 5in (12.5cm) high.
£2,000–2,500 *CSK*

A Royal Doulton figure,
'The Goose Girl' designed by
L. Harradine, HN559,
introduced 1923, withdrawn
1938, 8in (20.5cm) high.
£1,200–1,500 *LT*

A Royal Doulton figure,
'Ibraham', HN2095,
withdrawn 1955.
£350–400 *Bea*

A Royal Doulton figure,
'Farmer Bunnykins',
D3003, printed and painted
marks, 7in (18cm) high.
£1,000–1,200 *CSK*

A Royal Doulton figure,
'Abdullah', HN2104,
withdrawn 1962.
£350–400 *Bea*

A Royal Doulton figure,
'King Charles', designed by
C. J. Noke and H. Tittensor,
HN404, cane missing, printed
marks, 17in (43cm) high.
£350–400 *CSK*

A Royal Doulton figure,
'The Jester', HN1295,
withdrawn 1949,
signed 'C. J. Noke',
10in (25.5cm) high.
£800–1,000 *LT*

A Royal Doulton figure,
'Carpet Seller', HN1464,
withdrawn 1969.
£120–150 *Bea*

A Royal Doulton figure, '
The Alchemist', designed by
L. Harradine, HN1282, date code for
1937, introduced 1928, withdrawn
1938, 11½in (29cm) high.
£800–1,000 *P*

A Royal Doulton figure,
'Miss 1928', designed by
L. Harradine, HN1205,
withdrawn c1938,
7in (18cm) high.
£1,700–2,000 *LT*

A Royal Doulton figure, 'The Poke
Bonnet', HN612, 9½in (24cm) high.
£800–1,000 *LT*

A Royal Doulton figure, 'Delight', designer L. Harradine, HN1772, printed and painted marks, 7½in (19cm) high.
£120–150 *CSK*

A Royal Doulton figure, 'Easter Day', HN2039, withdrawn 1969.
£250–300 *Bea*

A Royal Doulton figure, 'The Wardrobe Mistress', HN2145, withdrawn 1967.
£200–250 *Bea*

A Royal Doulton figure, 'The Gaffer', HN2053, green printed marks to base, 7½in (19cm) high.
£250–300 *BWe*

r. A Royal Doulton figure, 'One of the Forty', designer H. Tittensor, HN677, introduced 1924, withdrawn 1938, 8½in (21.5cm) high.
£800–1,000 *LT*

l. A Royal Doulton figure, 'Mephistopheles & Marguerite', designed by C. J. Noke, HN775, withdrawn 1949, 8in (20.5cm) high.
£1,000–1,200 *LT*

A Royal Doulton pilot figure of a girl with a pink skirt and a pail under her right arm, 7in (17.5cm) high.
£800–1,000 *LT*

A Royal Doulton figure, 'Sweet and Twenty', designer L. Harradine, HN1360, printed marks, 6in (15cm) high.
£170–200 *CSK*

A Royal Doulton figure, 'Uriah Heep', HN2101, green printed marks to base, 7½in (19cm) high.
£250–300 *BWe*

A Royal Doulton figure, 'Quality Street', HN1211, introduced 1926, withdrawn 1938, 7in (18cm) high.
£800–1,000 *LT*

A Royal Doulton figure 'Midinette', designer L. Harradine, HN2090, printed marks, 7in (17.5cm) high.
£170–200 *CSK*

A Royal Doulton figure, 'Butterfly', designer L. Harradine, HN719, 6½in (16.5cm) high.
£1,500–2,000 *LT*

A Royal Doulton cabinet plate, painted and signed by W. E. J. Dean, dated '1916', 9in (23cm) diam.
£250–300 *TVA*

A Royal Doulton Holbein ware pottery vase, decorated by W. Nunn, in colours with 2 men seated drinking at a table, signed and impressed 'Doulton Ivory 1920B', printed mark in green, 9½in (24cm) high.
£350–400 *HSS*

A Doulton Lambeth plaque, decorated by Hannah Barlow, dated '1874', 9in (23cm) square.
£650–800 *Wai*

A Royal Doulton figure, 'The Curtsey', HN334.
£800–1,000 *GSP*

A Royal Doulton Art Nouveau vase, artists' monograms for Eliza Simmance and Bessie Newbery, incised date code for 1909, 15in (38cm) high.
£650–800 *TVA*

A Royal Doulton porcelain figure, 'Matador and Bull', designed by M. Davies, HN2011, printed and painted marks, 15½in (39.5cm) wide.
£1,000–1,200 *CSK*

A Royal Doulton jug, 'The Pied Piper', by H. Fenton, No. 252 of limited edition of 600, 10in (25.5cm) high.
£800–1,000 *P(M)*

A Royal Doulton Lambeth stoneware figure of Samuel, by George Tinworth, on an oval moulded base, impressed initials, 6in (15cm) high.
£800–1,000 *AH*

A Royal Doulton flambé model of a seated rabbit, restored, c1925, 4in (10cm) high.
£125–175 *TVA*

A Royal Doulton blue and white chamber pot, c1900.
£40–45 *OD*

l. A Royal Doulton figure, 'Henry Lytton as Jack Point', HN610, designed by C. J. Noke, introduced 1924, withdrawn 1949, 6½in (17cm) high.
£700–800 *LT*

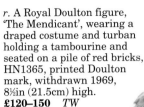

r. A Royal Doulton figure, 'The Mendicant', wearing a draped costume and turban holding a tambourine and seated on a pile of red bricks, HN1365, printed Doulton mark, withdrawn 1969, 8½in (21.5cm) high.
£120–150 *TW*

A Royal Doulton figure, 'Angela', HN1204, designed by L. Harradine, introduced 1926, withdrawn 1938, hairline crack to base, 7½in (19cm) high.
£400–500 *LT*

l. A Royal Doulton figure, 'Yeoman of the Guard', designed by L. Harradine, HN2122, introduced 1954, withdrawn 1959, 6in (15cm) high.
£600–700 *LT*

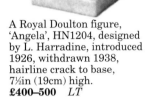

l. A Royal Doulton figure, 'Moorish Piper Minstrel', no number, designed by C. J. Noke, withdrawn 1938, 13½in (34.5cm) high.
£1,500–2,000 *LT*

r. A Royal Doulton figure, 'Lady Jester', designer L. Harradine, HN1222, introduced 1927, withdrawn by 1938.
£1,200–1,500 *LT*

Three miniatures, 'One of the Forty', decorated in gilt, designer H. Tittensor, no number, should be HN423, largest 3in (7.5cm) high.
£1,200–1,500 *LT*

A Royal Doulton figure, 'Mask Seller', designer L. Harradine, HN1361, introduced 1929, withdrawn by 1938, 8½in (21.5cm) high.
£800–1,000 *LT*

r. A Royal Doulton stoneware garden ornament, impressed monogram 'C.M. & I', 11½in (29cm) high.
£700–800 *P*

A porcelain group of 'Spooks', modelled as two elderly gentlemen wearing long turquoise coloured cloaks and black caps, by C. J. Noke, HN88, printed and painted marks, 'Royal Doulton, England' and 'Doulton & Co.' 7in (18cm) high.
£2,000–2,500 *CSK*

l. A Royal Doulton figure, 'Fox in Red Coat', seated, HN100, 6½in (17cm) high.
£800–1,000 *LT*

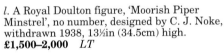

A Royal Doulton figure, 'Scotties', designed by L. Harradine, HN1281, introduced 1928, withdrawn 1938, slight damage, 5in (12.5cm) high.
£800–1,000   *WIL*

A Royal Doulton figure, 'Easter Day', designed by M. Davies, HN2039, introduced 1949, withdrawn 1969.
£160–200   *WIL*

A Royal Doulton figure, 'Griselda', 1947–53, 6in (15cm) high.
£200–220   *TRU*

A Royal Doulton figure 'Memories', 1949–59, 6in (15cm) high.
£250–300   *TRU*

A Royal Doulton figure, 'Modena', HN1846, withdrawn 1949, cracked.
£120–150   *Bea*

A Royal Doulton figure, 'Bess', HN2002, 7½in (18cm) high.
£250–300   *TW*

A Royal Doulton figure, 'Dreamland', HN1481, base cracked, printed marks in green script, impressed date '1931'.
£850–950   *SC*

A Royal Doulton figure, 'Bonnie Lassie', HN1626, introduced 1934, withdrawn 1953, 5½in (14cm) high.
£250–300   *Bea*

A Royal Doulton figure, 'Francine', designed by J. Bromley, introduced 1922, withdrawn 1981, 5½in (14cm) high.
£55–70   *TVA*

r. A Royal Doulton figure, 'The Orange Lady', HN1759, introduced 1936, withdrawn 1975, 9in (23cm) high.
£100–120   *TW*

l. A Royal Doulton figure of a seated bulldog, with a Union Jack flag draped over its back, printed factory marks, 4in (10cm) high.
£150–200   *CSK*

A Royal Doulton figure, 'Butterfly', HN1456, 6½in (16.5cm) high.
£1,500–2,000 *CSK*

A Royal Doulton double-sided figure, 'Mephistopheles and Marguerite', HN775, 8in (20.5cm) high
£1,000–1,500 *CSK*

A Royal Doulton figure, 'Angela', slight damage, painted title, HN1204, date code for 1929, 7in (18cm) high.
£1,000–1,500 *S*

A Royal Doulton figure of a girl, 'Negligée,' with coloured slip and red turban, on a multi-coloured cushion, HN1219, printed and painted marks, 5in (12.5cm) high.
£800–1,000 *CSK*

A Royal Doulton figure, 'Negligée', by L. Harradine, HN1272, impressed date '1.1.28'. 5in (12.5cm) high.
£800–1,000 *P*

l. A Royal Doulton figure, 'Columbine', designed by L. Harradine, BH1296, impressed date '2.9.29', introduced 1928, withdrawn 1938, 6in (15cm) high.
£800–1,000 *P*

A Royal Doulton figure, 'Geisha', by C. J. Noke, HN1292, impressed date '4.1.28', 7in (18cm) high.
£1,000–1,200 *P*

A Royal Doulton figure, 'Covent Garden', HN1339, 9in (23cm) high.
£800–1,000 *Bea*

Make the most of Miller's

Condition is absolutely vital when assessing the value of an antique. Items in good condition are more likely to appreciate than less perfect examples. Rare, desirable items may command higher prices even when in need of restoration.

A Royal Doulton figure, 'Pierrette', printed and painted marks, painted title, HN731, impressed date code for 1927, 7in (18cm) high.
£800–900 *S*

r. A Royal Doulton figure, 'Marion', HN1583, introduced 1933, withdrawn 1938, 6½in (16.5cm) high.
£500–600 *Bea*

A Royal Doulton figure, 'Marietta', HN1341, printed Royal Doulton marks, 8in (20.5cm) high.
£600–700 *CSK*

r. A Royal Doulton figure, 'Columbine', in a pink and yellow dress, seated on a green column, printed and painted marks, HN1439, 6in (15cm) high.
£800–1,000 *CSK*

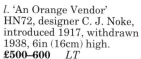

l. 'An Orange Vendor' HN72, designer C. J. Noke, introduced 1917, withdrawn 1938, 6in (16cm) high. **£500–600** *LT*

r. A Royal Doulton figure, 'Guy Fawkes', HN98, designer C. J. Noke, introduced 1918, withdrawn by 1949, 10½in (26.5cm) high. **£800–1,000** *LT*

A Royal Doulton figure, 'In The Stocks', 1st version, HN14/4, designer L. Harradine, introduced 1921, withdrawn 1938, 5in (12.5cm) high. **£1,500–1,800** *LT*

A Royal Doulton figure, 'A Jester', HN45, signed C. J. Noke, introduced 1915, withdrawn by 1938, 10in (25.5cm) high. **£800–1,000** *LT*

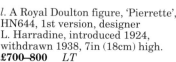

l. A Royal Doulton figure, 'Pierrette', HN644, 1st version, designer L. Harradine, introduced 1924, withdrawn 1938, 7in (18cm) high. **£700–800** *LT*

l. A Royal Doulton figure, 'Geisha', designer H. Tittensor, dated February 1927, 11in (28cm) high. **£2,000–2,200** *LT*

r. A Royal Doulton figure, 'Harlequinade Masked', designer L. Harradine, introduced 1925, withdrawn by 1938, 6½in (16.5cm) high. **£1,000–1,200** *LT*

A Royal Doulton figure, 'The Beggar', HN526, designed L. Harradine, introduced 1921, withdrawn by 1949, 6½in (16.5cm) high. **£350–400** *LT*

A Royal Doulton figure, 'Pierrette', pilot decoration, designer L. Harradine, introduced 1924, withdrawn by 1938, 7in (18cm) high. **£1,200–1,500** *LT*

A Royal Doulton figure, 'Butterfly', HN719, designer L. Harradine, 6½in (16.5cm) high. **£1,700–2,000** *LT*

A Royal Doulton figure, 'Judge and Jury', HN1264, designer J. G. Hughes, introduced 1927, withdrawn 1938, 6in (15cm) high. **£2,500–3,000** *LT*

A Royal Doulton figure, 'London Cry, Turnips and Carrots', HN752, designer L. Harradine, introduced 1925, withdrawn 1938, 7in (18cm) high. **£1,000–1,200** *LT*

A Royal Doulton figure, 'The Modern Piper', HN756, designer L. Harradine, introduced 1925, withdrawn by 1938, 8½in (21.5cm) high. **£1,000–1,200** *LT*

A Royal Doulton figure, 'Negligée', HN1219, designer L. Harradine, introduced 1927, withdrawn 1938, 5in (12.5cm) high. **£1,000–1,200** *LT*

A Royal Doulton figure, 'Gladys', designer L. Harradine, HN1740, introduced 1935, withdrawn by 1949, 5in (12.5cm) high.
£700–800 *LT*

A Royal Doulton figure, 'Veronica', designer L. Harradine, no number, should be HN1943, introduced 1940, withdrawn by 1949.
£350–400 *LT*

A Royal Doulton figure, 'Top o' the Hill', designer L. Harradine, HN1834, introduced 1937, 7in (18cm) high.
£45–60 *LT*

A Royal Doulton figure, 'Carmen', designed by L. Harradine, introduced 1928, withdrawn 1938, HN1267, 7in (18cm) high.
£800–1,000 *LT*

A Royal Doulton figure, 'The Awakening', 1st version, designer L. Harradine, HN1927, introduced 1940, withdrawn by 1949.
£1,200–1,500 *LT*

A Royal Doulton pilot figure of a boy carrying a lantern, wearing a red coat and tricorn hat, not produced, 6½in (16.5cm) high.
£700–1,000 *LT*

A Royal Doulton figure, 'The Bather', designer L. Harradine, no number, model as HN1708 but with different decoration, with check robe, black costume and blue base, 7½in (19cm) high.
£1,000–1,200 *LT*

l. A Royal Doulton figure, 'The Mask', designer L. Harradine, HN7333, introduced 1925, withdrawn by 1938, 7in (18cm) high.
£1,200–1,500 *LT*

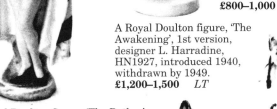

A Royal Doulton figure, 'Mantilla', designer E. J. Griffiths, HN2712, 12in (30.5cm) high.
£170–200 *LT*

Ellen Terry as Queen Catherine', by C. J. Noke, HN379, 12½in (32cm) high.
£1,000–1,200 *LT*

r. A Doulton figure, 'Spring', designed by Richard Garbe, modelled as a partially draped maiden holding flowers to her bosom as she is swept upwards, her drapery resting on a circular plinth above a stepped square section base, cream coloured glaze, in 2 sections with original screw and nut fixing, hand-painted signature, 'Potted by Doulton & Co. Edition Limited to 100, No. 61, "Spring" by Richard Garbe ARA', moulded artist's signature and date '1932' on the plinth, 21½in (54cm) high overall.
£2,700–3,000 *C*

A Royal Doulton figure, 'Coppelia', HN2115, 7in (18cm) high.
£300–350 *WIL*

A Royal Doulton pilot figure of an Elizabethan lady courtier, holding a rose, 10½in (26.5cm) high.
£1,000–1,200 *WIL*

Doulton

A London pottery firm, established in 1815, but important for its Art Pottery only from the 1860s, when it revived brown stoneware and saltglaze ware. Its leading potter was George Tinworth and the company had links with the Martin Brothers.
In the 1870s the Barlow sisters decorated ware with animals and scenes. In the 1880s and 1890s, many different artists made or decorated fancy ware, 'siliconware' or enamelled china. In 1902 Doulton received the Royal Warrant. Royal Doulton figures were introduced in 1913, since when more than 2,000 designs have been produced.

A Royal Doulton figure, 'Clemency', HN1633, 7½in (19cm) high.
£200–250 *WIL*

A Royal Doulton pilot figure of a young lady in a red dress, standing by a sundial, 7in (17.5cm) high.
£1,500–2,000 *LT*

A Royal Doulton figure. 'Sonia', HN 1692, 6½in (16.5cm) high.
£330–380 *LT*

r. A Royal Doulton miniature character jug, 'Pearly Girl'.
£2,500–3,000 *LT*

l. A Royal Doulton miniature character jug, 'Pearly Boy'.
£1,700–2,200 *LT*

A Royal Doulton musical mug, 'Old King Cole', with a yellow crown, fitted with a Thorens Swiss movement, No. D6014, 8in (20.5cm) high.
£1,000–1,200 *AH*

l. A Royal Doulton figure of a newsboy, HN2244, 8in (20.5cm) high.
£250–300 *LT*

r. A Royal Doulton character jug 'Old King Cole', with a yellow crown.
£800–1,000 *LT*

'Siesta', designer L. Harradine, HN1305, produced February 1931, 5in (12.5cm) high.
£1,500–1,800 *LT*

'Tulips', HN1334, introduced 1929, withdrawn 1938, 9½in (24cm) high.
£600–700 *LT*

A Royal Doulton figure, 'Lady Jester', designer L. Harradine, 2nd version, HN1284, introduced 1928, withdrawn 1938, 4in (10cm) high.
£800–1,000 *LT*

l. A Royal Doulton figure, 'Sweet Lavender', designer L. Harradine, HN1373, introduced 1930, withdrawn 1949, 9in (23cm) high.
£300–400 *LT*

'Folly', designer L.Harradine, HN1335, 1929–38, 9in (23cm) high.
£800–1,000 *LT*

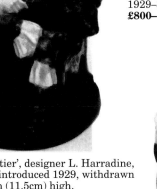

'The Courtier', designer L. Harradine, HN1338, introduced 1929, withdrawn 1938, 4½in (11.5cm) high.
£1,000–1,200 *LT*

l. A Royal Doulton figure, 'Doreen', designer L. Harradine, HN1389, introduced 1930, withdrawn 1938, 5in (12.5cm) high.
£400–500 *LT*

'Iona', designer L. Harradine, HN1346, introduced 1929, withdrawn 1938, 7½in (19cm) high.
£1,000–1,200 *LT*

A Royal Doulton figure, 'Phyllis', designer L. Harradine, HN1420, introduced 1930, withdrawn 1949, slight damage, 9in (23cm) high.
£300–350 *WIL*

A Royal Doulton figure, 'Calumet', designer C. J. Noke, HN1428, introduced 1930, withdrawn 1949, 6in (15cm) high.
£400–500 *LT*

r. A Royal Doulton figure, 'Tildy', designer L. Harradine, HN1576, introduced 1933, withdrawn 1938, 5½in (14cm) high.
£350–400 *LT*

r. 'Teresa', designer L. Harradine, HN1683, introduced 1935, withdrawn 1938, hair cracks, 6in (15cm) high.
£350–400 *LT*

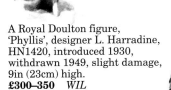

A Royal Doulton figure, 'Dreamland', designer L. Harradine, should be HN1473, introduced 1931, withdrawn 1938, 4½in (12cm) wide.
£2,000–2,500 *LT*

r. A Royal Doulton figure, 'Molly Malone', designer L. Harradine, HN1455, introduced 1931, withdrawn 1938, slight hair crack, 7in (18cm) high.
£1,000–1,200 *LT*

l. A Royal Doulton figure, 'Court Shoemaker', designer L. Harradine, HN1755, introduced 1936, withdrawn 1949, hair cracks to base, 7in (18cm) high.
£420–480 *LT*

A Royal Doulton figure, 'The Winner', No. 1407, 1930–38, 6in (15cm) high.
£1,200–1,500   *TP*

A Royal Doulton group, depicting a bay mare with her foal, No. 2522, 1938–60, 6in (15cm) high.
£350–450

A Royal Doulton figure, 'Town Crier', No. 2119, 1953–76, 8in (20.5cm) high.
£200–250   *TP*

A Royal Doulton 'Treasure Island' loving cup, from a limited edition of 600, c1934.
£800–1,000   *TP*

A Royal Doulton figure, 'The Organ Grinder', No. 2173, 1956–75, 8in (20.5cm) high.
£350–400   *TP*

A Royal Doulton figure of a seated collie, No. 47, c1920.
£350–400   *TP*

l. A Royal Doulton set of 'The Four Seasons', 2nd version, 'Autumn' HN2087, 'Winter' HN2088, 'Spring' HN2085, and 'Summer' HN2086, designer Margaret Davies, introduced 1952, withdrawn 1959, largest 8in (20.5cm) high.
£1,200–1,500   *LT*

l. A Royal Doulton figure, 'Spring Flowers', HN1945, designer L. Harradine, introduced 1940, withdrawn by 1949, 7in (18cm) high.
£200–250   *LT*

A Royal Doulton group, 'Afternoon Tea', HN1747, 5½in (14cm) high.
£150–200   *HCH*

A Royal Doulton pilot figure of a lady in a blue and pink ballgown, damaged, 9in (23cm) high.
£600–700   *LT*

A Royal Doulton figure, 'The Squire', HN1814.
£1,200–1,500 *LT*

A Royal Doulton figure, 'Miranda', designer L. Harradine, HN1819, 8½in (21.5cm) high.
£450–550 *LT*

A Royal Doulton figure 'Mariquita', designer L. Harradine, HN1837, 8in (20.5cm) high.
£800–1,000 *LT*

A Royal Doulton figure, 'Henry VIII', designer C. J. Noke, 2nd version, HN1792, No. 39 of 200, hair crack in base, 11½in (29cm) high.
£2,000–2,500 *LT*

l. A Royal Doulton figure, 'The Young Miss Nightingale', designer Margaret Davies, HN2010, 9in (23cm) high.
£400–500 *LT*

'The Corinthian', designer H. Fenton, no number, should be HN1973, 8in (20.5cm) high.
£800–1,000 *LT*

r. A Royal Doulton figure, 'Pearly Boy', 2nd version, designer L. Harradine, HN2035, 5½in (13.5cm) high.
£130–160 *WIL*

A Royal Doulton figure, 'Granny's Heritage', HN1873, 7in (18cm) high.
£500–600 *CDC*

A Royal Doulton figure, 'Promenade', designer Margaret Davies, HN2076, 8in (20.5cm) high.
£800–1,000 *LT*

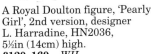

A Royal Doulton figure, 'St George', designer Stanley Thorogood, ARCA, HN2067, 16in (40.5cm) high.
£600–700 *LT*

A Royal Doulton figure, 'Pearly Girl', 2nd version, designer L. Harradine, HN2036, 5½in (14cm) high.
£120–160 *WIL*

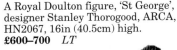

A Royal Doulton figure, 'Kathleen', designer L. Harradine, HN1252, printed and painted marks, 8in (20.5cm) high.
£350–400 *CSK*

A Royal Doulton figure, 'The Tailor', designer M. Nicoll, HN2174, 4in (10cm) high.
£500–600 *LT*

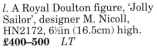

l. A Royal Doulton figure, 'Jolly Sailor', designer M. Nicoll, HN2172, 6½in (16.5cm) high.
£400–500 *LT*

A Royal Doulton figure, 'St George and the Dragon', designer W. K. Harper, 3rd version, HN2856, 16½in (42cm) high.
£600–700 *LT*

A Royal Doulton figure, 'Daffy Down Dilly', designed by L. Harradine, HN1712, introduced 1935, withdrawn 1975, 8in (20.5cm) high.
£200–250 *L*

A Royal Doulton figure, 'June', designed by L. Harradine, HN1691, withdrawn 1949, 7½in (19cm) high.
£300–350 *LT*

A Royal Doulton figure, 'Romany Sue', HN1758, 1936–49, hairline crack in shawl, 9½in (24cm) high.
£200–250 *Bon*

A Royal Doulton figure, 'Matilda', HN2011, printed and painted marks, 'COPR 1947', 10in (25.5cm) high.
£400–450 *SS*

A Royal Doulton figure, 'Spring Flowers', designed by L. Harradine, HN1807, withdrawn 1959, 7½in (19cm) high.
£150–180 *LT*

A Royal Doulton figure, 'The Leisure Hour', designed by Margaret Davies, HN2055, withdrawn 1965, 6½in (17cm) high.
£300–350 *LT*

An unissued porcelain figure of a young girl wearing a blue dress feeding a baby, printed 'Royal Doulton England' marks, HN2252, 5in (12.5cm) high.
£800–1,000 *CSK*

A Royal Doulton figure, 'Linda', HN2106, withdrawn 1976.
£100–120 *Bea*

A Royal Doulton figure, 'Sir Walter Raleigh', HN2015, withdrawn 1955.
£300–350 *Bea*

A Royal Doulton figure, 'Sleepy Head', HN2114, printed marks, 4½in (11.5cm) high.
£1,500–1,800 *CSK*

A Royal Doulton figure, 'Winter', from the Seasons series, HN2088, introduced 1952, withdrawn 1959.
£200–250 *TW*

r. A Royal Doulton figure, 'Masquerade', HN2251, circle mark, lion and crown, c1960, 8½in (21.5cm) high.
£200–250 *TVA*

A Royal Doulton figure, 'The Perfect Pair', 7in (18cm) high.
£400–450 PB

A Royal Doulton pilot figure, believed to be entitled 'The Logsman', not produced, Block No. 1767, 6in (15cm) high.
£1,500–1,800 LT

Four Royal Doulton character jugs.
l to r.
'Parson Brown'. £50–60
'White-haired Clown'. £300–350
'Toby Philpot'. £50–60
'Vicar of Bray'. £80–100 MGM

A Royal Doulton flambé Buddha, signed 'Noke', 8in (20.5cm) high.
£1,500–1,800 HCH

Three Royal Doulton character jugs:
l. 'Ard of 'Earing', designer D. Biggs, D6588, registered numbers 913137, 45356, 9681, 811/63, 7½in (19cm) high.
£600–700
c. 'The Clown', brown-haired version, designer H. Fenton, registered number 810520, 6in (15cm) high.
£1,200–1,500
r. 'Old King Cole, designer H. Fenton, 6in (15cm) high.
£100–120 GC

A Royal Doulton character jug, 'Lord Nelson', designer M. Henk, D6336, introduced 1952, withdrawn in 1969, 7in (18cm) high.
£150–250 WIL

l. A Royal Doulton flambé model of a leaping salmon, 12in (30.5cm) high.
£550–650
r. A Royal Doulton flambé model of a seated fox, 9in (23cm) high.
£550–650 MGM

A Royal Doulton 'Jester' wall mask.
£250–300 MGM

A Royal Doulton 'Lonsdale' leaf and floral decorated toilet jug and basin.
£200–250 PC

A Royal Doulton 'Kingsware' jug, decorated with embossed golfing figures in period costume, printed factory mark, c1935, 9in (23cm) high.
£500–600 WIL

A Royal Doulton Isaac Walton two-handled 'fishing pot', inscribed 'And when the Timorous Trout...', 6in (15cm) high.
£80–100 MN

A Royal Doulton model of a bulldog, HN1043, and a smaller bulldog.
£400–500 Bea

l. A Doulton figure of a mandarin, wearing a yellow tunic with circular motifs over a plain blue full length skirt, his jacket with larger motifs on a black ground, small chip to hat, dated '7.24', HN611, 10in (25.5cm) high.
£1,000–1,200
S(C)

A pair of Doulton Lambeth saltglazed stoneware bookends, one with a single monkey, the other with a monkey and infant, on a foliate base under a green glaze, stamped factory mark 'Doulton, Lambeth', c1890, 6in (15cm) high.
£600–700   *S(C)*

A 1930s style Doulton dinner service, entitled 'Dubarry', comprising: 4 tureens and covers, 2 ladles, 5 graduated meat plates, 2 sauceboats, 22 plates and 2 petal edged plates, on a cream ground, with a geometric pattern of intersecting lines and semi-circles edged in green with a central motif of a stylized flower in orange, some plates worn.
£300–400   *P(M)*

A Doulton Lambeth stoneware vase, decorated by Edith Lupton, carved and glazed with flowers and grasses over a beige background with painted florets, dated '1887', 16in (40.5cm) high.
£600–700   *PCh*

l. A Doulton figure, 'Contentment', designed by L. Harradine, HN395, decorated mainly in yellow, light green and pink, 7½in (18cm) high.
£1,000–1,200   *S(C)*

l. A Doulton saltglazed stoneware vase, by Hannah B. Barlow, impressed factory marks and date, incised monogram 'BHB' and 'LAB' for Lucy A. Barlow, c1884, 12in (30.5cm) high.
£1,200–1,500   *S(C)*

r. A Doulton baluster vase, decorated in black against a rich flambé ground, printed and impressed marks, 20in (51cm) high.
£300–350   *CSK*

A Doulton Lambeth jug, to commemorate Emin Pasha, Relief Expedition 1887–89, with a portrait of H. M. Stanley, 8in (20.5cm) high.
£250–300   *WIL*

'Philippa of Hainault', HN2008, 9½in (24cm) high.
£600–700
'Matilda', HN2011, 9in (23cm) high.
£400–500
'The Lady Anne Neville', HN2006, 9½in (23cm) high.
£550–650
'Margaret of Anjou', HN2012, 9in (23cm) high.
£500–600
'The Young Miss Nightingale', HN2010, 9in (23cm) high.
£400–500
'Mrs Fitzherbert', HN2007, 9in (23cm) high.
£400–500
'Henrietta Maria', HN2005, 9in (23cm) high.
£400–500   *EH*

A set of 8 Doulton Dickens characters, printed marks, 4in (10cm) high.
£300–350   *SC*

l. A Royal Doulton figure, 'Little Boy Blue', designed by L. Harradine, 6in (15cm) high.
£120–150   *TVA*

A Royal Doulton figure, 'Rosebud', designed by L. Harradine, HN1581, 3in (7.5cm) high.
£300–350   *P*

Locate the Source

The source of each illustration in *Miller's Art Nouveau & Art Deco Buyer's Guide* can be found by checking the code letters below each caption with the Key to Illustrations on pages 8–10.

A Royal Doulton
polychrome glazed
stoneware fountain
figure, designed by
Gilbert Bayes,
impressed signature
'Gilbert Bayes', 1934,
42in (106.5cm) high.
£2,000–2,500   *C*

A Royal Doulton figure,
'Fortune Teller', HN2159,
introduced 1955,
withdrawn 1967.
£300–350   *TW*

A Royal Doulton figure,
'The Puppetmaker', HN2253,
1962–73, 8in (20.5cm) high.
£200–250   *Bon*

A Royal Doulton figure,
'The Shepherd', M.17,
miniature, withdrawn 1938,
4in (10cm) high.
£400–500   *LT*

A Royal Doulton character jug,
'The Clown', modelled by
H. Fenton, red haired version,
printed mark and title in green,
c1940, 6½in (16.5cm) high.
£800–1,000   *SC*

A Royal Doulton character
jug, 'The White Haired Clown',
designer L. Harradine, D6322,
withdrawn 1955.
£300–350   *LT*

A Royal Doulton character mug,
'The Poacher'.
£60–70   *M*

l. A Royal Doulton character
mug, 'Friar Tuck'.
£150–180   *M*

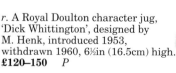

A Royal Doulton character jug,
'Punch & Judy Man', designed by
D. Biggs, D6590, introduced 1964,
withdrawn 1969, 7in (18cm) high.
£300–350   *WIL*

r. A Royal Doulton character jug,
'Dick Whittington', designed by
M. Henk, introduced 1953,
withdrawn 1960, 6½in (16.5cm) high.
£120–150   *P*

A Royal Doulton character jug,
'Drake', hatless version, date
code for 1940, 6in (15cm) high.
£1,500–1,800   *McC*

*This early version without a hat
was piloted but never actually
released for general production.
See* Character and Toby Jugs
*by Desmond Eyles, published by
Royal Doulton, 1979.*

A pair of Doulton dessert plates. **£75–100** *AOS*

A pair of inverted baluster form saltglazed stoneware vases, initials of Florence E. Barlow, assistant Eleaner Tosen, one rim chipped, c1902–5, 10½in (26.5cm) high.
£500–600 *CDC*

A Doulton 'fishing' plate, 10½in (26.5cm) diam.
£75–100 *RP*

l. A Doulton Lambeth stoneware oil lamp, by Florence and Lucy Barlow, with etched glass shade and chimney, impressed mark and initials, 25in (63.5cm) high.
£1,200–1,500 *DSH*

A pair of Doulton Burslem twin-handled vases, painted in green, pink, purple, white and brown with gilt highlights, against a background with gilt flowerheads on a light blue ground, printed and painted marks, 14½in (37cm) high.
£800–1,000 *CSK*

A Doulton Lambeth stoneware tobacco jar and cover, with applied decoration, painted in shades of buff and blue, outlined in white slip, all on a stippled green and brown ground, impressed factory mark, incised artist's monogram, c1925, 6in (15cm) high.
£60–70 *WIL*

A Doulton Lambeth dish, decorated by Linnie Watt, painted in shades of brown, yellow and blue, damaged, impressed and painted marks, 6in (15cm) wide.
£400–500 *CSK*

A Doulton Lambeth vase, damaged, impressed date '1885', monogram of G. H. Tabor.
£175–200 *SN*

A Lambeth vase, decorated in Art Nouveau style with mauve flowers on green ground, by Eliza Simmance, 14in (35.5cm) high.
£800–1,000 *LT*

A pair of saltglazed stoneware vases, grey-green with blue and ochre details, initials of Bessie Newbery, a supervisor at Doultons from 1911, c1912–18, 12in (30.5cm) high.
£200–250 *CDC*

A pair of Doulton Lambeth green and blue decorated tankards, 6in (15cm) high.
£150–180 *PC*

A Doulton Burslem vase, by W. Slater, with chrysanthemums in shades of yellow, blue, mauve and green on a mottled turquoise ground, signed, printed marks, 1890s, 19½in (49.5cm) high.
£600–700 *SS*

A pair of Doulton Burslem blue and white transferware soup plates, 'Madras' pattern, 10in (25.5cm) diam.
£15–20 *OD*

A Doulton vase, be G. H. Tabor, incised with blue flowerheads and dark green leaves and foliage on a green ground, impressed 'Doulton Lambeth 1881', 10½in (26.5cm) high.
£500–600 *CSK*

A Doulton Lambeth vase, by Hannah Barlow, decorated with an incised band of cattle, dated '1888', 7½in (19cm) high.
£600–700 *TVA*

A Doulton stoneware figure of a Merry Musician, by George Tinworth, inscribed with monogram 'T.G', 4in (10cm) high.
£500–600 *Bea*

A Doulton Lambeth stoneware group, modelled by George Tinworth, signed on base 'Doulton's Lambeth' and 'GT' monogram, 7in (18cm) high.
£3,000–3,500 *P*

A Royal Doulton stoneware jardinière and stand, in muted colours on a green ground, hair crack to rim, 37in (94cm)high.
£800–1,000 *Bea*

A Doulton Lambeth stoneware globular vase, by Eliza Simmance, glazed olive against a ground of slip-decorated petals, artist's monogram No. 875, dated '1886', 10½in (26.5cm) high.
£500–600 *P*

A Doulton Lambeth pottery lemonade jug, by Emily J. Partington, with silver-plated hinged cover and thumbpiece, decorated in low relief within oval buff reserve panels, on flower decorated green and blue ground, impressed mark and initials, 9in (23cm) high.
£500–600 *AH*

A pair of Doulton stoneware vases, decorated by Hannah Barlow, with bands of deer within stylized foliage borders, impressed mark and date '1885', 9½in (24cm) high.
£1,500–1,800 *SWO*

A Royal Doulton 'Chang' vase, covered in a thick crackled mottled white, black, red, ochre glaze running over mottled shades of ochre, red, blue and black, printed marks 'Chang, Royal Doulton, Noke', 4½in (11cm) high.
£800–1,000 *C*

A pair of Royal Doulton baluster vases, with mottled green glaze and raised design of stylized flowers and foliage.
£300–350 *LRG*

A Royal Doulton teapot and cover, commemorating Lord Nelson, blue ground with brown glazed rope-twist handle and spout, raised decoration of the head of the Admiral, the other side depicting HMS *Victory,* and inscribed around the neck, 'England Expects Every Man Will Do His Duty', monogrammed 'Ap', 5in (12.5cm) high.
£300–350 *RID*

A Royal Doulton urn, with Grecian figures, 13in (33cm) high.
£300–350 *ASA*

A Doulton Studio ware vase, c1930, 7in (18cm) high.
£75–95 *AOS*

A pair of Royal Doulton toy vases, hand-painted with a country scene, c1910, 1½in (4cm) high.
£200–250 *TVA*

A Royal Doulton vase, decorated with a continuous floral pattern in blue, white and gilt, against a shaded ground, 18½in (47cm) high.
£220–270 *RID*

A pair of Doulton stoneware vases, 11in (28cm) high.
£250–300 *ASA*

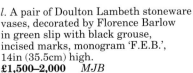

l. A pair of Doulton Lambeth stoneware vases, decorated by Florence Barlow in green slip with black grouse, incised marks, monogram 'F.E.B.', 14in (35.5cm) high.
£1,500–2,000 *MJB*

Two Doulton stoneware candlesticks, by George Tinworth, signed, c1900, 8in (20.5cm) high.
£1,000–1,500 *HER*

A Royal Doulton earthenware 'suffragette' inkwell, 3in (7.5cm) high.
£400–500 *GAK*

A Royal Doulton soap dish, specially designed and manufactured for the proprietors of Wright's Coal Tar Soap, c1920, 6in (15cm) wide.
£80–100 *POW*

A Royal Doulton fish ashtray, in green, blue, brown and grey, 6in (15cm) wide.
£100–120 *POW*

A Doulton bulldog, 'Old Bill', in a steel helmet with a rucksack, khaki glaze.
£300–350 *HER*

l. A Royal Doulton Art Deco coffee set, cream ground with a yellow, green, blue and orange C-scroll pattern, slight damage and losses.
£120–150 *GAK*

A pair of Royal Doulton pottery vases, brown ground with raised blue and light brown floral and leaf pattern, 12½in (32cm) high.
£200–250 *GAK*

l. A pair of Doulton faïence vases, c1880, 11½in (29cm) high.
£400–500 *HER*

A Royal Doulton earthenware 56-piece dinner service, designed by Sir Frank Brangwyn, cream ground with green geometric panels with green, yellow and blue foliage motifs, minor damage, printed marks 'Designed by F. Frank Brangwyn R. D., Royal Doulton, England', c1930, and a 23-piece part tea service, 'Harvest', designed by Sir Frank Brangwyn, incised and impressed decoration of fruit with foliage and sheaves of corn, polychrome on a cream ground, various printed Royal Doulton marks, minor damage, c1930.
£2,000–2,500 *C*

l. A Doulton Lambeth vase, by Hannah Barlow, with green ground and a band of ponies, 13in (33cm) high.
£800–1,000 *GAK*

A Royal Doulton glazed stoneware jardinière and stand, deep blue and mottled green glazed ground, minor damage, impressed lion, crown and circle mark, incised monogram 'MB' early 20thC, 42in (106cm) high.
£800–1,000 *S(S)*

A Doulton Lambeth stoneware vase, decorated in Art Nouveau style with seaweed fronds in blue, green and white on shaded brown and green ground, initialled 'MVM' for Mark V. Marshall, 17in (43cm) high.
£600–700   *MJB*

A pair of Doulton faïence vases, by A. Euphemia Thatcher, assisted by Elizabeth Shelley, 1880, 11in (28cm) high.
£500–600   *HER*

A Royal Doulton 'Chang' vase, 13½in (34.5cm) high.
£1,200–1,500   *LT*

A Doulton faïence moon flask, painted by Hannah Barlow, 1885, 11½in (29cm) high.
£1,000–1,200   *HER*

A Doulton Series ware vase, 'The Blue Children', with blue and white gilt rim, introduced in 1890, c1920.
£400–500   *HER*

A Doulton faïence vase, by Mary Butterton, dated '1879', 22in (56cm) high.
£650–750   *HER*

l. A pair of Doulton faïence vases, by M. M. Arding, ochre base, blue ground, c1883, 11in (28cm) high.
£500–600   *HER*

l. A Doulton faïence vase, painted by Mary Butterton, with 3 circular panels of white peonies on a yellow ground, on a reserve of overlapping palmettes in shades of brown and yellow, the neck with a band of butterfly-wing design, painted monograms, damaged, 24in (61cm) high.
£400–500   *C*

A pair of Doulton Lambeth vases by Frank Butler, 14in (35.5cm) high.
£1,200–1,500   *LT*

A Doulton Lambeth stoneware jug, by George Tinworth, with green scrolling foliage and applied flowerheads, mounted with silver rim and cover, hallmarks for Sheffield 1873, impressed marks and incised 'GT' monogram to base, 11½in (29cm) high.
£500–600 *CSK*

A Doulton Lambeth baluster jug, by Hannah Barlow, brown, green and cream, with a silver rim and cover, hallmarks for London 1894, restored, incised and impressed marks 'HBB', 7½in (19cm) high.
£200–250 *CSK*

A Doulton Lambeth stoneware jug, by George Tinworth, glazed in green, blue, brown and white, mounted with a silver rim and hinged cover, with Hukin & Heath Birmingham hallmarks for 1877, impressed and incised marks, 10in (25.5cm) high.
£500–600 *CSK*

A Doulton Lambeth stoneware silver-rimmed lemonade set, comprising a jug and a pair of beakers, all moulded in relief, jug 9½in (24cm) high.
£300–350 *Wor*

A Doulton Burslem dessert service, comprising: 5 cake stands and 12 dessert plates, painted in pink, purple, light green, blue and gilt, damaged, printed and painted marks, plates 8½in (21.5cm) diam.
£500–600 *CSK*

A Doulton Lambeth stoneware jug and 2 beakers, by George Tinworth, glazed in green, blue and brown, each with white metal mount to rim, 'G.T.' monogram to body, impressed date '1882', incised marks to base, 9in (23cm) high.
£800–1,000 *CSK*

A Doulton Lambeth faïence wall plaque, 'First Come First Served', painted by Esther Lewis in naturalistic colours, impressed and painted marks, numbers '242', 17in (43cm) diam.
£600–700 *CSK*

A Doulton Lambeth stoneware jug, by Hannah Barlow, incised with goats above a band of blue and green stylized leaves, Doulton Lambeth mark, dated '1878', incised 'HBB' and assistants, 8in (20.5cm) high.
£800–1,000 *CSK*

r. A Doulton faïence jardinière and stand, moulded in high relief with foliate rococo designs, the baluster stand with fluted waist, painted in muted enamel colours, slight restoration to bowl, late 19thC, 18in (45.5cm) high.
£800–1,000 *Bea*

A Royal Doulton jug, by Mark V. Marshall, with blue and brown foliage, impressed 'Doulton Lambeth England', 9½in (24cm) high.
£400–500   *CSK*

A Royal Doulton 'Sung' vase, ruby red, blue and green, marked 'Sung, Noke', 'FM', 5in (12.5cm) high.
£500–600   *P*

A pair of Royal Doulton vases, decorated by Frank Butler, ochre, lavender and green, on a blue and buff ground, marked, artists's monogram, '991', assistant's initials of Jane Hurst, date code for 1906, 18½in (47cm) high.
£1,500–2,000   *S*

A Royal Doulton stoneware vase, by Francis C. Pope, with white flowers in relief, brown foliage on a purple ground, signed 'F.C.P.', No. 537, date code for 1916, 16in (41cm) high.
£1,000–1,200   *P*

A Royal Doulton 'Chang' snuff bottle, with a cracked white glaze streaked in red, amber, blue, brown and green, marked 'C.M. Chang, Noke', monogram for Harry Nixon, date code for 1925, 2½in (6cm) high.
£500–600   *P*

A pair of Doulton Lambeth stoneware oviform vases, by Harry Simeon, blue, brown and mustard, impressed Lambeth faïence mark with 'Faïence' cancelled, signed 'HS', No. 369, 13in (33cm) high.
£1,500–1,800   *P*

A Doulton vase, by Mark V. Marshall, green and blue, impressed Lambeth mark and initials, No. 990, dated '1883', 10½in (26.5cm) high.
£1,000–1,200   *S*

A pair of Royal Doulton vases, incised by Francis C. Pope, green and blue against a tan ground, impressed marks, artist's assistant's initials, No. 98, date code for 1904, 15in (38cm) high.
£1,500–1,800   *S*

A Doulton Lambeth stoneware timepiece, by George Tinworth, modelled as a theatre, incised marks, 'GT' monogram, assistant's initials 'LB' and 'PK', 8½in (21cm) high.
£4,000–5,000   *P*

A pair of Doulton Lambeth faïence vases, decorated by Margaret E. Thompson, impressed and printed marks, No. L8095, artist's monogram, '14', c1900, 13in (33cm) high.
£1,600–1,800   *S*

A Doulton Lambeth faïence vase, probably decorated by Margaret E. Thompson, impressed and printed marks, No. L7782, c1910, 10½in (27cm) high.
£800–1,000   *S*

An early Doulton stoneware jug, by George Tinworth, in blue and brown, monograms 'GT' and 'SG' for Sarah Gathercole, impressed 'B', 9in (23cm) high.
£400–500   *P*

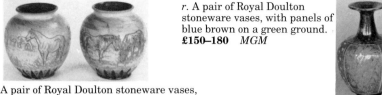

r. A pair of Royal Doulton stoneware vases, with panels of blue brown on a green ground.
£150–180 *MGM*

A pair of Royal Doulton stoneware vases, by Hannah B. Barlow and Florrie Jones, heightened in brown on a buff ground, the base with green and blue lappets, incised monograms 'H.B.B.' and 'F.J.', 5½in (14cm) high.
£1,000–1,200 *CSK*

r. A pair of Royal Doulton vases, initialled 'WB', c1925, 13in (33cm) high.
£200–250 *TVA*

A pair of Royal Doulton stoneware vases, incised monograms for Eliza Simmance and Bessie Newberry, early 20thC.
£800–1,000 *WIL*

A pair of Royal Doulton vases, decorated in the Art Nouveau manner in green and yellow on a gold-decorated ivory ground, c1900, 10½in (26.5cm) high.
£400–500 *Bea*

A pair of Royal Doulton stoneware vases, decorated on a blue ground.
£200–250 *MGM*

A Royal Doulton 'Chang' vase, covered in a thick multi-coloured crackled glaze, bearing the marks for Charles John Noke and Harry Nixon, 5½in (13.5cm) high.
£800–1,000 *Bea*

A Royal Doulton plate, depicting Porchester, signed 'A. Holdcroft', c1925, 10in (25.5cm) diam.
£120–140 *TVA*

A Royal Doulton 'Master of Foxhounds' presentation jug, No. 248 of a limited edition of 500, with original certificate of verification, 13in (33cm) high.
£1,000–1,200 *OL*

A Royal Doulton stoneware Dewar's Whisky jug, with green collar, c1895, 6½in (16.5cm) high.
£130–150 *CA*

l. A Royal Doulton buff stoneware jardinière, by Hannah Barlow, with olive green glazed neck, incised with sheep in panoramic landscape, 9in (23cm) diam.
£600–700 *WHB*

r. A Royal Doulton stoneware jardinière and stand, painted with deep blue and mottled green, stand chipped, late 19thC, 37½in (95cm) high.
£700–800 *Bea*

l. A set of 5 Royal Doulton plates, with gilded rims, the centres painted with flowers and fruit, signed 'A. Piper', 9½in (24cm) diam.
£400–500 *P(Re)*

An early Doulton
Lambeth stoneware jug,
decorated by Hannah
B. Barlow, with silver
collar and cover, artist's
monogram, London
hallmarks for 1872,
11½in (28cm) high.
£1,000–1,200   *P*

A Doulton stoneware jug, of tapering form
with skirted base, and a pair of beakers,
incised by Hannah Barlow, impressed
mark 'Doulton Lambeth 1878', and signed
'BHB', with silver mounts, London 1878,
jug 9½in (24cm) high.
£1,500–1,800   *L*

A Doulton Lambeth biscuit
barrel, with plated hinged top,
decorated with a sheepdog and
sheep by Hannah Barlow,
impressed mark and date '1873',
incised marks, 8½in (21cm) high.
£1,000–1,200   *DWB*

An early Doulton Lambeth
three-handled loving cup,
decorated by Hannah B.
Barlow, dated '1876',
artist's monogram, No.
'558', also signed on side,
6½in (16cm) high.
£800–1,000   *P*

A vase by Hannah Barlow,
incised with a band of
donkeys and 2 children,
impressed 'Doulton
Lambeth, 10½in (26cm) high.
£800–1,000   *CSK*

A Royal Doulton pottery
vase, decorated by Hannah
Barlow, with a fox attacking
sheep, 12in (30.5cm) high.
£1,000–1,200   *DSH*

A Royal Doulton stoneware vase,
by Frank A. Butler, incised with
dark green and brown spiky
bulbs with mottled green and
light blue centres, incised
artist's monogram, No. '996',
13in (33cm) high.
£800–1,000   *P*

A pair of baluster vases, by
Hannah Barlow, incised with lions,
impressed 'Doulton Lambeth
England' marks, 14in (35.5cm) high.
£3,000–3,500   *CSK*

A Doulton Lambeth faïence jardinière,
painted by Florence E. Lewis with
green and lemon ground, artist's
monogram, No. '317', 13in (33cm) high.
£400–500   *P*

l. A pair of Doulton Lambeth vases,
decorated by Frank A. Butler and
Mary Ann Thomson, all in olive
greens, blues, russet, brown, green
and white, dated '1885', with
'F.A.B.' monogram, No. '532' and
'MT' monogram on inner necks,
21½in (54cm) high.
£2,000–2,500   *P*

A Royal Doulton pilot
figure of a botanist,
6½in (17cm) high.
£1,500–1,800   *LT*

A Royal Doulton loving cup,
polychrome moulded in relief with
the Three Musketeers, No. 395 from
an edition of 600, printed marks,
10in (25.5cm) high.
£800–1,000   *Bon*

A Royal Doulton character jug,
''Ard of 'Earing', No. D6588.
£500–600   *LT*

A Doulton bust of Sir Winston
Churchill, one of only 3 made,
c1940, 8½in (21cm) high.
£1,400–1,800   *ARE*

A Doulton jardinière, signed
by George Tinworth, c1880,
12in (30.5cm) high.
£800–1,000   *HER*

A Doulton Lambeth biscuit barrel
by Florence Barlow, with plated
swing handle and lid, the mottled
brown body with incised acanthus
scroll and star decoration, incised
'FEB' mark to base.
£500–600   *Bon*

A Doulton siliconware owl, by J. A. Milne.
£600–700 *Bon*

A Doulton Lambeth stoneware Queen Victoria Jubilee commemorative jug, with a silver mounted neck, 7½in (19cm) high.
£200–250 *Re*

A Doulton group, modelled as 2 frogs attacking 2 mice, entitled 'The Combat', by George Tinworth, on an oval mound base, 4in (10cm) high.
£2,000–2,500 *CSK*

l. A pair of Doulton ivory earthenware 'Galleon' jugs, printed with 6 galleons in choppy seas, with dolphins on a lower frieze, c1885, 7in (17.5cm) high.
£500–600 *TW*

A Doulton Lambeth stoneware bowl, by Frank A. Butler, in green, pink and blue beneath a beaded band, with gilt-metal rim, impressed Doulton mark, incised monogram 'FAB', dated '1882', 9½in (24cm) diam.
£400–500 *Bon*

A Doulton Lambeth vase, by Florence E. Barlow, decorated with leaves and pâte-sur-pâte birds, on a brown ground.
£600–700 *LT*

A Doulton Lambeth stoneware figure, attributed to John Broad, impressed 'Doulton' on base, 18in (46cm) high.
£600–700 *P*

A Doulton character jug, 'Ugly Duchess', designed by M. Henks, D6603, printed marks, 4in (10cm) high.
£200–250 *CSK*

A Doulton Lambeth stoneware commemorative vase, by George Tinworth, glazed in shades of brown, green and blue, incised 'GT' monogram, 9in (23cm) high.
£600–800 *P*

l. A Doulton Lambeth vase, with incised panels of deer, by Hannah Barlow and assistant Annie Jentle, 1887, 11in (28cm) high.
£600–700 *LT*

A Doulton Lambeth teapot and cover, by Hannah Barlow, incised with goats.
£800–1,000 *WHB*

A pair of Doulton stoneware vases, incised by Hannah Barlow, brown and green, incised artist's mark, impressed factory marks, late 19thC, 11in (28cm) high.
£1,500–1,800 *SC*

A Royal Doulton vase, incised by Hannah Barlow, artist's and assistant's monogram for Florence E. Roberts, repair at base, 21½in (54.5cm) high.
£500–600 *Bon*

A Royal Doulton vase, by Hannah Barlow, monogram for Florence E. Roberts, 19½in (49.5cm) high.
£2,000–2,500 *Bon*

A Doulton Lambeth longcase clock, by Frank Butler, the caramel ground with stylized acanthus leaves and flowers, heightened in blue, chip to hood, incised 'Doulton Lambeth 1884', artist's monogram, 12in (30.5cm) high. **£1,200–1,500** *Bon*

A Doulton Lambeth stoneware vase, incised by Hannah Barlow, brown on a buff ground, with green and blue incised leaves and florets by Frank Butler, artist's monograms, assistant's mark for Emma Martin, dated '1876', 15in (38cm) high.
£1,500–1,800 *P*

A Royal Doulton stoneware vase, by Frank A. Butler, monogram 'F.A.B.', No. 347, 16in (40.5cm) high.
£1,000–1,200 *P*

A pair of Doulton vases, by Frank Butler, 19thC, 17½in (44.5cm) high.
£2,000–2,500 *SC*

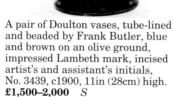

A pair of Doulton vases, tube-lined and beaded by Frank Butler, blue and brown on an olive ground, impressed Lambeth mark, incised artist's and assistant's initials, No. 3439, c1900, 11in (28cm) high.
£1,500–2,000 *S*

A Doulton vase, tube-lined by Frank Butler, glazed in blue and brown against an olive ground, impressed Lambeth mark, incised artist's and assistant's monograms, c1900, No. 58, 13½in (34.5cm) high.
£600–700 *S*

A Royal Doulton stoneware vase, by Mark V. Marshall, strawberry ground decorated in lilac and pale green, No. '96' and 'M.H.' possibly for Marion Holbrook, date letter for 1902, 12in (30.5cm) high.
£1,000–1,200 *P*

A Royal Doulton vase, tube-lined by Frank Butler, No. 647, marked, date code for 1902, 17½in (44.5cm) high.
£1,200–1,500 *S*

A Doulton menu-holder, by George Tinworth, the base titled 'I See No Reason Why Gunpowder Treason Should Ever Be Forgot', olive and ochre, impressed Lambeth mark, monogram, repaired, 1880s, 4½in (11.5cm) high.
£800–1,000 *S*

A Doulton stoneware mouse group, 'Waits', by George Tinworth, blue and ochre, impressed Lambeth mark, c1880, 5½in (14cm) high.
£2,000–2,500 *S*

A Doulton vase, painted by George White, with the legend of Orpheus and Eurydice in Hades, signed, incised 'No. 1210' and date code for 1911, one handle repaired, 16in (40.5cm) high.
£1,500–2,000 *S*

A Doulton three-handled mug, commemorating the 'Hoisting of the Flag at Pretoria', green and blue glazes, impressed marks, 10½in (26.5cm) high.
£300–350 *CSK*

A Doulton Burslem vase and cover, by George White, signed, printed mark, repaired, c1910, 21in (53cm) high.
£1,000–1,200 *S*

l & r. A pair of Royal Doulton 'Blue Children' oviform vases, the bases marked 'Royal Doulton Flambé', 11½in (29cm) high.
£1,200–1,400
c. A Royal Doulton 'Blue Children' globular vase, date code for 1931, 7in (17.5cm) high.
£400–500 *P*

A pair of Doulton Lambeth stoneware vases, by Hannah Barlow, in shades of blue and green, slight chips to rims, incised and impressed marks 'HBB', and assistant's marks, 8in (20.5cm) high.
£700–800 *CSK*

A Doulton Lambeth musical mice group, 'Happy Violincello', by George Tinworth, traces of monogram, inscribed title, 5in (12.5cm) high.
£1,500–1,800 *P*

l. A pair of Doulton vases, each printed and painted with Arabs on camels, in green, yellow and orange, printed and painted marks, 20thC, 9½in (24cm) high.
£400–500 *S*

A Doulton Lambeth jug, incised by Edgar Wilson, glazed in blue and green, impressed mark, No. '270', artist's monogram, dated '1882', 9½in (24cm) high.
£800–1,000 *S*

A pair of Doulton stoneware vases, by
Hannah Barlow, 1888, 7in (17.5cm) high.
£1,000–1,200 *DWB*

A Doulton Lambeth
stoneware three-handled
loving cup, by Florence
E. Barlow, decorated in
pâte-sur-pâte with silver
rim, 'F.E.B.' monogram,
6½in (16cm) high.
£800–1,000 *P*

A Doulton Lambeth lamp,
by Florence E. Barlow, with
3 pâte-sur-pâte panels,
'F.E.B.' monogram No. 571,
with 'R.B.' assistant's
monogram, dated '1884',
25in (63.5cm) high.
£2,000–2,400 *P*

A pair of Doulton vases, decorated by Hannah
Barlow and Florence Roberts, detailed in brown
glaze against a stippled buff ground between
tube-lined floral borders glazed in brown, pale
green and blue, one cracked, impressed Lambeth
mark, incised artists' monograms, No. 78 and
assistant's initials of Bessie Newbery, c1890,
12½in (32cm) high.
£1,200–1,500 *S*

A pair of Doulton vases, incised by
Hannah Barlow and Florence Roberts,
glazed in brown, olive and blue, minor
restoration to one rim, impressed lion,
crown and circle, incised artists'
monograms and numerals, date code
for 1903, 11in (28cm) high.
£1,800–2,200 *S*

A Doulton oviform
vase, outlined in white
on a green ground, by
Hannah Barlow,
impressed 'Royal
Doulton England',
11½in (29cm) high.
£800–1,000 *CSK*

r. A Doulton pottery
baluster vase, painted pâte-
sur-pâte, on a blue ground,
by Florence Barlow,
impressed 'Royal Doulton',
12in (30.5cm) high.
£600–700 *CSK*

*Florence more frequently
painted in slip, and also
worked on Doulton items
other than stoneware.*

l. A Doulton ewer, incised by
Hannah Barlow and Eliza
Simmance, glazed in shades
of green, brown and mauve,
impressed Lambeth mark,
incised artists' initials, 653 and
1000, dated '1877', minor chip
to foot, 14in (35.5cm) high.
£600–700 *S*

r. A Doulton jug, by
Hannah Barlow, incised
with a cat and 4 kittens,
in pale blue on a
stoneware ground, blue
and green foliage neck
and handle, impressed
'Doulton Lambeth', 1880,
9in (23cm) high.
£1,200–1,500 *CSK*

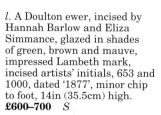

A Doulton Lambeth jug, by Arthur B. Barlow, glazed in shades of blue and brown, artist's monogram 'SG', No. 777?, assistant's mark, dated '1873', 6½in (17cm) high.
£400–500 *P*

A Doulton Lambeth stoneware jug, decorated by Hannah Barlow, Florence Barlow and Mark V. Marshall, glazed in greens, brown and beige, incised 'H.B.B.', monogram 'No. 214, F.E.B. No. 341, M.V.M. No. 3.', 9½in (24.5cm) high.
£1,500–1,800 *P*

A Doulton stoneware jardinière, in blues, browns and grey, incised 'H. Doulton Lambeth', 7½in (19cm) high.
£800–1,000 *C*

A Doulton stoneware jug, decorated by Hannah Barlow and probably Lucy Barlow, marked, dated '1884', 9½in (24cm) high.
£800–1,000 *Bea*

A Doulton tapering mug, decorated by Hannah Barlow, impressed 'Doulton Lambeth', incised 'H.B.B., 209', dated '1874', 4in (10cm) high.
£500–600 *CEd*

l. A Doulton stoneware vase, designed by Frank Butler, impressed Royal Doulton mark, incised artist's monogram 'F.A.B.', 18½in (47cm) high.
£3,000–3,500 *C*

r. A Doulton Lambeth stoneware baluster vase, by Florence E. Barlow and Frank A. Butler, in rich blues, browns and greens, the neck rim carved as a row of scrolls, 'F.E.B.' and 'F.A.B.' monograms, No. '345' and '385' and 'RHM' monogram of assistant, 21in (53cm) high.
£2,500–3,000 *P*

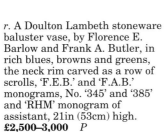

A Doulton Lambeth faïence tile panel, printed on reverse, indistinct painted monogram on one, 'R' to bottom tile, 24½in (61.5cm) high.
£600–700 *P*

A pair of Doulton Lambeth vases, by George Tinworth, in dark blue and with pale blue beadwork tendrils and flowerheads on an ochre coloured ground, both with incised monogram, 11in (28cm) high.
£1,500–1,800 *L*

r. A Doulton Lambeth siliconware vase, by Edith D. Lupton and Ada Dennis, in white, brown and blue, top reduced, 'E.D.L.' artist's monogram, numbered '378', 'AD' monogram, numbered '16', dated '1885', 8in (20.5cm) high.
£800–1,000 *P*

l. A Doulton Lambeth stoneware vase, by Mark V. Marshall, glazed in mottled brown, blue and cream, artist's monogram, No. 3 and assistant's mark, 10in (25.5cm) high.
£600–700 *P*

r. A Doulton Lambeth vase by Emily Stormer, glazed in blues, greens, white and brown, artist's monogram, No. '825' and 'EM' for Emma Martin, dated '1877', 9½in (24.5cm) high.
£500–600 *P*

A set of 3 Doulton Lambeth faïence tiles, by Florence E. Lewis, framed, painted artist's monogram, Minton & Hollins, each 8in (20.5cm) square.
£300–350 *P*

A pair of Doulton Lambeth stoneware and brass candlesticks, by Frank A. Butler, in olive greens, blues, brown and russet, artist's monogram and No. 550, 10in (25.5cm) high.
£1,200–1,500 *P*

A Doulton stoneware vase, decorated by Edith Lupton, in dark coloured glazes, impressed and incised marks and date '1888', 13in (33cm) high.
£700–800 *SC*

A pair of Doulton Lambeth stoneware jardinières, by Edith D. Lupton, incised with olive green foliate scrolls against deep blue, with artist's initials, No. 512 and 513, assistant's initials for Eliza J. Hubert, dated '1877', 8in (20.5cm) high.
£1,500–1,800 *P*

r. A Royal Doulton stoneware vase, by Mark V. Marshall, incised artist's initials, No. 685, assistant's mark for Emily Partington, date shield for 1907, 12in (30.5cm) high.
£800–1,000 *P*

A Doulton Lambeth jug, by Mark V. Marshall, incised artist's initials, No. 105, assistant's initials 'MH' and 'JBH', 9in (23cm) high.
£3,000–3,500 *L*

Doulton Glazing Techniques

- 'Sung' and 'Chang' wares draw upon old Chinese glazes with their bright mottled colours against a flambé ground.
- 'Titanian' wares, introduced in 1915, required a fine porcelain body, often with artist's illustrations under a blend of metallic pigments to form a silvery-blue glaze.
- 'Kingsware', the distinctive treacle brown glaze often found on flasks and bottles made for Dewar's Whisky, was made with a transparent ivory glaze fired over coloured slips.

A Doulton jug, by Mark V. Marshall, with a band of blue and brown foliage outlined in white on a stoneware ground, impressed mark, 10½in (26cm) high.
£400–500 *CSK*

A pair of Doulton stoneware vases, by Eliza Simmance, with stylized lily motifs on a streaked pale green ground, impressed mark, incised artist's initials, 1900s, 9in (23cm) high.
£1,500–1,800 *SS*

A Doulton Lambeth stoneware ewer, by Mark V. Marshall, in ochre, cobalt and green, shown at the 1893 Chicago Columbian World Fair, 72in (183cm) high.
£18,000–20,000 *Bon*

A pair of Royal Doulton vases, c1900, 11in (28cm) high.
£200–250 *HAE*

A pair of Doulton flambé models of penguins, set in an alabaster ashtray with silver mounts, with assay mark for London 1919, 6½in (17cm) high.
£500–600 *Bea*

A pair of Doulton saltglazed stoneware vases, by Hannah B. Barlow, in green and brown with tube-lined Art Nouveau swirling motifs in a band above and below, chip to rim of one, impressed factory marks, incised monogram 'BHB' and others of assistants, c1885, 11in (28cm) high.
£1,500–1,800 *S(C)*

l. A Doulton coffee service, 'Reynard the Fox' printed marks and pattern No. H4927.
£300–350 *DN*

A Doulton group, 'The Love Letter', HN 2149.
£200–250 *Bea*

A Doulton brown and white model of a standing bulldog, HN 1045.
£400–500 *Bea*

l. A large Doulton loving cup, produced to commemorate the Silver Jubilee of King George V and Queen Mary, No. 980 of a limited edition of 1,000.
£600–700 *Bea*

A Doulton white character jug, 'Simon the Cellarer', 3in (7.5cm) high.
£200–250 *DN*

A Doulton saltglazed metal-mounted stoneware biscuit barrel, highlighted in blue, with impressed factory mark and date, and incised monogram 'Hannah B. Barlow', 1880, 7½in (19cm) high.
£600–700 *S(C)*

A Doulton porcelain vase, by Arthur Leslie, decorated with a maiden holding a white dove in a landscape, dated '5.11', 9in (23cm) high.
£600–700 *S(C)*

A Doulton pottery vase, decorated with a hunting scene between bands of flowers, cracked, 22½in (57cm) high.
£200–250 *Bea*

A Royal Doulton limited edition loving cup to commemorate the reign of Edward VIII, by H. Fenton, No. 699 of 2000, printed inscription and factory mark, and a certificate signed by Charles J. Noke, 10in (25.5cm) high.
£600–700   *TW*

A Royal Doulton pottery 'Nelson' loving cup, inscribed 'I Was In Trafalgar Bay' and 'England Expects', decorated in colours and incised 'Fenton', the base with printed inscription and mark in green, No. 579 of limited edition of 600, 10½in (27cm) high.
£1,000–1,200   *HSS*

A Royal Doulton character teapot and cover, 'Old Charley', date code for 1939, introduced 1939, withdrawn 1960, 7in (17.5cm) high.
£600–700   *P*

A Royal Doulton character teapot and cover, 'Sairey Gamp', date code for 1939, introduced 1939, withdrawn 1960, 7in (17.5cm) high.
£600–700   *P*

A Royal Doulton mug, decorated in relief with golfers in period costume, glazed in colours, D5716, 6in (15cm) high.
£200–250   *P*

A Royal Doulton character jug, 'Mephistopheles', designed by C. J. Noke and H. Fenton, introduced 1937, withdrawn 1948, 6in (15cm) high.
£500–600   *P*

r. A 'Kingsware' whisky flask and stopper, printed Royal Doulton, England marks, 8in (20.5cm) high.
£200–250   *CSK*

A Doulton flambé figure, by Noke, the pagoda-like red silk and cream braid shade with metal-mounted faceted glass drops, printed mark and original printed label, c1930, 22½in (58cm) high.
£2,000–2,500   *C*

A pottery character jug, modelled as Santa Claus, D6690, printed Royal Doulton England marks, 7½in (19cm) high.
£80–100   *CSK*

l. A Royal Doulton 'Bunnykins' candleholder, with loop handle, 'Santa Claus' and 'Lambeth Walk', designed by Barbara Vernon, 'Bunnykins' back stamp, 1940–49, 7in (17.5cm) high.
£150–180   *P*

Restored or not Restored?

In salesrooms or at fairs, some readers may have seen potential buyers biting into pieces of Doulton with their teeth. They have not skipped lunch, they are testing for restoration. This can be detected as a soft putty on the surface of the glaze and hence will be soft to the teeth. A more hygenic method is to open a paper clip and gently prod the surface – any restoration should appear soft to the touch. Always ask the seller's permission as you risk defacing expensive restoration. Best of all, ask the seller to 'blue light' the piece for you; restoration will show up under an ultraviolet lamp.

A Royal Doulton figure, 'Smuts' designed by H. Fenton, 7in (18cm) high.
£500–600 *P*

A Royal Doulton figure, 'Dulicinea', designed by L. Harradine, HN1419, introduced 1930, withdrawn 1938, 5½in (14cm) high.
£1,500–1,800 *LT*

A Royal Doulton pottery character jug of 'Johnny Appleseed', printed marks, D6372, 6½in (16.5cm) high.
£100–120 *CSK*

A Royal Doulton 'Kingsware' Dewar's Whisky flask, with a figure of 'George the Guard', printed marks, 8½in (21.5cm) high.
£120–150 *Bon*

A Royal Doulton figure, 'Marquise Silvestra', c1920, 9in (23cm) high.
£5,000–6,000 *Bon*

A Royal Doulton figure, 'The Lilac Shawl', after a model by C. J. Noke, printed mark and title, HN44, date code for 1918, 8½in (21.5cm) high.
£800–1,000 *S*

A Royal Doulton 'Kingsware' Dewar's Whisky flask, decorated with a 16thC town crier, printed marks, 9in (23cm) high.
£150–180 *Bon*

A Royal Doulton figure, 'Lady Ermine', green painted mark, HN54, No. 15, dated '2.1918', 8½in (22.5cm) high.
£1,000–1,200 *SC*

A Royal Doulton figure, 'Robert Burns', HN42, inscribed 'E. W. Light Sc.' and 'No. 5', 14in (35.5cm) high.
£2,500–3,000 *P*

A Royal Doulton figure, 'Fruit Gathering', designed by L. Harradine, HN562, impressed date '9.23/8?', 8in (20.5cm) high.
£1,000–1,200 *P*

A Royal Doulton figure, 'Pretty Lady', HN70, date code for 1919, 9½in (24cm) high.
£800–1,000 *S*

r. A Royal Doulton model of a fox, lying curled with its tail around its head, with dark and light marking, HN147, impressed date '2.1.36', 3½in (9cm) wide.
£500–600 *P*

l. A Royal Doulton model, 'Character Owl', HN187, No. 228, 8in (20.5cm) high.
£1,500–1,800 *P*

r. A Royal Doulton figure, 'The Perfect Pair', designed by L. Harradine, HN581, impressed date '10.26', 7in (17.5cm) high.
£400–500 *P*

A Doulton Slaters patent vase, decorated with panels of charcoal-grey and royal blue, painted 'M.L.X1974', 12in (30.5cm) high.
£200–250 *P*

l. A Doulton Lambeth saltglazed figure of a Boer War soldier, designed by John Broad, on a green and caramel base, impressed marks, 12in (30.5cm) high.
£800–1,000
c. A Doulton Burslem urn, painted by D. Dewsberry, on an ivory ground, bordered by gilt friezes, printed mark, 14in (35.5cm) high.
£600–700
r. A Royal Doulton 'Chinese jade' vase, covered with a green streaked glaze, printed mark, 6in (15cm) high.
£800–1,000 *Bon*

A Doulton jug, with brown glazed borders, printed in black with 'The Handyman', a sailor from HMS *Powerful*, flanked by bust portraits of Capt. H. Lambton and P. M. Scott, impressed 'Doulton Lambeth England', 8½in (21.5cm) high.
£300–400 *CSK*

A Royal Doulton 'Chang' vase, glazed in shades of crimson, blue and green and over-painted with brightly coloured butterflies, faintly impressed and painted 'Doulton' and numerals, 9½in (24.5cm) high.
£1,500–1,800 *S*

A Royal Doulton Flambé 'Sung' vase, with a mauve, amber and crimson ground, mottled brown glaze, printed lion, crown and circle, impressed 'Doulton' and numerals, painted Sung script mark, No. 2653E, dated '3–224', 8in (20.5cm) high.
£600–700 *S*

A Doulton jug, 'Regency Coach', decorated in low relief and colours with a coach drawing up outside an inn, printed and painted marks, limited edition, No. 329, 10½in (26.5cm) high.
£600–700 *CSK*

A Doulton mug, decorated in 'Shakespeare's Knights' pattern, c1928, 5½in (14cm) high.
£40–50 *SN*

A set of 10 Doulton plates, decorated by Kelsall, painted in polychrome with gilt borders, chips to one plate, the majority with painted title on reverse and printed marks, 9in (23cm) diam.
£1,000–1,200 *CSK*

A Doulton two-handled loving cup, with King George VI and Queen Elizabeth, limited edition No. 949 of 2000, 1937.
£600–700 *MGM*

r. A Doulton jug, 'Chart of Treasure Island', decorated in colours and relief with Treasure Island characters, cracks to base, printed and painted marks, limited edition, No. 3, 7in (18cm) high.
£400–450 *CSK*

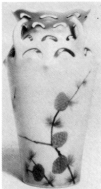

A pair of Royal Dux porcelain figural vases, modelled with scrolling golden leaves and pink tinged flowers, raised pink triangle mark, 16½in (42cm) high.
£300–350 *CSK*

A Royal Dux figure of a boy, picked out in pale colours and gilding, applied triangle mark and impressed '1810', c1900, 20½in (52cm) high.
£400–550 *SC*

A Royal Dux porcelain figure, seated on a green rocky base, marked 'P. Aichele, No. 1379', 18½in (47cm) high.
£900–1,000 *DSH*

A Rozenburg twin-handled pottery vase, by Jan van der Vet, printed crown and stork mark, artist's monogram, date code for 1902, 14in (35.5cm) high.
£850–1,000 *P*

l. A small Rozenburg 'egg-shell' vase, painted in greens, yellow, purple, black and orange, painted factory marks, numbered '1588' and date code for 1900, 5in (12.5cm) high.
£850–1,000 *P*

A pair of Royal Dux porcelain vases, with scrolling golden leaves and pink tinged flowers, raised pink triangle mark, 16½in (42cm) high.
£1,000–1,500 *CSK*

A Villeroy & Boch 'Mettlach' wall plaque, in pale pink, matt red and petrol blue, with a gilded rim, impressed factory marks and number '2549', 18in (45.5cm) diam.
£850–1,000 *P*

A Rozenburg dish, decorated with a Chinese dragon, the border with yellow geometrical pattern, repaired, marked 'Rozenburg Den Haag 758 NKx, 1896'. 17½in (44.5cm) diam.
£850–1,000 *C(Am)*

A Royal Dux bowl, painted in muted enamel colours and gold, 11in (28cm) wide.
£450–550 *Bea*

A Royal Dux figure, 'The Girl with the Golden Apple', c1920, 22in (56cm) wide.
£1,400–1,600 *BEV*

A pair of Martin Brothers stoneware panels, the arched forms impressed and incised with profile images of Cowper and Chaucer, each against a patterned background, covered in a salt glaze in shades of blue and brown, indistinct marks and date, 17in (43cm) long.
£800–950 *C*

A pair of Minton Art Pottery moon flasks, painted in blue with frogs and fish or birds and rabbits within chevron bands, the short cylindrical neck flanked by a pair of loop handles, impressed, printed and painted marks, c1870, 8½in (21.5cm) high.
£800–950 *S(S)*

A Martin Brothers jug, in a mottled blue-green on a brown ground, the neck with a band of vertical incised lines, incised 'Martin Bros., London & Southall, 2–1894', chip to spout, c1894, 8½in (21.5cm) high.
£400–480 *S(S)*

A Martin Brothers vase, painted with spiny fish and eels swimming among water weeds and other aquatic life, in shades of grey and brown on a buff ground, incised 'Martin Bros., London & Southall, 10–1891', repaired, 7½in (19cm) high, and a miniature Martin ware vase.
£500–600 *CSK*

A Linthorpe vase, by Christopher Dresser, shape No. 24, 12½in (32cm) high.
£400–500 *NCA*

A Martin Brothers stoneware tobacco jar and cover, modelled as a comic bird with curly plumage, standing erect with eyes closed, glazed in shades of blue and buff, base incised 'Martin Bros. London & Southall', cover incised 'Martin 30.8.81 London & Southall', repaired, 12in (30.5cm) high.
£6,500–8,000 *CSK*

A Minton Art Pottery Studio moon flask, one side with painted head and shoulders portrait of a girl in the style of W. S. Coleman, framed by a band of holly, the reverse in dark blue, impressed 'Minton 1498', and printed mark 'Minton's Art Pottery Studio Kensington Gore', damaged, 14in (35.5cm) high.
£800–950 *P(S)*

A set of 20 Minton stoneware tiles, designed by A. W. N. Pugin, the ochre ground with brown and black glazed decoration, quatrefoil reserve with central flowerhead within foliate motifs, reverse with moulded marks 'Minton & Co., Stoke-upon-Trent, Patent', each tile 6in (15cm) square.
£600–720 *C*

A Brannam pottery slipware vase, the red body overlaid with white slip, decorated with 3 sgraffito panels of armorial style beasts and foliage, flanked by foliate and geometric panels and borders, beneath a honey glaze, signed 'C. Brannam, Barum, N. Devon' and dated '1891', 'R' on neck, 15in (12.5cm) high.
£800–950   *P*

At this early date it is highly possible that C. H. Brannam himself threw and decorated this piece.

A Bretby 'jewelware' vessel, 16in (41cm) high.
£250–300   *ZEI*

l. A pair of Ault brown and black earthenware vases, c1930, 10½in (26cm) high.
£125–150   *OCA*

A pair of Fenton Sutherland Art Ware vases, by Frank Beardmore & Co, with pink, green and yellow decoration, 12½in (31.5cm) high.
£700–800   *ASA*

A Watcombe Pottery terracotta tea set, designed by Christopher Dresser, with bands of ridged decoration, comprising: a teapot and cover, milk jug, sugar basin, cup with saucer and tray with impressed 'W', teapot 3in (7.5cm) high.
£600–700   *C*

An Austrian wall plaque, by Boss, 6½in (16cm) high.
£170–200   *ASA*

A stoneware jug, both sides modelled with the face of a mildlly amused, overweight and ageing male, with strap handle, incised '10.12.1909 R. W. Martin & Brothers, London & Southall', 7in (17.5cm) high.
£1,000–1,200   *P*

A tapering jug, incised with a gentleman and companion in medieval costume, flanked by flowers and leaves on a brown ground, incised mark, 'R.W. Martin, London and Southall', and dated '15th July 1881', 8½in (21cm) high.
£270–320   *DN*

A Hadcote vase, with raised slip design in turquose, made for Liberty & Co, 7in (17.5cm) high.
£200–250   *ZEI*

A pair of Martin Brothers stoneware candlesticks, on sloping footed square bases, incised with panels of water birds, surmounted by twisted columns incised with foliage and the monogram 'PA', glazed in shades of green and blue, damaged, incised factory marks, 8in (20.5cm) high.
£500–600   *CSK*

A Martin Brothers stoneware double faced jug, inscribed on base 'R. W. Martin Brothers, London & Southall, 2.2.1903', 7in (17.5cm) high.
£2,000–2,500 *Re*

A Martin Brothers stoneware spirit flask, with a grinning face, and a silver-mounted stopper, inscribed on base 'R. W. Martin Brothers, London & Southall, 11.1901', 9½in (24cm) high.
£2,000–2,500 *Re*

A Martin Brothers stoneware jug, with mottled blue ground, incised and dated 1897', 10½in (26cm) high.
£1,250–1,500 *Re*

A stoneware vase, decorated with incised fish and water snakes among seaweed, in mottled brown glaze, incised 'R. W. Martin London & Southall, 3.1891', 7in (17.5cm) high.
£1,000–1,200 *CSK*

A stoneware jug, with incised decoration of an underwater scene, with grotesque fish in shades of brown, green and blue on a cream-coloured ground, inscribed 'Martin Bros. London & Southall, 1888', 9in (23cm) high.
£400–500 *CSK*

A Martin Brothers stoneware bottle vase, incised with 2 grotesque frogs painted in shades of green and brown against a light honey-coloured ground, incised 'Martin Bros. London & Southall 4.1913', 5in (12.5cm) high.
£650–800 *C*

A Martin Brothers stoneware bottle vase, incised with 2 frogs among grasses, painted in shades of green, brown and white, incised 'Martin Bros. London & Southall, 4.1913', 4in (10cm) high.
£600–700 *C*

r. A Martin Brothers stoneware sundial, the base glazed in various shades of brown, green, blue and yellow, below a brass sundial, incised 'R. W. Martin Brothers, London & Southall 4.1888', 33in (84cm) high.
£5,000–6,000 *CSK*

A Martin ware stoneware vase, painted with orchids in shades of ochre and pale lilac on a brown ground, inscribed 'Martin Bros. London & Southall 3.1898', 13in (33cm) high.
£850–1,000 *CSK*

A Martin Brothers stoneware grotesque double faced jug, in pale grey glaze mottled with brown, the hair and handle in darker brown, incised 'R. W. Martin Bros. London & Southall', c1900, 6in (15cm) high.
£1,500–1,800   *C*

A Martin Brothers stoneware vase, signed 'Martin Bros., London & Southall' and dated '8–1894', 14in (35.5cm) high.
£700–850   *P*

A Martin ware imp musician, 'Tambourine Player', modelled as a grotesque creature with exaggerated ears and grinning expression, signed on tambourine 'Martin Bros, London & Southall', 4½in (11.5cm) high.
£800–950   *P*

An early Martin ware jug, decorated in blues, brown and greens, signed 'R. W. Martin' and 'E9', 8½in (21.5cm) high.
£350–450   *P*

The form this decoration takes shows the obvious influence of the designs of Christopher Dresser, perhaps from The Art of Decorative Design *of 1862.*

A Martin ware pouring vessel, decorated with a sunburst centred with a grotesque face, all against a dark brown ground, signed 'Martin, London', 9in (23cm) high.
£900–1,100   *P*

A Martin Brothers fantastic animal, damaged, inscribed, 11in (28cm) high.
£5,000–6,000   *DWB*

A Martin ware vase, incised 'Martin Brothers, London, Southall', 7in (17.5cm) high.
£500–600   *CSK*

A Martin Brothers stoneware flower vase, with blue grey and brown glazes on a pricked surface, incised marks, 12⅛in (31cm) high.
£650–800   *CSK*

A stoneware vase, incised 'Martin Bros. London & Southall 3–1894', 9½in (24cm) high.
£600–720   *C*

r. A stoneware jardinière, glazed in blues and greys on a stone coloured ground, incised 'Martin Brothers, London & Southall 10–1892', 11in (28cm) high.
£2,000–2,400   *C*

Ferdinand Preiss
(German, 1882–1943)

The Preiss-Kassler Foundry was formed in Berlin in 1906. Preiss himself designed most of the models produced by the firm, although by 1914 there were about six designers working for him.

Most figures by Preiss are made of chryselephantine, a combination of bronze and ivory. He also made a few ivory figures, often small classical female nudes. The quality of his carving was usually very high, and he specialized in sporting figures, based on real sportsmen and sportswomen, and also actresses. His figures usually bear the 'PK' monogram, for the Preiss-Kassler Foundry, and the signature 'F. Preiss'. Copies do exist, often made from a softer type of stone that resembles onyx. Beware of any figures attributed to Preiss that have a very elaborate base. Most bases on Preiss figures are made of green, black, or a combination of green and black, Brazilian onyx, sometimes banded with black Belgian slate.

An ivory figure, 'Nude', carved after a model by Ferdinand Preiss, 17½in (44cm) high.
£5,000–6,000   *C*

An Art Deco jade, lapis lazuli and mother-of-pearl table clock, base repaired, signed by Cartier, No. 1216.
£12,000–15,000   *CNY*

Three gilt-bronze and ivory figures, after models by A. Gory:
l. 'Exotic Dancer' inscribed in the bronze 'A. Gory', 15in (38cm) high.
£2,000–2,500
c. 'Flower Girl', inscribed 'A. Gory', 14in (35.5cm) high
£1,200–1,500
r. 'Flower Seller', inscribed 'A. Gory', 15in (38cm) high.
£1,000–1,200   *C*

Cartier

Cartier made a variety of timepieces, usually desk and carriage clocks, or wristwatches. The firm treated the clock almost as a sculpture, and it is not always immediately apparent what the piece's function is. Designs were often exotic or Oriental. Chinoiserie forms and decorative motifs with a Chinese influence are common. Semi-precious stones were often embellished with fine quality gems.

Clocks can be dated by their serial number, which can be checked with Cartier, who keep a record of everything they make. Pieces which come from Cartier in Paris carry more of a premium than those from Cartier in either New York or London.

A calendar table clock, with adjustable day and date, marked 'Cartier', stand stamped 'Cartier 2324 Paris', 4½in (11cm) high.
£4,500–5,000   C

r. A Swiss lapis lazuli and jade table clock, face gilded, c1925, 10in (25.5cm) wide.
£5,000–6,000   CNY

A black lacquered metal, mother-of-pearl and glass table clock, inscribed 'Cartier No. 1074, Made in France', 5in (12.5cm) high, with original battery movement and fitted case.
£5,000–6,000   CNY

l. A cloisonné box, brass inlaid with a geometric design, incised 'Jean Goulden CVIII 30', and stamped 'J', 5in (12.5cm) wide.
£2,500–3,000   C

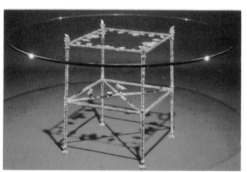

A bronze and glass dining table, by Diego Giacometti, the glass top with 4 frogs for attachment above a gilt leaf band, signed 'Diego', 60in (152cm) diam.
£90,000–100,000   CNY

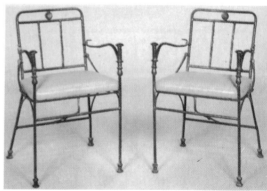

Two bronze armchairs, by Diego Giacometti, the arms formed by the front leg rising to a button top, 32in (81cm) high.
£15,000–18,000   CNY

A black vase, 'Martins Pêcheurs', moulded with songbirds in flowering branches, with impressed signature 'R. Lalique', 9½in (23.5cm) high.
£5,000–6,000   C

An ebonised and rosewood cabinet by Carlo Bugatti, with brass, pewter and ivory inlay, 35½in (30cm) wide.
£9,000–10,000   C

A leaded glass window, designed by Frank Lloyd Wright, c1900, 41½ x 27in (105 x 68cm).
£3,500–4,500   CNY

An oak dining table and 8 chairs, designed by Frank Lloyd Wright, c1903, table 54½in (138cm) wide.
£350,000+   CNY

r. A cameo glass bowl, by Thos. Webb & Sons, with silver rim, London 1901, 8in (20.5cm) diam.
£1,700–2,000   SWO

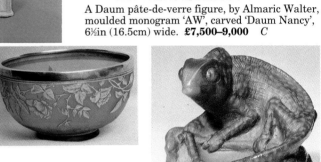

A Daum pâte-de-verre figure, by Almaric Walter, moulded monogram 'AW', carved 'Daum Nancy', 6½in (16.5cm) wide. **£7,500–9,000   C**

above right. A pâte-de-verre paperweight, designed by H. Bergé, with moulded signature 'A. Walter Nancy H Bergé', 3in (7.5cm) high.
£10,000–12,000   C

An oak side chair, by Charles Rohlfs, Buffalo NY, 1901, 47in (119cm) high.
£16,000–19,000   CNY

An oak side chair, designed by Frank Lloyd Wright, c1902.
£14,000–16,000   CNY

r. A Tiffany Favrile glass vase, inscribed 'L. C. Tiffany E136', c1896, 20in (51cm) high.
£4,000–5,000   CNY

A silver and ivory tea service, the hammered bodies raised on 4 short feet, impressed mark of Gorham and Martelé '9584 WDL', the samovar with stand, 13in (33cm) high, 218oz.
£11,000–13,000   *CNY*

Two earthenware vases, by Rookwood, c1910, 14in (35.5cm) high.
l. Designed by Carl Schmidt. **£3,500–4,000**
r. Designed by Edward Diers. **£600–800**   *CNY*

l. and r. Two Guild of Handicraft mustard pots, one by C. R. Ashbee, stamped 'CRA', c1900, largest 3½in (9cm) high, 4oz 11dwt. **£12,000–15,000**
c. A box and cover, designed by C. R. Ashbee, stamped 'G of H Ltd.', c1900, 8in (20.5cm) high, 16oz 15dwt.
£5,000–6,000   *C*

An enamelled three-piece demi-tasse service, by Tiffany & Co, New York, bearing touchmark of Pan-American Exposition in Buffalo, NY, 1901, marked on base, coffee pot 9in (23cm) high, 37oz 10dwt.
£17,000–19,000   *CNY*

A Liberty & Co silver bowl with matching spoon, designed by Archibald Knox, stamped 'L & Co', Cymric and Birmingham 1899, 4in (10cm) wide, 21oz.
£5,000–6,000   *C*

An earthenware vase, by Rookwood, designed by Carl Schmidt, 1900, impressed firm's mark, 8½in (21.5cm) high.
£4,500–5,500   *CNY*

A Doulton Lambeth faïence tile panel, 'Sleeping Beauty – the Fairies at the Christening', painted by Margaret E. Thompson, signed, 41 x 55in (104 x 139.5cm).
£5,000–6,000   *P*

l. A Martin Brothers stoneware model of a grotesque bird, with removable head, signed on neck, rim and base 'R. W. Martin & Bros', dated '12-1900', 15in (38cm) high.
£6,500–8,000   *P*

A silver sugar bowl and teapot, by Tiffany & Co, with a green stone finial and applied with insects, 1877–91.
Sugar bowl: 3in (7.5cm) high, 13oz. **£7,000–8,000**
Teapot: 5in (12.5cm) high, 115oz. **£12,000–14,000**   *CNY*

A pâte-de-verre glass vase, by
G. Argy-Rousseau, marked, c1920,
4in (10cm) high.
£8,500–10,000 *S*

A clear and frosted Alexandrite vase,
'Tortues', intaglio moulded 'R. Lalique',
10½in (26cm) high. **£6,500–8,000** *Bon*

A Müller Frères cameo
glass vase, cameo mark,
12in (30.5cm) high.
£1,600–2,000 *S*

An opalescent vase, 'Bacchantes',
engraved signature 'R. Lalique, France',
9½in (24cm) high. **£6,500–8,000** *C*

A glass and earthenware table lamp shade, by Tiffany,
base by Ruth Erikson. **£6,750–10,000** *CNY*

A double overlaid and etched glass
table lamp, cameo signature
'Müller Frères, Luneville', 21½in
(54cm) high. **£6,000–7,500** *CNY*

A glass scent flaçon, 'Bouchon Müres',
chip to underside, moulded 'R. Lalique',
4½in (11cm) high.
£10,000–12,000 *Bon*

l. A pâte-
de-verre
table
lamp, by
G. Argy-
Rousseau,
marked
on shade
and base,
15½in
(39.5cm)
high.
**£26,000–
30,000**
C

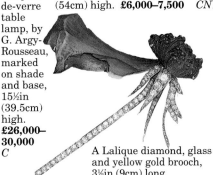

A Lalique diamond, glass
and yellow gold brooch,
3½in (9cm) long.
£45,000–50,000 *CNY*

A glass vase, 'Penthièvre', stencilled
'R. Lalique', 10in (25.5cm) high.
£5,000–6,000 *Bon*

A glass table, 'Cactus', by Lalique et Cie,
engraved 'No. 37 le 3/12/82', 60in (152cm) diam.
£15,000–18,000 *CNY*

A Pilkington Royal Lancastrian lustre vase, decorated by Wm. S. Mycock, potted by E. T. Radford, marked, 1929, 15½in (39.5cm) high.
£1,200–1,400   C

A leaded glass and bronze table lamp, by Duffner & Kimberly, 29in (73.5cm) high.
£4,000–5,000   CNY

A majolica simulated basket jardinière, by Holdcroft, on a shaped stand, late 19thC, 11in (28cm) high.
£500–600   PCh

A Royal Doulton vase, inscribed 'Presented to Mr A. Baldwin by his colleagues at Royal Doulton Potteries on the occasion of his marriage, 2nd Sept. 1925', signed by his colleagues.
£200–250   PCh

A Martin Brothers stoneware bird, signed and dated 9-1898', 14½in (37cm) high.
£6,000–7,000   P

A daffodil leaded glass and bronze table lamp, impressed 'Tiffany Studios, New York, 25882', 22in (56cm) high.
£6,000–7,000   CNY

A Royal Doulton character jug, 'Paddy', with a musical box playing an Irish jig.
£400–450   PCh

An Art Deco glass table lamp, acid-etched with geometric panels, signed 'Daum Nancy France' on base and shade.
£5,000–6,000   P

A stoneware Toby jug, signed 'Martin Bros. London & Southall', dated '11-1903', 10in (25.5cm) high.
£3,000–3,500   P

r. A Royal Doulton figure, 'Europa and the Bull', impressed 'H. Tittensor, Noke', and '203', 10½in (26cm) wide.
£2,500–3,000   P

A stained glass window, 'Minstrel with Cymbals', designed by William Morris, 10in (25.5cm) high. **£10,000–12,000** *C*

A Daum etched and wheel-carved vase, 12in (30.5cm) high. **£10,000–12,000** *CNY*

An Emile Gallé vase, c1902, 11in (28cm) high. **£28,000–32,000** *S*

A Daum cameo glass vase, decorated with irises, signed 'Daum Nancy', 16in (41cm) high. **£2,500–3,000** *E*

A Gallé enamelled glass liqueur set, inscribed 'E. Gallé', 1890, decanter, 8½in (21cm) high. **£10,500–12,000** *S(NY)*

A Morris & Co stained glass window, designed by Edward Burne-Jones, 41in (105cm) high. **£12,000–15,000** *C*

A Sabino opalescent glass lamp, 'Suzanne au Bain', by R. Lalique, chipped, c1930, 10in (25.5cm) high. **£1,200–1,500** *S*

A Gallé cameo glass vase, minor fleck at base, c1900, 13½in (34cm) high. **£2,800–3,200** *S(NY)*

A Gallé cameo glass pilgrim vase, signed in cameo, c1900, 17in (43cm) high. **£6,500–8,000** *S(NY)*

A Koloman Moser sherry jug, for E. Bakalowits & Söhne, in dimpled glass with electroplated metal mounts, c1900, 10in (25.5cm) high. **£5,000–6,000** *S*

A blue iridescent glass vase, inscribed 'Steuben Aurene 2479', c1910, 12½in (31.5cm) high.
£1,500–2,000   *S(NY)*

A Loetz glass bowl, the design attributed to Koloman Moser, decorated internally with bubbles and silver iridescence, 11in (28cm) diam.
£2,000–2,500   *P*

A Steuben Aurene glass jar with cover, inscribed, c1910, 14in (36cm) high.
£1,500–2,000

l. An iridescent glass vase, signed 'Quezal/937', c1920, 11in (28cm) high.
£1,500–2,000
S(NY)

A Tiffany Favrile iridescent glass vase, signed, numbered 'E1630', 9in (23cm) high.
£1,000–1,200   *P*

A cameo glass and wrought-iron lamp and shade, the shade supported on 3 iron arms, the yellow glass overlaid and etched with brown and orange, etched 'Daum Nancy', 17½in (44cm) high.
£6,000–7,500   *Bon*

A Loetz iridescent glass bowl, supported on a pad foot by a twisted stem, 8½in (21.5cm) high.
£2,500–2,800   *P*

l. A Tiffany Favrile glass vase, signed, numbered 'E1630', 9in (23cm) high.
£750–850   *P*

A pâte-de-verre coup, by G. Argy-Rousseau, Fers de Lance (bloch Dermant 30.04), moulded 'F. Argy-Rousseau', 1930, 7in (17.5cm) diam.
£7,500–9,000   *S(NY)*

A Daum wheel-carved cameo glass vase, inscribed 'Daum Nancy', c1900, 10½in (26cm) high.
£3,750–4,500   *S(NY)*

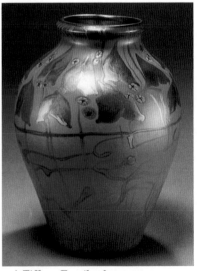

A Tiffany Favrile glass vase, with thick rolled rim, inscribed 'Louis C. Tiffany 865N', c1919, 13in (33cm) high.
£11,000–13,000   *S(NY)*

A Gallé double overlaid and etched glass chandelier, the domed shade with frosted ground overlaid and etched to depict blossoms, cameo signature, 17½in (44.5cm) wide.
£3,500–4,000   *CNY*

l. A Daum etched and enamelled glass vase, signed, 19½in (49cm) high.
£10,000–12,000 *CNY*

A glass vase, signed 'Daum Nancy', 9½in (24cm) high.
£2,500–3,000   *P*

A Daum glass vase, with Cross of Lorraine, 7½in (19cm) high.
£14,000–17,000   *P*

A Gallé carved and acid etched glass chandelier, cameo signatures, 18in (45.5cm) diam.
£5,000–6,000   *C*

A Gallé overlaid glass lamp, 22in (56 cm) high.
£8,000–10,000   *CNY*

A Gallé overlaid and etched glass chandelier, cameo signatures, 18in (45.5cm) diam.
£10,000–12,000   *CNY*

A Gallé overlaid glass lamp, 22in (56cm) high.
£8,000–10,000   *CNY*

A Gallé carved and acid etched double overlay table lamp, signed.
£14,000–17,000   *C*

A Gallé double overlaid etched glass lamp, 25in (63.5cm) high.
£12,000–14,000   *CNY*

A Gallé carved and acid etched triple overlay lamp.
£12,000–14,000   *C*

A Gallé carved, acid etched and fire polished double overlay table lamp, signed.
£10,000–12,000   *C*

A Gallé carved and acid etched table lamp, 15½in (39cm) high.
£15,000–20,000   *C*

l. A bronze and ivory figure, by F. Preiss, 'Sonny Boy', restored, 8½in (21.5cm) high.
£1,800–2,200
c. A bronze and ivory figure of a Japanese lady, by C. Jaeger, 10½in (26.5cm) high.
£2,000–2,500
r. A bronze and ivory figure by F. Preiss, 'Con Brio', 14½in (37cm) high.
£10,000–12,000   *C*

A copper urn, designed by Frank Lloyd Wright, by James A. Miller, c1903, 18in (45.5cm) high.
£57,000–63,000   *CNY*

r. A polished bronze head of a woman, 'Divinité Solaire', from a model by Gustave Miklos, early 20thC, 25½in (64.5cm) high.
£28,000–32,000   *CNY*

A painted bronze and ivory figure, stamped with 'PK' monogram, signed on base 'F. Preiss'.
£5,000–6,000   *P*

r. A bronze and ivory figure, 'Bayadère', by D. H. Chiparus, 20½in (52.5cm) high.
£7,000–8,500   *C*

A bronze group, from a model by Jean Lambert-Rucki, 23in (58cm) high.
£9,000–10,000   *CNY*

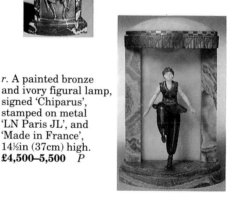

r. A painted bronze and ivory figural lamp, signed 'Chiparus', stamped on metal 'LN Paris JL', and 'Made in France', 14½in (37cm) high.
£4,500–5,500   *P*

A bronze card holder, by Diego Giacometti, 'Chat Maître d'Hotel', impressed 'Diego', 11½in (29cm) high.
£25,000–28,000   *CNY*

A bronze group of an amorous dancing couple, from a model by Bruno Zach, early 20thC, 10in (25.5cm) high.
£3,000–3,500   *CNY*

A lacquered metal bowl, on a raised foot, with flaring body and everted rim, distressed gold body and coral red interior, signed in red lacquer 'Jean Dunand', c1925, 4in (10cm) high.
£1,000–1,200   *C*

A ginger jar and cover, 'Floral Comets', enriched with gilt decoration, printed marks 'Carlton Ware, Made in England, Trade Mark', 12in (30.5cm) high.
£1,200–1,500   *C*

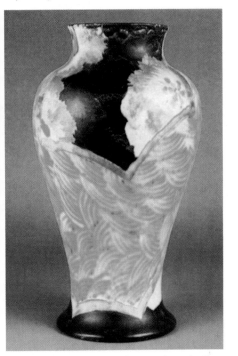

A Clarice Cliff vase, hand painted marks 'Inspiration by Clarice Cliff Newport Pottery, Burslem England', signed, c1930, 16in (40.5cm) high.
£2,500–3,000   *C*

A pâte-de-verre vase, with stylized moulded decoration of fish swimming through waves, moulded signature 'G. Argy-Rousseau', c1925, 6in (15cm) high.
£2,500–3,000   *C*

A Lalique butterscotch glass statuette, 'Thais', inscribed 'R. Lalique', 9in (23cm) high.
£3,000–3,500   *CSK*

Three Fauré vases, silver and thick enamel, with geometric abstract designs, signed 'C. Fauré, Limoges', c1925.
£1,500–2,000   *C(Am)*

Two René Lalique drinking services:
l. 18 pieces, after 1934. **£1,000–1,200**
r. 29 pieces, after 1924. **£2,500–3,000**   *S*

A René Lalique opalescent
glass vase, 'Orleans',
marked, 8in (20.5cm) high.
£800–1,000   *S*

An opalescent glass
clock, 'Inseparables',
by René Lalique, after
1926, 4½in (11.5cm) high.
£1,200–1,400   *S*

A Lalique moulded, frosted and
enamelled glass vase, introduced
in 1926, inscribed 'R. Lalique',
7in (17.5cm) high.
£4,000–5,000   *S(NY)*

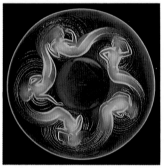

A René Lalique opalescent
glass plate, 'Assiette Calypso',
stencilled mark, after 1930.
£1,600–2,000   *S*

l. A Lalique glass vase 'Tournesol',
after 1927.
£1,200–1,500
r. A Lalique perfume bottle.
£600–750   *S*

A René Lalique glass and nickel-
plated metal plaque, moulded
mark, slightly polished, c1925,
16in (40.5cm) high.
£3,000–3,500   *S*

A René Lalique table decoration, 'Faisans',
comprising: 2 glass candelabra and a serving dish,
dish with engraved mark, chips to dish, after 1942.
£1,200–1,500   *S*

A Lalique moulded
and frosted glass vase,
1914 model, moulded
and inscribed.
£1,200–1,500   *S(NY)*

A René Lalique glass vase 'Aras',
moulded mark 'R. Lalique',
after 1924, 9in (23cm) high.
£3,750–4,500   *S*

A Lalique moulded
glass perfume bottle,
1926 model,
3in (7.5cm) high.
£1,600–2,200   *S(NY)*

A black enamelled clear glass vase, wheel cut
'R. Lalique', and engraved 'France No. 970',
8in (20.5cm) high.
£1,500–1,800   *CNY*

l. A glass vase, designed by Koloman Moser, 7in (17.5cm) high.
£1,300–1,600
c. A glass vase, by Loetz, 8in (20.5cm) high.
£1,200–1,400
r. A Ferdinand Poschinger Glasshütten vase, engraved
signature and marked 'Bayern No. 189', 10in (25.5cm) high.
£1,200–1,400 *C*

A Daum cameo glass vase,
9in (23cm) high.
£1,400–1,600 *PSG*

A Gallé cameo glass vase,
10in (25.5cm) high.
£2,200–2,500 *PSG*

A Gallé cameo glass vase,
12in (30.5cm) high.
£1,400–1,600 *PSG*

A glass vase, overlaid on amber with a design of lilies and lotus rising form a pond, signed 'Gallé', c1900, 8½in (21.5cm) high.
£1,400–1,600 *PSG*

A mould-blown double overlay elephant glass vase, with incised signature 'Emile Gallé', 15in (38cm) high.
£40,000–50,000 *CNY*

A glass vase, overlaid with a design of clematis, signed 'Gallé', c1900, 12½in (32cm) high.
£1,800–2,000 *PSG*

A glass vase, engraved with silver scrolling flowers and foliage, inscribed 'Loetz, Austria', 9in (23cm) high.
£1,800–2,200 *Bea*

A glass vase, with red flowering creeper overlaid on amber, signed 'Gallé', c1900, 9in (23cm) diam.
£1,600–2,000 *PSG*

A wheel-carved cameo glass vase, signed 'Daum, Nancy', 8in (20.5cm) high.
£30,000–33,000 *P*

A wheel-carved and enamelled cameo glass vase, by Daum, Nancy, c1900, 5in (12.5cm) high.
£2,800–3,200 *PSG*

An internally decorated glass vase, by Daum, 14in (35.5cm) high.
£30,000–35,000 *C*

A wheel-carved cameo glass vase, 10in (25.5cm) high.
£14,000–16,000 *P*

Two glass vases, decorated with spring flowers, signed 'Gallé', c1900.
l. 14in (35.5cm) high. **£2,000–2,200**
r. 8in (20.5cm) high. **£1,200–1,500** *PSG*

l. A plum mould-blown triple overlay glass vase, by Emile Gallé, 13in (33cm) high. **£8,000–10,000**
r. An apple mould-blown triple overlay glass vase, by Emile Gallé, 11½in (29.5cm) high. **£10,000–12,000** *CNY*

A bronze-mounted 'veilleuse', with 3 dragonflies forming the stand, with carved signature of 'Gallé', 7in (17.5cm) high. **£6,500–7,500** *C*

l. A vase, modelled as a Fu Dog, clear glass with blue and gilt enamelling, engraved with a grasshopper enriched with gilding, engraved 'EG' and Cross of Lorraine, c1875, 6in (15cm) high. **£8,000–10,000** *C*

A blow-out vase, with moulded decoration of clematis flowers, moulded 'Gallé' signature, 10in (25.5cm) high. **£6,000–7,500** *C*

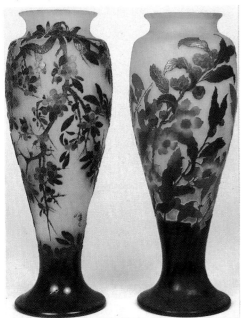

Two cameo baluster vases, with carved 'Gallé' signatures, 23in (58.5cm) high. **£9,000–11,000 each** *C*

A cameo glass vase, overlaid with amethyst tone acid-etched flowers and leaves, signed in cameo form 'Gallé', 16in (40.5cm) high. **£2,000–2,400** *P*

An Art Nouveau leaded stained glass panel, signed 'Jacques Gruber', dated '04', 101in (256cm) high. **£10,000–12,000** *C*

Two Minton majolica cockerel
and hen planters, designed by
David Henck.
£5,000–6,000   *PCh*

A Gouda pottery charger, in 'Syncap'
design, c1927, 12in (30.5cm) diam.
£200–250   *OO*

A Doulton Luscian ware
vase, by H. Piper, c1895,
8in (20.5cm) high.
£275–325   *HER*

A Gouda pottery vase,
marked 'Zuid (Holland)',
c19200, 10in (25.5cm) high.
£275–325   *OO*

A Rosenthal porcelain
ginger jar and cover, by
Kurt Wendler, c1920.
£900–1,000   *S(NY)*

A Carlton Ware butter dish, c1940,
10½in (26cm) wide.
£800–950   *ARE*
This item was part of the Elton John collection.

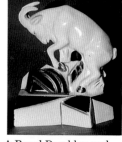

A Doulton ball teapot, decorated with flowers
and butterflies, c1916, 5½in (14cm) high.
£125–150   *HER*

A Gouda pottery vase, from
the Goedewaagen factory,
c1915, 4½in (11cm) high.
£100–120   *OO*

A Royal Dux blue and
gilt-decorated figure of
a ram, 7in (17.5cm) high.
£100–125   *PCh*

Four Royal Doulton figures, 'Veronica', HN 1517, 8in (20.5cm) high,
'Aileen', HN 1645, 6in (15cm) high, 'Prue', HN 1996, 7in (17.5cm) high,
and 'Easter Day', HN 2039, 7½in (18cm) high.
£100–150 each   *CAG*

A Foley Intarsio clock,
designed by Frederick
Rhead, c1900,
9in (23cm) high.
£450–550   *AJ*

A Martin Brothers jug, incised and dated '20 12 1898', 8½in (21cm) high.
£2,000–2,500 *DWB*

A Martin ware triple bird group, each with a removable head, signed on heads and base, 'R. W. Martin & Bros. Southall' and 'B–37', 7in (17.5cm) high.
£5,000–6,000 *P*

This piece is an example of the work produced by Clement Martin in collaboration with Captain H. Butterfield.

A Martin Brothers stoneware model of a grotesque bird, signed 'R. W. Martin & Bros. London & Southall', dated '5-1884', 13in (33cm) high.
£8,000–9,500 *P*

A Martin Brothers stoneware vase, incised and glazed in shades of blue, on a pitted brown and biscuit ground, incised 'R. W. Martin & Bros. London & Southall 2–1892', 17½in (45cm) high.
£850–1,000 *CSK*

A Robert Wallace Martin & Brothers stoneware face jug, matt ochre glaze, incised 'R. W. Martin & Bros. London & Southall, 1–1–1903', 6in (15cm) high.
£1,700–2,000 *CSK*

A Martin Brothers face jug, the eyes black and white against the buff glaze, incised marks and dated '8–(18)98', spout chipped, 8in (20.5cm) high.
£850–1,000 *SS*

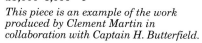

A Martin Brothers pottery vase incised 'R. W. Martin & Bros. London & Southall' '4–1887', 8in (20.5cm) high.
£800–950 *P*

A pair of Martin Brothers stoneware slender baluster vases, incised and painted in shades of brown and green with exotic birds, incised 'Martin Bros. London & Southall, 6–1897', 10in (25.5cm) high.
£600–700 *C*

r. A Martin Brothers pottery vase, incised 'Martin Bros. London & Southall, 10–1901', 7in (17.5cm) high.
£300–350 *P*

r. A Martin Brothers pottery vase, incised 'Martin Bros. London & Southall, 10–1901', 7in (17.5cm) high.
£2,000–2,500 *DWB*

A Martin Brothers stoneware face jug, incised and dated '3-1-1903', 9in (23cm) high.
£2,500–3,000 *CSK*

l. A Martin Brothers pottery vase, coloured in shades of brown, against a buff ground, incised 'Martin Brothers London & Southall, 4–1890', 5in (12.5cm) high.
£600–700 *P*

A Martin Brothers vase, green, blue and brown on a buff ground, incised mark, dated '8–1885', minor chip, 7½in (19cm) high.
£550–650 *S*

A pair of Martin Brothers vases, with honey coloured glaze, incised marks and dated '6–1904', 10in (25.5cm) high.
£750–850 *S*

A Martin Brothers 'Gourd' vase, incised and dated '9–1899', 8½in (21.5cm) high.
£450–500 *S*

l. A Martin Brothers bowl, glazed in brown against a washed blue and green ground, incised mark, dated '7–1911', 9½in (24cm) diam.
£500–600 *S*

A Robert Wallace Martin Brothers stoneware jug, incised 'R. W. Martin & Bros, London & Southall 2–1887', 8½in (21cm) high.
£500–600 *CSK*

A De Morgan lustre dish, impressed '17', 1898–1907, 14⅛in (37cm) diam.
£2,000–2,400 *S*

A De Morgan lustre dish, decorated in ruby, salmon-pink and buff, impressed numerals '24', 1898–1907, 14in (35.5cm) wide.
£2,000–2,400 *S*

A De Morgan lustre dish, impressed '17', painted 'EK' initials, late Fulham period, 14in (35.5cm) diam.
£2,500–3,000 *S*

An early Martin Brothers clock-case, incised 'R. W. Martin Fulham, 6', restored, c1874, 11in (28cm) high.
£1,500–1,800 *S*

Two De Morgan lustre dishes, one decorated in ruby lustre with a griffin, the other with an infant, the latter painted 'ad infinitum' mark, 1898–1907, 12in (30.5cm) diam.
£700–850 each *S*

A Martin ware tile picture, depicting grotesque fish, painted in muted enamel colours, some damage, each inscribed, 14½ x 17½in (37 x 44.5cm).
£1,500–1,800 *Bea*

A De Morgan lustre dish, ruby and salmon-pink, cracked, 1898–1907, 14in (35.5cm) diam.
£1,000–1,200 *S*

A stoneware double bird vase, one half of the vessel formed by the body of a bird with 'shifty' expression, the other squinting, their plumage picked out in browns, ochre, beige, blue and black, signed on base 'R. W. Martin & Brothers, London & Southall', dated '3–1892', 8½in (21cm) high.
£2,500–3,000   *P*

A stoneware bird, with removable head, resembling a duck with beak parted to reveal a tongue, the creature glazed dark brown and resting on a circular wooden base, signed on neck and near base 'Martin Brothers, London & Southall', indistinct date, 8in (20.5cm) high.
£1,500–1,800   *P*

A C. H. Brannam sgraffito six-handled vase, fish motif with trailed organic Art Nouveau forms, 5in (12.5cm) high.
£200–250   *L&E*

Martin Brothers
The pottery firm owned by the Martin Brothers was active in London between 1873 and 1914. It was best known for its grey stoneware, often in grotesque shapes or with incised decoration.

l. A stoneware bird, with removable head, modelled with broad beak, heavy head plumage resembling eyebrows, in browns, ochre and beige with areas of pale blue, signed on neck and base, 'R. W. Martin & Bros, London & Southall' dated '3-101', 12in (30.5cm) high.
£7,000–8,400   *P*

A stoneware flask, finely incised on one side with an amusing face of the Sun, the reverse side showing a bearded Man in the Moon amid stars and comets signed 'Martin Bros, London & Southall', and dated '11-1891', 6½in (16.5cm) high.
£2,000–2,400   *P*

A. C. H. Brannam vase, designed by F. Braddon, 1906, 11in (28cm) high.
£250–300   *ZEI*

A stoneware face jug, both sides modelled with a face of a grinning, chubby cheeked fellow, incised '3-1891, Martin Brothers, London & Southall', 7in (17.5cm) high.
£1,500–1,800   *P*

l. A Minton Secessionist jardinière and stand, tube-lined with stylized vertical floral banding in mauve and pale blue enhanced with sinuous green tendrils on a blue round, marked 'Minton Ltd., No. 72' to each base, slight repair, 40in (102cm) high.
£1,500–1,800   *P*

A stoneware effigy of a boy sleeping, in blue, brown and cream, incised 'He rests, He sleeps, nor dreams of any harm', Edwin Bruce Martin, R. Wallace, Martin S. C., original plaster cast, modelled in Wandsworth Road, c1962.
£900–1,100   *Bon*

A biscuit tin, by W. R. Jacobs & Co, moulded in a Moorcroft shape and transfer-decorated with the 'Pomegranate' design, 6in (15cm) high.
£125–150   *WIL*

r. A Moorcroft MacIntyre 'Yellow Cornflower' design tobacco jar, c1910, 6in (15cm) diam.
£600–700   *LIO*

A Moorcroft MacIntyre 'Blue Poppy' design salad bowl and servers, c1902, 10in (25.5cm) diam.
£850–1,000   *LIO*

A Moorcroft two-handled 'Blue Pansy' design biscuit barrel, c1929, 7in (17.5cm) high.
£600–700   *LIO*

A Moorcroft 'Spanish' pattern oviform vase, in reds, butterscotch and pale brown against a shaded beige/blue ground, signed 'W. Moorcroft' and part of Liberty retail label, 10½in (27cm) high.
£1,500–1,800   *P*

r. A Moorcroft MacIntyre vase, heightened with ruby lustre against deep blue in panels, and olive green ground, MacIntyre mark, signed 'W. Moorcroft' and 'M2980', repaired, 6in (15cm) high.
£250–300   *P*

A Moorcroft vase, in shades of deep rose, ochre and olive on a mottled blue/green ground, impressed 'Moorcroft Burslem', slight damage, painted signature in green, c1910, 12½in (32cm) high.
£800–950   *S*

l. A pair of Moorcroft vases, painted in the 'Pomegranate' pattern in shades of pink, green and purple on an inky blue ground, impressed marks, signed in green, 15in (38cm) high.
£1,500–1,800   *CSK*

A Moorcroft exhibition ginger jar, 'Pomegranate' design, 1927, 12in (30.5cm) diam.
£3,300–4,000   *LIO*

A Moorcroft MacIntyre blue teapot, 18thC design, c1906.
£450–550   *LIO*

A MacIntyre footed bowl, the exterior decorated with sprays of pansies on a green ground, impressed factory marks, signed in green, rim restored, 9in (23cm) diam.
£250–300   *CSK*

Three Moorcroft MacIntyre Florian Ware vases.
£2,500–3,000 each *SWO*

A Moorcroft vase with loop handles, with 'Poppy' design, c1925, 12in (30.5cm) high.
£1,250–1,500 *PGA*

A Moorcroft MacIntyre 'Peacock' pattern candlestick c1900, 13½in (34.5cm) high.
£800–900 *PGA*

A pair of Moorcroft vases, decorated with 'Spanish' pattern trailed in white slip with scrolling flowers and foliage, picked out in dark glazes, green script signature, impressed Burslem mark, c1920, 12½in (31.5cm) high.
£3,300–4,000 *PGA*

A Moorcroft vase, with 'Claremont' design on a mottled green ground, c1915, 9in (23cm) high.
£2,500–3,000 *PGA*

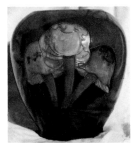

A Moorcroft vase, with toadstool design under a brown lustre glaze, 8in (20.5cm) high.
£1,700–2,000 *PGA*

A Moorcroft jardinière, with the 'Claremont' toadstool design, with green signature, c1905, 7in (17.5cm) wide.
£2,500–3,000 *PGA*

A Moorcroft Tudric 'Hazeldene' bowl, decorated internally and externally with stylized trees in the 'Eventide' palette, raised on a Tudric pewter base, stamped 'Tudric Moorcroft 01311', 10½in (26.5cm) diam.
£900–1,100 *P*

A Moorcroft Burslem vase, with a flambé fish design on blue/lilac ground, c1910, 12⅜in (31.5cm) high.
£2,500–3,000 *PGA*

A Moorcroft Florian Ware vase, painted in lilac pattern in shades of blue, printed marks and inscribed 'W.M.', 7in (17.5cm) high.
£750–900 *CSK*

A Moorcroft pottery vase, painted on a mottled blue/green ground, blue signature, impressed Royal marks, 7in (17.5cm) high.
£400–480 *P(Re)*

A Moorcroft vase, with a fish design, on a pale flambé ground, c1930, 12in (30.5cm) high.
£1,700–2,000 *PGA*

A Moorcroft vase, painted with a fish, in yellow and green on a green to blue ground, impressed marks, signed in green, 12in (30.5cm) high.
£1,000–1,200   *CSK*

A Moorcroft MacIntyre Florian Ware vase, with slip-trailed decoration of dark blue flowers, green painted 'W. Moorcroft' signature, printed mark, c1900, 12½in (31.5cm) high.
£1,500–1,800   *C*

A MacIntyre Aurelian Ware tazza and cover, attributed to William Moorcroft, dark blue ground, gilded panels with orange flowers and leaves, printed 'MacIntyre Burslem England', monogram, marked 'Made for Ward & Son, Doncaster', c1898, 12in (30.5cm) high.
£650–800   *C*

r. A Walter Moorcroft ginger jar and cover, with a turquoise and blue mottled ground, painted initials impressed facsimile signature, factory mark and 'potter to the Queen', c1945, 11in (28cm) high.
£500–600   *WIL*

A pair of MacIntyre Florian Ware vases and covers, decorated by William Moorcroft and anemones in blue and green, on an ivory ground, one with slight hair crack, 8½in (21.5cm) high.
£1,500–1,800   *Bea*

r. A Moorcroft vase, 10½in (26cm) high.
£350–400   *SBA*

A Moorcroft pottery vase, painted with green trees on a yellowy blue ground, green painted signature and printed 'Made for Liberty & Co.', mark to base, 9in (23cm) high.
£2,000–2,400   *BWe*

A Moorcroft vase, c1912, 10in (25.5cm) high.
£700–800   *SBA*

A Moorcroft Florian Ware vase, signed, c1895, 10in (25.5cm) high.
£700–800   *SBA*

A pair of Moorcroft MacIntyre vases, signed, c1898, 10in (25.5cm) high.
£1,250–1,500   *SBA*

r. A Moorcroft Florian Ware vase, signed, 12in (30.5cm) high.
£1,000–1,200   *SBA*

l. An early Moorcroft vase, with the 'Pomegranate' pattern, c1912, 10½in (26cm) high.
£700–800   *SBA*

A Moorcroft pottery vase, decorated in the 'Claremont' pattern with toadstools in shades of red, yellow, green and blue, printed marks, signed in green, 6in (15cm) high.
£1,000–1,200 *CSK*

l. A Moorcroft vase, in the 'Dawn' pattern, painted in blue against a pale sky, impressed marks, 3½in (9cm) high.
£600–700 *CSK*

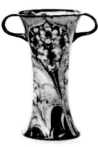

A Moorcroft Florian Ware twin-handled vase, decorated in white, yellow, blue and pale green, reserved against a shaded blue ground, signed 'W. Moorcroft des.', printed mark, 8in (20.5cm) high.
£1,000–1,200 *P*

r. A trumpet-shaped vase, with grape and 'Pomegranate' decoration, backstamp 'Moorcroft Burslem', c1914, 10½in (26.5cm) high.
£800–950 *LT*

A Moorcroft pottery vase, decorated in the 'Hazeldene' pattern, in shades of yellow, green and blue, painted signature, c1915, 6in (15cm) high.
£1,500–1,800 *TW*

A Moorcroft 'Tudor Rose' pattern vase, decorated in white tube-lining, glazed in green, blue and heightened with red and reserved against a turquoise ground, signed 'W. Moorcroft des.', printed 'Made for Liberty & Co, Rd. No. 431157', 10in (25.5cm) high.
£800–950 *P*

A Moorcroft 'Waratah' plate, decorated with 3 white and red flower blooms and green leaves against a green ground, impressed facsimile signature, 'Potter to H.M. The Queen, Made in England', 9in (23cm) diam.
£1,500–1,800 *P*

A Martin Bros. stoneware vase, brown and buff glazed, with decoration of flowering tendrils, mark to base 'R. W. Martin & Bros, London and Southall, 8/84'.
£200–250 *A*

A pair of MacIntyre plates attributed to William Moorcroft, decorated in white slip trailing with blue irises and green leaves against an off-white ground, printed MacIntyre marks, Rd No. 211991, 8in (20.5cm) diam.
£200–250 each *P*

A Moorcroft 'Spanish' pattern pot pourri, decorated with blue and green flowers on green scrolling stems, on a pale green ground, signed 'W. Moorcroft 12/1911', impressed '189 W', 4in (10cm) high.
£500–600 *P*

A Moorcroft wheatear motif vase, with green and purple tones on an off-white ground, blue signature, 13½in (34.5cm) high.
£1,500–1,800 *LE*

A William Moorcroft 'Claremont' pattern bowl, slip-trailed with red flushed toadstools on a mottled green/blue ground, facsimile signature, Liberty mark, early 20thC, 10½in (26cm) wide.
£800–950 *SS*

A Moorcroft tobacco jar and cover, painted with the 'Cornflower' pattern, purple flowers amongst green scrolling foliage on a creamware ground, impressed mark and signed 'W. Moorcroft' in green, 5½in (13cm) high.
£700–850 *CSK*

A Moorcroft vase, painted in
shades of red, green, yellow,
white and blue on a dark blue
ground, impressed marks,
17in (43cm) high.
£900–1,100   CSK

A Moorcroft MacIntyre vase, painted
with red and purple cornflowers
with green foliage, MacIntyre trade
mark on base and green signatures,
10in (25.5cm) high.
£1,500–1,800   P(M)

A pair of Moorcroft Tudric vases,
decorated with trees against a dark
blue ground, with flared pewter
bases, No. 01310, 9in (23cm) high.
£2,000–2,400   HCC

A Moorcroft 'Eventide' pottery vase,
decorated with green and brown
trees and green hills, against a
flame coloured sky, stamped marks,
signed in blue, 10in (25.5cm) high.
£1,500–1,800   CSK

A Moorcroft two-handled pottery
vase, decorated in the 'Claremont'
pattern, with toadstoools under a
deep flambé glaze, impressed marks,
signed in green, 7in (17.5cm) high.
£2,000–2,400   CSK

A pair of Moorcroft
pottery vases, decorated
in the 'Hazeldene'
pattern, with tall blue
and green trees and
hilly landscape, on a
yellow/green ground,
cracks to the body of
one, printed marks for
Liberty & Co., signed in
green 'W. Moorcroft
des.', 9½in (24cm) high.
£3,000–3,500   CSK

A Moorcroft pottery vase,
decorated with poppies on a
dark blue ground, impressed
marks 'Made in England,
Potter to H. M. Queen',
signed 'W. Moorcroft',
factory paper label,
15in (38cm) high.
£600–750   AGr

A Moorcroft 'Eventide' pottery vase,
decorated with green and brown
trees and green hills against a flame
coloured sky, impressed marks,
signed in blue, 9½in (23cm) high.
£2,000–2,400   CSK

A deep flared bowl, by Moorcroft,
painted in the 'Claremont' design
with pink, yellow and blue
toadstools on a mottled blue/green
ground, the border inscribed 'Facta
non verba vincit omnia veritas',
impressed 'Moorcroft, Made in
England', green painted signature,
14in (35.5cm) diam.
£2,000–2,400   C

l. A Moorcroft Macintyre Florian Ware two-handled vase, decorated with Peacock pattern, the rim glazed in blue, yellow, grey and green, printed mark, green-painted mark 'W. M. des.', c1902, 5in (12.5cm) high.
£1,000–1,200

r. A Moorcroft Macintyre vase, decorated with Daisy pattern, in blue, green and white, green-painted mark 'W. Moorcroft des.', c1900.
£1,500–1,800 *Bon*

A Moorcroft flared-rim vase, decorated with Moonlit Blue pattern, in blue and green, impressed Royal Warrant, signed 'W. Moorcroft', c1925, 9½in (24cm) high.
£2,000–2,400 *S*

A Moorcroft vase, decorated with Pomegranate pattern, in puce, green, red and blue, signed 'W. Moorcroft', c1910, 12½in (32cm) high.
£2,000–2,400 *C*

l. A Moorcroft Burslem candlestick, decorated with 'Cornflower' pattern, c1914, 9in (23cm) high.
£800–950 *Bon*

A Moorcroft Florian Ware jardinière.
£1,500–1,800 *DM*

A Moorcroft bottle vase, decorated with 'Pomegranate', impressed marks, painted signature, 10½in (26.5cm) high.
£600–700 *Bea*

A Bernard Moore lustre vase, painted with scrolling foliage beneath the glaze, 6in (15cm) high.
£300–350 *CDC*

A pair of Moorcroft Florian Ware candlesticks, decorated with Poppy pattern, c1904.
£800–950 *DM*

l. A Moorcroft cylindrical pewter-mounted vase, decorated with 'Eventide' pattern, in red and orange, made for Liberty & Co, restored, c1928, 7½in (19cm) high.
£800–950 *S(C)*

A two-handled bottle vase, decorated after Christopher Dresser, facsimile signature, 29½in (75cm) high.
£650–750 *SS*

A Moorcroft jardinière, decorated
with flowers, 5½in (14cm) high.
£300–350 *PCh*

A Moorcroft 'Flamminian' dish, c1905,
12in (30.5cm) diam.
£300–350 *CSK*

A Moorcroft Florian Ware vase,
decorated with 'Poppy' pattern,
in shades of blue, signed, c1898,
11½in (29cm) high.
£800–950 *OBJ*

A Moorcroft Florian Ware jug,
with silver-plated lid, decorated
in shades of blue, stamped,
signed, c1898, 8in (20.5cm) high.
£400–450 *OBJ*

A Moorcroft vase, decorated with
'Claremont' pattern, made for
Liberty & Co, signed, c1903,
6in (15cm) high.
£1,500–1,800 *OBJ*

A Moorcroft vase, decorated with
'Cornflower' pattern, in red, beige
and purple, signed in green,
c1912, 12in (30.5cm) high.
£1,000–1,200 *P(M)*

A Moorcroft plate, decorated with
'Yacht' pattern, mid-1930s,
6in (15cm) high.
£80–100 *BRE*

A Moorcroft Florian Ware
vase, decorated with 'Iris'
pattern, stamped, signed,
c1900, 6in (15cm) high.
£450–550 *OBJ*

l. A Moorcroft Florian
Ware vase, decorated
with 'Cornflower'
pattern, in shades of
blue, signed, c1900,
5in (12.5cm) high.
£400–480 *OBJ*

A Moorcroft vase,
signed and dated 1929,
22in (56cm) high.
£1,200–1,500 *SWO*

r. A Moorcroft Macintyre
Florian Ware vase,
10in (25.5cm) high.
£800–900 *PBJ*

A Moorcroft Macintyre two-handled vase, decorated with 'Pansy' pattern, printed mark, signed, dated '1912', 12in (30.5cm) high.
£1,000–1,200 *SC*

A Moorcroft bowl, decorated with 'Pomegranate' pattern, on a blue/green ground, signed 'W. Moorcroft', 10in (25.5cm) diam.
£500–600 *CSK*

A Moorcroft vase, decorated with a fish pattern, on a pale brown ground, impressed, signed 'WM', c1930, 7in (18cm) high.
£1,500–1,800 *P*

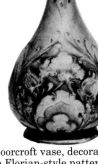

A Moorcroft vase, decorated with Florian-style pattern, printed Liberty mark, signed, c1910, 10in (25.5cm) high.
£800–950 *S*

A Moorcroft Macintyre vase, decorated with 'Pansy' pattern, printed mark, signed, dated '1912', 11in (28cm) high.
£1,000–1,200 *SC*

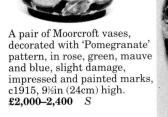

A pair of Moorcroft vases, decorated with 'Pomegranate' pattern, in rose, green, mauve and blue, slight damage, impressed and painted marks, c1915, 9½in (24cm) high.
£2,000–2,400 *S*

l. A William Moorcroft vase, decorated with 'Poppy' pattern, in purple, pink and green, impressed and painted marks, c1939, 14½in (37cm) high.
£400–450 *WHL*

A Moorcroft vase, decorated with 'Hazeldene' landscape pattern, in blue, impressed, signed and inscribed, dated '1920', 18½in (47cm) high.
£3,000–3,500 *P*

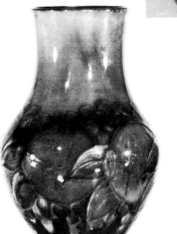

A Moorcroft vase, decorated with 'Pomegranate' pattern, in orange, red, ochre, cinnamon and blue, impressed 'Burslem' mark, signed in green, 1920s, 8½in (21.5cm) high.
£400–450 *CSK*

A Moorcroft Florian Ware vase, decorated with daffodil pattern, signed, c1900, 6in (15cm) high.
£800–950 *LT*

l. A Moorcroft vase, decorated with flowers, in pink, green and dark blue, impressed mark, painted signature and label, c1940, 3½in (9cm) high.
£100–120
r. A Moorcroft vase, decorated with flowers, in red and dark blue, label covering impressed and painted marks, c1940, 3½in (9cm) high.
£100–120 *TW*

A Moorcroft meat dish,
decorated with 'Yacht' pattern,
c1934, 16½in (42cm) wide.
£100–120 *LIO*

*The 'Yacht' pattern was introduced
by William Moorcroft in 1934,
taken from an original sketch
by his daughter, Beatrice.*

A Moorcroft two-handled
jardinière, decorated with Florian-
style daisy and poppy pattern,
in green, blue and yellow,
impressed Cambridge factory
mark, painted signature, c1916,
10in (25.5cm) wide.
£1,500–1,800 *AH*

A Moorcroft jardinière, decorated
with 'Blue Pansy' pattern, c1928,
4in (10cm) high.
£250–300 *LIO*

A Walter Moorcroft mug, decorated
with 'Caribbean' pattern, c1962,
4½in (11.5cm) high.
£200–250 *LIO*

A Moorcroft Macintyre
Florian Ware jug,
decorated with 'Blue
Tulip' pattern, c1901,
12in (30.5cm) high.
£1,000–1,200 *LIO*

r. A Moorcroft vase,
decorated with 'Claremont
Toadstool' pattern, in
yellow mauve, blue and
green, signed, impressed
'Moorcroft Burslem', 1914,
4½in (11.5cm) high.
£800–950 *WIL*

A Moorcroft Macintyre
coffee pot, decorated with
'Aurelian' pattern, c1897,
7in (17.5cm) high.
£350–400 *LIO*

A Lisa B. Moorcroft plaque,
decorated with 'Toadstool' pattern,
dated 1990, 16in (40.5cm) diam.
£250–300 *LIO*

*Lisa B. Moorcroft is the daughter
of Walter Moorcroft, who ran the
factory from 1945–86, and the
granddaughter of the founder,
William Moorcroft. She works as
an independent art potter.*

A Moorcroft 'Pink Flamminian'
teapot with cup, saucer and
plate, c1914.
£350–450 *LIO*

A Moorcroft teapot,
decorated with a blue
glaze, c1918,
6in (15cm) high.
£50–60 *LIO*

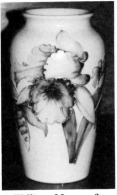

A William Moorcroft
saltglazed vase,
decorated with 'Orchid'
pattern, c1930,
7in (17.5cm) high.
£700–800   *RUM*

A William Moorcroft clock,
with original movement, the case
decorated with 'Poppy' pattern,
c1920, 5in (12.5cm) high.
£1,700–2,000   *RUM*

A Moorcroft Macintyre teapot and
stand, decorated with 'Seaweed'
pattern, c1902.
£800–900   *RUM*

A Walter Moorcroft cup and
saucer, decorated with 'Orchid'
pattern, c1930, 7in (17.5cm) high.
£180–200   *RUM*

A Moorcroft Macintyre
vase, decorated with
'Peacock' pattern,
on a celadon ground,
signed, c1900,
10in (25.5cm) high.
£2,500–3,000   *RUM*

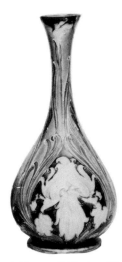

A Moorcroft Florian Ware
vase, decorated with 'Iris'
pattern, in green, blue and
yellow, printed and
painted marks, c1910,
10in (25.5cm) high.
£800–950   *S*

A Moorcroft Macintyre Florian
Ware vase, decorated with 'Poppy'
pattern, c1904, 3½in (9cm) high.
£350–400   *RUM*

A Moorcroft Macintyre vase,
decorated in green, blue and
yellow, printed Macintyre
mark, 7in (17.5cm) high.
£1,000–1,200   *S*

A Moorcroft Macintyre tea
kettle, decorated with
'Pomegranate' pattern, c1912.
£1,700–2,000   *RUM*

l. A Moorcroft
Macintyre vase,
decorated with Florian
pattern and gilt, incised
'W. M. Des', c1898,
9in (23cm) high.
£1,700–2,000   *RUM*

A Moorcroft ovoid footed bowl
with inverted rim, decorated with
fish and water weeds, in shades
of green, blue and yellow,
impressed factory marks,
signed in green, 6in (15cm) high.
£800–950 *CSK*

A Moorcroft Macintyre Florian
Ware vase, with blue and yellow
flowers, c1903, 6in (15cm) high.
£850–1,000 *RUM*

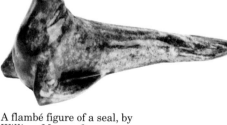

A flambé figure of a seal, by
William Moorcroft,
8in (20.5cm) long.
£1,000–1,200 *LT*

A Moorcroft Macintyre Florian
Ware 'Poppy' pattern jug,
with simulated bamboo moulded
handle, EPNS mount,
hinged cover and thumbpiece,
damaged, printed mark in
brown, initialled 'WM' in green,
early 20thC, 8½in (21.5cm) high.
£350–450 *HSS*

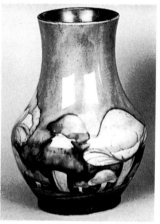

A Moorcroft 'Claremont' pattern
vase, designed by William
Moorcroft, the swollen cylindrical
form with flared neck and everted
rim, blue and green mottled with
yellow, pink, green and blue
mushrooms, restored, impressed
'Moorcroft, Made in England',
green signature 'W. Moorcroft',
c1920, 6½in (16.5cm) high.
£800–950 *C*

l. A William Moorcroft
saltglaze 'Fish' design vase,
c1928, 9in (23cm) high.
£1,700–2,000 *RUM*

A Macintyre 'Claremont'
pattern bowl, designed by
William Moorcroft, the green
and blue streaked ground with
crimson, blue and green
mushrooms, printed marks
'Made for Liberty & Co',
registered No. 420081, signed,
c1903, 8½in (21.5cm) high.
£2,000–2,400 *C*

A Moorcroft MacIntyre tobacco
jar and cover, with a celadon
ground and red flowers, c1903,
5in (12.5cm) high.
£850–1,000 *RUM*

A William Moorcroft 'Pansy'
design vase, on a blue ground,
c1925, 9in (23cm) high.
£500–600 *RUM*

l. A Macintyre Florian Ware 'Iris'
pattern vase, designed by William
Moorcroft, on a flared foot, with
everted rim, blue ground with
raised slip decoration of cartouches
of green and yellow irises, brown
printed 'Macintyre Florian Ware'
stamp, green signature 'W.
Moorcroft', c1900,
6½in (17cm) high.
£450–550 *C*

A Moorcroft bowl, painted with red and green toadstools on a mottled green ground, printed marks and signed in green, 8in (20.5cm) diam.
£800–950 *CSK*

A pair of Moorcroft 'Dawn' pattern vases, painted in deep blue against a pale blue sky, between chevron borders of blue and cream, painted initials in blue, impressed 'Moorcroft, Made in England', 8in (20.5cm) high.
£2,000–2,400 *L*

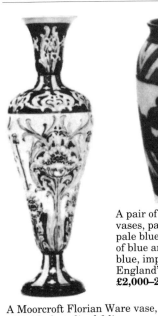

A Moorcroft Florian Ware vase, with black stylized foliage on a white and black ground, printed marks, signed in green, 12½in (32cm) high.
£600–700 *CSK*

A Moorcroft 'Brown Cornflower' vase, decorated in reds, blue, orange and beige, impressed 'Moorcroft Burslem' and signed 'W. Moorcroft', 8in (20.5cm) high.
£600–700 *P*

A Moorcroft Macintyre tobacco jar, decorated in reds, blues, browns, greens and apricot, Macintyre marks and signed 'WM', 4½in (11.5cm) high.
£500–600 *P*

A Moorcroft two-handled trumpet-shaped vase, with a matt blue ground, signed, 1898–1900, 10in (25.5cm) high.
£1,000–1,200 *LT*

A Moorcroft Macintyre vase, with Florian-style decoration, full signature, c1900, 7in (18cm) high.
£600–700 *LT*

William Moorcroft (1872–1945)

From 1898, William Moorcroft headed the Art Pottery department of Macintyre & Co, the Staffordshire pottery firm established in about 1847 at Burslem. His early designs, known as Aurelian wares, were generally printed in underglaze blue with overglaze iron-red and gilt, and decorated with designs reminiscent of the textiles of William Morris. His later work for Macintyre, retailed as Florian Ware, was possibly the foremost British contribution to Art Nouveau ceramics.

r. A Moorcroft 'Claremont' pattern vase, decorated on a green-blue ground, base chipped, impressed 'Moorcroft Burslem England 1440' and with green painted 'W. Moorcroft' signature, 8in (20.5cm) high.
£1,000–1,200 *C*

l. A Moorcroft Macintyre baluster vase, decorated in blue-green and gold against olive green, Macintyre marks signed 'W.M. des.' and Rd. No. '404017', 12½in (32cm) high.
£600–700 *P*

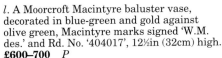

A Moorcroft vase, decorated with 'Anemone' pattern, on a red ground, 6½in (16.5cm) high.
£260–300   *Bea*

A Moorcroft Macintyre pottery baluster vase, with 2 loop handles, polychrome floral decoration on a white ground with gilt banding, 7½in (19cm) high.
£800–950   *AH*

A Moorcroft flambé 'Eventide' vase, tube-lined with trees in a hilly landscape and richly coloured in mauve, orange and red, minor chip restored on foot, impressed 'Moorcroft, Made in England' and signed in blue 'W. Moorcroft', 8in (20.5cm) high.
£2,000–2,400   *S*

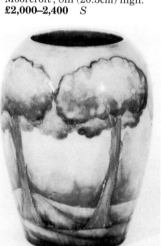

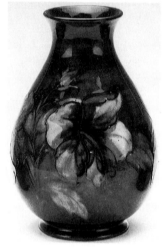

A Moorcroft pottery vase, painted with 'Hibiscus' pattern, on a deep red ground, impressed marks and painted signature, 8½in (21.5cm) high.
£300–350   *Bea*

A Moorcroft vase, painted with 'Pomegranate' pattern on a blue ground, impressed marks and painted signature, 6½in (17cm) high.
£200–250   *Bea*

A Moorcroft 'Eventide' vase, decorated with green and brown trees and hills against a flame-coloured sky, impressed mark, signed, 5½in (14cm) high.
£1,000–1,200   *AH*

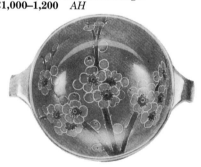

A Moorcroft 'Apple Blossom' bowl, tube-lined with branches of flowers and berries in green, hair crack, impressed 'Moorcroft Burslem 1914', signed 'W. Moorcroft', dated '1914', 10in (25.5cm) high.
£1,000–1,200   *S*

A Moorcroft Florian Ware bottle vase with fluted rim, decorated with 'Poppy' design, in blue and green, pattern No. 401753, printed mark, signed, 6in (15cm) high.
£800–950   *Bea*

A Moorcroft Florian Ware vase, tube-lined with yellow and blue flowerheads and green foliage on a blue ground, printed mark, signed 'W. Moorcroft', c1902, 11½in (29cm) high.
£1,500–1,800   *S*

l. A Moorcroft Macintyre Florian Ware blue 'Landscape' pattern vase, signed 'W. Moorcroft', c1903, 12in (30.5cm) high.
£1,700–2,000 *RUM*

A William Moorcroft Flambé 'Landscape' vase, c1928, 12in (30.5cm) high.
£3,300–4,000 *RUM*

l. A Moorcroft Macintyre Florian Ware vase, tube-lined in white, decorated in green and gilt on a blue ground, printed mark and pattern No. 'M2019', 9in (23cm) high.
£500–600 *DN*

A Walter Moorcroft 'Bougainvillea' design vase, on a green ground, c1955, 10in (25.5cm) high.
£450–550 *RUM*

l. A William Moorcroft 'Claremont' design vase, 7in (17.5cm) high.
£800–950 *LT*

A Walter Moorcroft 'Bougainvillea' design vase, on a green ground, c1955, 10in (25.5cm) high.
£600–700 *RUM*

l. A Walter Moorcroft 'Hibiscus' design vase, on an ivory ground, c1955, 8in (20.5cm) high.
£260–300 *RUM*

A Moorcroft vase, decorated in 'Cornflower' pattern with blue flowers and leaves reserved against a pale blue ground, impressed marks, signed in blue, paper label, 12½in (32cm) high.
£650–750 *P*

A Macintyre Florian 'Peacock' pattern vase, designed by William Moorcroft, blue ground with raised slip decoration of blue, green and yellow stylized peacock eyes, with brown printed Macintyre Florian Ware stamp, Reg. No. 347807, green monogram 'W.M.', c1900, 3½in (9cm) high.
£800–950 *C*

A William Moorcroft 'Pansy' design vase, on green ground, impressed 'Burslem', signed, c1913, 5in (12.5cm) high.
£1,000–1,200 *RUM*

r. A Moorcroft Macintyre Florian Ware vase, decorated with cornflowers and butterflies, outlined in white slip and coloured in shades of blue, factory mark 'W.M. Des', painted in green 'M757', 8½in (21.5cm) high.
£750–850 *P*

A Linthorpe pottery bowl, designed by Christopher Dresser, with silver rim, impressed mark and signature, 10in (25.5cm) diam.
£300–350   *DN*

A Bretby figure of a fisher boy, standing on a rock, c1895, 35in (89cm) high.
£500–600   *OCA*

A Linthorpe pottery ewer, designed by Christopher Dresser, the red body covered with a streaked milky green-brown glaze, facsimile Dresser signature 'HT' monogram for Henry Tooth and numbered '502', 8½in (21.5cm) high.
£600–700   *P*

A Gallé faïence cat, painted with polychrome floral sprays on a yellow ground, wearing a pendant and floral scarf, green glass eyes, some damage, 13in (33cm) high.
£1,500–1,800   *Bon*

l. An Austrian 'Femme Fleur' pottery vase, glazed in green and beige, impressed marks, 16½in (42cm) high.
£500–600   *P*

A Minton Secessionist jug, with green, yellow and grey glaze, 11½in (29cm) high.
£450–500   *ZEI*

A pair of Brannam pottery vases, by James Dewdney, sgraffito-decorated with birds, in red slip against stippled white, beneath a blue glaze, incised 'C.H. Brannam, Barum J.D. 1888', 'R' to necks, 14½in (37cm) high.
£300–350   *P*

An Art Nouveau hanging plaque, 9in (23cm) diam.
£200–250   *ASA*

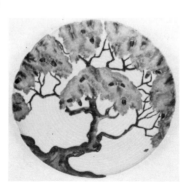

r. A Carlton Ware charger, 13in (33cm) diam.
£170–200   *ASA*

A Brannam pottery slipware vase, sgraffito-decorated with birds, the red body overlaid with white slip, beneath a honey-coloured glaze, signed 'C. H. Brannam, Barum, N. Devon', dated '1881', 'R' on neck, 15in (38cm) high.
£700–800   *P*

l. A Continental green boat vase, 16in (40.5cm) wide. **£70–80** *THA*

A jug and basin, with green and pink embossed design, jug 12½in (32cm) high. **£120–140** *PAR*

A Foley plate, produced for the American market, signed 'F. Micklewright', c1893, 9in (23cm) diam. **£120–140** *AJ*

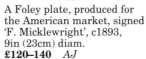

Two Foley Intarsio Toby jugs, John Bull and Scotsman, 7½in (19cm) high. **£350–400 each** *AJ*

An Eichwald tazza, c1920, 11in (28cm) high. **£170–200** *BEC*

r. Two early E. Radford Burslem vases, tallest 6½in (16.5cm) high. **£50–60 each**

A pair of Eichwald vases, 12in (30.5cm) high. **£100–120** *BEV*

An E. Radford 'Anemone' pattern jug, 6½in (16.5cm) high. **£40–50** *MA*

An E. Radford 'Strawberry' pattern vase, 9in (23cm) high. **£50–60** *MA*

An early E. Radford 'Ranunculus' pattern jug. **£100–120** *MA*

l. An early E. Radford 'Anemone' pattern vase. **£75–85** *MA*

l. An E. Radford cheese dish and toast rack, decorated with 'Anemone' pattern. **£35–40 each** *MA*

l. A pair of William de Morgan tiles, with Isnik style decoration, on a pale green ground, framed, each 8in (20.5cm) square.
£400–450   *C*

A Linthorpe pottery pouring vessel, designed by Christopher Dresser, the brown body streaked milky-green with yellow speckling, 'Linthorpe Chr. Dresser' mark, 'HT' for Henry Tooth and '267', 5½in (14cm) high.
£400–450   *P*

A Pilkington 'Royal Lancastrian' vase, by William Salter Mycock, painted in gold and ruby lustres on a shaded blue ground, impressed rosette mark, incised 'E. T. R.' for E. T. Radford, artist's monogram and date code for 1933, 8½in (21.5cm) high.
£800–950   *P*

A Mintons Secessionist ware garden stool, decorated in raised outline against a printed ground of flowers and foliage, glazed in turquoise, green, brown and yellow, impressed marks, date code for 1908, 21in (53.5cm) high.
£600–700   *P*

Above. A Mintons Secessionist jardinière and stand, probably designed by John Wadsworth and Leon Solon, in pink, red, yellow and green, on cylindrical stand, printed marks and date code for 1902, 42in (106.5cm) high overall.
£1,500–1,800   *P*

A Maw & Co vase, designed by Walter Crane, painted in olive green, signed on base, 13in (33cm) high.
£2,000–2,400   *P*

l. A Mintons Secessionist ware jardinière, decorated in green slip-trailing with cream/amber stylised buds on blue stems, reserved against a purple ground, stamped marks and printed mark 'NO.1', 10½in (26.5cm) high.
£350–400   *P*

A Mintons Art Studio Pottery twin-handled moon flask, in the style of Christopher Dresser, decorated in greey, white and gilt, on a chocolate-brown ground, circular 'Kensington Gore' marks, impressed 'Minton' with date code for 1872, printed marks 'S.122' and 'K92', 13in (33cm) high.
£500–600   *P*

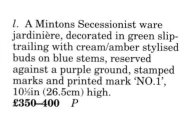

Four William de Morgan tiles, ruby lustre on a cream ground, c1890, each tile 6in (15cm) square.
£500–600 each   *C*

A William de Morgan ruby lustre charger, decorated with a peacock, c1900, 14in (35.5cm) diam.
£2,000–2,400   *C*

A pair of Foley Intarsio wall plates, designed by Frederick Rhead, printed factory marks and 'Rd Nos. 330399' for 1898–99, 12in (30.5cm) diam.
£900–1,100   *P*

A Gallé cat, with yellow ground, c1900, 13½in (33.5cm) high.
£1,700–2,000   *GCA*

A Gallé cat, with tartan coat, c1900, 13in (33cm) high.
£1,700–2,000   *GCA*

l. A terracotta bust of a lady, signed 'Lefevre', c1900.
£500–600   *Phi*

An Ault pottery vase, designed by Christopher Dresser, the magnolia-coloured body painted possibly by Clarissa Ault, impressed facsimile signature and 'No. 247', 27½in (69.5cm) high.
£600–700   *P*

A Linthorpe pottery ewer, designed by Christopher Dresser, with linear decoration beneath a streaked honey, green, blue and grey glaze, factory marks, facsimile signature and 'HT' for Henry Tooth, 9in (23cm) high.
£350–450   *P*

A Christopher Dresser Linthorpe pottery pot pourri vase and cover, silver-mounted with blue glazed underside, the pierced silver cover with fluted dome and ball finial, impressed marks and 'No. 277', c1900, 9½in (23.5cm) diam.
£400–450   *TW*

A Linthorpe pottery tobacco jar, the brown glazed body with electroplated rim and swing handle, impressed mark, Henry Tooth monogram and shape 'No. 913', late 19th C, 5in (12.5cm) high.
£50–60   *TW*

l. A globular green glazed bowl, designed by Christopher Dresser, impressed with facsimile signature, 5½in (14.5cm) high.
£1,000–1,200   *C*

A Christopher Dresser Linthorpe vase, decorated in plum and green crackle effect glaze, impressed marks and shape 'No. 875', late 19thC, 12in (30.5cm) high.
£200–250   *TW*

Above left. A pottery plate, designed by Christopher Dresser, with a speckled jade green glaze, impressed 'Linthorpe', monogram 'HT' for Henry Tooth, and facsimile 'Dresser' signature, 11½in (29cm) diam.
£200–250

Above centre. A Della Robbia vase and cover, slip decorated in sgraffito against a shaded turquoise ground, Galleon mark, initials for George Seddon and painted by Liz Wilkins, No. '744A/74B', 11½in (29cm) high.
£400–450

Above right. A Pilkington Lancastrian circular wall plate, by William Salter Mycock, impressed Bees mark but later signed with 'WSM' monogram, dated '1919', 13in (33cm) diam.
£300–350   P

A Brannam/Barnstaple vase, incised signature and date '1916', 20in (51cm) high.
£300–350   SC

A Wedgwood vase, decorated by Alfred Powell, the body painted in shades of blue, green, brick-red and bronze-lustred mauve, impressed 'Wedgwood', incised 'P.21', painted monogram and '89', c1910, 15in (38cm) high.
£700–800   S

A Ruskin vase, turquoise and lavender, impressed oval mark, dated '1907', 8½in (21.5cm) high.
£800–950   S

A Louis Wain pottery figure, 'The Lucky Haw-Haw Cat', with an aperture in the back possibly for a vase, 5in (12.5cm) high.
£250–300   CSK

r. A Burmantofts faïence Art Nouveau jardinière and stand, decorated in blue, yellow and turquoise, impressed marks and numbered '2273/4', 39in (99cm) high.
£300–350   P

r. A Louis Wain model of a pig, with green and lemon body, facsimile signature and 'Made in England', 4½in (12cm) high.
£300–350   P

Above left. A Minton's Art Pottery jardinière, c1890, 9½in (24cm) high.
£300–350

Above right. A Minton's Secessionist pottery jardinière, 1900–08, 10in (25.5cm) high.
£400–450   CDC

l. A Royal Copenhagen group, entitled 'The Rock and the Wave', depicting a man tethered to a rock and a woman rising from the waves, wave mark and 'ØF' in underglaze blue, incised '1132A.W.', and monogram 'T.L.', dated '1897', 18½in (47cm) high.
£800–950   SS

A William de Morgan Art Pottery dish, decorated with a dragon in ruby copper lustre on a white ground, 14½in (36cm) diam.
£2,500–3,000   *Bea*

A Goldscheider porcelain head of a woman, printed 'Goldscheider U.S.A.', 11½in (29cm) high.
£300–350   *CSK*

A Mintons Secessionist jardinière and stand, with tube-lined decoration, printed and impressed marks 'Minton Ltd.', c1910, 41½in (103.5cm) high.
£1,500–1,800   *C*

A Mintons Seccessionist jardinière, outlined in relief, green transfer and impressed mark to base, early 20thC, 17in (43cm) diam.
£400–450   *WIL*

A Pilkington's Royal Lancastrian vase, in yellow, blue and ruby lustre, decorated by Gordon M. Forsyth for Pilkington's, impressed Bee mark, 'VIII, England 218', 8in (20.5cm) high.
£800–950   *C*

A William de Morgan tile, impressed 'DM98' in circle, and another tile with stylized carnations and leaves, impressed 'Sand's End Pottery' marked, both 6¼in (15.5cm) square.
£100–200 each   *P*

A Pilkington's Royal Lancastrian vase, decorated by Gordon M. Forsyth, with lions in silver mottled lustre against a bright blue ground, printed marks, artist's monogram on base, c1905, 11½in (29cm) high.
£600–700   *HSS*

A Pilkington's Royal Lancastrian highly decorated lustre bowl, by Mycock, c1900, 5in (12.5cm) diam.
£300–350   *ASA*

l. A Pilkington's Royal Lancastrian wall plaque, possibly by Gladys Rodgers, impressed 'Royal Lancastrian, Made in England', 10½in (26cm) diam.
£300–350   *P*

A Minton's moon flask, painted by W. S. Coleman, neck damaged, signed, 17in (42.5cm) high.
£1,500–1,800   *PWC*

l. An Austrian vase,
12in (30.5cm) high.
£250–300 *ASA*

A Royal Dux ceramic figure on
a sea shell, 14in (36cm) high.
£450–500 *ASA*

A Goldscheider terracotta
lamp, 28in (71cm) high.
£2,500–3,000 *ASA*

A pair of German tiles, both
depicting maidens with flowing
hair, in coloured glazes, depicting
the Muse of Dancing, and the
Muse of Music playing a harp,
5in (12.5cm) wide.
£700–800 *P*

A pair of Zuid Holland vases,
with 4 undercut edges and
applied handles, painted with
pendant stylized flowers on the
neck, painted mark 'Made in
Zuid, Holland 'J.H.' and incised
'213', 8½in (22cm) high.
£300–350 *S(S)*

A Reps and Trinte pottery
clock case, the base
supporting a female bust
flanked by 2 floral buttresses
beneath triangular face,
impressed marks and incised
'Stellmacher', damaged, early
20thC, 21in (53cm) high.
£600–700 *S(S)*

A Clement Massier
turquoise glazed
earthenware jardinière
and stand, moulded in
relief with leaves, flowers
and branches, the oviform
bowl on cylindrical stand,
impressed factory marks,
37in (94cm) high.
£1,000–1,200 *CSK*

A Rozenburg vase, painted in
rich polychrome colours, black
printed factory mark and year
symbol of a flower, 'Rozenburg,
den Haag', a cross in a square,
'372', c1913, 6in (15cm) high.
£450–550 *S(S)*

A pair of Rozenburg
vases, decorated in rich
polychrome colours, black
painted factory mark and
year symbol of a flower,
'Rozenburg, den Haag',
cross in a square, '472',
c1913, 8½in (21.5cm) high.
£750–900 *S(S)*

An Elton ware jardinière, with triple loop handles, signed 'Elton', 10in (25.5cm) high.
£500–600 *HOD*

An Elton ware pre-Columbian shaped jug, with floral decoration and butterflies in shades of green, c1885, 8½in (22cm) high.
£200–240 *OBJ*

An Elton ware jug, with fruit design in shades of green and red, c1890, 6½in (16cm) high.
£200–240 *OBJ*

r. An Elton ware vase in gold 'crackle' with black slip underneath, c1910, 5½in (14cm) high.
£400–450 *OBJ*

l. An Elton ware vase, decorated with sunflowers in shades of blue, c1900, 9in (23cm) high.
£200–240 *OBJ*

Sir Edmund Harry Elton (1846–1920)

English art potter who, in 1883, inherited Clevedon Court in Somerset. With an assistant potter, G. Masters, he made earthenware vessels decorated with flower patterns in coloured slips (blue, red or green).
His products, known as 'Elton ware', were shown at the Arts and Crafts Exhibition Society, of which he was a member.

An Elton ware trefoil-shaped jug, in shades of purple and red, c1900, 6in (15cm) high.
£400–450 *OBJ*

An Elton ware jug, in green slip with gold 'crackle', c1910, 6½in (16cm) high.
£250–300 *OBJ*

An Elton ware vase, with daffodil design in shades of blue, green and brown, c1890, 7in (17.5cm) high.
£100–120 *OBJ*

l. An Elton ware 'crackle' jug, c1921, 7in (17.5cm) high.
£300–350 *OBJ*
This jug was made by his son after Elton had died, and is signed 'Elton' with a cross.

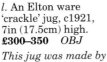

An Elton ware gourd shaped vase, with insects design in shades of purple and red, c1885, 9½in (24cm) high.
£200–240 *OBJ*

An Elton ware vase, with bird and leaf design in shades of green, blue and yellow, c1900, 10in (25.5cm) high.
£300–350 *OBJ*

A dish, with a figure of a lady in the centre, by Ernst Wahllis, Vienna, c1900, 8½in (21.5cm) high.
£600–700   *ASA*

A William de Morgan tile, painted in brown and yellow with a sailing boat, impressed Sand's End mark, mounted as a teapot stand, 7in (17.5cm) high.
£500–600   *P*

A William de Morgan tile, painted in red lustre with stylized carnations, with painted signature, 'W. de Morgan & Co, Fulham, London', 8in (20.5cm) square.
£200–250   *C*

l. An Elton ware jug, with central gold lustre decoration of a fish and wings, base with monogram for George Masters, 7in (17.5cm) high.
£700–800   *HOD*

l. A lustre pottery vase, attributed to William de Morgan, painted by Frederick Passenger, in pink and ruby lustres on a white ground, blue painted initials 'FP' on base, 7in (17.5cm) high.
£500–600   *CSK*

l. A Dutch jardinière and stand, decorated in batik style with flowers, foliage and trellis panels, supported on a broad cylindrical stand, signed 'Corona Holland', 39in (99cm) high.
£700–850   *P*

A Bretby jardinière, decorated with fish.
£750–900   *ASA*

An Elton ware jar and cover, with floral design in shades of blue and green, c1890, 6½in (16.5cm) high.
£200–240   *OBJ*

A Watcombe Pottery vase, decorated in green and red, 8in (20.5cm) high.
£100–120   *STU*

A Linthorpe Pottery ewer, designed by Christopher Dresser, the reddish body streaked with milky-green and brown, marked 'Linthorpe HT', and facsimile signature, 9½in (24cm) high.
£300–350   *P*

A William de Morgan tile, painted in black with a stylized dodo, impressed Sand's End pottery mark, mounted as a teapot stand, 7in (17.5cm) high.
£500–600   *P*

A Wade vase, with floral decoration, c1930, 9in (23cm) high.
£85–100   *STU*

A French stoneware figural vase, by James Vibert, glaze shaded turquoise and brick red, signed 'J. Vibert' on the handle, 'E. Muller' as maker, 6½in (16.5cm) high.
£600–700 *P*

James Vibert was born in Switzerland in 1872, and in 1892 was employed in the workshops of Rodin.

A Burmantofts faïence plaque, painted by William Neatby, impressed 'Burmantofts Faïence', signed 'Wm. Neatby', dated '1887', 16in (40.5cm) high.
£600–700 *P*

A Riessner, Stellmacher and Kessel Art Nouveau porcelain vase, coloured in green, yellow and gilding against a shaded yellow and white ground, impressed crown mark, 'Amphora, Austria, 15024-46', 15in (38cm) high.
£300–350 *P*

A Theodore Deck faïence circular wall plate, 'Phryne', impressed 'T. H. Deck', signed 'R. Collin' (?), 24⅖in (62cm) high.
£1,500–1,800 *P*

An Austrian lustre glazed porcelain pitcher, by Ernst Wahliss, c1900.
£400–450 *VAS*

A Pilkington Royal Lancastrian vase, painted by Richard Joyce, in golden lustre and red against a powder blue ground, impressed rosette mark and artist's monogram, 12in (30.5cm) high.
£1,500–1,800 *P*

A Hancocks Morris Ware vase, designed by George Cartlidge.
£1,000–1,200 *THA*

A Della Robbia clock case, designed by Ruth Bare and decorated by Alice Jones, painted ship mark flanked by 'DR' above artist's monogram 'LJ' and '57', c1904, 18in (45.5cm) high.
£1,500–1,800 *SC*

The inscription is linked with Ruth Bare's involvement with the Positivist Movement.

A pair of Rozenburg pottery vases, with a green ground, painted marks and date mark for 1898, 9½in (24cm) high.
£800–950 *C(Am)*

l. A pair of Mettlach Villeroy & Boch vases, each incised and painted in ochre, red and green on a blue ground, rim chip to one, incised marks and '2416', 16in (40.5cm) high.
£1,000–1,200   *CEd*

An early Rozenburg pottery wall plate, attributed to Th. A. C. Colenbrander, signed on base 'Rozenburg, den Haag', date letter for 1890, 15in (38cm) diam.
£1,000–1,200   *P*

An early Rozenburg pottery wall plate, attributed to Th. A. C. Colenbrander, probably painted by W. F. Abspoel, 'WG' mark for W. von Gudenberg, den Haag, date letter for 1888, and artist's device, 15in (38cm) diam.
£1,000–1,200   *P*

r. A vase by Jessie Marion King, cracked, 'J.M.K.' marks, 6in (15cm) high.
£350–450   *CEd*

An Austrian porcelain coffee set, painted in mauve, green and yellow with delicate flowers, and further embellished with gilding, factory marks for Carl Knoll of Karlsbad, Austria.
£1,500–1,800   *P*

A Minton Art Studio jug, in turquoise and honey colours, restored, c1875, 8in (20.5cm) high.
£300–350   *CEd*

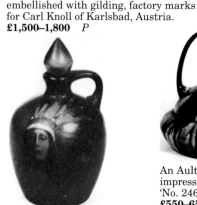

A William de Morgan tile panel, made from 2 large tiles, painted in red and pink lustres, framed.
£1,000–1,200   *P*

An Ault pottery vase, marked, impressed 'C. W. Dresser', and 'No. 246', 7in (17.5cm) high.
£550–650   *HOD*

A Rookwood Pottery 'Indian' flask and stopper, decorated by Harriet Elizabeth Wilcox, with a treacle coloured ground, impressed factory mark, date code for 1898, artist's initials, 7½in (18cm) high.
£2,000–2,400   *P*

An Ault pottery twin-handled vase, designed by Christopher Dresser, decorated in red, white and apple green, factory mark, No. 246, facsimile signature, 7in (17.5cm) high.
£800–950   *P*

An Ault pottery freeform vase, designed by Christopher Dresser, impressed facsimile signature, 12½in (32cm) high.
£350–450   *P*

An Elton ware vase, decorated with gold and platinum crackle glaze, base with signature, 21½in (54cm) high.
£800–900   *HOD*

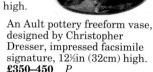

l. A Brannam pottery vase, decorated in sgraffito by James Dewdney, in red, blue and yellow glaze giving the appearance of green and brown colouring, signed and dated '1898', 19½in (49cm) high.
£650–800   *P*

r. A Dalpayrat high-fired porcelain vase, the white body glazed in shades of sang-de-boeuf, mauve, eau-de-nil, and blue, signed, numbered '12', 2in (5cm) high.
£300–350   *P*

A Foley China 'Harjian' vase, with 3 loop handles, decorated in brown, white, turquoise and green, with a frieze of dancing Negro figures, printed Foley Art China and rope mark and 'Harjian', 10½in (27cm) high.
£450–550 P

A Linthorpe earthenware jug, designed by Dr Christopher Dresser, covered in a streaked lustrous olive brown and turquoise glaze, impressed 'Linthorpe', with facsimile signature, 'Chr. Dresser', 7½in (19.5cm) high.
£600–700 C

A Carlton Ware limited edition punch bowl, moulded in relief with a frieze of Henry VIII and his wives and children, glazed in bright colours and heightened with gilding, with full inscription on base, numbered 50 of an edition of 250, 8in (20.5cm) high.
£600–700 P

A ceramic câchepot, by Max Lauger, the celadon ground decorated with green branches and black fruit, hairline crack, impressed mark on the base, 8in (20.5cm) high.
£600–700 CG

A William de Morgan deep bowl, decorated by Fred Passenger in copper, blue and silver lustre, the exterior in golden and ruby lustre with scroll motif, painted marks 'W. de Morgan, Fulham FP', 16½in (41.5cm) wide.
£2,500–3,000 C

A Scottie Wilson ceramic plate, painted in colours, signed on the plate 'Scottie', 14in (35.5cm), mounted, framed and glazed.
£200–250 P

An Austrian 'tube line' decorated plant trough, 11in (28cm) wide.
£130–160 ASA

A Carlton Ware plaque, painted in gilt, orange, blue, green and white, printed mark, design No. 7898, 3787, 15½in (39cm) diam.
£400–450 CEd

An Ernst Wahliss pottery wall plaque, in muted naturalistic colours, stamped 'Made in Austria', Ernst Wahliss, Turn-Wien', 20in (51cm) high.
£280–340 P

l. A Bing & Grøndahl porcelain model of a monkey, factory marks, signed beneath glaze 'Dahl Jensen 1902', 'R' on tortoise, 13in (33cm) high.
£450–550 P

A Goldscheider pottery bust, impressed factory mark, 14½in (36.8cm) high.
£600–700 P

l. Three pieces of Radford ware, decorated with 'Ranunculus' pattern. **£25–100 each** *MA*

An E. Radford 'coaching jug', 10½in (26.5cm) high. **£100–120** *MA*

An E. Radford moulded vase, 'Rose' pattern, 6in (15cm) high. **£60–70** *MA*

An early E. Radford, Burslem teapot, 5½in (12.5cm) high. **£85–100** *MA*

An E. Radford moulded jug, decorated with 'Indian Tree' pattern, 8½in (21.5cm) high. **£70–80** *MA*

Two E. Radford vases, decorated with 'Anemone' pattern, largest 10in (25.5cm) high. **£40–60 each** *MA*

An early E. Radford, Burslem jug, 7in (17.5cm) high. **£80–90** *MA*

An E. Radford plate and vase, vase 8in (20.5cm) high. **£40–60 each** *MA*

Two E. Radford wall pockets, decorated with 'Anemone' pattern, 4½in (11.5cm) high. **£40–60 each** *MA*

An early E. Radford, Burslem table lamp base. **£70–80** *MA*

A Royal Doulton miniature cup, impressed '7498', incised 'CA', 2in (5cm) high.
£25–30 *HM*

A blue and white faïence dish and cover, painted with a crest and 'Pour n'Oublié', marked 'Gallé Nancy St Clement', 1880s, 10in (25.5cm) wide.
£500–600 *SB*

A Zsolnay centrepiece, in green-blue and golden purple lustre glaze, moulded circular 'Zsolnay' mark, 21½in (54.5cm) high.
£1,500–1,800 *C*

A faïence seated cat, black glazed, painted with amber and gilt scroll motifs, one flank painted with a crest, slight damage, 13in (33cm) high.
£1,500–1,800 *C*

A French pottery bust of an Arthurian style lady, after Jacob, shaded in turquoise and rose, picked out in gold, impressed mark, 8in (20.5cm) high.
£350–450 *SBe*

A French pottery plate, with a design by Alphonse Mucha and painted in colours, marked 'Mucha 97', and on reverse 'Au Grand Depot, 21 rue Drouot, Paris', 12in (30.5cm) diam.
£900–1,100 *P*

A Koenig & Lengsfeld ceramic figure of a young woman peeking into a mirror, in shades of grey and lavender, impressed 'Koenig & Lengsfeld, Koln Lindenthal 2687, 27½in (70cm) high.
£1,000–1,200 *C*

A Scottish painted low relief plaster panel, incised initials 'GAW', c1905, 12in (30.5cm) wide.
£300–350 *SB*

A Della Robbia earthenware cream glazed vase, decorated by Liza Wilkins, incised mark, painted initials, 10½in (26.5cm) high.
£350–450 *CSK*

An Arte Della earthenware vase, impressed and painted factory insignia, c1905, 13½in (34.5cm) high.
£900–1,100 *SB*

A Royal Dux earthenware mirror, impressed factory mark, numbered '1098', c1900, 21½in (54.5cm) high.
£800–950 *SB*

A Clement Massier lustre glazed earthenware vase, decorated with green, pink and peacock metallic lustre, painted mark 'M.C. Clement Massier Golfe Juan a.m.', c1900, 12in (30.5cm) high.
£1,000–1,200 *SB*

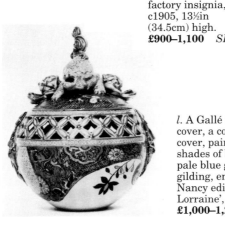

l. A Gallé faïence pot pourri and cover, a copy of a Kutani *koro* and cover, painted in Japanese style in shades of blue and rust against a pale blue ground, detailed with gilding, enamelled mark 'Gallé Nancy editeur St Clement terre Lorraine', 1870s, 10in (25.5cm) high.
£1,000–1,200 *SB*

A Wedgwood Fairyland lustre 'Elves and Bell Branch' bowl, after a design by Daisy Makeig-Jones, decorated with elves and fairies dancing among tall grass against a black ground with a gilt spider's web, printed Portland vase mark, painted number 'Z4968', minor rubbing, c1920, 3in (7.5cm) high.
£900–1,100   *S(S)*

A pair of Shelley Intarsio vases, after a design by Walter Slater, decorated with stylized pink flowerheads among foliage in green, brown and blue, printed mark 'Late Foley', Shelley, England, Intarsio', and painted number '544 3617', c1915, 6½in (16.5cm) high.
£300–350   *S(S)*

A Rye Pottery vase, with flared neck, applied with daffodils and leaves, marked on base 'Sussex Ware, Rye', 6in (15cm) high.
£150–170   *RAG*

A pair of Wedgwood Fairyland lustre vases, after a design by Daisy Makeig-Jones, each decorated with the 'Imps on a Bridge and Tree House' pattern, against a flame red ground, Portland vase mark 'Wedgwood Made in England', and painted number 'Z5481', c1920, 10in (25.5cm) high.
£3,500–4,000   *S(S)*

A Pilkington's Royal Lancastrian lustre wall plaque, after a design by Walter Crane and painted by Charles E. Cundall, in copper lustre with red details on a mauve ground, the reverse with 4 copper lustre floral motifs, damaged, impressed factory 'P' and Bee mark, 'VII', and lustre monograms, c1907.
£2,300–2,800   *S(S)*

A Wileman & Co Intarsio jug, after a design by Frederick Rhead, modelled as the body of a bird with an Egyptian-style head, raised on 3 feet, printed factory mark, registration No. 330274, painted number '3076', c1900, 5in (12.5cm) high.
£350–400   *S(S)*

A Rye Pottery bowl, the brown body profusely covered with applied green hops, the rim banded with leaves, marked on base 'Rye Sussex', dated '1919', 8in (20.5cm) diam.
£350–400   *RAG*

A Wedgwood Fairyland lustre 'Woodland Bridge' bowl, after a design by Daisy Makeig-Jones, decorated outside with orange, yellow, green and purple shrubs on a black ground, the interior with the 'Fairy with Large Hat' pattern, cobwebs in the trees, fairies and elves among the toadstools on the banks of a river, gilt printed factory mark and painted number 'Z4968', c1920, 6in (15cm) diam.
£2,000–2,400   *S(S)*

A tapering vase, applied with branches, acorns and oak leaves, marked on base 'S. R. W. Rye', 4in (10cm) high.
£75–90   *RAG*

r. A Wileman & Co Intarsio jardinière, after a design by Frederick Rhead, decorated with a frieze of geese between foliate bands, in typical colours printed factory mark, registration No. 330400, printed number '3143', c1900, 7in (17.5cm) high.
£700–850   *S(S)*

A vase by C. H. Brannam,
c1885, 10in (25.5cm) high.
£200–250 *NCA*

A blue frog, by C. H. Brannam,
3in (7.5cm) high.
£100–120 *NCA*

A green vase, by C. H. Brannam, with
6 handles, 1903, 6½in (16.5cm) high.
£85–100 *NCA*

A pair of candlesticks/spill
vases, by C. H. Brannam,
10in (25.5cm) high.
£300–350 *NCA*

A Bretby 'copperette' jug,
12in (30.5cm) high.
£140–150 *NCA*

A Watcombe cheese dish,
attributed to Christopher Dresser,
6½in (16.5cm) high.
£160–180 *NCA*

A Burmantofts vase, decorated
with dragons, by V. Kremer,
9½in (24cm) high.
£450–500 *NCA*

A Bretby spill vase, decorated
in yellow with a stork and
bamboo, 12in (30.5cm) high.
£120–150 *NCA*

An early Burmantofts turquoise blue
planter, No. 1082, 7in (17.5cm) high.
£170–200 *NCA*

A figure of 'The Brighton Wet
Nurse', with nodding head and
suspended body, dressed in a
cloak and gown baring a bosom
to a babe in arms, base marked
'Rye B4', 6in (15cm) high.
£320–370 *RAG*

A collection of William de Morgan tiles, decorated with a parrot, flowers, guinea fowl, great curassow, pelican with fish and ships, some lustre and some polychrome, various marks, two 8in (20.5cm) square, the others 6in (15cm) square.
£3,500–4,500 *CSK*

r. A Pilkington's shaped vase, 6in (15cm) high.
£130–150 *AOS*

'Ruskin Pottery' high-fired stoneware lettering, the speckled green glaze with areas of cloudy blue, mounted on copper panels, c1905, each letter 7in (17.5cm) high.
£3,500–4,000 *C*

These are the original letters that were used at the Ruskin Pottery factory.

A Pilkington's Royal Lancastrian orange vermilion glazed vase, moulded with fish amongst waves on a green ground under a speckled orange glaze, impressed factory marks, c1920, 8in (20.5cm) high, and a similar vase, after a design by William S. Mycock and thrown by E. T. Radford, with a mottled green and speckled orange glaze, impressed factory marks 'E.T.R.', painted monogram and year cypher, c1929, 7in (17.5cm) high.
£250–300 *S(S)*

A Royal Lancastrian uranium glazed vase, by Richard Joyce, 5in (12.5cm) high.
£250–300 *NCA*

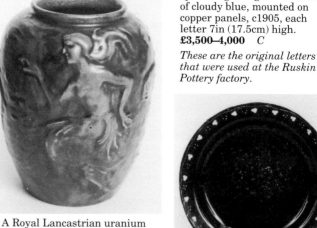

A Ruskin plate, with incised mark, 6in (15cm) diam.
£80–100 *AOS*

A Ruskin lustre vase, dated '1922', 8in (20.5cm) high.
£170–200 *AOS*

A Ruskin blue vase, c1930, 5½in (14cm) high.
£130–150 *AOS*

A Rye Pottery 'Sussex Pig', lead glazed mainly in blue, with a hook-on head, inscribed 'Wun't be druv', 4½in (11.5cm) long.
£200–240 *RAG*

A Mintons Secessionist jardinière, decorated in purple, turquoise and green, repeated around the body, impressed and printed factory marks 'Mintons, No. 72', c1910, 13in (33cm) high.
£600–700 *S(S)*

A Mintons stoneware bread plate, designed by A. W. N. Pugin, inscribed 'Waste Not, Want Not', with rust and blue encaustic glazes, stamped '430', 13in (33cm) diam.
£900–1,100 *C*

A William de Morgan two-tile panel of a manned galleon within a classical harbour, with green, turquoise, amethyst and yellow glazes, c1880, 12in (30.5cm) wide.
£1,200–1,500 *C*

A William de Morgan deep red lustre bowl, decorated by Fred Passenger, with decoration of an eagle attacking a grotesque lizard within a scrolling foliate border, painted 'FP' initials, c1890, 10in (25.5cm) diam.
£1,500–1,800 *C*

A Mintons Secessionist jardinière, after a design by Léon V. Solon and John W. Wadsworth, decorated in turquoise above printed scrolling green foliage, damaged, moulded 'Minton's, England', impressed factory marks and date cypher, 12½in (32cm) high.
£300–350 *S(S)*

A William de Morgan dish, painted by Frederick Passenger, in ruby lustres against white, signed 'FP', 14½in (37cm) diam.
£2,000–2,400 *P*

r. A William de Morgan four-tile panel depicting 2 snakes among flowering foliage against turquoise ground, with green, puce and amethyst glazes, chipped, each impressed 'WM', Merton Abbey seal, c1882, 16in (40.5cm) square.
£1,400–1,700 *C*

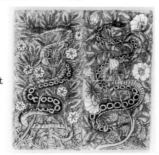

A Pilkington's red vase, 5½in (14cm) high.
£80–100 *AOS*

A Bernard Moore enamelled flambé plate, the centre painted and enamelled with the bust of a female figure, the face in profile, hands clasped in prayer, with an inscription in a halo, on a flambé ground, overpainted hands and face, painted monogram 'B.M.', circular frame, 10in (25.5cm) diam.
£700–800 *C*

A Pilkington's Royal Lancastrian lustre charger, by Mycock, inscribed on reverse, c1900, 11½in (29cm) diam.
£1,700–2,000 *ASA*

A Pilkington's Royal Lancastrian vase, signed, 6½in (16.5cm) high.
£80–100 *AOS*

An Ault vase, by Christopher Dresser, 12in (30.5cm) high.
£180–200　*NCA*

A pair of Bretby pottery vases, with applied horn and insect decoration, No. 1470, 14in (35.5cm) high.
£250–300　*NCA*

A Burmantofts pottery ewer, 10in (25.5cm) high.
£150–180　*NCA*

A Burmantofts green pottery vase, with Gothic decoration, 9½in (24cm) high.
£180–200　*NCA*

A vase by Thomas Forester, 8in (20.5cm) high.
£120–150　*AOS*

A Linthorpe pouring vessel, designed by Christopher Dresser, with a mottled and streaked green glaze, impressed 'Linthorpe, 312', facsimile signature 'Chr. Dresser' with Linthorpe Pottery seal, 6½in (16.5cm) high.
£800–950　*C*

A Linthorpe pottery vase, after a design by Christopher Dresser, in a streaked brown glaze, with a pierced flower and foliage in the centre in green, stamped 'Chr. Dresser, HT', c1880, 8½in (21.5cm) high.
£450–550　*S(S)*

A Minton porcelain vase, designed by Christopher Dresser, painted in gold, green, yellow, blue, black and orange enamels, restored, 11½in (29cm) high.
£2,000–2,400　*C*

A Linthorpe vase, by Clara Pringle, 9½in (24cm) high.
£280–300　*NCA*

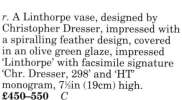

r. A Linthorpe vase, designed by Christopher Dresser, impressed with a spiralling feather design, covered in an olive green glaze, impressed 'Linthorpe' with facsimile signature 'Chr. Dresser, 298' and 'HT' monogram, 7½in (19cm) high.
£450–550　*C*

A Brannam beaker, part of a
lemonade set, with inscription.
£80–100 *BLO*

A Quimper cup and saucer, c1905,
saucer 7in (17.5cm) diam.
£50–60 *VH*

An Elton ware loving cup,
c1890, 8½in (21.5cm) high.
£325–375 *SAI*

l. A Ruskin green cup and
saucer, 5½in (14cm) diam.
£80–90 *PC*

A Brannam blue Toby jug,
4in (10cm) high.
£40–50 *BLO*

A pair of Foley Intarsio ewers,
designed by Frederick Rhead,
c1880, 11in (28cm) high.
£800–900 *BEV*

A Brannam puffin jug,
c1900, 8in (20.5cm) high.
£170–200 *BLO*

A Barum jug, 'The Lundy
Parrot', 5in (12.5cm) high.
£130–150 *BLO*

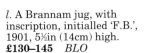

l. A Brannam jug, with
inscription, initialled 'F.B.',
1901, 5½in (14cm) high.
£130–145 *BLO*

A Ruskin dark green cup
and saucer, from the
Ferneyhough collection,
saucer 6in (15cm) diam.
£90–110 *PC*

A Barum blue puzzle jug,
with inscription,
5in (12.5cm) high.
£35–40 *BLO*

A Sèvres Art Pottery bowl,
decorated in blue tones
sponged with yellow, c1930,
11in (28cm) diam.
£80–100 *HOW*

A Sèvres Art Pottery dish, decorated in
red, green and brown, 7in (17.5cm) diam.
£55–65 *HOW*

A Brannam pink dog with
toothache, 6½in (16.5cm) high.
£130–150 *BLO*

A Brannam green owl jar with lid,
made for Liberty, 5in (12.5cm) high.
£70–80 *BLO*

A Brannam cat, green with black
markings, 11in (28cm) high.
£200–220 *BLO*

An Upchurch Pottery bowl with
three handles, in blue and grey,
7in (17.5cm) diam.
£60–70 *BLO*

A Brannam flower holder, initialled
'BW', c1900, 10in (25.5cm) wide.
£175–200 *BLO*

A Brannam blue frog,
2½in (6.5cm) high.
£65–80 *BLO*

A Brannam chamberstick,
initialled 'SW', 4in (10cm) high.
£130–150 *BLO*

A Bretby apple vase,
3½in (9cm) high.
£35–45 *BLO*

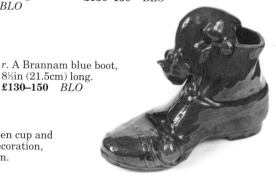

r. A Brannam blue boot,
8½in (21.5cm) long.
£130–150 *BLO*

l. A Ruskin green cup and
saucer, with decoration,
3½in (9cm) diam.
£65–80 *PC*

A Bretby bowl, c1895, 8½in (21.5cm) diam.
£90–110 *BLO*

A Bretby jardinière, decorated with fish.
£700–800 *ASA*

A William de Morgan tile, painted in red lustre with stylized carnations, painted signature 'W de Morgan & Co, Fulham, London', 8in (20.5cm) square.
£150–180 *C*

A Bretby earthenware 'bamboo' stick stand, with a seated monkey at the base, his arms wrapped around the stand, the monkey painted in naturalistic colours, the stand shading from yellow to amber and green, rim cracked, impressed mark, 23in (58.5cm) high.
£350–400 *Bon*

A William de Morgan red lustre vase and cover, the white ground decorated in red, cover restored, the base impressed 'W de Morgan, Sand Pottery', with Morris & Co. paper label, 13in (33cm) high.
£4,500–5,500 *C*

A pair of Bretby vases, c1885, 14in (35.5cm) high.
£500–600 *BLO*

A pair of Bretby vases, with grey metal finish, c1900, 8½in (22cm) high.
£40–50 *STU*

A William de Morgan jar, decorated in the Persian style, in turquoise, blue, dark purple and grey with stylized floral arabesques, 16in (41cm) high.
£3,750–4,500 *P*

A pair of steel candle sconces, attributed to Edward Spencer and the Artificers Guild, 12in (30.5cm) high.
£3,000–3,500 *P*

l. A Minton pottery plaque, painted by W. S. Coleman, in pastel colours, printed 'Minton Art Pottery Studio, Kensington Gore', c1870, 18in (46cm) wide.
£3,000–3,500 *Bon*

A Barum jardinière, the green ground with fish decoration, some damage, late 19thC, 9in (23cm) high.
£100–120 *PCh*

A Della Robbia vase, marks include 'AB' and 'CEMB', 9in (23cm) high.
£200–250 *BLO*

A pair of Brannam vases, with sgraffito design in brown and blue on a cream ground, initialled 'WB' and dated 1889, 10in (25.5cm) high.
£500–600 *BLO*

A Gouda vase, c1925, 13in (33cm) high.
£170–200 *BEV*

A Gouda vase, c1920, 7½in (19cm) high.
£50–60 *BEV*

r. A Barum vase, decorated with a lizard in relief.
7in (17.5cm) high.
£130–150 *BLO*

A Gouda vase, c1925, 10in (25.5cm) high.
£130–150 *BEV*

A Gouda vase, c1900, 14in (35.5cm) high.
£300–350 *BEV*

A Lauder vase, with sgraffito fish design, 6½in (16.5cm) high.
£130–150 *BLO*

A Bretby jug, with flowing
glaze spout, copperette handle
and body, 12in (30.5cm) high.
£140–160 *BLO*

A jug, by Louis Desmant, Normandy,
with scenes from the Bayeux Tapestry,
5½in (14cm) high.
£65–80 *BLO*

A Lauder green jug,
8in (20.5cm) high.
£100–110 *BLO*

A Barum green frog
candle holder,
6in (15cm) high.
£170–200 *BLO*

A Belgian pottery
candle holder,
11½in (29cm) high.
£50–60 *BLO*

A Gouda ceramic
candle holder, c1920,
8½in (21.5cm) high.
£100–120 *BEV*

A Ruskin candlestick, marbled
grey with burgundy trim,
marked, 3in (7.5cm) high.
£230–250 *PC*

A Wardle mauve candle holder,
9in (23cm) high.
£50–60 *BLO*

A Frederick Rhead candle holder,
15in (38cm) high.
£250–300 *BEV*

A Chameleon ware
container with lid,
8½in (21.5cm) high.
£130–150 *BEV*

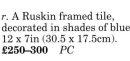

r. A Ruskin framed tile,
decorated in shades of blue,
12 x 7in (30.5 x 17.5cm).
£250–300 *PC*

A pair of Villeroy
& Boch vases,
10½in (26.5cm) high.
£420–500   *BEV*

A Boch blue and white vase,
c1930, 12in (30.5cm) high.
£300–350   *BEV*

An E. B. Fisher vase,
8½in (21.5cm) high.
£130–150   *BLO*

A Maw's pink
vase, c1900,
12½in (32cm) high.
£120–140   *THA*

An early Frederick Rhead
vase, 10in (25.5cm) high.
£300–350   *BEV*

An Upchurch pottery vase,
decorated in pink and grey,
10in (25.5cm) high.
£70–80   *BLO*

l. A majolica vase, c1880,
6in (15cm) high.
£170–200   *HOW*

An Ault pottery vase,
designed by Christopher
Dresser, covered with
liver-red glaze, impressed
facsimile signature on
base, 20in (51cm) high.
£550–600   *P*

A Bretby deep
blue vase,
12in (30.5cm) high.
£200–250   *BLO*

A pair of Ault vases, decorated
with pansies, one signed by
William Ault, 9½in (24cm) high.
£85–100   *BLO*

l. A pair of Bretby vases, painted
with ships on a chocolate coloured
field, 13½in (34.5cm) high.
£85–100   *BLO*

r. An Ashby Potters'
Guild pink vase,
8in (20.5cm) high.
£170–200   *BLO*

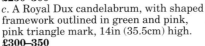

A Carlton Ware lustre pottery
vase, painted with a bold
chequered and geometric
design in vivid orange, yellow,
tan and black, printed mark,
10in (25.5cm) high.
£350–450 CSK

l. A Royal Dux tazza, pink triangle mark,
6½in (16.5cm) high.
£250–300
c. A Royal Dux candelabrum, with shaped
framework outlined in green and pink,
pink triangle mark, 14in (35.5cm) high.
£300–350
r. A Royal Dux figure of a girl, partially
covering her body with a puce and green
robe that her pet dog tries to remove,
pink triangle mark, 14½in (37cm) high.
£400–450   P

A Royal Dux part bisque
figure, 10in (25.5cm) high.
£200–220   CDC

A Jean Mayodon Art Deco
faïence vase, impressed
monogram 'J.M.', c1925,
11in (28cm) high.
£300–350   S

A Hutschenreuther
porcelain figure of
Mephistopheles,
by K. Tutler,
factory marks,
11in (28cm) high.
£300–350   P

A Royal Dux figure
of a dancer, in a
revealing blue dress,
12in (30.5cm) high.
£300–350   Re

A Zsolnay lustre ewer, in
the form of a bird, spires
mark and 'Zsolnay Pecs',
13in (33cm) high.
£600–700   P

A Goldscheider figure of a
dancer, impressed marks,
16½in (42cm) high.
£800–950   N

An Art Deco pottery vase,
incised and painted in brown
with stylized flamingoes on a
turquoise mounds, on a cream
ground, inscribed 'Simone
Liarrieu', 12in (30.5cm) high.
£300–350   CSK

An Art Deco Goldscheider
pottery figure, by Claire Weiss,
impressed marks, inscribed
'C. Weiss', 12½in (32cm) high.
£500–600   CSK

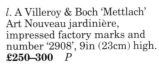

l. A Villeroy & Boch 'Mettlach'
Art Nouveau jardinière,
impressed factory marks and
number '2908', 9in (23cm) high.
£250–300   P

A Shelley tea set, in yellow and black on a white ground,
comprising: teapot, sugar bowl, milk jug, 2 square
sandwich platters, 12 cups and saucers, 9 side plates,
printed mark, Reg. No. 723404, c1930,
teapot 5in (12.5cm) high.
£800–950   C

A Beswick teapot, in the form of a panda, c1930.
£200–250   BRI

A Goldscheider pottery head
of a woman, 9½in (24cm) high.
£200–220   CDC

A Shelley part tea set, decorated in black, orange
and beige with sunburst motifs against a white
ground, comprising 6 cups, 5 saucers, 5 side plates
and a sugar bowl, printed factory marks,
Rd. No. 756533.
£900–1,100   P

A Louis Wain model of a cat,
with a lemon, green, yellow
and red coloured body,
printed and painted marks,
6½in (16.5cm) high.
£400–450   CSK

A Shelley Mode tea set, decorated in grey and acid green
on a white ground, comprising: milk jug, sugar bowl,
6 cups and saucers, 6 side plates, printed 'Shelley England',
Rd. No. 756533, c1930.
£1,000–1,200   P

A Shelley three-piece pottery nursery
tea set, designed by Mabel Lucie
Attwell, decorated in bright colours
on a white ground, each piece signed,
c1925, largest 7½in (19cm) high.
£600–700   C

An Art Deco ceramic night
light holder.
£40–50   ASA

An ashtray, formed of inter-
linked circles with a recess in
the rim, applied with a female
head with orange curly hair on
the edge, stamped 'Goldscheider
Wien', c1925, 10in (25.5cm) wide.
£300–350   S(S)

A Shelley lustre ware bowl, signed by Walter Slater, c1920, 12in (30.5cm) diam.
£130–150   *AJ*

A Shelley Harmony ware strainer, c1930, 8in (20.5cm) diam.
£60–70   *AJ*

A Carlton Ware 'Apple Blossom' breakfast set, c1930.
£300–350   *RO*

r. A Shelley 22-piece teaset, with orange, silver and black geometric decoration, comprising: teapot, milk jug, sugar basin, 6 cups, saucers and plates, and a cake plate.
£1,500–1,700   *TW*

A wall mask, by Leonardi, with a mushroom-coloured face and green scarf, Reg. No. 825795, c1930, 20½in (52cm) high.
£170–200   *AW*

A Shelley ginger jar, decorated in orange and yellow, c1930, 8½in (21.5cm) high.
£170–200   *AJ*

A Quimper cup, decorated with 'Pêcheur' pattern, signed, 2in (5cm) high.
£15–20   *VH*

A Robj earthenware bowl and cover, formed as a Native American's head, with dark red glazed feather head-dress, impressed mark 'Robj Paris, Made in France', 8in (20.5cm) high.
£400–450   *C*

A Lenci bust, by Essevi Samdo Vachetti, 8½in (21.5cm) high.
£350–400   *BEV*

A Lenci bust, by Essevi Samdo Vachetti, c1938, 7in (17.5cm) high.
£350–400   *BEV*

A Jean Luce 55-piece dinner service.
£900–1,100   *C*

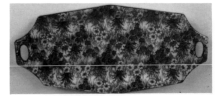

A Royal Winton tray, c1940.
£40–45   *CIR*

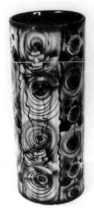

A stylized floral
ceramic umbrella
stand, probably
French, c1920.
£100–120   *ST*

A Shelley plate, decorated with
Melody pattern, 7in (17.5cm) diam.
£12–15   *CIR*

A Crown Ducal bowl, designed by
Charlotte Rhead, decorated in the
'Manchu' pattern in green, blue,
orange and gilding on a green ground,
printed factory marks, signed
'C. Rhead', 10in (25.5cm) diam.
£150–180   *P*

A Shelley vase,
6in (15cm) high.
£40–45   *CIR*

A Gray's Pottery plate, signed
'Nite', with clipper mark.
£90–110   *DEC*

A Gray's Pottery plate, with clipper
mark, 10½in (26.5cm) diam.
£55–65   *DEC*

l. A Mott hand-
painted jardinière,
8in (20.5cm) diam.
£90–110   *DEC*

r. A Carlton Ware vase,
with lid, chipped,
12in (30.5cm) high.
£130–150   *CIR*

A Pilkington's Lancastrian vase,
with everted rim, designed by
Walter Crane in yellow lustre on
a blue/green ground, impressed Bee
mark, painted artist's monogram,
wheatear motif, 10½in (26.5cm) high.
£1,300–1,500   *C*

A Crown Devon porcelain bridge set, with black and gilt
geometric decoration, comprising: 4 coffee cups and saucers,
2 ashtrays, and a card box, printed marks 'Crown Devon
Fieldings, Made in England, 2714', in original box.
£275–350   *C*

A wall face mask, by
C. Copes & Co, c1930,
7in (17.5cm) high.
£85–100 *BEV*

A milk jug,
2½in (6.5cm) high.
£8–10 *BEV*

r. A Carlton Ware vase,
decorated on a mottled
purple and white ground,
enriched with gilding,
marked 'Carlton Ware,
Made in England,
Trade Mark', c1930,
10½in (26.5cm) high.
£300–350 *C*

A Gray's Pottery jug,
No. A923, 7½in (19cm) high.
£45–50 *DEC*

A Japanese flask, entitled
'Just a Little Nip', c1900.
£50–60 *BEV*

A Susie Cooper coffee pot,
5in (12.5cm) high.
£30–35 *PC*

A Barker Bros.
hand-painted jug,
6in (15cm) high.
£45–50 *DEC*

A Susie Cooper tea cup and coffee cup.
£12–15 *BEV*

A Hancock's Ivory ware
jug, decorated in blue,
yellow and green,
8½in (21.5cm) high.
£25–30 *CIR*

A Susie Cooper coffee set, pot 8in (20.5cm) high.
£170–200 *CIR*

A Shelley 22-piece tea service, decorated with
Phlox pattern in yellow.
£250–300 *CIR*

A Carlton Ware bowl and drainer, with 'Water Lily' design, bowl 9½in (24cm) wide.
£55–65 each   *ADC*

A Burleigh jug, decorated with 'Parrot' design, c1930, 8in (20.5cm) high.
£170–200   *AOS*

A Burleigh jug, decorated with 'Kingfisher' pattern, c1930.
£170–200   *AOS*

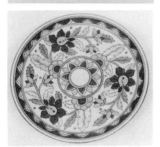

A Royal Cauldon fruit bowl, c1935, 9in (23cm) diam.
£100–120   *AOS*

l. A Burleigh jug, decorated with a fox and stork, 8in (20.5cm) high.
£120–140   *AOS*

A Hancock vase, decorated with 'Autumn' design, 7in (17.5cm) high.
£130–150   *AOS*

A Charlotte Rhead Crown Ducal plaque, decorated in light and dark pink and grey on a cream ground, No. 6778, 12½in (32cm) diam.
£250–300   *ADC*

A Carlton Ware dish, with 'Pink Daisy' design, 4½in (11.5cm) wide.
£20–25   *ADC*

A pair of Shelley banded vases, 8in (20.5cm) high.
£85–100   *AOS*

r. A Carlton Ware blue toilet jug and bowl set, decorated with chinoiserie pattern, printed mark in blue.
£300–350   *HSS*

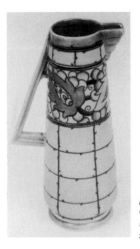

l. A Charlotte Rhead Crown Ducal jug, No. 5623, 9½in (24cm) high.
£85–100   *ADC*

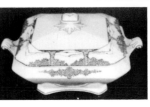

l. A Crown Ducal vegetable dish, decorated in a red trees pattern, c1925.
£35–40   *AOS*

A pair of cantilever nickel-plated steel, leather and glass chairs, and a coffee table, by Josef Müller, Berlin, glass replaced, table 24in (61cm) diam. **£45,000–55,000** *S*

An Eavestaff six-octave mini piano, in an Art Deco walnut case, 51in (129.5cm) wide, and a matching stool. **£700–800** *PCh*

A satinwood and walnut 'Stafford' wardrobe, by Gillow & Co, in 3 sections, stamped 'L5778', 87½in (222cm) high. **£5,000–6,000** *C*

An inlaid mahogany and metal-mounted bureau, by W. J. Neatby, c1903. **£4,500–5,500** *S*

A wrought-iron and gilt-bronze firescreen, by Edgar Brandt, c1925, 33in (84cm) high. **£9,000–10,000** *S(NY)*

A rosewood, parchment and marble dining room suite, by Gio Ponti, c1935, table 87½in (222cm) long. **£13,000–15,000** *S(NY)*

A firescreen, by Edgar Brandt. **£10,500–12,000** *S(NY)*

A wrought-iron hall stand, attributed to Paul Kiss, c1925. **£7,250–8,500** *S(NY)*

A carved mahogany dining table and 18 chairs, with carved foliate frames and upholstered in tooled leather, c1910. **£12,000–14,000** *CNY*

A wrought-iron firescreen, c1925, 31in (79cm) wide. **£3,000–3,500** *S*

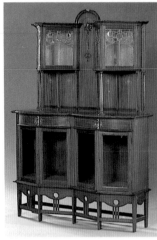

A mahogany and stained glass cabinet, by George Ellwood, for J. S. Henry, c1900, 77½in (197cm) high.
£2,000–2,400 *S*

A pair of Art Deco stained oak bergère chair, re-upholstered, c1925, 33in (84cm) wide.
£3,500–4,000 *S*

An oak dresser, by Shapland & Petter, inlaid with pewter, mother-of-pearl and brass, possibly designed by Baillie-Scott, c1890.
£2,300–2,800 *S*

An ebonized and painted corner cabinet, designed by Charles Rennie Mackintosh, with a painted panel by Margaret Macdonald Mackintosh, c1897, 72½in (183cm) high.
£25,000–30,000 *C*

An oak and brass cabinet, with double doors, attributed to Léon Jallot, c1907, 76in (193cm) high.
£2,300–2,800 *S*

A pair of Heal's oak and rush ladderback armchairs, c1905.
£2,200–2,600 *S*

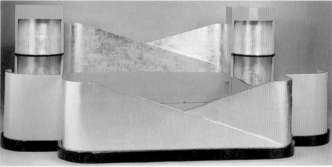

A lacquered, gilt and silvered wood double bed, by Paul Poiret, with nightstands and stools, c1929, 82in (208cm) long.
£4,500–5,500 *S(NY)*

A thuya wood side cabinet, c1870, 40in (101.5cm) high.
£2,000–2,400 *S*

An oak and rush high back armchair, c1907.
£2,500–3,000 *S*

An oak and brass buffet, attributed to Léon Jallot, c1907, 52in (132cm) high.
£2,000–2,400 *S*

An Aesthetic Movement ebony
and lacquer cabinet, signed and
stamped 'Gregory & Co',
62in (158cm) wide.
£3,000–3,500 *C*

r. An American Arts & Crafts clock,
with a brass face, c1910.
£850–1,000 *ST*

An ebonized, rosewood and vellum-
covered games table, by Carlo
Bugatti, the top with 4 covered wells
and inlaid with a pewter chessboard,
inlaid signature, 31½in (79cm) wide.
£10,000–12,000 *C*

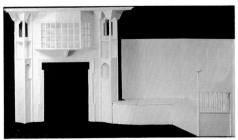

A white painted fire surround and inglenook,
designed by M. H. Baillie-Scott, c1898,
83in (211cm) high.
£8,500–10,000 *C*

A walnut and yew dining suite, labels
for Russell & Sons, Broadway, Worcs.,
c1920, table 66in (167cm) long.
£12,000–14,000 *P*

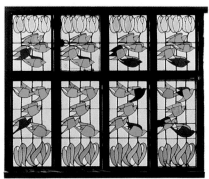

A lead and stained glass window, designed by M. H. Baillie-
Scott, with a wooden frame, c1898, 70in (177.5cm) high.
£14,000–16,000 *C*

An ebonized and painted sideboard,
the painting attributed to Henry Stacy
Marks, 78in (198) wide.
£3,000–3,500 *P*

A Morris & Co. green stained oak centre table, the design attributed to Philip
Webb with George Jack, 125in (320cm) wide.
£20,000–25,000 *P*

A pair of beechwood open armchairs, designed by
J. Hoffman, branded 'J & J Kohn, Wien, Austria'.
£4,000–4,500   *C*

A glass and chromed metal dining table, inlaid with panels by Lalique,
and 8 chairs, all by Asprey.
Table: **£100,000+**   Chairs: **£28,000–30,000**   *C*

Josef Hoffman (Austrian, 1870–1956)

Originally trained as an architect, Josef Hoffman was influenced by Charles Rennie Mackintosh and the Glasgow School. In 1897 he founded the Vienna Secession, an association of artists and architects disillusioned with the work of the Viennese Society of Visual Artists. Inspired by the attempts of the Vienna Secessionists to bring more abstract and purer forms to design, in 1903 Hoffman founded the Wiener Werkstätte, or Vienna Workshops. Associated designers included Josef Olbrich and Koloman Moser and, as well as buildings and furniture, the group designed silver, glass, ceramics and metalwork.

Hoffman's furniture designs were mainly geometric in form, and were mostly executed by one of the largest Viennese furniture manufacturers, Jacob & Josef Kohn, together with another large Viennese firm, the Thonet Brothers.

l. The Gerrit Rietveld '1919 Red/Blue Chair', by G. A. van der Groenekan, in beech and plywood.
£3,000–3,500   *C*

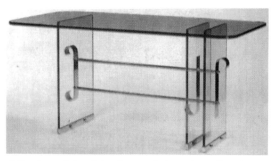

A Fontana Arte plate glass and chromium-plated table, c1935, 67in (170cm) wide.
£4,000–4,500   *C*

A wrought-iron and mahogany table, by Pierre Chareau, 19½in (49.5cm) wide.
£12,000–15,000   *CNY*

A bentwood salon suite, designed by Josef Hoffman, made by J. & J. Kohn, c1905, settee 47½in (121cm) wide.
£7,000–8,000   *CNY*

A pair of Art Deco burr-walnut bedside
cabinets, by Mercier Frères,
23in (58.5cm) wide.
£3,500–4,000 *C*

An oak sewing cabinet, by
Gustav Stickley, with red
decal, c1905, 20in (51cm) wide.
£3,500–4,500 *CNY*

A walnut, maple and chrome
display cabinet, by Gordon
Russell workshops, c1930.
£4,500–5,500 *S*

An oak smoker's cabinet,
by Gustav Stickley, c1903,
17in (43.5cm) wide.
£4,000–4,500 *CNY*

A carved mahogany
and marquetry cabinet,
by Louis Majorelle,
25in (63.5cm) wide.
£30,000–35,000 *CNY*

An inlaid oak music
cabinet, designed by
Harvey Ellis for
Gustav Stickley, c1903.
£6,500–8,000 *CNY*

A carved mahogany
and marquetry
cabinet, by Louis
Majorelle, 68in
(172.5cm) high.
£20,000–25,000 *CNY*

A mahogany and marquetry side
cabinet, c1900, 55in (139.5cm) wide.
£3,000–3,500 *S*

An oak trophy cabinet, by Gustav
Stickley, c1904, 60½in (172.5cm) high.
£6,000–7,000 *CNY*

An Art Deco three-piece bedroom
suite, comprising: grand lit and
2 bedside tables, branded 'Leleu'.
£6,500–7,500 *C*

A mahogany and marquetry
cabinet, by Louis Majorelle,
boldly carved and inlaid,
75in (190.5cm) high.
£30,000–35,000 *CNY*

An Art Deco Macassar ebony and
vellum daybed, 86in (218.5cm) long.
£5,500–6,500 *C*

r. A Guild of Handicraft oak cabinet, designed by C. R. Ashbee, with two drawers below a pair of doors inlaid in fruitwood with stylized flowers, the inner face veneered in satinwood and painted and gilt with flowers, silver lamp fitting above, writing flap extending on to hinged supports, the pair of doors enclosing a fitted shelf, the hinge and key plates pierced with stylized flowers, stamped 'The Guild of Handicraft Ltd, Essex House, Bow E.', c1900, 41½in (105cm) wide. **£35,000–45,000** *S*

r. A Gordon Russell walnut and mahogany writing cabinet, the panelled fall-front inlaid in ebony with fine stringing, enclosing a writing compartment, above 3 drawers edged with ebony stringing and with ebony knobs, on octagonal legs linked by cross-stretchers, paper label 'This piece of furniture design No. 570 was made throughout in The Russell Workshops, Broadway, Worcestershire Designer: Gordon Russell Foreman: Edgar Turner Cabinet Maker: T. Lees Metal Worker: D. Keen Timber used: English Walnut and White Mahogany Date: 15/2/27', 47in (120cm) wide. **£7,500–9,000** *S*

An oak director's table, by Gustav Stickley, with brand mark, c1912, 72in (182cm) wide. **£8,000–9,500** *CNY*

A walnut and marquetry étagère, by Louis Majorelle, 48½in (123cm) high. **£2,000–2,500** *C*

A two-tier table, marquetry-inlaid with flowers and leaves, signed 'Gallé, Nancy', 17in (43cm) wide, **£3,000–3,500** *CNY*

A pair of steel and marble consoles, 32in (81cm) high. **£9,000–10,000** *CNY*

A burr-walnut and marquetry centre table, designed by Oscar Kaufmann, 41⅓in (105cm) diam. **£4,000–4,500** *C*

r. A carved mahogany side table, by Louis Majorelle, 39in (99cm) high. **£4,000–4,500** *CNY*

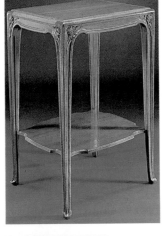

An oak library table, by Gustav Stickley, the 2 drawers with hand-forged oval pulls, model No. 461, c1905, 54in (137cm) wide. **£7,500–9,000** *CNY*

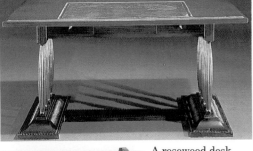

A rosewood desk, by Jacques-Emile Ruhlmann, the top inset with a leather panel, fitted with 2 drawers, brand mark, c1925, 60in (152cm) wide. **£150,000–180,000** *CNY*

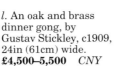

l. An oak and brass dinner gong, by Gustav Stickley, c1909, 24in (61cm) wide. **£4,500–5,500** *CNY*

An oak tile-top table, by Gustav Stickley, labelled, c1905, 24in (61cm) wide. **£9,000–11,000** *CNY*

l. A longcase clock, by Gustav Stickley, labelled, model No. 3, 72in (182.5cm) high. **£30,000–35,000** *CNY*

Two chairs by the Bookcase & Chair Co,
Grand Rapids, under the label 'Lifetime', c1912.
£2,500–3,000   *ST*

A teak garden table and 4 chairs, from a design by
Ambrose Heal.
£1,200–1,500   *ST*

An American Arts & Crafts Movement
extending oak dining table.
£2,500–3,000   *ST*

An oak dining table, probably by Liberty & Co, c1885.
£1,800–2,400   *ST*

l. An American Arts &
Crafts Movement oak
display cabinet, c1905.
£1,500–1,800   *ST*

r. An American Arts
& Crafts Movement
telephone table and
window seat, c1900.
£250–350 each   *ST*

An oak chair, by Stickley Bros,
Grand Rapids, c1910.
£600–750   *ST*

l. An American Arts & Crafts
Movement oak chair, by Morris
& Co, c1905.
£1,200–1,500   *ST*

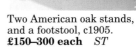

Two American oak stands,
and a footstool, c1905.
£150–300 each   *ST*

A French Art Nouveau
armoire, c1900,
105in (266.5cm) high.
£5,000–6,000 *S(NY)*

Art Nouveau furniture

The French were the forerunners of the Art
Nouveau style, and adapted the organic elements
of Arts & Crafts to sculptural Art Nouveau
forms, rather than use the strict carpentry forms
of the English. There were two distinct schools
of French Art Nouveau, one based in Paris, the
other in Nancy. The Nancy School, epitomized by
the work of Emile Gallé and Louis Majorelle, was
more prolific and consequently seen to be more
readily synonymous with Art Nouveau design.
It was this school that first used marquetry
panels, often created from local woods and
depicting flora and fauna.

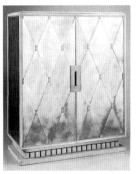

A mirrored, bronze and
painted wood wardrobe,
and a pair of night tables,
by Archibald Taylor, c1940.
£4,000–4,500 *S(NY)*

A Scottish mahogany
hammered copper
and leaded glass
firescreen, c1900.
£1,000–1,200 *S(NY)*

A mahogany and marquetry-
inlaid bed, and a pair of night
tables, by Louis Majorelle, c1900.
£22,000–28,000 *S(NY)*

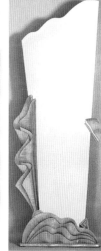

An Austrian
Biedermeier-
style painted
wood corner
étagère, c1920.
£3,000–3,500
S(NY)

A Marsh & Jones
inlaid linen press,
attributed to
Charles Bevan,
89½in (227cm) high.
£2,500–3,000 *C*

A mirror, by John
Cederquist.
£3,000–3,500
S(NY)

An Art Nouveau mahogany, fruitwood
marquetry and mother-of-pearl inlaid
cabinet, School of Nancy, c1900.
£11,000–13,000 *S(NY)*

r. An Art Deco bronze-mounted, stained oak
and marble sideboard, attributed to Krass,
Lyon, c1928, 77in (195.5cm) wide.
£3,500–4,000 *S(NY)*

A set of 8 Everaut pressed metal stacking chairs, c1930.
£4,000–4,500   *S*

A pair of Apelli and Varesio side chairs, by Carlo Mollino, c1945.
£9,000–11,000   *C*

A 'Cloud' suite of leather furniture, comprising: a three-seater sofa and 2 armchairs, c1930.
£2,500–3,000   *S*

An aluminium chair, designed by Frank Lloyd Wright for the H. C. Price Company tower.
£9,000–10,000   *CNY*

A 'Kota' chair, by Sue Golden, made from fibreboard and steel.
£900–1,100   *C*

Frank Lloyd Wright (American, 1867–1959)

Frank Lloyd Wright was the foremost exponent of the Prairie School, an American Modernist movement in domestic architecture established c1895, and his furniture shows an architectural influence. His pieces were usually made from oak, and often hand-made. Shapes and motifs are commonly cubistic or angular, many reflecting a Mayan, Aztec or Japanese influence.

An Art Deco 'Cloud' suite of leather furniture, comprising: a three-seater sofa and 2 armchairs.
£3,500–4,000   *C*

A Cassina chaise longue.
£1,200–1,400   *S*

An inlaid oak side chair, designed by Harvey Ellis, made by Gustav Stickley, model No. 338, c1904.
£3,000–3,500   *CNY*

An Irish Art Nouveau pearwood three-piece suite, by James Hayes, upholstered in brown leather, labelled 'Millar & Beatty Ltd', c1902.
£6,000–7,000   *C*

A Carlo Bugatti painted vellum ebonized and inlaid side chair, seat restored, painted signature.
£4,000–4,500   *C*

A pair of Liberty and Co. oak armchairs, with leather upholstery, each labelled.
£2,500–3,000   *C*

A set of 6 dining chairs, by Gustav Stickley, designed by Harvey Ellis, model Nos. 353 and 353A, c1910.
£7,500–8,500   *CNY*

An inlaid oak double bed, by Gustav Stickley, used in his home at Morris Plains, New Jersey, c1909, 58in (147cm) wide.
£12,000–15,000 *CNY*

An oak double bed, by Gustav Stickley, c1901, 58in (147cm) wide.
£8,000–9,000 *CNY*

A pair of oak beds, by Gustav Stickley, c1909, 45in (114cm) wide.
£3,500–4,500 *CNY*

l. A Macassar ebony bed, by Emile Jacques Ruhlmann, 43in (109cm) wide.
£20,000–25,000 *C*

A walnut and ebonized bedroom suite, designed by Gio Ponti.
£3,000–3,500 *C*

A 'Tutankhamun' gilt decorated mahogany daybed, in the style of J. Moyr-Smith, with a cushion and bolsters, 69½in (176cm) long.
£3,000–3,500 *C*

An oak bookcase, by Gustav Stickley, for his Craftsman Farms home, Morris Plains, New Jersey, c1909, 62in (157cm) wide.
£3,000–3,500 *CNY*

A chestnut bookcase, in 2 sections with adjustable shelves, by Gustav Stickley, c1909, 94½in (239cm) wide.
£6,500–8,500 *CNY*

r. An oak book rack, by Gustav Stickley, c1909, 33in (84cm) wide.
£2,500–3,000 *CNY*

An oak book shelf and cabinet, by Gustav Stickley, with adjustable shelves, c1904, 38in (96.5cm) wide.
£4,000–4,500 *CNY*

A Continental mahogany display cabinet, c1900, 81in (205.5cm) high.
£12,000–15,000 *CNY*

l. An oak armoire, by Gustav Stickley, for his Craftsman farms home, Morris Plains, New Jersey, c1909, 77in (195cm) high.
£7,500–9,000 *CNY*

An inlaid mahogany music cabinet, by Gustav Stickley, designed by Harvey Ellis, c1904, 48in (122cm) high.
£6,500–7,500 *CNY*

A set of 6 painted oak side chairs, by J. Walden, design attributed to Wm. Burgess.
£2,000–2,500 *C*

A cast-iron, enamel and bronze clock, by Albin Müller, 21½in (54.5cm) high. **£6,000–7,000** *C*

An Austrian Secessionist lacquer and pewter cabinet, inlaid with mother-of-pearl, 64in (162.5cm) wide.
£5,000–6,000 *C*

A laminated birchwood sideboard, designed by Gerald Summers, 54in (137cm) wide.
£3,000–3,500 *C*

A rosewood and tooled vellum side chair, by Carlo Bugatti, with copper and pewter.
£2,000–2,500 *C*

An oak lath armchair, designed by Marcel Breuer for the Bauhaus, Weimar, original fabric replaced, 1924.
£45,000–60,000 *C*

An oak bookstand, by Morris & Co, the rest surmounted with carved and turned ball and foliate finials, 73in (185cm) wide.
£4,500–5,000 *C*

A military chair, by Gerrit Rietveld.
£11,000–12,000 *C*

A set of 6 Art Deco Macassar ebony armchairs, attributed to Paul Kiss, the backs formed as 3 upholstered panels with hammered brass top rails.
£6,000–7,000 *C*

An oak buffet, designed by M. H. Baillie-Scott, c1898, 128in (324.5cm) wide.
£7,500–8,000 *C*

A pair of laminated birchwood open armchairs, designed by Gerald Summers.
£14,000–15,000 each *C*

A painted vellum, tooled copper, brass and wood desk and side chair, by Carlo Bugatti, the chair signed, c1902.
£20,000–25,000 *S(NY)*

A stained oak and beech desk, by Marcel Louis Baugniet, c1935, 55in (139.5cm) wide.
£1,400–1,800 *S(NY)*

A French rosewood, mahogany and leather desk, c1935, 75in (190.5cm) wide.
£5,500–6,500 *S(NY)*

An inlaid mahogany desk, by Louis Majorelle, c1900, 57½in (145cm) wide.
£12,000–14,000 *S(NY)*

A green lacquered wood and gilt iron desk, by André Arbus, c1940, 51in (129.5cm) wide.
£20,000–25,000 *S(NY)*

An Arts & Crafts writing desk, with a folding flap, 33in (84cm) wide.
£450–550 *E*

An armchair, by Ludwig Mies van der Rohe, c1927.
£12,000–15,000 *S(NY)*

A French oak partners' desk, and a leather upholstered armchair, c1930, desk 82½in (209cm) wide.
£5,000–6,000 *S(NY)*

A pair of French mahogany and leather armchairs, c1930.
£4,500–5,000 *S(NY)*

A bentwood half barrel chair, c1904.
£2,800–3,200 *S(NY)*

An Art Nouveau mahogany
hall stand, c1900,
104in (264) high.
£3,700–4,500   *S*

An oak and leather chair, by
Frank Lloyd Wright, c1904.
£14,000–16,500   *S*

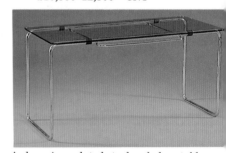

Two armchairs, by Alvar Aalto for
Finmar Ltd, maker's stamps, c1931.
l. **£800–950**
r. **£1,500–1,800**   *S*

An oak drop-front desk, by Charles
Rohlfs, with stylized monogram,
maker's logo, dated '1902',
36in (91.5cm) wide.
£10,500–12,500   *CNY*

Four mahogany and rosewood
barrel chairs, by Joubert et
Petit, c1930.
£3,700–4,500   *S(NY)*

A pair of wood and leather
upholstered 'Cloud' armchairs,
some wear, c1930.
£700–800   *S*

A bronze and marble low table, by Armand-Albert Rateau,
raised on bird form supports, 40in (101.5cm) wide.
£120,000–140,000   *S(NY)*

A chromium-plated steel and glass table,
'B 19', by Marcel Breuer for Thonet, original
label, c1928, 55in (139.5cm) wide.
£5,000–6,000   *S*

A mirrored glass and pale wood
laminate coffee table, c1930.
£900–1,100   *S*

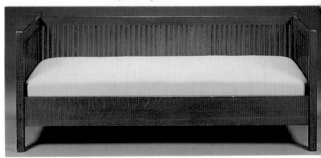

An oak settle, by Gustav Stickley, model No. 291, with firm's red
decal, c1908, 78in (198cm) wide.
£8,500–11,000   *CNY*

An oak wardrobe,
by Peter Waals.
£3,000–3,500 C

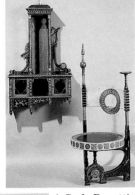

A Carlo Bugatti
shelf and chair.
£4,000–5,000 each
CNY

A 'Metropole' Memphis
clock, designed by
George J. Sowden,
made in Italy.
£1,500–1,800 C

An oak mirror, by C. F. A.
Voysey, 1906, 23in (58cm) wide.
£3,000–3,500 S

An oak blanket chest, by Gordon
Russell, dated '20.6.27',
65in (166cm) wide. £4,500–5,000 C

An oak sideboard, by Gustav Stickley, No. 804,
marked, 54in (137cm) wide. £8,000–9,500 S

A Carlo Bugatti
ebonized pedestal,
51in (130cm) high.
£3,000–3,500 C

A Liberty & Co oak
revolving bookcase, c1900.
£3,500–4,500 S

A black lacquered dining table, the top
with curved corners, on a U-shaped
base, c1930, 66in (168cm) wide.
£2,000–2,500 S

Carlo Bugatti
(Italian, 1855–1940)

Bugatti's designs looked back to
13th and 14thC Moorish Spain
and North Africa for inspiration,
and his decorative approach was
highly original.

An oak serving table, by Gustav
Stickley, marked, c1912.
£3,000–3,500 CNY

A spruce coffee table, designed by Frank
Lloyd Wright, c1950, 74in (188cm) wide.
£8,500–9,500 CNY

A mahogany and
marquetry cupboard,
by Louis Majorelle,
46in (117cm) wide.
£6,000–7,000 CNY

A mahogany and marquetry
sideboard, by Louis Majorelle, signed.
£8,000–9,500 CNY

Louis Majorelle
(French, 1859–1926)

Majorelle was a member of the
Nancy School and was influenced
by Gallé. His individual, elegant
designs were either architectural
in form, with inlaid decoration,
or sculptural, with mainly
carved decoration.

l. A Shapland & Petter oak
sideboard, the central reserve
decorated with a copper relief
panel of stylized flowers,
90in (228cm) wide.
£5,000–6,000 C

An inlaid oak piano and bench, designed by
Harvey Ellis, executed by Gustav Stickley,
with stylized brass and wood inlay,
unsigned, c1904, 62½in (159cm) wide.
£10,000–12,000 *CNY*

A walnut fishing tackle cabinet, by Ernest
Gimson, with barber's pole inlay, the brass
mounts by Alfred Bucknell, the bottom
drawer inlaid with fruitwoods, dated '1913',
79in (200.5cm) high.
£15,000–18,000 *C*

An oak and leather hexagonal table,
Model No. 624, by Gustav Stickley,
with original finish, leather and tacks,
part of craftsman's paper label, c1910,
48in (122cm) wide.
£12,000–14,000 *CNY*

A walnut bureau cabinet-
on-stand, by Ernest Gimson,
with fitted interior, the
frieze drawer with barber's
pole inlay, on a black
painted stand, c1906,
39in (99cm) wide.
£15,000–18,000 *C*

A walnut bookcase,
by Sidney Barnsley,
with 2 glazed doors
above 2 panelled doors
with rosewood handles,
42in (106.5cm) wide.
£10,000–12,000 *C*

Two oak high spindle back chairs, designed
by Frank Lloyd Wright, probably executed
by Neidecken-Wallbridge Co, for Ray
Evans House, Chicago, Illinois, c1908,
45in (114cm) high.
£30,000–35,000 each *CNY*

A set of 7 high backed dining chairs,
by L. & J. G. Stickley, Nos. 814 and 812,
including one carver, with original finish
and original leather drop-in seats, c1910,
45½in (115cm) high.
£12,000–14,000 *CNY*

A Carlton Ware dish, designed as pear fruit, flowers and leaves, c1935, 4½in (11.5cm) high.
£50–60 *BRI*

A 15-piece Carlton Ware coffee service, brightly painted with exotic birds and clouds, with gilt interiors and highlights.
£350–450 *P(Re)*

A Carlton Ware cream jug, decorated with anemones in relief on a yellow ground, c1930, 3in (7.5cm) high.
£60–70 *BRI*

l. A Carlton Ware oviform vase, the dark and pale blue ground with purple, lavender and green zig-zag motif outlined with gilt, printed marks 'Carlton Ware, Made in England, Handcraft 8490', 5in (12.5cm) high.
£450–550 *C*

r. A Carlton Ware lustre jug, with gilt loop handle, painted and gilded with stylized floral and fan decoration, 5in (12.5cm) high.
£350–450 *P(Re)*

A Shorter toast rack, decorated with purple anemones on a green base, c1930, 6in (15cm) long.
£30–35 *BRI*

A Goldscheider wall mask of a lady holding beads, various makers' marks, c1930.
£400–500 *ASA*

A Swedish pottery Modernist bust, modelled as a girl with green curly hair, orange necklace and lips, covered in speckled green glaze, impressed 'b' in a crowned shield, 12in (30.5cm) high.
£600–700 *P*

A Carlton Ware dish decorated with clematis on a green ground, c1930, 7in (17.5cm) diam.
£50–60 *BRI*

A Carlton Ware sugar sifter, with flowers and leaves in relief, c1930, 5in (12.5cm) high.
£100–120 *BRI*

A Carlton Ware beaker, decorated with anemones on a yellow ground, c1930, 4in (10cm) high.
£60–70 *BRI*

Insurance values

Always insure your valuable antiques for the cost of replacing them with similar items, regardless of the original price paid. Both auctioneers and dealers will provide a valuation service for a fee.

A Czechoslovakian coffee service, decorated in yellow, silver-gilt and black.
£100–120 *CIR*

A Burleigh ware coffee set, decorated with 'Dawn' pattern.
£250–300 *DEC*

A Carlton Ware tea set for 2 people, with fin handles.
£300–350 *BEV*

A Shelley vase, 6½in (16.5cm) high.
£30–35 *CIR*

A Crown Derby vase, decorated in autumn colours, 6in (15cm) high.
£40–45 *CIR*

A Gray's Pottery jug, A. 2447, 5in (12.5cm) high.
£50–60 *DEC*

A Shelley jug, decorated in shades of green, 9½in (24cm) high.
£50–55 *CIR*

A Falcon Ware jug, 7in (17.5cm) high.
£60–65 *CIR*

A Crown Devon dark red jug, with gilt trim, 5in (12.5cm) high.
£45–50 *CIR*

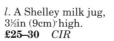

A Gray's Pottery flower trough, 9in (23cm) wide.
£85–100 *BEV*

l. A Shelley milk jug, 3½in (9cm) high.
£25–30 *CIR*

A Crown Devon Lotus-type jug, c1930, 13in (33cm) high.
£200–225 *CIR*

A Shelley tea set for 2, with green leaf motif, No. 12387, c1935.
£250–300 *AOS*

A Radford ware jug and vase, c1930.
£40–45 *AOS*

A Wedgwood 44-piece dinner service, 'Travel', designed by Eric Ravilious, grey ground transfer-printed in black and heightened in blue enamel, printed marks 'Travel, designed by Ravilious, Wedgwood of Etruria & Barlaston, Made in England', c1953, dinner plate 10in (25.5cm) diam.
£2,500–3,000 *C*

A Shelley banded jam pot, 4½in (11.5cm) high.
£25–30 *AOS*

A Poole Pottery teapot stand, c1930.
£25–30 *AOS*

A Shelley nursery plate, with Mabel Lucie Attwell design, printed in colours with a girl standing with her doll beneath an umbrella, watching a parade of pixies, inscribed 'Fairy folk with tiny wings flying all over my plates and things', printed factory marks, 8in (20.5cm) diam.
£100–120 *CSK*

A Staffordshire model of a cat, after a design by Louis Wain, in green, yellow, red blue and black, slight rubbing, impressed and overpainted facsimile signature on the back, stamped 'Made in England' and impressed registration mark, 1920s, 5in (12.5cm) high
£450–500 *S(S)*

A Czechoslovakian vase, 8in (20.5cm) high.
£65–75 *AOS*

A W. H. Grindley coffee sevice, comprising 15 pieces.
£110–125 *AOS*

A Carlton Ware teapot, milk jug and sugar bowl, decorated in 'Water Lily' pattern, c1930.
£150–180　*AOS*

A Carlton Ware blue coffee service, decorated in jewelled enamels and gilt with wisteria and exotic birds, with gilt interiors, comprising: coffee pot, two-handled sucrier and cover, cream jug and 6 coffee cups and saucers, printed mark in black.
£450–500　*ASA*

Three Gray's Pottery Paris jugs, with geometric design by Susie Cooper.
£250–300 each　*CAR*

A Hancock's part coffee service.
£150–175　*AOS*

l. A Gray's Pottery plate and bowl, by Susie Cooper, bowl 5in (12.5cm) wide.
Plate　**£150–180**
Bowl　**£250–300**　*CAR*

A Carlton Ware tête-à-tête, each piece with a speckled pale blue ground heightened with gilding, applied with solid gilt ribbed handles, comprising: teapot, 2 cups and saucers, jug, sugar bowl, jam pot and cover, plate and biscuit barrel, printed marks, 1930s.
£700–800　*S(S)*

A pair of Compton Pottery stoneware bookends, each trefoil form with relief decoration of a butterfly, on a semi-circular base, covered in matt green glaze with black, ochre and yellow painted decoration, impressed seal 'Compton Pottery, Guildford', c1945, 5in (12.5cm) high.
£150–180　*C*

A Susie Cooper cased part coffee set, each piece painted with wash and solid bands in mixed grey, brown and blue, comprising: 6 coffee cans, saucers and electro-plated shell moulded spoons with blue bead ends, in a fitted case, printed factory marks 'A Susie Cooper Production, Crown Works, Burslem, England', coffee cans 2in (5cm) high.
£150–180　*S(S)*

A Maling ware fruit bowl, 8in (20.5cm) diam.
£120–145　*AOS*

A Maling ware oval dish in the 'Stork' design, decorated by Janet Taylor, c1932, 10in (25.5cm) wide.
£120–140 *IS*

A Hancock bowl, decorated with 'Pomegranate' pattern, 9in (23cm) diam.
£110–125 *AOS*

A pair of Hancock vases, in 'Cremorne' pattern, 11in (28cm) high.
£250–275 *AOS*

A Gray's Pottery lamp base, painted with golfers, c1930, 6in (15cm) high.
£750–800 *CAR*

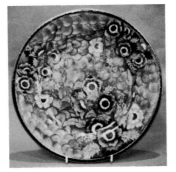

A Maling ware wall plaque, decorated with 'Anemone' pattern, c1936, 11in (28cm) diam.
£180–220 *IS*

A Gray's Pottery teapot, with Cubist face design in orange and yellow enamel, 4⅓in (11.5cm) high.
£200–250 *CAR*

A Maling ware ginger jar, c1950, 8in (20.5cm) high.
£60–85 *AOS*

A Hancock bowl, decorated with 'Water Lily' pattern, 9in (23cm) diam.
£110–125 *AOS*

A Poole Pottery jug, with geometric design, 6in (15cm) high.
£70–85 *AOS*

A Maling ware oval bread basket in the 'Gladioli' pattern, c1936, 11in (28cm) wide.
£150–180 *IS*

A Maling ware wall pocket, in the 'Michaelmas Daisy' pattern, c1938, 9in (23cm) high.
£170–200 *IS*

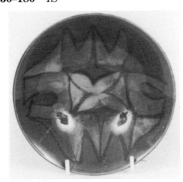

A Poole Pottery bowl, 1960s.
£10–12 *AOS*

A Radford ware vase, with 'Tree' design, c1930, 10in (25.5cm) high.
£80–95 *AOS*

A Gouda vase, decorated with 'Rembrandt' design, c1927, 6½in (16.5cm) high.
£100–110 *OO*

A Poole Pottery tin-glazed doorstop, designed by Harold Stabler, modelled as a galleon in full sail, in blue, green, yellow and white, 21in (53.5cm) high.
£1,000–1,200 *CSK*

A Dutch Arnhem Factory vase, decorated in 'Isolda' design, with green background, c1920, 14in (35.5cm) high.
£180–200 *OO*

A Shelley Art Deco coffee service, decorated in orange and black, comprising: coffee pot, sugar bowl, cream jug, 6 cups and saucers, pattern No. 11792, coffee pot 7½in (19cm) high.
£1,000–1,200 *AG*

A Charlotte Rhead dressing table set, decorated in the Trellis pattern, in shades of orange, yellow, green and coffee lustre on a cream ground, comprising: tray, powder bowl and cover, 2 squat candlesticks, and 4 other items, printed factory marks.
£250–300 *CSK*

A Shelley China Mode shape part tea service, lightly printed in black and overpainted in bright blue, green, black and orange, comprising: 4 tea cups and saucers, 6 tea plates, sugar basin and milk jug, printed mark in green, registered No. 756533, pattern No. 11755, inscribed in burnt orange.
£350–450 *HSS*

A Gouda vase, decorated with 'Bochara' design, c1920, 9in (23cm) high.
£150–170 *OO*

A Gouda vase, decorated with 'Kalman' design, c1929, 8in (20.5cm) high.
£80–90 *OO*

Locate the Source

The source of each illustration in *Miller's Art Nouveau & Art Deco Buyer's Guide* can be found by checking the code letters below each caption with the Key to Illustrations.

A Poole Pottery fruit bowl, with fruit design in brown and coral, impressed mark, c1926, 13in (33cm) diam.
£50–55 *OCA*

A Gouda jardinière, 'Marga' design, c1921, 6½in (16.5cm) high.
£160–180 *OO*

A French porcelain golfing flask and stopper, signed 'E. Marquis' and 'P. Bastard, Editeur, Paris, France', on base, 11in (28cm) high.
£350–450 *P*

A Poole Pottery historic plaque, entitled 'Poole Whaler, 1783', inscribed on reverse 'This dish was made and painted at the Poole Pottery in the year 1932, ship drawn by Arthur Bradbury, painted by Margaret Holder', 14½in (37cm) diam.
£500–600 *MSL*

A Poole Pottery 'Festival of Britain 1951' presentation bowl, with broad everted rim painted with rose, shamrock, thistle and daffodil symbolizing unity in the British Isles during Festival year, the centre with Poole's coat-of-arms in red, green, blue, yellow and mauve, 17in (43cm) diam.
£500–550 *P*

Probably designed by Claude Smale, this piece would have been part of the small output of presentation pieces granted to the pottery under licence during Festival year, and is possibly unique in representing the town of Poole itself.

A Carlton Ware Rouge Royale ginger jar and domed cover, the mottled maroon glaze with gilt and polychrome enamel decoration of pagodas and scenes of Oriental life, printed factory marks, 10½in (26.5cm) high.
£350–400 *C*

A Carlton Ware ginger jar and cover, decorated with coloured enamels in a chinoiserie pattern featuring a repeating scene of an Oriental couple in traditional costume amid pagodas, birds and trees, in orange, blue, green, mauve and yellow on a brown ground heightened with gilt, marked 'W. & R. Carlton Ware' on base, 12in (30.5cm) high.
£450–550 *P*

A French Art Deco crackle glazed ceramic group, modelled as a lady wearing a full ball gown of cream and gold, with Harlequin standing behind her in black, silver and cream, marked 'C. H. France', and 'G. Deblaze', 14in (35.5cm) high.
£350–450 *P*

A Poole Pottery historic plaque, entitled 'Waterwitch, built by Meadus, Poole 1871, 207 tons, Master Captain C. H. Deacon, drawn by Arthur Bradbury, 1932', painted by Ruth Paveley, 14½in (37cm) diam.
£500–600 *MSL*

A Carlton Ware pottery Glamour tea set for two.
£350–450 *W*

l. A Robj Art Deco porcelain figural lamp, modelled as a woman with gold bobbed hair, standing swathed in a long white robe and holding a bunch of flowers, with a depression for aromatic oils, with flowers at her feet, painted with gilt highlights, printed 'Robj, Paris, Made in France', 13in (33cm) high
£500–600 *P*

A Shelley Gainsborough trio, decorated in 'Classical' design, c1918.
£40–45 *AJ*

A Shelley Regent trio, decorated in 'Yellow Phlox' design, c1933.
£30–35 *AJ*

A Poole Pottery cream ribbed vase, c1925.
£40–45 *OCA*

A Poole Pottery blue and white geometric vase, 10in (25.5cm) high.
£800–1,000 *CHa*

r. A Shelley Vincent trio, decorated with Dorothy Perkins (yellow rose) pattern, No. 1168/2, c1920.
£25–30 *A*

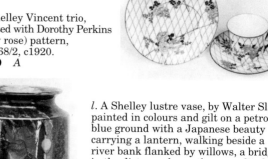

l. A Shelley lustre vase, by Walter Slater, painted in colours and gilt on a petrol blue ground with a Japanese beauty carrying a lantern, walking beside a river bank flanked by willows, a bridge in the distance, beneath a moonlit sky, printed factory marks and facsimile signature, 15½in (39.5cm) high.
£400–450 *CSK*

A Royal Dux figural vase, the twin-handled vessel formed as a tree trunk with green leaf and mistletoe embellishment, supporting to one side the standing figure of an Art Nouveau maiden in long flowing green dress, pink triangular mark to base, 26in (65.5cm) high.
£800–1,000 *P*

r. A Poole Pottery vase, the design attributed to Truda Carter, painted in pink, grey, orange, pale green and white with zig-zags, stylized leaves and flowers, reserved against a pale pink ground, impressed 'Poole, England', 10in (25.5cm) high.
£300–350 *P*

A Radford ware dish,
11in (28cm) diam.
£40–45 *AOS*

A Radford ware jug, decorated with
carrots, c1930, 6½in (16.5cm) high.
£40–45 *AOS*

A Charlotte Rhead jug,
6in (15cm) high.
£55–65 *AOS*

A Radford ware two-handled vase,
10in (25.5cm) high.
£60–75 *AOS*

A Charlotte Rhead Crown Ducal
vase, No. 5623, 7in (17.5cm) high.
£120–135 *ADC*

A pair of Charlotte Rhead vases,
7in (17.5cm) high.
£450–500 *HEW*

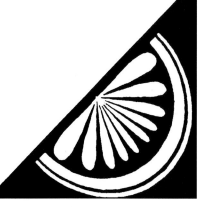

A Rosenthal porcelain figure,
naturalistically coloured and
modelled as a female nude reclining
on a rock, green printed and painted
marks, c1934, 16in (40.5cm) wide.
£1,000–1,200   *S(S)*

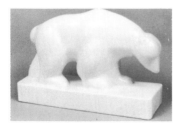

A Saint Clement Ged Condé polar
bear, c1920, 11in (28cm) wide.
£240–265   *POW*

A Saint Clement Ged Condé fish,
with white crackle glaze, c1920,
10½in (26.5cm) high.
£170–185   *POW*

A Royal Dux porcelain group,
in dark blue with gilt detail,
on a scallop-edged circular
base, applied pink triangular
mark, stamped 'Made in
Czechoslovakia, 2993 4',
c1930, 12in (30.5cm) high.
£450–500   *S(S)*

A Rosenthal porcelain figure of Pierrot,
12in (30.5cm) wide.
£1,000–1,200   *ASA*

r. A Boch Frères Keramis Ch.
Catteau figure of 'The Skaters',
13in (33cm) high.
£260–285   *POW*

A French white porcelain
figure, signed,
13in (33cm) high.
£400–450   *ASA*

A Lenci earthenware
group, modelled as a
naked girl seated at
the foot of a kneeling
woman wearing a
flowing blue robe and
cream scarf, minor
glaze chips, painted
factory mark, 1938,
16in (40.5cm) high.
£650–800   *CSK*

A Goebels Pottery set of ashtrays, and
a jockey cigarette box, decorated in orange
and black, box 6in (15cm) high.
£30–50 each   *ASA*

r. A Goldscheider
Butterfly model of
a figure, after a
design by Lorenzl,
incised marks
'Goldscheider,
Wien, Lorenzl,
5917 515 4',
facsimile signature
on base, 1930s,
10in (25.5cm) high.
£1,000–1,200   *S(S)*

A Gouda jug, 'Peter' design, c1923,
11in (28cm) high.
£120–130 *OO*

A Gouda vase, 'Westland'
design, c1927,
12in (30.5cm) high.
£160–180 *OO*

A Gouda vase, 'Ali' design,
c1924, 6½in (16.5cm) high.
£100–120 *OO*

A Gouda wall vase, 'Paula' design,
c1920, 6in (15cm) high.
£100–110 *OO*

r. A Carter Stabler Adams
Poole Pottery dish, a variation
on Truda Carter's spotted deer,
the centre painted in colours
with a spotted deer amid
flowering branches,
impressed pottery marks,
15in (38cm) diam.
£600–700 *P*

An Art Deco pottery
flat-backed bust of a
sailor, advertising
Senior Service cigarettes,
14in (35.5cm) high.
£250–300 *GAK*

A Gouda jug, 'Costia'
design, c1926,
7½in (19cm) high.
£85–100 *OO*

l. A Gouda bowl,
'Collier' design, c1922,
8in (20.5cm) high.
£140–150 *OO*

A Myott & Son hand-painted yellow and black vase, 8½in (21.5cm) high.
£70–85   *LB*

A Beswick wall mask, with brown hair, wearing a green and yellow necklace, with blue and yellow flowers behind, impressed 'Beswick, Made in England, 4360', late 1930s, 12in (30.5cm) high.
£250–300   *S(C)*

A Pilkington's Royal Lancastrian lapis-ware wall plate, decorated by W. S. Mycock in grey on an orange ground, with impressed Pilkington mark and artist's monogram, 12½in (32cm) high.
£250–300   *C*

A Charlotte Rhead Burslem jug, c1920, 9in (23cm) high.
£65–70   *SCO*

A Pilkington Royal Lancastrian vase, decorated by W. S. Mycock, 8½in (21.5cm) high.
£700–800   *ASA*

A Shelley Regent-shape coffee service, transfer-printed with a Lakeland scene, comprising: coffee pot, milk jug, sugar basin, 6 cups and saucers, printed factory mark 'Shelley, England', registration No. 781613, painted No. 12336, c1935.
£450–550   *S(C)*

A Shelley porcelain tea service, each piece decorated with irises and stylized flowers on a pink and white ground, comprising: teapot, hot water jug, sugar basin, milk jug, 2 bread and butter plates, 12 tea plates, teacups and saucers, slight damage to sugar basin.
£450–550   *Bea*

A Pilkington's Royal Lancastrian vase, decorated by W. S. Mycock, 8½in (21.5cm) high.
£700–800   *ASA*

A Pilkington Royal Lancastrian vase, decorated by Charles Cundall, 9in (23cm) high.
£600–700   *ASA*

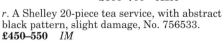

r. A Shelley 20-piece tea service, with abstract black pattern, slight damage, No. 756533.
£450–550   *IM*

A Goldscheider model of a dancing girl, by Lorenzl, with mauve, blue and black skirt, on circular base, signed 'Lorenzl', painted factory marks and impressed '5581 1828', 9½in (24cm) high.
£700–850 *P*

A Goldscheider figure of an Eastern dancer, by Kostial, with mauve pantaloons and flared skirt, artist's signature, factory marks, impressed '5549 48 8' to base, 17½in (44.5cm) high.
£1,500–1,800 *P*

A Goldscheider figure of a dancer, after Lorenzl, with a peacock design dress in mottled blue and green glaze, on a domed circular base, transfer-printed and impressed marks, 15in (38cm) high.
£650–750 *W*

l. A Carlton Ware 'Tutankhamun' ginger jar and cover, decorated in colours and gilding on a powder-blue ground, factory marks on base, 15½in (39.5cm) high.
£3,500–4,500 *P*

r. A Susie Cooper pottery bowl, by Crown Works, Burslem, 9½in (24cm) diam.
£130–150 *HM*

An Art Deco pottery ornament, depicting a leaping ibis, by Vago-Weiss, 18in (46cm) wide.
£100–120 *GAK*

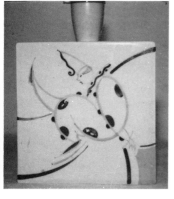

l. A Susie Cooper Art Deco table lamp base, 5in (12.5cm) high.
£850–950 *LT*

l. A Foley china part tea service, designed by Paul Nash, factory marks, facsimile signature, cake plate 9in (23cm) diam.
£1,000–1,200   *P*

A Foley Intarsio character teapot, designed by Frederick Rhead, No. 3359, late Foley mark, Rd. No. '363131', 4½in (11.5cm) high.
£650–750   *P*

A Foley Intarsio vase, designed by Frederick Rhead, decorated in brown with 4 yellow 'scaled' panels, with mauve irises on a green ground below, factory marks, numbered '3003', 8½in (21.5cm) high.
£300–350   *P*

A Foley Art China coffee set, designed by George Logan, comprising: 6 cups and saucers, 6 side plates and a sandwich plate, decorated in green and lilac on a white ground, printed mark 'Foley Art China Peacock Pottery'.
£500–600   *C*

A Foley china 'Dainty White' shape part teaset, comprising: 12 cups and saucers, 12 plates, 2 cake plates, milk jug and slop bowl, decorated in pink, red, green, blue and fawn on a white ground, printed factory marks, Rd. No. 272101, 1896.
£200–250   *P*

A Foley Intarsio vase, in blue, white, pink, green and brown, printed factory marks, No. 3469, 9in (23cm) high.
£250–300   *P*

A Shelley 23-piece tea service, 1930s.
£150–180   *Re*

l. A Shelley Mode shape 'Sunray' pattern coffee set, decorated in beige, yellow and black on a white ground, printed factory marks, Rd. No. 76533.
£1,500–1,700   *P*

r. A Foley Intarsio tapering cylindrical vase, printed marks, 8½in (21.5cm) high.
£350–450   *CSK*

A Shelley Mode shape 'Butterfly Wing' pattern part tea set, comprising: 6 cups and saucers, 6 plates, a cake plate, milk jug and sugar bowl, each piece decorated in green, black and grey on a white ground, printed factory marks, Rd. No. 756533.
£1,500–1,800   *P*

A Carlton Ware coffee service, decorated with pale primrose glaze, comprising: coffee pot, cream jug, covered sugar bowl and 6 cups and saucers, printed marks.
£250–300   *Bon*

A Shelley 22-piece tea service, low Queen Anne Shape, 'English Cottage' design.
£400–500 *AJ*

A Shelley 22-piece tea service, with green and silver pattern, c1933.
£250–300 *AJ*

A Wedgwood stoneware vase, designed by Keith Murray, of globular form, with cylindrical neck, ribbed body and emerald green glaze, inscribed facsimile signature 'Keith Murray, Wedgwood, Made in England', 7½in (19cm) high.
£300–350 *C*

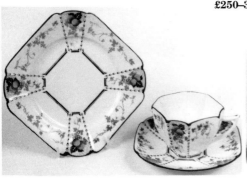

l. A pair of Wedgwood green-glazed bookends, designed by Keith Murray, with fluted decoration, stamped 'Wedgwood', 5½in (14cm) high.
£300–350 *C*

A Shelley 21-piece tea service, with teapot, low Queen Anne shape, with peaches and grapes design, c1920.
£350–400 *AJ*

Above. A Shelley tea service, 'Apple Blossom' pattern, comprising: 12 cups and saucers, 12 square plates, 2 bread plates, teapot, hot water jug, cream jug, sugar bowl and teapot stand, pattern No. 12287, Rd. No. 756533.
£450–550 *AG*

A Shelley 21-piece tea service, 'Sunburst' pattern, c1931.
£1,000–1,200 *RO*

A Wiener Keramik coffee service, decorated by Ida Schwetz, with a flower pattern in grey and black on a cream ground, with scalloped borders and handles, impressed 'Wiener Keramik' marks and decorator's monogram 'IS', coffee pot 8in (20.5cm) high.
£450–500 *C*

r. A Linthorpe vase, designed by Christopher Dresser, decorated with 4 grotesque heads, each forming a handle, covered in a streaky green glaze, running and pooling, impressed facsimile signature 'Chr Dresser 254', 9in (23cm) high.
£1,500–1,800 *C*

A Linthorpe jug, by Christopher Dresser, shape No. 346, 10in (25.5cm) high.
£600–700 *BLO*

A Shelley white porcelain coffee set, painted in orange, black and silver, comprising: coffee pot, 6 cups with solid triangular handles, 6 saucers, cream jug and sugar bowl, printed marks.
£700–850 *CSK*

A Brannam egg separator, c1910.
£125–150 *BLO*

A Goldscheider ceramic wall mask, c1930.
£450–500 *ASA*

A Carlton Ware figure, 'Mrs Bun', designed by John Hassell.
£300–350 *BEV*

A Goldscheider 'Bacchus' mask, signed 'Lorenzac'.
£200–250 *CS*

A Rosenthal figure, by Boehs, c1920, 9in (23cm) high.
£450–500 *BEV*

A Rosenthal figure of a child with a bird, by Liebermann, c1920.
£400–450 *BEV*

l. A Goldscheider earthenware figure of a woman, wearing a pink and grey skirt, the rose bodice with pink halter neck, restored, printed factory mark, 'Made in Austria', signature and impressed No. 6126 42 6', 15in (38cm) high.
£400–450 *HSS*

Three figures, 'Egg Men', by John Hassell: a boy scout, a country yokel and a policemen, all with painted marks, signed 'J. Hassell', 6in (15cm) high.
£300–400 each *CSK*

r. An Imperial amphora bowl, designed by Louis Wain, modelled as a stylized seated cat of Cubist inspiration, in orange, purple, black and blue on an acid green ground, printed mark 'Imperial Amphora', painted facsimile mark 'Louis Wain', 6in (15cm) high.
£2,300–2,800 *C*

A Goldscheider figure, from a model by Lorenzl, printed marks, inscribed 'Lorenzl', 13in (33cm) high.
£800–950 *CSK*

A Goldscheider pottery figure of a dancing girl, designed by Lorenzl, base impressed 'Lorenzl', printed marks, 16in (40.5cm) high.
£1,000–1,200 *CSK*

A Lenci centrepiece, modelled as a young naked girl, inscribed 'Lenci, Made in Italy Torino', 18in (45.5cm) high.
£2,300–2,800 *C*

A Lenci figure, modelled as a naked girl, marked 'Lenci, Made in Italy,' and printed paper label, 12in (30.5cm) wide.
£2,300–2,800 *C*

A Berlin white porcelain figure of a nymph with a deer, designed by Gerhard Schliepstein, inscribed 'G. Schliepstein', underglaze blue sceptre mark and impressed 'MZ 12050', 8in (20.5cm) high.
£300–350 *C*

A Katschutte porcelain figure, marked, 20½in (54.5cm) high.
£750–900 *ASA*

An Italian china 'Gallé' figure of a kneeling semi-clad female, 1950s, 18in (45.5cm) high.
£600–700 *Re*

A Royal Dux figure of Ghandi, c1950, 12in (30.5cm) high.
£240–280 *CS*

A Royal Dux pottery group, raised triangular mark, 13½in (34.5cm) high.
£350–450 *CSK*

l. A Wiener Keramik polychrome figure by Gudrun Baudisch, some damage, impressed 'WW' monogram and artist's mongram 'GB', 7½in (19cm) high.
£900–1,000 *C*

A Torquay pottery jug,
5in (12.5cm) high. **£30–35** *CIR*

A green teapot, modelled as
a car, c1930.
£100–120 *CIR*

A Gray's Pottery dish,
14in (35.5cm) wide.
£85–100 *DEC*

A Lingard ware yellow teapot,
7½in (19cm) high.
£70–80 *HOW*

An orange cube teapot, by G. Clews
Ltd, c1930, 4in (10cm) high.
£70–80 *CIR*

A Simple Simon teapot.
£100–120 *BEV*

A Carlton Ware grey teapot, c1950,
9½in (24cm) high. **£70–80** *CIR*

A Burleigh Ware biscuit
barrel, with plated lid and
handle, 7½in (19cm) high.
£85–100 *DEC*

A Myott biscuit barrel,
7½in (19cm) high.
£50–60 *DEC*

A Shelley tea cup, saucer and plate.
£30–35 *CIR*

A Burleigh Ware plaque in the form
of a galleon, with matt green glaze,
13in (33cm) diam.
£70–80 *CDC*

A Gray's Pottery jam pot, with
Pharaoh's mark, 4½in (11.5cm) high.
£25–30 *DEC*

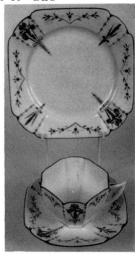

A Shelley 'Blue Iris' design
tea cup, saucer and plate.
£30–35 *CIR*

l. A KPM white porcelain mask, by Hubatsch, blue printed 'KPM' device and moulded signature 'Hubatsch 1930', 9½in (24cm) high.
£650–800   *C*

r. A Ruskin high-fired transmutation glaze vase and matching circular stepped stand, with cloudy deep purple glaze with green mottling and speckling over a mottled pale grey ground, vase and stand impressed 'Ruskin England', c1930, 14½in (36cm) high including stand.
£2,300–2,800   *C*

A Sèvres porcelain lantern, with bronze tassel, designed by Henri Rapin, glazed in dark celadon and amber on a cream ground and embellished with gilding, circular red printed 'manufacture Nationale Décoré à Sèvres 1923', and black rectangular 'S 1923DN' marks, 20in (51cm) high.
£800–950   *C*

An Amphora vase, polychrome on a white porcelain ground, enriched with gilding, impressed 'Amphora' and printed 'Turn Teplitz R. St.K' with maker's device and 'D.464', c1930', 7in (17.5cm) high.
£1,500–1,800   *C*

A Berlin KPM porcelain box and cover in colours and gilding, with oval intaglio panels of birds and flowers, sceptre mark and 'KPM' and orb inside cover, 'SR' on base, 8½in (21.5cm) high.
£300–350   *P*

A Rosenthal ginger jar designed by Kurt Wendler, with abstract design in blues, red and green heightened with gilding on a white ground, printed 'Rosenthal Selb Bavaria' mark and artist's signature, 'Kurt Wendler', c1925, 8½in (21.5cm) high.
£450–550   *C(Am)*

r. A Brannam green glazed model of a dragon, with yellow and blue markings, incised marks, 8in (20.5cm) high.
£150–180   *P*

A Fraureuth porcelain box and cover, decorated in blue and white with black and gilt stylized foliate hand-painted decoration, printed mark 'Fraureuth Kunstabteilung', c1920, 8½in (21.5cm) high.
£300–350   *C*

A Limoges porcelain box and cover designed by Sandoz, decorated with white and yellow plumage and blue beak, 6½in (16cm) high and another similar, 2in (5cm) high, both with printed marks, signed 'Sandoz'.
£350–450   *CSK*

A Fornasetti porcelain plate, printed in black against white, 'eye' mark, 'Tema E. Variazioni, Fornasetti-Milano, Made in Italy', No. '94', 10½in (26.5cm) high.
£100–120   *P*

A Limoges Art Deco coffee set,
marked with a cockerel and 'T.L.B.'
for Touze, Lemaitre Frères &
Blancher, pot 9in (23cm) high.
£200–250 *P*

A Carlton Ware vase, with
stylized flowerheads in
polychrome enamels,
c1930, 9in (23cm) high.
£600–700 *CAR*

A porcelain lamp,
modelled as a girl
standing beside a
porcelain and brass
lamp post supporting
a fabric 'umbrella'
shade, printed factory
marks, 'Fraureuth
Künstableitung',
20in (51cm) high.
£150–180 *P*

A Royal Dux figure, by Schaff,
wearing blue and gilt trousers,
signed 'Schaff', pink triangle
mark, printed 'Made in
Czechoslovakia, No. 3101',
17½in (44.5cm) wide.
£300–350 *P*

A Royal Dux figure,
hollowed for use as
a vase, covered with
foliage, pink
triangle mark, '440',
15in (38cm) high.
£350–450 *P*

A Boulogne pottery
figure, 'La Soie',
designed by Marcel
Renard, the crackle
glazed body partially
clad in a gilt and
mauve mottled robe,
impressed factory
marks, signed in gilt
'Marcel Renard',
19in (48.5cm) high.
£900–1,100 *P*

A Goldscheider earthenware
mask, printed factory mark,
No. '7888', c1920,
12in (30.5cm) high.
£300–350 *SB*

l. An earthenware teapot, modelled as
an aeroplane, yellow crackle glaze with
silver details, impressed 'T. Plane Made
in England', 1930s, 9½in (24cm) long.
£350–450 *S*

A Goldscheider 'Bat Girl', the
blue wings veined with yellow,
inscribed 'Lorenzl', impressed
5230/422/16, printed factory
mark, 18½in (47cm) high.
£1,500–1,800 *CSK*

A pottery wall mask,
moulded as a girl's head with
a pink sun-bonnet, marked
'Royal Doulton', c1930,
8in (20.5cm) high.
£200–250 *EEW*

A Derny earthenware figure
of a baboon, matt brown-black
glaze, incised signature 'Derny',
1920s, 9in (23cm) wide.
£300–350 *S*

l. A Goldscheider porcelain head
of a young woman, in 1940s style,
stamped, circular mark, impressed
'507', 11½in (29.5cm) high.
£300–350 *C*

FURNITURE

One of the biggest influences on people buying furniture is the architectural style of their homes. They may be attracted to a certain maker, or to the workmanship and quality, but very few buy furniture in the way that others collect Royal Doulton or wine glasses. The basic criteria may be the same (authenticity and condition) but with one additional factor: does it fit?

The slowness of the housing market over the last few years has had an effect on the sale of furniture recently, as people are not so readily changing either their home or their furniture. This may well not be the case in the very top echelons where items will always change hands for many thousands of pounds, but it does apply to that middle range of selective buying. Prices have not changed as dramatically in the last few years as they did from 1979 to 1989 when the job and housing markets seemed more secure, and the notion of collecting antiques was taken up by a wider audience.

In the middle of the last century, John Ruskin and William Morris bemoaned the lack of style and taste of applied arts in this country, and so began the 'alternative' to mainstream Victorian art and artefacts. The Gothic revival was inspired by what was considered the last great age of British architecture namely medieval; the Aesthetic Movement was influenced by Oriental design with the opening up of Japan in the 1860s; and the Arts & Crafts movement grew out of Morris's teachings of simplicity and integrity: 'fitness for purpose'. These 'movements' did not remain static, they took from each other, grew and were adapted. Out of them came Art Nouveau, the designs of Mackintosh and the Vienna Secession, which in turn became Art Deco and Modernism. The latter could not have evolved from mainstream Victorian art.

What seems striking now, in retrospect, is that here began the age of the 'designer'. Most of the prominent creative figures in these movements were architects or artists, but now they were interested in interior aesthetics as well as buildings or pictures. The work of these leading designers is also the most sought after today: names such as Burgess, Godwin, Talbert, Morris, Voysey, Gallé, Mackintosh, Hoffmann, Moser, Ruhlmann, Lloyd Wright, Breuer, Aalto and many others – all these will make a great deal of difference to the price you may have to pay for a piece of furniture.

Apart from the name of the designer or maker and the condition of a piece, the factors that will make the most difference to the price will be the quality and style. Style is particularly important when considering the age in which it was made. Not all furniture made in the 1920s or 1930s is 'Art Deco' or 'modern'; some will be reproductions of earlier styles, other pieces may reflect the period but will be tame and bland in design. Art Deco, for example, is collected because it is different from any other style, as is Art Nouveau, and the closer an item is to the epitome of the style at its best, the more collectable the piece becomes.

However desirable a piece of furniture, before making your final commitment to buy because of its aesthetic appeal, make certain of the item's condition and authenticity. The auction house or dealer should be happy to give condition reports, answer any questions, and give the assurances you need. But it is always good to look oneself.

When assessing the item's condition ask yourself 'what is it made of, how is it constructed and what could go wrong?' If it is wood it could split, be scratched or stained, or have woodworm, and the joints could be loose. If they are, is it just a question of the restorer re-glueing them or are they actually broken? Does it have sturdy legs? If a piece is veneered, is the veneer intact? A little piece missing on an edge may not be a big problem, but damage to larger areas can be more serious and may prove costly because of the difficulty in matching the veneer.

If it is a glazed cabinet, are all the panes present and intact? What type of glass is it, would it be difficult to match? For furniture made from laminated woods look carefully at the structure. Is id still strong and flexible? Look out for splits and 'tiredness'. If an item has metal in it, be it wrought iron or steel, with or without nickel or chromium plating, again think about the material and what could go wrong with it. Is it split, badly dented, rusted or the plate flaking? Generally, when considering restoration, bear in mind how extensive it needs to be to restore the item to its former glory, and how this will affect its authenticity and perhaps its selling price later on.

One of the advantages of buying items of antique or 'old' furniture is that they generally maintain their value better than brand new 'department store' pieces. Usually one can trade them in more easily for different or more valuable items – this is not only an enjoyable way of working to enhance your home but, in this world of diminishing resources and materials, it is also a very 'green' approach. **Fiona Baker**

An Arts & Crafts-style ebonized side cabinet, inset with blue and cream glazed pottery tiles, 37in (93cm) wide.
£600–700 *HSS*

A glazed cabinet, c1910, 63in (160cm) wide.
£1,200–1,500 *SV*

An Edwardian mahogany display cabinet, inlaid with a stylized peacock in various woods, 48in (120cm) wide.
£1,200–1,500 *TW*

An Aesthetic Movement mahogany corner desk, 30in (75cm) wide.
£450–550 *P*

An Aesthetic Movement simulated satinwood bedroom suite, by Gillows & Co, with wardrobe, dressing table, washstand and bedside cabinet, stamped 'Gillow & Co'.
£700–800 *MSh*

A late Victorian Arts & Crafts ebonized and pollard oak sideboard, 90in (228.5cm) wide.
£600–750 *CDC*

A late Victorian Arts & Crafts oak kneehole pedestal desk, 57½in (144cm) wide.
£1,300–1,500 *CSK*

An Arts & Crafts oak desk, attributed to the workshops of L. & J. G. Stickley, 38⅛in (96cm) wide.
£700–850 *P*

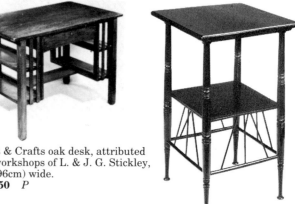

An Aesthetic Movement ebonized occasional table, after a design by E. W. Godwin, 26½in (67.5cm) wide.
£450–550 *P*

A Gallé marquetry two-tier tea table, the satinwood top inlaid with fruitwoods, bronze handles, 31in (79cm) wide.
£1,500–1,800 *P*

A mahogany armchair, 48in (122cm) high.
£250–300 *OB*

An oak and copper hall seat and chest, embellished in copper with plant form panels and studded edging, 30½in (77.5cm) wide.
£350–450 *P*

A set of 6 Arts & Crafts teak chairs, c1900.
£900–1,100 *ST*

An oak bookcase, with copper handles, by the Stickley Brothers, Grand Rapids, Michigan, c1910.
£2,500–3,000 *ST*

A wrought-iron and glass side table, 22½in (63cm) high.
£1,700–2,000 *C*

A beech armchair, by Liberty & Co, with label.
£550–650 *P*

An Arts & Crafts oak hall stand, with copper fittings, c1905, 78in (198cm) high.
£900–1,100 *ST*

A set of 6 teak dining chairs, in the style of A. W. Simpson.
£900–1,100 *ST*

r. An oak bookcase, attributed to Bruce Talbert, stamped 'Gillow L 3867', 56in (142cm) high.
£2,500–2,800 *C*

A mahogany, ebonized and marquetry jardinière, in the style of Charles Bevan, with 9 marquetry panels inlaid with various fruitwoods, zinc liner and later burr-walnut chamfered cover, 29in (73.5cm) wide.
£2,800–3,200 *C*

A mahogany open armchair, inlaid with marquetry and white metal.
£550–700 *LRG*

An Arts & Crafts coal scuttle.
£150–180 *ST*

l. A mirror attributed to Bugatti, decorated with beaten copper and inlaid with copper and pewter , c1900, 26in (66cm) high.
£2,000–2,500 *C*

l. An Arts &
Crafts desk,
by Shapland
& Petter of
Barnstaple,
c1905.
£900–1,100
ST

A Gallé walnut and fruitwood
marquetry side table, signed
'Gallé', 21in (53cm) wide.
£900–1,100 *C*

A limed oak dining room suite,
by Heal's, comprising: dining
table, sideboard, 6 chairs,
including one armchair, and
a serving trolley, with inset
manufacturer's label, c1935.
£3,200–3,800 *C*

An Arts & Crafts armchair, c1900.
£700–850 *ST*

An American Arts & Crafts
mahogany occasional table, c1910.
£325–400 *ST*

A Victorian Aesthetic
Movement ebonized
chair, similar to a
Fred Maddoz design
for Floris & Co.
£350–450 *ST*

An Arts & Crafts oak chair,
Glasgow School, c1900.
£500–600 *ST*

l. An oak revolving bookcase,
the design attributed to Richard
Norman Shaw, the top with
carved inscription 'The Tabard
Inn, the true university of these
days is a collection of books',
73in (185.5cm) high.
£1,300–1,600 *C*

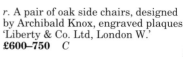

r. A pair of oak side chairs, designed
by Archibald Knox, engraved plaques
'Liberty & Co. Ltd, London W.'
£600–750 *C*

l. A William Birch oak armchair,
the tapering back splat with
heart-shaped piercing, the
out-curving arms and rush
seat on square section legs
joined by plain stretchers.
£650–800 *C*

A pair of limed oak chairs,
by Heal's, c1908.
£350–450 *ST*

r. An oak stool, by Grand Rapids
Bookcase and Chair Co, c1910.
£250–300 *ST*

l. An oak stool, by the Stickley
Brothers, Grand Rapids, c1905.
£400–450 *ST*

A set of 6 Finmar stained birch chairs, designed by Alvar Aalto, with Finmar Ltd label.
£200–250   *P*

A walnut side cabinet, with a grey slate top, 4 cupboard doors, inlaid with slate panels, 1900–20, 58in (147cm) wide.
£650–800   *S*
The small plate panels are replacements, presumably instead of the original pietra dura panels.

A pair of 'Fledermaus' side chairs, designed by Josef Hoffmann, with J. & J. Kohn label beneath upholstery, c1907.
£650–700   *S*

A French oak dining chair, designed by Charles Plumet and Anthony Selmersheim. £400–500   *P*

An oak settle, by Walter Cave, the fabric designed by C. F. Voysey, c1900, 54in (137cm) wide.
£3,500–4,500   *S*

An oak chair, by Wylie and Lochhead, the design attributed to E. A. Taylor.
£450–550   *C*

A corner chair, by Bugatti, the sides slung with beaten copper and kid drums, inlaid with pewter and ivory.
£2,000–2,500   *CSK*

An inlaid satinwood stand, and a pair of chairs.
£400–450   *LRG*

A bentwood rocking chair, by Thonet, c1904.
£350–400   *CNY*

l. A mahogany and marquetry settle, the top and frieze inlaid with various fruitwoods, c1890, 73in (185cm) wide.
£1,400–1,700   *C*

An oak 'Granville' chair, by Edward Pugin, stamped 'P.O.D.R.', mark for 1870.
£2,700–3,200   *S*

An Arts & Crafts oak smoking cupboard, with coppered hinges, marked 'Rd 39192', c1885, 12in (30.5cm) wide.
£100–120   *ROW*

An oak writing desk, designed by George Walton, with 3 drawers, on square tapering supports, c1900, 37in (94cm) high.
£800–950   *C(S)*

A pair of ash high-backed armchairs, by Clisset, designed by Ernest Gimson, with ladderbacks above rush seats, on turned tapered legs joined by stretchers.
£1,200–1,500   *C*

A mahogany gateleg table, by Kenton & Co, designed by Ernest Gimson, the sides with rose and briar palmwood inlay, c1891, 32in (81.5cm) long extended.
£4,500–5,500   *C*

A Thebes mahogany stool, 17in (43cm) square.
£500–600   *APO*

An oak side table, designed by Gordon Russell, 33½in (85cm) wide.
£550–700   *C*

r. An Arts & Crafts ebonized card table, 36in (91.5cm) wide.
£450–500   *APO*

An Arts & Crafts hall table/bureau, in the manner of Gustav Stickley, the 2 drawers with copper handles, 49in (124.5cm) wide.
£650–800   *APO*

l. An oak chequered inlaid wardrobe, possibly designed by M. H. Baillie-Scott, 85in (216cm) wide, and a matching chest with 2 hinged lids above a pair of doors and 3 drawers, on octagonal supports, 55in (139.5cm) high, both with copper curved handles.
£2,500–3,000   *C(S)*

A mahogany and cane newspaper basket, designed by Sir Edwin Lutyens, with carved 'rope' decoration and cane panels, on 4 square section legs, each pair joined with a single plain stretcher, on casters, 32in (81cm) wide.
£4,500–5,000   *C*

This newspaper basket was designed by Sir Edwin Lutyens for his own use, certainly at 13 Mansfield Street, where he lived from September 1919. However, it may have been designed earlier while he was living in Bedford Square. His daughter, Mary Lutyens, remembers the piece being in constant use.

A mahogany and satinwood breakfront cabinet, the design attributed to Thomas E. Collcutt, the marquetry to Stephen Webb, with original red velvet interior, stamped 'Collinson & Lock, 1900', c1885, 65in (165cm) wide.
£3,000–3,500 *C*

A corner cabinet, by Heal & Son, on a plinth base, 21½in (54cm) wide.
£450–550 *C*

Four dining chairs and one carver, by George Walton, 40in (101.5cm) high.
£750–900 *APO*

An oak low chair, by Arthur Simpson of Kendal, the curving arched back with pierced motif, with similarly curved seat on square section arched legs, damaged.
£700–850 *C*

A pair of upholstered oak side chairs, designed by J. P. Seddon, the moulded arched backs with carved leaf motifs, stamped 'Seddon, New Bond Street, 9969',
£2,000–2,500 *C*

An Arts & Crafts dark oak high-backed elbow chair, with solid seat.
£150–180 *LF*

A set of 7 Arts & Crafts oak dining chairs, including an open armchair.
£1,000–1,200 *CSK*

A set of 6 oak side chairs, designed by A. W. N. Pugin, on turned and chamfered legs joined by chamfered stretchers, upholstered in brown hide, with casters on front legs.
£2,000–2,500 *C*

An oak tea table, inlaid with ebony, with 4 fold-down shelves.
£400–450 *ST*

A Gustav Stickley oak armchair, c1903.
£700–850 *ST*

A Gustav Stickley oak settee, c1903.
£1,800–2,200 *ST*

r. A stained beech table, of pegged construction, by Liberty's, c1905.
£350–400 *ST*

An Arts & Crafts mahogany armchair, 1900.
£350–450 *ST*

A set of 5 Gordon Russell oak dining chairs and an armchair, with drop-in seats, on tapering square section legs joined by plain stretchers.
£1,800–2,200 *C*

An American Arts & Crafts oak magazine/book rack, by the Lake Craft Shops, Sheboygan, Wisconsin, c1905.
£900–1,100 *ST*

An oak occasional table, by Heal's.
£300–350 *ST*

Above & below. An oak sofa/table, the table top swivels to reveal a sofa, c1910.
£500–600 *ST*

l. An inlaid mahogany writing desk, 33in (84cm) wide.
£550–650 *IM*

An oak plant stand, with copper banding, c1900, 36in (91.5cm) high.
£180–220 *ST*

Furniture

Perhaps in no other area than furniture is the divergence of paths taken by Art Nouveau designers so evident. Exponents of the new art, turning their backs on classical precedent, introduced an entirely new sculptural element into their furniture.

While all Art Nouveau is based upon themes drawn from nature, the French and Southern European designers accentuated the swirls and sensuous curves that are the external, visible characteristics of natural growth. The Scottish and other Northern European schools sought a more abstract and usually austere form of expression, suggesting, rather than describing, their theme.

The latter groups often worked in oak, while the opulence of the more flamboyant Continental styles were generally captured in more decorative, and sometimes exotic, timbers. Not uncommonly, metals, ceramics, leather and even parchment were used for decorative embellishment in addition to the more traditional inlays of ivory and contrasting wood veneers.

Not all furniture is representative of the 'high' Art Nouveau styles. Much that is in keeping with today's taste can be bought at prices which are not unreasonable considering the consistently high standards of workmanship and materials that characterize them.

An Art Nouveau mahogany display cabinet, inlaid in horn and various coloured woods, with flower motifs, 47½in (121 cm) wide.
£1,200–1,400 C

A mahogany 'Quaint' side cabinet, designed by Adam Galt, c1910, 76in (193cm) wide.
£1,800–2,200 S

Adam Galt was an Edinburgh designer. This cabinet combines a traditional Edwardian Art Nouveau shape with a strong Glasgow School influence in the glazing.

A mahogany and marquetry hall cupboard, inlaid in a variety of stained woods, the umbrella wells stamped, 'Williamson and Sons, Worcester', early 20thC, 50in (127cm) wide.
£1,000–1,200 SBA

An Art Nouveau mahogany and brass-mounted music cabinet, 26in (66cm) wide.
£400–450 WHL

An Art Nouveau mahogany tri-form harpist's seat, c1910.
£450–550 SS

l. A small marquetry chest, with inlaid signature 'Emile Gallé', c1900, 27½in (69.7cm) wide
£6,500–7,500 SB

An Art Nouveau mahogany breakfront display cabinet, with boxwood stringing and marquetry panels of river scenes and wooded landscapes in copper, pewter and various woods, 66½in (169cm) wide.
£1,300–1,700 C

An Art Nouveau mahogany sideboard, decorated with satinwood crossbanding, with Robson & Sons, Newcastle, trade label, 78in (198 cm) wide.
£1,000–1,200 AG

An Art Nouveau Viennese-style mahogany table cabinet, with 2 brass handles, the amboyna wood veneered doors inlaid in brass, the rosewood interior fitted with 3 compartments and one drawer, 14½in (37cm) high.
£320–380 C

A William Birch oak armchair.
£650–750   *C*

A Gallé marquetry side table, hinged top opening to form X-shaped surface, incised 'E. Gallé Nancy' with Croix de Lorraine, 1900–10, 30in (76cm) high.
£1,300–1,700   *S*

An inlaid grey walnut table, probably by Wylie and Lochhead and designed by George Logan, inlaid in silver metal and mother-of-pearl, stamped '121688', c1900, 33in (84cm) wide.
£1,500–1,800   *S*

Two 'Fledermaus' chairs, designed by Josef Hoffmann, J. & J. Kohn label, c1905, 31½in (80cm) high.
£650–800   *S*

Two 'Fledermaus' chairs, designed by Josef Hoffmann, J. & J. Kohn labels, c1905, 31⅛in (91.5cm) high.
£1,000–1,200   *S*

A Liberty and Co. oak wardrobe probably designed by Leonard F. Wyburd, c1899, 36in (91.5cm) wide.
£1,000–1,200   *C*

A Liberty and Co. oak wardrobe, with copper hinges, c1900, 78in (198cm) wide.
£900–1,100   *S*

A mahogany bureau de dame, the upper shelf inlaid in various woods, incised signature on drawer, 'L. Majorelle, Nancy', 28½in (72cm) wide.
£3,000–3,500   *C*

r. A Louis Majorelle table, the top inlaid with stylised leaves in various fruitwoods, branded mark 'L. Majorelle, Nancy', c1900, 28½in (72cm) wide.
£1,200–1,400   *S*

A carved mahogany table, in the style of Louis Majorelle, with later turntable top, c1900, 29½in (75cm) high.
£450–550   *S*

A Gallé table, the top inlaid with oak, beech and other woods, with the legend 'Quand ce coq chante aura mon amitie pour finira', signed 'Gallé', 28½in (72cm) high.
£1,000–1,200   *P*

A French Art Nouveau fruitwood and maple vitrine, in the style of Louis Majorelle, 26in (66cm) wide.
£1,000–1,200   *CSK*

A 'Culloden' oak sideboard, by Liberty & Co, the superstructure with central shelving, cupboard door missing, flanked by an open shelf on either side, with copper strapwork hinges and door furniture, 80in (203cm) wide.
£1,300–1,600 *P*

A mahogany salon suite, probably by J. S. Henry, comprising: a two-seater settee, 2 armchairs and 6 side chairs, inlaid with stylized flowers in fruitwoods and lightwood stringing, the seats and backs upholstered with a Secessionist-style fabric.
£2,700–3,200 *P*

A hexagonal coffee table, by Heal's, with an undershelf and supported on 6 legs of triangular section with rounded fluted sides, 28½in (72cm) wide.
£400–450 *P*

A set of 6 oak dining chairs, by Johnson of Renfrew.
£700–800 *TRU*

A French Art Nouveau carved walnut armchair and footstool, the serpentine seat front and rail conforming to the shaped stool, upholstered in beige silk, c1900, 53in (135cm) long.
£4,500–5,500 *S(NY)*

An Art Nouveau walnut armchair, probably by Bath Cabinetmakers, with a pair of matching side chairs, the pierced backs inlaid with lightwood stringing and a floral motif highlighted with mother-of-pearl, the central splat carved with stylized flowers, on square section tapering legs, the seats upholstered with a Secessionist-style fabric.
£450–550 *P*

A French Art Nouveau walnut writing table, the rectangular top above a shaped and carved apron, set with a pair of drawers, on moulded legs rising to carved whiplash scroll brackets, 39in (99cm) wide.
£600–700 *P*

r. An Art Nouveau mahogany display cabinet, probably by J. S. Henry, with a glass fronted door above a bowfronted cupboard, with overhanging cornice, the legs with claw feet, the carcase inlaid with stylized floral designs in fruitwoods, 64in (162.5cm) high.
£1,300–1,600 *P*

A set of 8 mahogany dining chairs, designed by G. M. Ellwood for J. S. Henry, comprising: 2 carvers and 6 upright chairs, each with a circular panel at the top inlaid with pale wood, pewter and brass foliate motifs, with vertical slatted back, upholstered lower back and seat with compressed ball feet, square back legs.
£7,000–8,000 *P*

A marquetry cabinet,
profusely decorated.
£2,500–3,000 *ASA*

An inlaid armchair, 22in (56cm) wide.
£450–500 *APO*

A Glasgow-style mahogany
display cabinet, with a pair of
stained and leaded glass doors,
69in (175cm) high.
£1,500–1,800 *C(S)*

l. A breakfront cabinet, on arched trestle
ends, with a metal plaque, 'Liberty & Co.
London', 48in (122.5cm) wide.
£1,200–1,400 *C*

A polished mahogany bedroom
suite, designed by Carlo Zen,
comprising: a pair of bedside
cabinets, each set with a marble
plaque, and a shaped panelled
cupboard door carved with
stylized floral motifs, on arched
bracket feet, with original labels,
17in (43.5cm) wide.
£2,000–2,500
A matching double bed, the front
panel elaborately carved with a
flowerspray, the back panel with
original label, 46in (117cm) wide.
£3,000–3,500
A large matching wardrobe,
with floral brass lockplates,
77in (196cm) wide.
£3,000–3,500 *C*

A carved mahogany mirror,
by V. Epeaux, the glass
enclosed in a curvilinear
framework of apple blossom,
63½in (161.5cm) high.
£3,500–4,000 *C*

l. A black and white painted
cabinet, by the Wiener
Werkstätte, designed by
Josef Hoffmann, c1910,
34in (86cm) wide.
£1,200–1,400 *C*

*This piece is part of a suite
of furniture designed for
Heinrich Bohler, Vienna.*

An oak adjustable open armchair, upholstered in embroidered fabric, supported by Y-shaped arm and leg sections carved and pierced, on brass casters, late 19thC.
£1,000–1,200   C

A set of 8 chairs, including 2 carvers, by Ernest Gimson, with barber's pole inlay, tapering grille backs and upholstered drop-in seats, 38in (96.5cm) high.
£3,500–4,000   Bon

An oak 'Manxman' piano, by John Broadwood & Sons, designed by M. H. Baillie-Scott, with wrought-iron hinge plates and drop handles, brass and wrought-iron candle brackets, the case inscribed 'J. B. & Sons', movement No. 95972, c1899, 56½in (143.5cm) wide.
£6,500–8,000   C

A walnut occasional table, with ebony feet, by Gordon Russell, 23in (58cm) wide.
£000–1,100   C

George Henry Walton (1867–1933)

Closely associated with the Arts & Crafts movement, George Walton spent the first ten years of his career in Glasgow.

In 1888, after little formal training, he established retail premises and a workshop for his own business, George Walton & Co, Ecclesiastical and House Decorators.

Design commissions from this period included Clutha glass for James Couper & Son, stained glass panels for William Burrell, furniture and interiors for Liberty & Co, and the refurbishment of Miss Cranston's Tearooms in Argyll Street and Buchanan Street, Glasgow.

In 1898 Walton moved to London and at the same time set up in business in York. He received a major commission to redesign a series of interiors for Kodak in Glasgow, Brussels, Vienna, Milan, Moscow, Leningrad and London, and later widened his range of activities by turning his hand to architecture, designing and building houses in Oxfordshire, London, Wales and France.

A pine wardrobe, designed by E. W. Godwin, the panelled front with 2 studded brass bands and central cupboard door enclosing a single fitted shelf, above a long drawer with central circular escutcheon and drop ring handles on channelled square section legs and casters, 60in (152.5cm) wide.
£15,000–18,000   C

This wardrobe was probably designed for Castle Dromore, County Limerick, Ireland. The door fittings are identical to those illustrated in the drawings of Godwin's door furniture for Dromore in the Drawings Collection at the Royal Institute of British Architects.

An Arts & Crafts mahogany framed four-fold draught screen, with embossed board panels decorated and gilt with pomegranates and meandering foliage, 75in (190.5cm) wide.
£750–950   C(S)

An Arts & Crafts oak sideboard, the finialled ledge back with copper panel, quadrant tiers and slatted sides above a rectangular top, 2 frieze drawers and arched recess below, flanked by 2 panelled doors with carved tree motifs, on block feet, stamped 'Maple & Co. Ltd', in drawer and 'Nos. 4053, 2547, 1' to the reverse.
£1,000–1,200   CSK

An Art Nouveau inlaid
mahogany armchair.
£250–300   *Ph*

An Arts & Crafts oak chair.
£180–240   *Ph*

A pair of upright metal chairs,
of almost Gothic style.
£300–350   *P*

A set of 6 mahogany
dining chairs, the central
splat carved with an
elaborate dragon motif.
£600–750   *P*

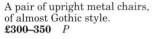

An Art Nouveau mahogany settle,
inlaid in various fruitwoods, c1890,
73in (185.5cm) wide.
£1,000–1,200   *C*

A beech settle, by J. & J. Kohn,
the design attributed to Gustav Siegel,
48½in (121.5cm) wide.
£900–1,100   *P*

A Louis Majorelle mahogany
and walnut armoire, Les
Clématites, carved with
frieze of clematis, c1900,
73½in (187cm) wide.
£3,000–3,500   *C*

A French Art
Nouveau walnut
buffet, attributed
to Maison Diot,
54in (135cm) wide.
£1,000–1,200   *P*

An oak vitrine, c1900,
25in (63.3cm) wide.
£1,000–1,200   *C*

A Peter Waals walnut library
bookcase, with ebony and
boxwood stringing, early 20thC,
76in (193cm) wide.
£12,000–15,000   *L*

An Aesthetic Movement ebonized
mahogany cabinet, 34in (86.5cm) wide.
£350–400   *L*

An Aesthetic Movement
ash wardrobe, 51in
(127.5cm) wide, and a
similar dressing table.
£800–1,100   *Re*

A Scottish Arts & Crafts oak bureau bookcase, by G. Laird, Glasgow.
£750–900 *GIL*

An oak bureau, by Sidney Barnsley, with a fitted interior, frieze drawer and 2 panelled cupboard doors, on moulded trestle ends with arched apron, 34in (86cm) wide.
£3,200–3,800 *C*

An Arts & Crafts buffet, 55in (139.5cm) wide.
£500–575 *APO*

A neo-Gothic carved and inlaid oak hanging cabinet, 41in (104cm) wide.
£3,200–3,700 *C*

A pair of oak side cabinets, with parquetry decoration, stamped 'Gillow & Co. 2344', 65in (164.5cm) wide, with single pedestal en suite stamped 'Gillow & Co. 2343'.
£5,000–6,000 *C*

An Arts & Crafts oak bureau, with a fitted interior of pigeonholes and 2 drawers, above 3 long similarly panelled drawers, on bracket feet, 36in (91.5cm) wide.
£1,000–1,200 *C*

An Arts & Crafts oak bureau, standing on 4 reeded legs, 27in (68.5cm) wide.
£450–550 *GAK*

l. An oak inlaid dwarf cabinet, by J. P. White, designed by M. H. Baillie-Scott, the cupboard door with pewter and fruitwood inlay, c1904, 20in (51cm) wide.
£1,800–2,200 *C*

An & Arts & Crafts oak dining table, by E. G. Punnett for William Birch, 54in (137.5cm) wide.
£1,200–1,500 *C*

An Arts & Crafts ash table, 31in (78.5cm) high.
£200–250 *OCA*

An Arts & Crafts gateleg dark stained oak table, the 2 end legs formed as shaped planks with a club motif, 47in (119.5cm) extended.
£550–650 *P*

An Arts & Crafts Glasgow School oak settle, 46½in (117cm) wide.
£450–550 *P*

An Arts & Crafts inlaid oak secrétaire, inlaid in ebony and pewter with stylized flower motifs within ebony and ivory inlaid borders, twin drawers below, on square supports united by stretchers, brass pulls and further chequer inlay, 41in (104.5cm) wide.
£900–1,100 *P*

A late Victorian Arts & Crafts mahogany and ebonized wardrobe, by Christopher Pratt & Sons, with a dog-tooth cornice above a mirrored door, flanked by 2 foliate carved panelled doors on stile feet brass fittings, with paper label, 66in (167.5cm) wide.
£1,000–1,200 *CSK*

An Arts & Crafts carved oak plant stand, c1890, 35½in (90cm) high.
£180–220 *OCA*

A late Victorian oak washstand, attributed to E. & J. Jones of Oswestry, with raised tiled back, Cararra marble top, above 3 frieze drawers on ring turned tapering legs, c1870, 48in (122cm) wide.
£900–1,100 *CSK*

Edward Jones, of Leeds and Oswestry, took over the firm of John Kendall & Co. in 1864, in partnership with John Marsh. During the following decade, the name appears variously as Edward Jones, Marsh & Jones, and Marsh, Jones & Cribb. The firm was associated with the designers Charles Bevan and Bruce Talbert.

An Arts & Crafts oak corner cabinet, possibly Newlyn, the door having 4 panels inset with copper, depicting stylized acorns and squirrels, with copper shaped strap hinges, 24in (61cm) wide.
£700–850 *P*

An Arts & Crafts copper mirror, possibly by Pearson or Newlyn, the glass mounted in a wooden frame, faced with copper and heavily embossed with stylized flowers and leaves against a hammered ground, 25½in (65cm) wide.
£600–750 *P*

An Arts & Crafts oak bookcase, with unusual copper metalwork and leaded light panels in the doors, probably Liberty's, c1900, 85½in (217cm) wide.
£2,000–2,500 *ST*

An Arts & Crafts oak sideboard, by Liberty's, probably designed by Leonard Wyburd, with geometric leaded glass and copper strapwork handles, c1895, 94in (238cm) wide.
£2,500–3,000 *ST*

A walnut cabinet, 66in (167.5cm) high.
£900–1,100 *RG*

r. A mahogany display cabinet, 48in (122cm) wide.
£1,300–1,700 *CEd*

An inlaid mahogany display cabinet, with enclosed shelves, inlaid in fruitwoods with Art Nouveau foliage and flowers.
£1,000–1,500 *P*

r. A mahogany display cabinet, 54½in (138cm) wide.
£1,000–1,500 *CEd*

r. An Arts & Crafts ebonized oak book cabinet, with brass panel inscribed 'Studies Serve for Delight', 50in (127cm) wide.
£1,000–1,500 *P*

An Edwardian oak bureau, probably for Liberty & Co, c1910, 54½in (138cm) wide.
£900–1,100 *N*

r. An Arts & Crafts-style mahogany display cabinet, marked '634145768', 53in (134.5cm) wide.
£700–1,000 *P(CW)*

Two Arts & Crafts armchairs, with 4 matching side chairs.
£1,000–1,200   *ARF*

A Liberty & Co tub chair, by Liberty & Co.
£500–600   *ARF*

An Arts & Crafts chair.
£170–200   *ARF*

A set of 8 Arts & Crafts rush-seated chairs, including 2 carvers.
£1,000–1,200   *ARF*

A set of 6 Arts & Crafts chairs.
£700–800   *ARF*

A Gothic chair.
£150–200   *ARF*

A set of 8 Arts & Crafts chairs, by William Birch.
£1,500–1,800   *ARF*

A set of 4 Arts & Crafts chairs.   **£400–450**   *ARF*

An Arts & Crafts pot cupboard, 32½in (82cm) high.
£250–300   *ARF*

A Gothic style bedroom suite comprising: pot cupboard, wardrobe and dressing table.
£2,500–3,000   *ARF*

A pair of Arts & Crafts adjustable book shelves, 36in (92cm) high.
£300–350 each   *ARF*

A pair of Gothic oak pillars, with painted decoration, 49in (124.5cm) high.
£700–750   *ARF*

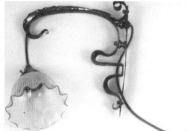

An Arts & Crafts copper wall light.
£200–250   *ARF*

A Newlyn copper repoussé tray, 17½in (44.5cm).
£450–500   *BLO*

A pair of Arts & Crafts oak reclining chairs, c1920.
£450–550 *OCA*

An Arts & Crafts oak armchair, attributed to William Birch.
£450–550 *P*

A William Birch oak armchair, attributed to E. Punnett, the back inset with 2 rush panels above a rush seat and 4 rectangular section legs with an H-shaped stretcher.
£1,500–1,800 *C*

A pair of oak reclining chairs, with 2 cushions, c1920.
£450–500 *OCA*

An Arts & Crafts oak chest, attributed to Heal's, with 3 long drawers beneath an enclosed cupboard, the doors set with fielded chestnut panels, with exposed joints throughout.
£1,500–1,800 *P*

An Arts & Crafts oak reclining armchair, attributed to William Birch, the ladder back with turned uprights, with an adjustable rod support, shaped armrests, turned front and square back supports united with stretchers, with William Morris fabric cushions.
£800–1,000 *P*

An Arts & Crafts mahogany display cabinet, in the style of J. S. Henry, the angled glazed doors separated and bounded by planks inlaid with stylized floral patterns in fruitwood, supported above a pointed pedestal base by 3 groups of 2 frontal columns and a solid back.
£1,300–1,600 *P*

A Fradgley Arts & Crafts three-piece salon suite, comprising: a two-seater settee and a pair of armchairs, inlaid with ebony stringing and fruitwood stylized floral inlay.
£1,800–2,200 *P*

r. An Arts & Crafts oak dining table, the top made from 3 pieces of wood, 84½in (214cm) long.
£800–950 *P*

A Gothic-style oak side table, in the manner of Pugin, 42½in (107cm).
£700–800 *P*

An Austrian mahogany kneehole desk, attributed to Otto Wagner, the top inset with green leather, with brass gallery, on flared brass feet, 47⅓in (121cm) wide, and a matching mahogany revolving chair, on similar brass supports.
£2,500–3,000 *P*

A mahogany and marquetry buffet, attributed to Louis Majorelle, with bronze mounts and marble tops, the gallery with a narrow shelf at the top, 56in (143cm) wide.
£900–1,100 *C(Am)*

An Arts & Crafts pollard oak bedroom suite of 8 pieces, in the manner of C. F. A. Voysey.
£2,500–3,000 *P(Re)*

An Arts & Crafts oak sideboard by Stanley Davis of Windermere, maker's monogram 'SDW 1927', and 'J.E.O.,' 4in (137cm) wide.
£800–950 *P*

An Aesthetic Movement walnut hanging cabinet, with hand-painted panel, c1875.
£350–400 *P(Re)*

r. An Aesthetic Movement corner cupboard, the bowfronted doors enclosing 3 shelves and painted in colours, one door unfinished, on a three-legged base with a single drawer and undertier, 27in (69cm) wide.
£350–450 *P*

A Dutch Arts & Crafts tea buffet, designed by Jac. van den Bosch for 'het Binnenhuis', with a metal tag 't Binnenhuis Raadhuisstraat, Amsterdam', and with branded monogram 'J.v.d. Bosch' and '848', 61½in (156cm) high.
£1,300–1,500 *C(Am)*

r. An Arts & Crafts oak dresser, with brass hinges, 50in (127cm).
£1,300–1,700 *RG*

A mahogany escritoire, with a marquetry panel, by Shapland & Petter, Barnstaple, c1905.
£1,500–1,800 *ST*

An Amsterdam School rosewood sideboard, bordered in coromandel, 65in (165cm) wide.
£350–400 *C(Am)*

A tubular chromium-plated chaise
longue, designed by Le Corbusier and
Charlotte Perriand, upholstered in
ponyskin, on a black painted steel base.
£2,500–3,000 *C*

A burr-maple sideboard,
the design attributed to Ray Hille,
54in (137cm) wide.
£700–800 *C*

A walnut cabinet, by A. J. Rowley,
the stepped top above 3 mirrored
compartments, the central one inset
with carved panel, on silvered plinth
base, with printed label 'Rowley ,
Church Street, Kensington, Est.
1898', 35in (89cm) wide.
£2,000–2,500 *C*

A mahogany dressing table,
51½in (130cm) wide.
£700–800 *P*

A French daybed, the mattress covered in black and
white zebra skin, with a matching cylindrical cushion,
on 4 tapering fluted legs, 1930s, 74in (188cm) long.
£1,500–1,800 *C*

l. A six-piece 'Cloud' suite, veneered
in walnut and re-upholstered in cream
leather, c1930, sofa 65in (165cm) wide.
£3,500–4,000 *ST*

A two-tier occasional table,
designed and labelled by Waring
& Gillow, 21in (53cm) high.
£200–250 *ARF*

An Art Deco nest of tables,
30in (76cm) diam.
£300–350 *ARF*

An Art Deco circular occasional
table, 36in (91.5cm) diam.
£750–900 *ARF*

r. An Art Deco walnut
and glass coffee table,
21in (53cm) high.
£170–200 *ARF*

A Modernist chrome and glass coffee table, 1940s, 24in (61.5cm) diam.
£400–450   *S*

A Barcelona chair and stool, by Mies van der Rohe, 1929, made post-1960, 28½in (73cm) high. **£400–450**   *S*

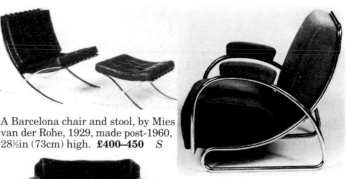

A pair of Modernist cantilever armchairs, 1930s, 30in (76cm) high.
£800–950   *S*

A Modernist chromed tubular steel sofa, 1930s, 63½in (161cm) wide.
£800–1,100   *S*

A pair of French Art Deco arm-chairs, c1920, 28½in (73cm) wide.
£800–1,000   *S*

A coffee table, in pale burr-wood 1930s, 40in (101cm).
£450–550   *S*

A Bauhaus bedroom suite comprising: cabinet, chair, dressing table, 2 single bed-ends, 2 bedside tables, 1930s, tables 23in (58.5cm) high.
£1,200–1,500   *S*

l. An Art Deco grand lit en lac d'or, 71in (180cm) wide.
£1,300–1,700   *C*

Three Modernist side tables, 1930s, 23½in (60cm) diam.
£700–800   *S*

An Art Deco dressing table, veneered with Macassar ebony, 1930s, 47½in (120.5cm) wide.
£900–1,100   *S*

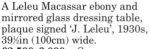

A Leleu Macassar ebony and mirrored glass dressing table, plaque signed 'J. Leleu', 1930s, 39½in (100cm) wide.
£2,500–3,000   *S*

A Finmar Ltd plywood armchair, designed by Alvar Aalto, Finmar label, 1930s, 23½in (60.5cm) high.
£200–250   *S*

A set of 6 Finmar Ltd plywood dining chairs, designed by Alvar Aalto, Finmar labels, stamped 'Aalto Design Made in Finland', 31½in (80cm) high.
£450–500   *S*

An Art Deco cabinet, 24in (61.5cm) wide.
£250–300 *ARF*

An Art Deco bedroom suite, comprising: a dressing table, bedside cupboard and large cupboard in oyster maple, 48in (122cm) wide.
£800–1,000 *ARF*

A chestnut wardrobe, the top with chamfered finials above 2 panelled cupboard doors, on octagonal section legs, printed paper label 'Design No. 101/1283, Designer Gordon Russell, Date 27.11.30', stamped 'E. A. Dorley', 76in (193.5cm) high.
£2,500–3,000 *C*

A Rowley bedroom suite, with illuminated panels, dressing table 34in (86cm) wide.
£700–800 *ARF*

A chrome bar stool, made by PEL, c1930, 30in (76cm) high.
£70–80 *ARF*

An Art Deco chrome stool, 37in (94cm) high.
£45–50 *ARF*

An Art Deco chrome and maroon glass cocktail trolley, 25½in (65cm) high.
£155–185 *ARF*

A Rowley Gallery corner unit, with inset picture of lion killing a deer, 44in (111.5cm) wide.
£750–900 *ARF*

A Robert 'Mouseman' Thompson oak wardrobe, with beaten iron fittings, on short square section legs, with mouse signature carved in intaglio, 48in (122cm) wide.
£3,000–4,000 *C*

An occasional table designed by Piero Fornasetti, the wooden top covered in black lacquer printed sun and ray motif, on tripod steel legs modelled with nodules, with printed paper label, 29½in (75cm) high.
£900–1,100 *C*

A French Art Deco table, c1930, 24in (61.5cm) high.
£150–180 *ARF*

An Art Deco rosewood, burr-maple and walnut centre table, in the style of Emile Ruhlmann, inlaid with ivory lattice stringing above plain frieze and chamfered legs, 33in (84cm) wide.
£2,000–2,500 *C*

An Art Deco copper and brass mantel clock, with French, 10½in (26.5cm) wide.
£70–80   *HM*

A silver-mounted mantel clock, the face set in an engine-turned surround, on a glass base, decorated with cutting and black enamel, maker's mark 'S. & M. Birmingham 1935', 4½in (11.5cm) high.
£100–120   *SBe*

An Art Deco table, 32in (81.5cm) diam.
£500–600   *ARF*

A French Art Deco bureau de dame, decorated in matt crackled polish and painted in relief, fitted interior, 47in (120cm) high.
£1,000–1,200   *C*

An Edward Barnsley walnut breakfront bookcase, made by Charles Bray, 1932, 89in (226cm) wide.
£7,500–9,000   *SB*

An Art Deco blonde wood bookshelf/display cabinet, 1930s, 31½in (80cm) high.
£600–700   *SB*

An oak chair, with label 'Designed by Frank Brangwyn RA, Manufactured by E. Pollard & Co Ltd', monogram 'FB', c1930, 42in (106cm) wide.
£500–600   *C*

A pair of tub-shaped easy chairs, attributed to Mercier Frères c1928, 28½in (73cm) high.
£800–950   *SS*

An Art Deco maple shagreen and ivory cocktail cabinet, panelled in a pale green shagreen, twin doors below, the top opening out, 1930s, 22in (56cm) wide.
£1,500–1,800   *SB*

An oak chest of drawers, designed by Robert 'Mouseman' Thompson, c1930, 36in (91.5cm) wide.
£1,000–1,200   *SB*

A black leather-covered desk, early 1930s, 57in (145cm) wide.
£650–750   *SB*

A Strohmenger small grand piano, the sycamore casing with double satinwood banding, numbered 'S 16413', 1930s.
£2,500–3,000   *SB*

A Gordon Russell oak bedroom cabinet, with walnut knobs, 73in (185cm) wide.
£2,500–3,000 *C*

An Epstein & Goldbart mahogany cocktail cabinet, veneered in sycamore, with a fitted interior, 60½in (153cm) high.
£650–750 *CSK*

l. A white painted side chair, by Edmund Moiret, with triple bar stretcher, c1907.
£1,500–1,800 *C*

Edmund Moiret, 1883–1967, was born in Budapest and became a leading member of the Hungarian Secession Movement. He began his studies at the Academy of Art in Budapest but went on to study in Vienna and Brussels. He was awarded a major prize at the Budapest Winter Salon in 1910 and settled in Hungary where he taught sculpture from 1911 at the Budapest Technische Hochschule. He later lived and worked in Vienna. In 1985 a commemorative exhibition was held at the Osterreichisches Museum für Angewandte Kunst.

A sycamore kneehole desk, with 2 slide pulls, 7 drawers and one false drawer, inset with a circular printed ivory label, 'Tottenham Court Road, Heal's, London W1', 28in (71cm) high.
£1,300–1,700 *C*

A set of 4 walnut side chairs.
£1,200–1,400 *C*

A set of 8 dining chairs.
£1,100–1,300 *C*

A Robert 'Mouseman' Thompson, oak writing desk, signed with a carved mouse, 72in (182cm) wide.
£1,200–1,500 *C*

A Heal's oak writing desk, designed by Ambrose Heal, with fall flaps at each end, enclosing 6 file trays, inlaid with printed ivory label 'Heal & Son Ltd London N.W', 60in (152cm) wide.
£3,500–4,000 *C*

A walnut dressing table, by Peter Waals, 46in (116cm).
£1,300–1,800 *C*

A coffee table, with a parquetry top, on 4 scrolling wrought iron legs, 31½in (79.5cm) diam.
£500–600 *C*

r. A bird's-eye maple dining suite, comprising: a table, serving table, 10 chairs upholstered in green leather, and a sideboard, 1930s, table 120in (305cm) long.
£3,000–3,500 *CSK*

A French rosewood dining table, c1928, 63in (160cm) wide.
£3,000–3,500 *CNY*

An occasional table, veneered and inlaid with ebony, boxwood, satinwood and oysterwoood, 25in (63.5cm) high.
£600–700 *ASA*

A quartered oak dining table, designed
by Gordon Russell, made by G. Cooke,
with label to underside, c1923,
66in (167cm) wide.
£2,500–3,000 *HCH*

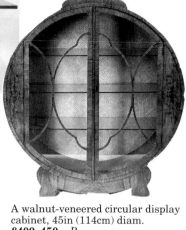

A burr-walnut veneered drinks
cabinet, with 4 cupboards and
a slide, 42in (106cm) wide.
£700–800 *P(Ch)*

A walnut-veneered circular display
cabinet, 45in (114cm) diam.
£400–450 *P*

A gilt salon chair, attributed
to Jules Leleu, upholstered
in beige fabric.
£1,700–2,000 *C*

An Austrian Secessionist painted writing
table and chair, 23in (58cm) high.
£2,700–3,200 *C*

An oak cabinet, designed by
Ambrose Heal, manufacturer's
label 'Heal & Son Makers,
London W', 44in (113cm) wide.
£2,500–3,000 *C*

A walnut-veneered dining table,
71in (180cm) long.
£700–800 *C*

A maple-veneered side table,
40in (102cm) wide.
£650–800 *P*

l. An oak and chestnut sideboard,
by Gordon Russell, cabinet maker
P. J. Wade, c1927, 52⅜in (136cm).
£3,500–4,500 *HCH*

A limed oak Ashanti-style stool,
stained black, 20½in (52cm) high.
£250–300 *P*

A walnut centre table,
31in (78.5cm) high.
£700–800 *C*

An Egyptian style bed, the headboard
with a beaten copper panel,
42in (107cm) wide.
£600–700 *C*

A set of 4 chairs, designed by
Ludwig Mies van der Rohe.
£1,000–1,200 *C*

An Art Deco three-piece red leather upholstered 'Cloud suite', comprising 2 armchairs and a sofa each with scallop shaped backs and curved sides, sofa 66in (167.5cm) wide.
£1,500–1,800 *CSK*

A French Art Deco calamander table, part veneered, the oval top supported on 4 stocky legs with a cross-stretcher between, the legs and feet carved with Oriental scrolls, 59in (150cm) long.
£650–750 *P*

An Art Deco burr-walnut cocktail cabinet, the central cupboard with twin fluted doors enclosing shelves, flanked by stepped side cupboards enclosing shelves, on arched supports on a solid ebonized base, 47½in (119.5cm) wide.
£1,600–2,000 *P*

An Art Deco cocktail cabinet, by Epstein, veneered in light walnut, the panelled doors enclosing a fitted pink mirrored interior, on slender carved floral and acanthus supports, 46in (116.5cm) wide.
£650–800 *MSL*

An Art Deco inlaid walnut fire screen, 34½in (87cm) wide.
£150–180 *OCA*

l. An Art Deco D-shaped wrought-iron console table, with a partly painted marble top, in the manner of Edgar Brandt, 42in (106.5cm) wide, and a matching overmantel.
£700–800 *CSK*

r. An Art Deco bird's-eye maple dining room table, with a glass cover, on 2 U-shaped supports on solid feet united by a stretcher, 78in (198cm) long.
£1,200–1,500 *P*

A French Art Deco wrought-iron, marble and wood mirrored console, in the style of Paul Kiss, the rectangular mirror plate within a simple hammered framework, the lower D-shaped black marble shelf with a single support composed of stylized floral devices, raised on a moulded wooden plinth, c1925, 72in (183cm) high.
£4,000–4,800 *S(NY)*

l. An Art Deco-style gilt-metal and glass dining table, with inset square top, the frieze cast with Greek key motifs, raised on 4 curved legs similarly cast, conjoined to a stepped square base, raised on 4 feet, 48in (123cm) square.
£3,700–4,200 *S(NY)*

An Art Deco cherrywood sofa, with carved
back rail and cornucopia arm supports,
covered in original patterned silk upholstery.
£600–700   *LRG*

An Art Deco birch-veneered sofa
and chair, byHille, upholstered in
muted pink fabric with small dots,
sofa 66½in (171cm) wide.
£3,500–4,000   *P*

An Art Deco Macassar ebony
bedroom suite, comprising:
a double bed, 63in (160cm) wide,
bedside cabinets, 20in (51cm)
wide, and a large wardrobe,
75in (109cm) high.
£2,700–3,200   *C*

An Art Deco gilt armchair, in the
manner of Maurice Dufrêne,
upholstered in green velvet, with
a matching footstool and cushions.
£1,000–1,200   *P*

An Art Deco three-piece 'Cloud'
suite, upholstered in cream
coloured leather, on casters.
£2,000–2,500   *P*

r. A pair of Art Deco armchairs,
the reclining backs and seats
upholstered in original beige and
brown fabric, each arm enclosing
a magazine rack and bookshelves,
with diamond motif frieze at the
front, stamped at the back
'W. Hudson 2842'.
£400–500   *P*

An Art Deco walnut suite,
possibly designed by Paul Follot,
comprising: a canapé and
2 bergère chairs, with yellow/
gold patterned velvet upholstery,
each piece with a shaped
upholstered cushion.
£3,500–4,500   *P*

An Arts & Crafts mahogany secrétaire, the fall flap enclosing a central cupboard with mother-of-pearl inlay, 48in (122cm) wide. **£1,500–1,800** *P*

A walnut and marquetry bookcase, inlaid in fruitwoods, on a later revolving base, inlaid 'Gallé' signature, 20in (51cm) wide. **£7,000–8,500** *C*

A three-fold wood-framed and leather-covered screen, decorated across the top with a tooled and gilded frieze of seagulls, with sailing boats below, the lower frieze depicting fish, crabs and shells, 70in (177.5cm) high. **£1,300–1,700** *P*

An Austrian mahogany desk and chair, attributed to Otto Wagner, with ivory inlay, satinwood stringing and bronze plaques, 48in (122cm) wide. **£3,000–3,500** *P*

Arts & Crafts furniture

The exponents of the Arts & Crafts Movement strove to incorporate the ideals of the hand craftsmanship of the medieval age into the 19th-century world of the machine. Furniture became heavier, with oak the preferred wood and styles that looked back nostalgically to medieval England. English-born architect and furniture designer, Harvey Ellis (1852–1904), worked with Gustav Stickley from 1902. He often used Jugendstil-style motifs inlaid in contrasting materials, such as ivory or darker woods, as well as pewter and copper. Other motifs include stylized flowers and Viking ships. Most inlaid Stickley pieces were designed by Ellis – in fact, his designs are so popular that some Stickley items have modern inlay. These can usually be identified by the poor quality of the work.

An oak bookcase, by Gustav Stickley, designed by Harvey Ellis, model No. 700, c1903, 36in (91.5cm) wide. **£9,000–11,000** *CNY*

r. An ebonized and rosewood lady's writing desk, by Carlo Bugatti, with pewter and ivory inlay, signed 'Ricardo Telligrini 1897', 30in (76cm) wide. **£5,000–6,000** *C*

A mahogany display cabinet, designed by
Carl Davis Richter, 65in (165cm) wide.
£3,000–3,500 *C*

An Ernest Gimson bureau, with an elaborately
fitted interior, barber's pole inlay, made by
Sidney Barnsley, 33in (83.5cm) wide.
£10,000–12,000 *C*

l. A Sidney Barnsley walnut
dresser, with diamond pattern
moulding, 75in (190.5cm) wide.
£8,000–9,500 *C*

r. An oak daybed,
by Charles Eastlake,
with panelled sides,
the headrest carved with
daisies, with a Gothic
roundel, upholstered in
green velvet, on turned
legs, 73in (185cm) long.
£4,000–5,000 *C*

A Gustav Siegel leather upholstered stained bentwood and brass seating group, made by J. & J. Kohn, c1905, settee 48in (122cm) wide.
£7,000–8,500   *S(NY)*

An Austrian burr-maple settee, upholstered in khaki twill, c1920, 55in (139.5cm) wide.
£4,250–5,000   *S(NY)*

A French Art Deco parcel gilt mahogany five-piece salon suite, upholstered in silk moiré, c1925, settee 50in (127cm) wide.
£6,000–7,500   *S(NY)*

A pair of Jacques Adnet black lacquered wood 'cube' club chairs, upholstered in beige canvas, c1930.
£10,000–12,000   *S(NY)*

A Josef Hoffman leather upholstered bentwood 'Buenos Aires' three-piece seating group, made by J. & J. Kohn, c1904, settee 52in (132cm) wide.
£10,500–11,500   *S(NY)*

A marquetry cabinet, by Louis
Majorelle, inlaid with flowers and
butterflies, the upper section with
a mirror, 39½in (100cm) wide.
£15,000–18,000   *CNY*

r. A marquetry cabinet, 'Aux
Grenouilles', with carved frog
feet, inlaid panels with
dragonflies and mushrooms,
marquetry 'Gallé' signature,
26in (66cm) wide.
£15,000–18,000   *CNY*

A pair of oak beds, designed by Frank
Lloyd Wright, probably by Niedecken-
Walbridge Co. for Ray Evans House,
Chicago, c1909, 47in (119cm) wide.
£6,000–7,000   *CNY*

A carved and marquetry-
inlaid vitrine, branded
'L. Majorelle, Nancy',
31in (78.5cm) wide.
£8,000–9,500   *CNY*

An upholstered mahogany three-piece salon suite, by Louis
Majorelle, carved with ferns and 2 snails, settee 54½in (138cm) wide.
£5,000–6,000   *CNY*

Two inlaid oak armchairs, designed by
Harvey Ellis, made by Gustav Stickley,
c1904, 47in (119cm) high.
£12,000–15,000 each   *CNY*

A marquetry umbrella stand,
with original tin liner,
marquetry 'Gallé' signature,
21in (53cm) wide.
£18,000–20,000   *CNY*

A pair of French
mahogany upholstered
club chairs, c1935.
£2,500–3,000   *S(NY)*

A Bruno Paul maple
armchair, restored
manufacturer's
monogram, Munich, 1901.
£12,000–15,000   *S(NY)*

A pair of Josef
Hoffmann stained
bentwood and brass
side chairs, by J. & J.
Kohn, Austria, c1901.
£9,000–11,000   *S(NY)*

The Aesthetic Movement

The 1870s and 1880s saw a growth in the
Aesthetic Movement in Britain, with
designers producing ebonized furniture in
simple forms, and decoration restricted to
confined areas rather than applied all over.
Unnecessary ornament was rejected as
vulgar. William Morris and his company
were the most important retail outlet for
Aesthetic-style furniture, while the Japanese
influence was particularly evident in the
work of Edward Godwin. The Aesthetic style
was especially popular in the United States,
where it was adopted with great success by
the Herter Brothers.

An Aesthetic
Movement ebonized
and inlaid open
armchair, c1870.
£2,000–2,500   *C*

A painted deal 'Berlin'
chair, designed by Gerrit
Rietveld in 1923, branded
label, made by Gerard
van de Groenekan, c1960.
£10,000–12,000   *S(NY)*

A Josef Hoffman bentwood
670 'Sitzmachine',
by J. & J. Kohn, c1905.
£12,000–15,000   *S(NY)*

A pair of French upholstered
club chairs, attributed
to André Arbus, c1945.
£4,000–4,500   *S(NY)*

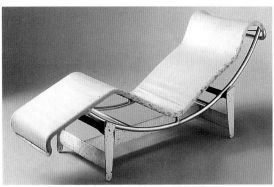

A white painted metal and canvas chaise longue, by
Le Corbusier, Pierre Jeanneret and Charlotte Perriand,
manufactured by Thonet, designed c1928,
63in (160cm) wide.
£35,000–40,000   *S(NY)*

A 'Red/Blue' chair, in beech and deal,
by Gerrit Rietveld, designed in 1918,
executed in 1919.
£30,000–35,000   *S(NY)*

A painted steel and
leather side chair,
by Frank lloyd
Wright, c1904.
£3,500–4,000   *S(NY)*

Henri van de Velde
(Belgian, 1863–1957)

Henri Clemens van de Velde trained as a painter, architect
and graphic designer in Antwerp and Paris, and was
instrumental in the evolution of the Belgian Art Nouveau
style. He designed all manner of items. including whole
interiors, but was particularly influential in the fields of
furniture, ceramics, jewellery and metalwork. His furniture
often combines innovative elements with tradition. It tends to
be substantial, concentrating on restrained, sculptural, well
balanced forms for interest, rather than the applied decoration
and inlay commonly used by adherents of the Nancy School.

A pair of oak side chairs,
with rush seats, designed by
Peter Behrens.
£5,500–7,000   *C*

A stained mahogany side chair,
by Richard Riemerschmid,
manufactured by B. Kohlbecker
& Sohn, Munich, 1903.
£1,800–2,400   *S(NY)*

A mahogany and leather
armchair, by Henry van de Velde,
designed for the Haby Salon,
Berlin, 1901.
£10,000–12,000   *S(NY)*

A pair of French upholstered
palmwood side chairs, c1930.
£3,000–3,500   *S(NY)*

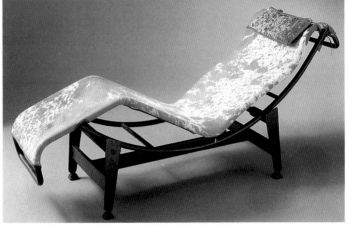

l. An ash and painted canvas
armchair, by Wharton
Esberick, signed 'Hedgerow/to
Jasper MCMXXXVII Wharton'.
£7,000–8,000   *S(NY)*

A black metal and ponyskin chaise longue,
by Le Corbusier, Pierre Jeanneret and
Charlotte Perriand, manufactured by
Embru Corporation, Switzerland, c1932.
£7,000–8,500   *S(NY)*

An Art Deco maple three-piece suite, comprising: sofa and 2 armchairs, the design attributed to Maurice Adams, the sofa with a waved padded back, rounded upholstered seat and scroll-end arms, on a platform base, sofa 71½in (179cm) wide.
£6,500–8,000 *C*

r. A Carlo Bugatti ebonized, inlaid and painted vellum side chair and table.
Chair **£4,500–5,500**
Table **£7,000–8,000**
C

l. An Edwin Lutyens 'Napoleon' chair, 38½in (98cm) wide.
£6,500–8,000 *C*

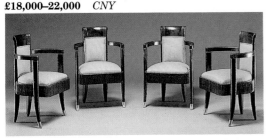

A carved mahogany dining table and 12 dining chairs, by the firm of Louis Majorelle, the table with 3 additional leaves, table 117in (297cm) wide, extended.
£18,000–22,000 *CNY*

A set of 6 carved mahogany 'Clematis' side chairs, by the firm of Louis Majorelle, 37in (94cm) high.
£3,000–3,500 *CNY*

l. A beechwood and mahogany 'Sitz machine' chair, c1912, 39in (99cm) high.
£9,000–11,000 *CNY*

A set of 4 mahogany dining chairs, from the ocean liner *Normandie*, 35in (89cm) high.
£12,000–14,000 *CNY*

A chair, known as the 'Barcelona Chair', designed by Ludwig Mies van der Rohe, No. MR90, c1931.
£60,000–80,000 *C(Am)*

l. An inlaid oak armchair, designed by Harvey Ellis, c1904. **£9,000–11,000** *CNY*

An aluminium chaise longue, designed by Marcel Breuer, Director of the Bauhaus furniture workshop 1925–28, the arm supports set with wooden handles, c1935, 53in (135cm) long.
£12,000–15,000 *C(Am)*

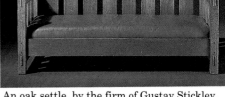

An oak settle, by the firm of Gustav Stickley, with branded mark, model No. 208, c1912, 76in (193cm) wide.
£10,000–12,000 *CNY*

l. A walnut stool, designed by Pierre Chareau, with moulded shell-shaped top, 18in (45.5cm) high.
£10,000–12,000 *CNY*

An Emile Gallé glass and
wrought-iron table lamp,
with cameo signature,
20½in (52cm) high.
£6,000–7,500   *CNY*

An Emile Gallé double overlaid and etched glass table
lamp, 11in (28cm) high.
£4,000–5,000   *CNY*

A Daum etched glass table
lamp, 165in (38cm) high.
£8,000–10,000   *CNY*

An Edgar Brandt gilt-
bronze table lamp,
20in (51cm) high.
£6,000–7,500   *CNY*

An etched and enamelled
glass vase, signed 'Daum
Nancy', 28in (71cm) high.
£13,000–15,000   *CNY*

An etched and enamelled
table lamp, signed on
base 'Daum Nancy',
14in (35.5cm) high.
£8,000–10,000   *CNY*

A Daum etched and
enamelled glass 'Rain' table
lamp, 14in (35.5cm) high.
£12,000–15,000   *CNY*

A Pairpoint reverse-painted
blown-out glass and patinated
metal lamp, unsigned, c1915,
17½in (44.5cm) high.
£3,000–4,000   *S(NY)*

l. A cameo glass
plafonnier,
signed in cameo
'Gallé', c1900,
16in (40.5cm) diam.
£3,500–4,000
S(NY)

l. A Gallé cameo glass and bronze
boudoir lamp, shade and base
signed, c1900, 10½in (26cm) high.
£3,000–3,500   *S(NY)*

A white 'Wisteria' leaded glass and bronze table lamp, the shade impressed '1073', the bronze tree-form base impressed 'Tiffany Studios New York 27770', 26½in (67.5cm) high.
£100,000–120,000 *CNY*

A 'Nasturtium' leaded glass and bronze table lamp, the shallow domed shade impressed 'Tiffany Studios New York', the base similarly impressed '8620', 24in (61cm) high.
£30,000–35,000 *CNY*

l. A 'Daffodil' leaded glass and bronze table lamp, the shade unsigned, the twisted vine base impressed 'Tiffany Studios New York 443', 25½in (65cm) high.
£15,000–18,000 *CNY*

A 'Banded Poppy' leaded glass and bronze floor lamp, the shade impressed 'Tiffany Studios New York 1597', the base 'No. 376', 79in (200.5cm) high.
£120,000–150,000 *CNY*

A 'Rosebush' leaded glass and gilt-bronze table lamp, the shade impressed 'Tiffany Studios New York 1915', the base 'No. 367', 30in (76cm) high extended.
£30,000–40,000 *CNY*

l. A leaded glass and earthenware table lamp, the shade impressed 'Tiffany Studios New York', the base 'Grueby Pottery Boston USA', 21in (53.5cm) high.
£5,500–6,500 *CNY*

A Tiffany Favrile glass and bronze 'Poinsettia' border lamp, c1910.
£17,000–20,000 *S(NY)*

A Tiffany Favrile glass and bronze 'Peony' floor lamp, shade impressed 'Tiffany Studios/New York 1505', c1910, 65in (165cm) high.
£50,000–55,000 *S(NY)*

A Tiffany Favrile glass and bronze 'Dogwood' border lamp, c1910, 23½in (59.5cm) high.
£12,000–15,000 *S(NY)*

A Tiffany Favrile glass and bronze 'Poinsettia' border lamp, c1910.
£17,000–20,000 *S(NY)*

A Tiffany Favrile glass and bronze 'Lily' lamp, c1915, 25in (63cm) high.
£14,000–17,000 *S(NY)*

A Tiffany Favrile glass and bronze 'Cyclamen' lamp, c1910.
£15,000–18,000 *S(NY)*

A Tiffany Favrile glass and gilt bronze 'Lily' lamp, inscribed and impressed marks, 23in (58.5cm) high.
£25,000–30,000 *S(NY)*

A Tiffany Favrile glass and bronze 'Lotus' lamp, c1915, 25in (63.5cm) high.
£17,000–23,000 *S(NY)*

r. A Tiffany Favrile glass and bronze 'Turtle-back' tile standard lamp, c1915, 67½in (170cm) high.
£13,500–17,000 *S(NY)*

A Tiffany Favrile glass and bronze 'Turtle-back' tile geometric chandelier, shade impressed 'Tiffany Studios/New York', c1915, 20in (51cm) high.
£8,000–10,000 *S(NY)*

Tiffany lamps

Tiffany table lamps were made in two sections: the base and stem, and the shade. Shades consist of many pieces of favrile (meaning hand-made) glass set in a bronze framework of irregular lozenge shapes, with decoration often inspired by organic and naturalistic motifs. Dragonflies are common, as are Renaissance, zodiacal, bamboo and medieval motifs. Bases are bronze or gilt-bronze, and often incorporate tile or mosaic work. Shades are sometimes crimped to resemble silk, others have pierced bronze bases with glass blown into the frames. Larger leaded shades may have supporting struts on the interior. Being handmade, no two shades are identical.

A Tiffany Favrile glass and gilt-bronze 'Turtle-back' tile geometric lamp, c1915, 26in (66cm) high.
£10,000–12,000 *S(NY)*

A Tiffany Favrile glass and bronze 'Dragonfly' lamp, impressed marks, c1910, 21in (53.5cm) high.
£17,000–20,000 *S(NY)*

A Cameo glass table lamp, the conical shade acid etched with pendant branches of honeysuckle, shade and base signed in cameo 'Gallé', 8½in (21.5cm) high.
£5,000–6,000   *P*

A copper and mica table lamp, the base of trumpet form, stamped 'Dirk van Erp', c1915, 22in (56cm) high.
£8,000–12,000   CNY

An earthenware and glass table lamp, by Fulper, the shade of mirrored black glaze over green flambé inset with leaded glass, base and shade marked, 15½in (39.5cm) high.
£6,000–7,500   CNY

A 'Woodbine' leaded glass chandelier, impressed 'Tiffany Studios New York 2-609', 27in (68.5cm) diam.
£25,000–30,000   CNY

A 'Trumpet Vine' double overlay and etched glass table lamp, with cameo signature 'Gallé', 26½in (67.5cm) high.
£10,000–12,000   CNY

A 'Hanging Head Dragonfly' leaded glass and bronze table lamp, shade and base impressed 'Tiffany Studios New York, 1507', and '7984', 32½in (82.5cm) high.
£25,000–30,000   CNY

An 'Oriental Poppy' glass and bronze floor lamp, impressed 'Tiffany Studios New York 2404 and 378', 76in (193cm) high.
£80,000–100,000   CNY

l. A 'Woodbine' leaded glass and bronze table lamp, the shade and base stamped 'Tiffany Studios New York', 21in (53.5cm) high.
£20,000–25,000   CNY

A copper and mica table lamp, stamped 'Dirk van Erp', c1910, 25½in (65cm) high.
£20,000–25,000   CNY

A 'Turtle-back' tiled, leaded glass and bronze table lamp, stamped 'Tiffany', 22in (56cm) high.
£12,000–14,000 *CNY*

A 'Laburnum' leaded glass and bronze table lamp, stamped 'Tiffany Studios New York, 397', 27in (68.5cm) high.
£50,000–60,000 *CNY*

A 'Daffodil' leaded glass and bronze table lamp, stamped 'Tiffany Studios', 22in (56cm) high.
£10,000–12,000 *Bon*

A Favrile glass and bronze table lamp, small repair, stamped 'Tiffany Studios D856', 25in (63.5cm) high.
£7,000–8,500 *CNY*

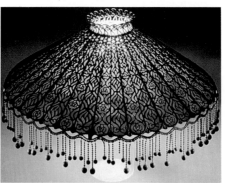

A leaded glass and filigree bronze lamp shade, by Tiffany Studios, 19in (48.5cm) diam.
£4,000–5,000 *CNY*

A Tiffany Favrile 'Lily' glass and bronze twelve-light table lamp, 19½in (49.5cm) high.
£20,000–25,000 *CNY*

r. A Tiffany 'Turtle-back' tile and bronze chandelier, 27in (68.5cm) diam.
£10,000–12,000 *CNY*

A 'Wisteria' leaded glass and bronze table lamp, stamped 'Tiffany Studios New York, 7806', 27½in (70cm) high.
£85,000–100,000 *CNY*

r. A 'Magnolia' leaded glass and bronze lamp, stamped 'Tiffany Studios', 77½in (197cm) high.
£150,000–200,000 *CNY*

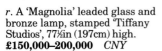

l. A carved and acid etched glass triple overlay table lamp, engraved 'Gallé', 23½in (59.5cm) high.
£10,000–15,000 *Bon*

r. An applied, carved and etched glass table lamp, shade carved 'Daum Nancy', 14in (35.5cm) high.
£16,000–20,000 *Bon*

A 'Peacock' table lamp, the base impressed 'Tiffany Studios New York 23923', 26in (66cm) high.
£50,000–60,000 *CNY*

A 'Magnolia' leaded glass and bronze floor lamp, the shade impressed 'Tiffany Studios New York 1599', the base cast with a band of leaves and impressed, numbered '379', 80in (203cm) high.
£150,000–180,000 *CNY*

A 'Peony' leaded glass and bronze table lamp, by Tiffany & Co, the shade and base impressed with maker's marks and numbered '1505' and '550' respectively, 31in (78.5cm) high.
£65,000–75,000 *CNY*

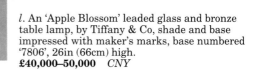

l. An 'Apple Blossom' leaded glass and bronze table lamp, by Tiffany & Co, shade and base impressed with maker's marks, base numbered '7806', 26in (66cm) high.
£40,000–50,000 *CNY*

A 'Dragonfly' leaded glass and gilt-bronze table lamp, stamped 'Tiffany Studios New York', 23in (58.5cm) high.
£17,000–20,000 *CNY*

A Handel reverse-painted glass and cold-painted metal lamp, c1920.
£8,000–10,000 *S(NY)*

A Handel reverse-painted glass and patinated-metal lamp, c1915.
£3,500–4,500 *S(NY)*

A leaded glass and bronze table lamp, 'Favrile Fabrique', by Tiffany Studios.
£7,000–8,500 *CNY*

A Handel reverse-painted glass and patinated-metal lamp, c1920.
£8,000–10,000 *S(NY)*

A leaded glass and bronze floor lamp, by Tiffany Studios.
£8,000–10,000 *CNY*

A Tiffany Favrile and bronze 'Poinsettia' border lamp shade and base, c1910.
£15,000–20,000 *S(NY)*

A Tiffany Favrile glass and bronze 'Peony' lamp, c1910, 23in (58.5cm) high.
£40,000–55,000 *S(NY)*

A Tiffany Favrile glass and gilt-bronze 'Poppy' filigree lamp, c1920.
£25,000–30,000 *S(NY)*

l. A Pairpoint reverse-painted glass 'Scenic Seagull' lamp, c1915, 25in (63.5cm) high.
£3,500–4,500 *S(NY)*

A Gallé carved and acid etched double overlay table lamp, carved signature, 25½in (65cm) high.
£10,000–12,000 *C*

A Gallé carved, acid etched and fire polished double overlay table lamp, 23in (58.5cm) high.
£22,000–26,000 *CNY*

A double overlay and etched glass table lamp and shade, both parts signed 'Gallé' in the overlay, 10½in (26.5cm) high.
£8,000–9,000 *HFG*

A double overlay and etched glass table lamp, cameo signature 'Gallé', 22in (56cm) high.
£8,000–10,000 *CNY*

An overlaid and etched glass table lamp, cameo signature 'Gallé' on shade and base, 20in (51cm) high.
£12,000–15,000 *CNY*

A double overlay and etched glass table lamp, with original bronze mounts, cameo signature 'Gallé' on shade and base, 30in (76cm) high.
£70,000–85,000 *CNY*

A 'Dragonfly' leaded glass and bronze table lamp, shade and base stamped 'Tiffany Studios', 18in (45.5cm) high.
£30,000–40,000 *CNY*

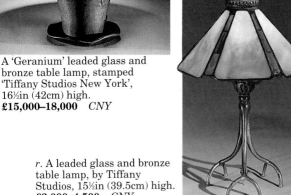

A 'Geranium' leaded glass and bronze table lamp, stamped 'Tiffany Studios New York', 16½in (42cm) high.
£15,000–18,000 *CNY*

A Favrile glass and metal table lamp, stamped under fuel canister 'Tiffany Studios', 20½in (52cm) high.
£8,000–9,500 *CNY*

r. A leaded glass and bronze table lamp, by Tiffany Studios, 15½in (39.5cm) high.
£3,000–4,500 *CNY*

r. An 'Autumn Leaf' leaded glass and bronze table lamp, by Tiffany Studios, 31in (78.5cm) high.
£25,000–30,000 *CNY*

A Daum etched glass and copper lamp, shade and base, engraved 'Daum Nancy France', 1920s, 16½in (42cm) high.
£3,500–4,000 *S*

A pâte-de-verre and wrought-iron tree lamp, by G. Argy-Rousseau, base and shade signed, 1926, 14½in (37cm) high.
£7,000–8,500 *S(NY)*

A Favrile 'Lily' ten-light glass and bronze table lamp, by Tiffany Studios.
£14,000–18,000 *CNY*

A Daum etched and enamelled glass table lamp, signed on base, 12½in (32cm) high.
£6,000–7,500 *CNY*

A Tiffany Studios 'Lotus' bell leaded glass and bronze table lamp, base stamped 'Tiffany Studios New York 6874', 18in (45.5cm) high.
£14,000–16,000 *CNY*

A Le Verre Français cameo glass and wrought-iron mushroom lamp, 1920s.
£1,600–2,000 *S*

A Daum etched glass and wrought-iron chevron lamp, shade and base, engraved mark 'Daum Nancy France', 1920s, 12in (30.5cm) high.
£4,000–5,000 *S*

A pair of Albert Cheuret gilt-bronze and alabaster tulip lamps, each inscribed, c1925.
£6,000–7,500 *S(NY)*

A Pairpoint reverse painted blown out and patinated metal boudoir lamp, c1920.
£2,500–3,000 *S(NY)*

A Daum etched, applied and wheel carved 'snail' vase, 10½in (27.5cm) high.
£8,000–12,000 *CN*

LOUIS COMFORT TIFFANY & TIFFANY STUDIOS

Associated mostly with his leaded glass table lamps and windows, Louis Comfort Tiffany's talent and restless energies led him into numerous disciplines within the decorative arts, including windows, lamps, vases, enamels, ceramics, bronzes, fancy goods, art jewellery, paintings and mosaics. Objects manufactured at Tiffany Studios were of the highest artistic and technical level and were produced in a variety of shapes and designs, incorporating a mixture of materials such as bronze, mosaic, enamel and glass.

For well over twenty years, prices for Tiffany Studios objects have continued to strengthen in the art market, mostly thanks to the auction house which has played an integral role in establishing prices. Auctions, traditionally the market place for dealers, began to attract private collectors from the mid-1970s. The booming economy of the late 1980s, which generated such high spirits and spending on Wall Street, exploded into the art world and sent auction salerooms into a frenzy. Spectacular prices for Tiffany lamps, generated in part by overseas purchasers, were evident both in auction rooms and through dealers. Enormous interest from Japanese buyers pushed prices for Tiffany lamps to levels never before imagined. Although the market saw a rapid decline in late 1990 as prices tumbled as quickly as they had risen, it stabilized within two years.

In 1992, Sotheby's New York sold a Tiffany leaded glass and mosaic 'Spider' lamp for $770,000 (£513,300), which established a new world record at auction. That record was broken in April 1995 when a unique model, a Virginia Creeper table lamp, sold at Sotheby's New York for $1.1 million (£733,300) – the first lamp to break the million dollar barrier at public auction. A highly important 'Cobweb' table lamp in the same sale realized $783,500 (£522,300), making it the second highest price paid at auction for a Tiffany lamp. The current record is held by Christie's New York who sold a pink 'Lotus' lamp for over $2.8 million (£1.8 million) including premium of 10%, in December 1997.

Collectors continue to favour the highly colourful floral lampshades, such as the 'Peony', 'Poppy' or 'Dogwood' models, although Arts and Crafts enthusiasts have created a solid market for the geometric and turtle-back models which complement the simplistic proportions of that style's interiors. Some of the most desirable lamps, including the 'Magnolia', 'Wisteria', 'Laburnum', 'Oriental Poppy' and elaborate 'Peony' models, rarely decrease in value, and important examples of these steadily continue to escalate in price.

Prices for Tiffany objects no longer categorize them as the bargains that they were thirty years ago, but there is still the opportunity to build good collections. Although availability of high-quality lamps and windows does make this increasingly difficult, the firm produced such a broad selection of high-quality items, including glassware, candlesticks and desk sets, that such objects can still be purchased at affordable prices.

Fakes and Reproductions

The problem of wrong attribution is commonplace for the collector and the issue of evaluating a Tiffany work of art for authenticity poses a constant concern in a market that has its fair share of fakes and forgeries. Fraudulent lamps (or 'fakes') are becoming more evident, no doubt because prices have been increasing steadily for nearly thirty years. While imitation is a recognized form of flattery, Mr Tiffany would no doubt find these imitation lamps – many bearing his trademark signature – a serious form of deception. Before purchasing a Tiffany Studios lamp (or any object that the firm produced) a wise collector must consider several points. Issues such as age, condition, material and provenance are serious factors to address when examining an object.

One must examine the glass quite carefully as no one, despite many attempts, has yet been able to achieve quite the qualities that Tiffany perfected in this medium. Condition is also an important factor when considering a lamp. Due to their age and fragility, many shades have cracks in the glass. While minor cracks do not affect a lamp's value, a shade which has numerous cracks throughout the design can decrease its worth. However, a lamp that has neither cracks, dirt nor any sign of age whatsoever could possibly reveal that it is a reproduction, as Tiffany lamps should show some signs of age. Also, beware of lamps sold at prices that seem too good to be true. With the widely recorded prices for lamps today, it is very difficult (if not impossible) to find a real bargain. If one is offered a lamp for $5,000 (£3,000), when a similar one sells at auction for $20,000 (£13,000), be wary.

It is always a good idea to ask questions about the history of an object. The better the provenance, the better off one is. If it was bought through auction, ask to see the catalogue. If the lamp has ever been appraised or insured, ask to review the documentation. Knowledge and curiosity are the best tools to become a wise collector. Try to see as many authentic works as possible: museums, auction houses and reputable dealers continue to serve as good sources of study. The more lamps one sees and examines, the more one learns about the medium and the marketplace. There have been numerous books written on Louis Comfort Tiffany and Tiffany Studios that prove to be valuable references in learning about the firm's production and the techniques that were used. It is always a good idea prior to acquiring any antique of value to seek the professional advice of a recognized authority who knows the market and can offer a valuable knowledge in his/her area of expertise. **MaryBeth McCaffrey**

A Daum winter landscape glass table lamp, the mottled orange and yellow body acid etched, signed on underside of base 'Daum Nancy', 16in (40.5cm) high.
£8,000–10,000 *P*

A Müller Frères glass and gilt-bronze chandelier, the central domed glass shade of mottled pink, green, blue and white, supported by foliate bronze mounts, each shade marked 'Müller Frères, Lunéville', 27½in (70cm) high.
£1,200–1,400 *P*

A Daum cameo glass table lamp, the predominantly yellow body shading to amethyst at the edges and overlaid with streaked red, grey and blue, signed in cameo on shade and base 'Daum Nancy', 26in (66cm) high.
£12,000–15,000 *P*

l. A Daum glass table lamp, the white flecked body shading to amethyst, acid etched and painted in natural colours with violets and leaves, signed on base 'Daum Nancy', 14½in (37cm) high.
£12,000–14,000 *P*

A Gallé cameo 'Magnolia' table lamp, the amber tinted body overlaid with tones of ruby glass, acid-etched with branches of magnolia, signed in cameo on base and shade 'Gallé', 23in (58.5cm) high.
£15,000–18,000 *P*

r. A reproduction glass and bronze floor lamp, in the style of Edgar Brandt and Daum, cast as a cobra rising from a basketwork base, its neck coiled around a mottled, frosted orange glass shade with wide everted rim, 64in (162.5cm) high.
£1,500–2,000 *Bon*

l. A Müller Frères cameo glass table lamp, the glass yellow-streaked with colours, overlaid with red and brown glass, acid etched with anemones, signed in cameo 'Müller Frères, Lunéville', 29in (73.5cm) high.
£5,000–7,000 *P*

A Gallé cameo glass table lamp and shade, purple on a yellow stained and frosted ground, each piece signed 'Gallé', 13in (33cm) high.
£5,000–6,000 *HAM*

A leaded glass lampshade, attributed to Tiffany, 12in (30.5cm) high.
£1,200–1,400 *P*

An Almeric Walter pâte-de-verre panel, mounted as a table lamp, the amber glass tinged with amethyst, moulded decoration of fish and seaweed, fitted for electricity, moulded signature 'A. Walter Nancy', 8½in (21.5cm) high.
£3,000–3,500 *C*

A Tiffany-style pewter table
lamp, stamped on base 'C. I. D.',
26in (66cm) high.
£600–700 *MPHS*

A Tiffany Studios bronze table
lamp, the semi-opaque glass
shade in yellow tones against
a variegated green ground,
stamped and applied marks,
c1900, 21½in (54.5cm) high.
£9,500–10,500 *SS*

A Tiffany Studio bronze and
leaded glass table lamp, with
'Dogwood' border, the shade
with green, pink, mauve and
blue glass panels, shade stamped
'Tiffany Studios, New York',
some damage, 22in (56cm) high.
£8,000–9,500 *SBe*

An 'Acorn' leaded glass and
bronze table lamp, by
Tiffany Studios, the shade
with segments of green and
amber glass, impressed
'Tiffany Studios, New York',
18½in (47cm) high.
£5,000–6,000 *C*

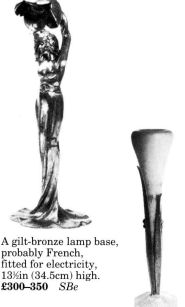

A gilt-bronze lamp base,
probably French,
fitted for electricity,
13½in (34.5cm) high.
£300–350 *SBe*

A French iron and
glass lamp, with a
mottled orange glass
centre, signed 'Roby,
Paris', c1900,
23½in (59.5cm) high.
£200–250 *SSS*

A patinated metal and glass table
lamp, the shade with panels of
cream and orange marbled glass,
25½in (65cm) high.
£400–450 *SBe*

An electroplated table lamp,
modelled in the form of
a young woman, fitted for
electricity, 18½in (47cm) high.
£250–300 *SBe*

A cut-glass biscuitière, with
silver-plated mount and
cover, 8½in (21.5cm) high.
£250–300 *SBe*

A bronze table lamp,
the leaded glass shade
streaked white and beige,
the rim with pink flowers
amid green foliage, c1900,
23in (58.5cm) high.
£1,200–1,600 *SBe*

An etched glass and wrought-iron table lamp, with mottled orange glass shade, the shade etched 'Daum Nancy, France', base stamped 'Katona', 12in (30.5cm) high.
£3,000–3,500 *Bon*

An Arts & Crafts American Prairie School wall lantern, c1900.
£300–400 *ST*

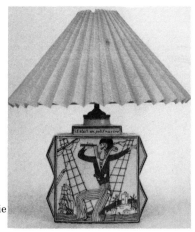

A Lallemant vase mounted as a table lamp, with polychrome painted decoration illustrating a nursery rhyme, with painted signature 'T.R. Lallemant, France', 9½in (24cm) high.
£200–250 *C*

A green patinated, bronzed metal figural lamp, on a veined marble base, inscribed 'Guerbe', stamped 'Le Verrier Paris', shade etched 'Daum Nancy, France', 15in (38cm) high.
£800–900 *Bon*

An Art Deco Limousin spelter table lamp, 16½in (42cm) high.
£200–250 *CDC*

A 'Le Verre Français' cameo glass and wrought-iron table lamp, designed by Schneider, the pale green ground overlaid and etched with thorny berry-laden branches, striped cane signature on base, 15½in (39.5cm) high.
£2,000–3,000 *C*

A Tiffany bronze table lamp base, with pineapple decoration with brown patina, stamped 'Tiffany Studios New York 366', 23½in (59.5cm) high.
£3,000–3,500 *CNY*

An American copper table lamp, in the form of a Doric column, with 2 lamp holders, the shade in leaded green glass, the stepped base marked 'Gorham Co, Q497', and trademark, 19in (48.5cm) high.
£400–500 *P(S)*

An Austrian bronze lamp, the shade set with coloured stones, c1900, 20in (51cm) high.
£500–600 *ASA*

A Tiffany Studios bronze desk lamp, the iridescent peacock blue glass shade with radiating bands of silver dots, inscribed 'L. C. T. Favrile', the base impressed 'Tiffany Studios, New York 327 11413', 15in (38cm) high.
£8,000–9,500 *CNY*

A German silvered pewter and nautilus shell desk lamp, designed as either a wall or table lamp, marked 'MH' and maker's symbol, c1900, 11in (28cm) high.
£1,500–1,800 *C*

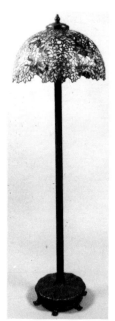

A Tiffany Studios bronze floor lamp, with 'Laburnum' pattern leaded glass shade, yellow flowers and green leaves on a blue ground, impressed mark, 63in (160cm) high.
£20,000–25,000 *CNY*

An Agate Favrile glass and bronze table lamp base, by Tiffany Studios, the deep amber body banded with blue and ochre between opalescent ribs, impressed mark, 14½in (37cm) high.
£900–1,000 *CNY*

l. A decorative gilt-metal table lamp, modelled as a maiden, on a marble base, 29in (73.5cm) high.
£600–700 *P*

A gilt-bronze table lamp, inscribed 'Raoul Larche', and impressed with the Siot Deceaville foundry seal, cast from a model by Raoul François Larche, wired for electricity, early 20thC, 17in (43cm) high.
£9,000–10,000 *CNY*

This is one of several models by Raoul Larche of 'La Loie' which were wired as table lamps. Known for her dramatic use of lighting and swirling scarves in her stage performances, Loie Fuller (1862–1928) was a great inspiration to artists in all media at the turn of the century.

An alabaster lamp, c1900, 36in (91.5cm) high.
£450–500 *SS*

A spelter figure, 'Libellule', designed as a lamp cast after a model by Auguste Moreau, printed metal tag 'Libellule par Aug. Moreau', c1900, 46in (117cm) high.
£1,200–1,400 *C*

A Sabino glass wall light, internal moulded mark, c1930, 10in (25.5cm) high.
£1,000–1,200 *SB*

A glass hanging shade, with 6 pointed shades attached to a central hexagonal body, stencilled mark 'R. Lalique', 1920s, 31in (78.5cm) wide.
£2,500–3,000 *SB*

An iridescent glass shade, with feathered panels of blue and gold lustre against a white lustre ground, engraved mark 'Quezal', c1910, 6in (15cm) high.
£150–180 *SB*

A spelter figurural lamp, partly gilded, 1930s, 24in (61cm) high.
£200–250 *F*

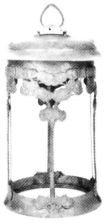

A March Bros copper hanging lantern, 15in (38cm) high.
£100–120 *P*

A bronze and ivory lampstand, 1930s, 23½in (59.5cm) high.
£800–1,000 *SKC*

An Art Deco lamp, with pewter base and hessian shade covered in plastic, 24in (61cm) high.
£50–60 *LEX*

A bronze lamp, with beaten copper shade, c1900, 23in (58.5cm) high.
£300–350 *SB*

An Art Deco alabaster, marble and spelter lamp, 1930s, 15in (38cm) high.
£100–150 *F*

A bronze figural lamp, c1900, 19in (48.5cm) high.
£800–1,000 *SB*

A bronze and glass lamp, the shade signed 'Arsoli', the bronze signed 'Zach', fitted for electricity, c1910, 30in (76cm) high.
£800–1,000 *SB*

A Lalique 'Soleil' amber glass chandelier, moulded with stylised flowerhead, with 4 original cords, moulded mark 'R. Lalique', 12in (30.5cm) high.
£800–1,000 *CSK*

A Maignan gilt-bronze lamp, signed in the maquette, foundry mark 'Eug. Blot Paris', c1900, 13½in (34.5cm) high.
£400–500 *SB*

DECORATIVE GLASS

The last twenty years have been something of a roller coaster ride in terms of keeping in touch with Art Nouveau and Art Deco glass. Rapidly rising prices, followed by the big splash of the recession when prices dropped alarmingly, have recently been followed by a steady haul back to a more level and stable situation.

Until 1985, the market leaders – Gallé, Daum, Lalique and Argy-Rousseau – were a firmly established collecting area and their pieces were already relatively highly priced. A steady year-by-year increase in both demand and value was noticeable. It was a healthy situation, so it was not entirely welcome when the second half of the 1980s saw prices accelerating so strongly that by 1989/90 it was almost a monthly occurrence. During this period, those of us actively buying and selling glass had to contend with a situation where it was never possible to replace stocks with similar pieces at similar prices. Wherever good examples were available, the prices had always increased.

It did not take long to realize what was happening. Along with the other areas of art and antiques, Art Nouveau and Art Deco glass had become a 'commodity', another form of investment. This became clear to see when dark-suited gentlemen, previously unknown to the Decorative Arts market, appeared and bought very determinedly over a short period of time, then disappeared. I shall always remember a conversation with one such gentleman when meeting him for the first time. His interest lay with Argy-Rousseau glass and he let it be known he had 'a little over 500 pieces'! Thinking he must have been collecting for a considerable time, I was dumbstruck to learn that he had, in fact, only been buying for just over a year. An amazing example, his investment in Argy-Rousseau would have been at least £1million, possibly a great deal more!

Another significant factor in this phenomenon was the spectacular auction in 1988 in London of the Elton John collection of Art Nouveau and Art Deco, which included many fine examples of glass. Buyers flew in from all over the world – thus promoting very high prices. The down-side to this situation was that prices really were rising too fast and, with hindsight, one can see that even if the recession had not brought everything to a halt, the market would inevitably have crashed through its own momentum. Towards the end of 1990 this is exactly what happened.

At this time good middle-range items in the £2,000–20,000 price bracket dropped to around 45–50% of the 1990 highs, the lowest point being reached in 1992. However, making price comparisons can only be a generalization in such a diverse and varied field, and there are many exceptions.

Least affected by the recession are the very rare pieces that exhibit important techniques or designs. For example, the 'Rose de France' vase by Gallé which incorporates the marqueterie-sur-verre technique, together with applied and carved work in high relief, an example of which recently sold for £135,000. Such rare and important items may actually have increased in value through better appreciation as a result of the middle range items no longer being over-valued. Conversely, examples of Gallé's 'Rhododendron' lamp, which reached an astonishing £250,000, have recently sold for between £60,000 and £70,000! It will always be a very beautiful lamp, but for an item produced nearly 20 years after Gallé's death (1904), an Art Nouveau 'stray' in the Art Deco period, its 1990 price was perhaps somewhat unrealistic. It may be that a finer discernment has come into play in addition to the effects of the recession.

Not until the end of 1993 could one feel any confidence that the worst was over and that prices had, at last, 'bottomed out'. It is now evident that that has happened, as once again it has become easier to anticipate the prices at which items will sell and that confirms that the market has stabilized – albeit at the new lower level of prices. Currently, middle-range items are probably up to 50–60% of 1990 values. The well-known 'Snail' vases by Daum, for example, usually sell at £8,000–12,000 as against £16,000–20,000 in 1990. However, there remain anomalies such as the 'Snail' vase which sold at Sotheby's New York in 1998 for over £60,000 which ensure that the exciting unpredictability of buying and selling at auction continues.

These same prices can also be applied to Lalique's popular 'Bacchantes' vase and 'Suzanne' figure (in opalescent glass). Glass by Argy-Rousseau was less affected due to its extra rarity and prices are probably around 70% of 1990 levels. Also less affected are those items in the £500–1,500 range, probably due to the greater number of buyers in this area.

The new lower, perhaps more realistic, level of prices is also an encouragement to new buyers who, understandably, may have been intimidated by the high figures of the late 1980s. Now, a beautiful example of Gallé or Lalique at, say, £1,500, that has been impossible to acquire for almost twice that amount, should be a very pleasing prospect to a serious collector. **Patrick Gould**

A Lalique frosted and clear glass oval dish, etched 'R. Lalique', etched script mark 'France', slight reduction at rim, 17in (43cm) wide.
£300–350 *Bon*

A Lalique black glass box and cover, 'Pommier du Japon', moulded on the top with branches of prunus blossom, the sides finely ribbed, moulded on the base 'R. Lalique' and 'Arys', 3½in (9cm) diam.
£700–850 *P*

A Lalique frosted and blue-stained perfume burner, 'Hygenie', No. 10, with original bronze base, 6½in (16.5cm) high.
£500–600 *Bon*

A Lalique 'Quatre Moineaux du Japon' frosted glass clock, electric movement by ATO, enamelled chapter ring, marked 'No. 3' and 'France', 7in (18cm) high.
£1,200–1,400 *Bon*

A Lalique black glass ring, 'Fleurs', with solid domed top and intaglio moulded with florets and stems picked out with white enamelling.
£800–1,000 *P*

A Lalique clear and satin-finished glass car mascot, 'Levrier', moulded signature 'R. Lalique, France', 2½in (6.5cm) high.
£1,800–2,200 *C*

A Lalique frosted and clear glass clock, the electric movement marked 'ATO', No. 10, 4½in (11.5cm) high.
£800–1,000 *Bon*

A Lalique frosted glass ceiling dome, 'Charmille', minor damage, 13½in (34.5cm) diam.
£800–1,000 *Bon*

A Lalique box and cover, 'Enfants', moulded with a band of naked children on a blue-stained ground, the lid moulded with 5 tiers of rose bands, stencilled mark 'R. Lalique, France', c1930, 3in (7.5cm) high.
£400–500 *S(S)*

A Lalique 'Moineaux' frosted glass clock, the electric movement marked 'ATO', No. 3, with 'France', 8½in (21.5cm) wide.
£1,200–1,500 *Bon*

r. A Lalique 'Quatre Moineaux du Japon' clock, the circular dial with black enamelled chapters, engraved 'R. Lalique, France', with chrome base enclosing light fitting, 7in (18cm) high.
£1,400–1,800 *C(S)*

l. A Lalique frosted glass vase, 'Archers', moulded with naked male archers, etched 'R. Lalique, France', 10½in (26.5cm) high. **£1,800–2,000** *P*

A Lalique enamelled vase, 'Baiez', moulded overall in shadow relief with thorny branches and berries, heightened with black enamel, moulded 'R. Lalique' on base, 10½in (26.5cm) high. **£6,000–7,000** *P*

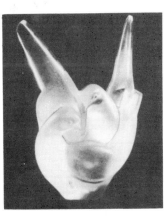

A Lalique blue opalescent glass vase, 'Ceylan', engraved 'R. Lalique, France', 9½in (24cm) high. **£1,800–2,000** *AG*

r. A Lalique 'Avallon' vase, moulded with birds, incised 'R. Lalique, No. 986, France', 5½in (14cm) high. **£800–1,000** *C(S)*

A Lalique smoky-grey glass vase, 'Archers', moulded with naked male archers, moulded 'R. Lalique', 10½in (26.5cm) high. **£1,800–2,000** *P*

A Lalique green glass vase, 'Druides', signed 'R. Lalique France No. 937', 7in (18cm) high. **£1,500–1,800** *P*

A Lalique amber glass 'Archers' vase, impressed 'R. Lalique', 10½in (26.5cm) high. **£900–1,000** *SB*

A Cristal Lalique frosted glass vase, 'Sylvie', in the form of two doves, signed 'Lalique, France', modern, 9½in (24cm) high. **£250–300** *N*

Six Lalique sherry glasses, 'Bourgueil', 3¼in (8.5cm) high. **£180–200** *CSK*

l. Three Lalique perfume bottles, for Worth, in deep blue, clear and star-moulded glass, stoppers moulded 'R. Lalique', tallest 5in (12.5cm) high. **£200–250** *S*

Two Lalique blue-tinted glass perfume bottles with stoppers, engraved 'R. Lalique', tallest 5in (12.5cm) high.
l. Petites Feuilles **£400–500**
r. Trois Guêpes **£800–1,000** *S*

A Lalique frosted and clear glass vase,
'Pierrefonds', one handle slightly ground on top,
Mk. No. 3, 6in (15cm) high.
£1,500–1,800 *Bon*

A Lalique frosted and clear glass
vase, 'Bellecour', slight damage,
Mk. No. 2, marked 'France No.
9**', 11in (28cm) high.
£3,000–3,500 *Bon*

A Lalique frosted glass vase,
'Douze Figurines avec Bouchon',
with stopper, Mk. No. 2, marked,
11½in (29cm) high.
£2,000–2,500 *Bon*

A Lalique frosted and black
stained glass lamp, 'Paons',
Mk. No. 10, 16in (40.5cm) high.
£12,000–15,000 *Bon*

A Lalique frosted glass
statuette, heightened
with sienna stain, 'Source
de la Fontaine', Mk. No. 3,
marked 'France',
28in (71cm) high.
£4,000–5,000 *Bon*

A Lalique frosted and clear glass
bowl, 'Chiens', moulded in relief
with hounds, Mk. No. 12, marked
'France', 9½in (24cm) diam.
£375–450 *Bon*

A Lalique grey frosted glass
vase and cover, 'Tourterelles',
No. 2, 11½in (29cm) high.
£2,000–2,500 *Bon*

A Lalique opalescent glass deep
bowl, 'Ondine Ouverte', moulded
with sirens, acid-etched 'R. Lalique,
France', 12in (30.5cm) diam.
£800–1,000 *CSK*

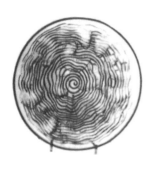

l. A Lalique opalescent glass bowl,
'Dauphins', No. 3, marked 'France',
11in (28cm) diam.
£400–500 *Bon*

A Lalique turquoise-tinted
frosted and opalescent glass
vase, 'Ceylan', No. 3, period
lamp fitting with clear celluloid
shade painted with parakeets,
18⅓in (47cm) high.
£2,000–2,500 *Bon*

A Lalique clear and satin glass car mascot, 'Longchamps', moulded signature 'R. Lalique, France', 5in (12.5cm) high.
£2,000–2,500 *C*

A Lalique clear and satin glass car mascot, 'Archer', etched 'R. Lalique France', 4½in (11.5cm) high.
£1,000–1,200 *C*

René Lalique

The work of René Lalique spans both the Art Nouveau and Art Deco periods. He began his career designing jewellery in the 1890s, and was an innovator among goldsmiths being more concerned with the crafts-manship and decorative elements of the work than its intrinsic value. His pieces at this time are recognized as the finest examples of Art Nouveau jewellery. By the 1900 Paris Exposition – 'the triumph of Art Nouveau' – the movement was actually on the wane. This, combined with the fact that he had more commissions than he could cope with and that numerous imitations of his work were appearing, made him turn elsewhere for inspiration. He found it in glass, and exhibited some pieces at the Salon in 1902. In the same year he designed a new studio and set up a workshop where his most notable cire-perdue and glass panels were produced.

A Lalique clear and satin glass plafonnier, acid stamped 'R. Lalique, France', 5in (12.5cm) high.
£1,000–1,200 *C*

A pair of Lalique opalescent glass plafonniers, each bowl signed 'R. Lalique France', 16½in (42cm) diam.
£1,800–2,000 *C*

He was introduced to commercial glass production around 1907 when François Coty asked him to design labels for perfume bottles. In fact, Lalique designed the bottles as well. These were manufactured by Legras et Cie, until he opened his own small glassworks at Combs le Ville in 1909 to cope with the demands of this and other work. After WWI he opened a larger glassworks from which the bulk of his output was produced.

A Lalique amber plafonnier, 'Saint Vincent', moulded 'R. Lalique', signed 'France', 13½in (34.5cm) wide.
£800–1,000 *C*

A yellow frosted glass plafonnier, 'Lausanne', moulded 'R. Lalique, France', 15in (38cm) wide.
£1,200–1,400 *C*

Just as Lalique had triumphed at the 1900 Paris Exposition with his Art Nouveau jewellery, so he dominated the 1925 Exposition, establishing himself as the leading exponent of mass-produced glassware. His designs by now were in the Art Deco style, but the earlier Art Nouveau influence was still apparent in some of the decorative elements. He was very much concerned with the commercial mass-production of his designs and should be remembered as much as a pioneer of mass-produced art glass as for his earlier imaginative jewellery.

A Lalique clear and satin glass car mascot, 'Perche', engraved 'Lalique France', 3½in (9.5cm) wide.
£600–750 *C*

A Lalique glass St. Christopher car mascot.
£700–850 *AAA*

Beware of full crystal items produced during the 1950s, which have intaglio-moulded signatures. Pre-WWII examples in demi crystal are not as white.

Make the most of Miller's

When a large specialist well-publicised collection comes on the market, it tends to increase prices.

Immediately afterwards, prices can fall slightly due to the main buyers having large stocks and the market being 'flooded'. This is usually temporary and does not affect very high quality items.

l. A Lalique opalescent glass vase, 'Formose', signed 'R. Lalique', 6½in (16.5cm) high.
£600–750 *C*

A Lalique brown glass vase, 'Milan', engraved 'R. Lalique, France', No. 1025, 11in (28cm) high.
£800–1,000 *C*

A Lalique amber glass vase, 'Avalon', moulded with birds, incised 'R. Lalique, France 986', c1930, 5½in (14cm) high.
£1,600–2,000 *SBe*

A Lalique cobalt blue glass pendant, 'Guepes', inscribed 'R. Lalique, France', 2in (5cm) wide.
£600–750 *C*

l. A pair of Lalique blue glass knife rests, intaglio moulded with a dragonfly, engraved 'R. Lalique', c1920, 4in (10cm) wide.
£200–250 *S*

A Lalique amber glass vase, 'Formose', impressed 'R. Lalique', c1920, 7in (18cm) high.
£2,000–2,500 *SB*

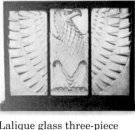

A Lalique glass three-piece panel, c1920, 11⅛in (29cm) high.
£1,800–2,000 *SB*

A Lalique glass vase, 'Oran', engraved 'R. Lalique, France', c1930, 10in (25.5cm) high.
£8,000–10,000 *SS*

A pair of Lalique glass candlesticks, damaged, 9in (23cm) high.
£1,000–1,200 *C*

A Lalique opalescent glass vase, 'Borromee', the milky body with blue staining, marked 'R. Lalique, France No. 1017', c1925, 9½in (24cm) high.
£2,000–2,500 *SB*

l. A Lalique opalescent glass inkwell and cover, 'Sirènes', moulded 'Lalique', 6½in (16.5cm) diam.
£600–750 *SB*

A Lalique glass vase, 'Marisa', with graduated bands of fish, damaged, engraved 'R. Lalique, France, No. 1002', 9in (23cm) high.
£2,500–3,000 *C*

A Lalique glass statue 'Source de la Fontaine', wheelcut 'R. Lalique France', mounted on a polished stone plinth, 22in (56cm) high.
£4,000–5,000 *Bon*

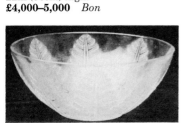

A Lalique box and cover, 'Roger', moulded with long-tailed exotic birds perched in branches among clear glass discs, engraved 'Lalique, France', c1927, 5in (12.5cm) diam.
£300–350 *S(S)*

A Lalique glass bowl, 'Filix', the deep well moulded outside with a band of large fern leaves picked out with frosting, wheel engraved 'R. Lalique, France', c1927, 13in (33cm) diam.
£300–400 *S(S)*

A Lalique frosted and clear glass vase, 'Danaides', 7in (17.5cm) high.
£1,200–1,600 *Bon*

A Lalique moulded glass vase, 'Bacchantes', in satin finished glass with blue staining, incised signature, 'R. Lalique France', c1930, 10in (25.5cm) high.
£2,200–2,600 *C*

A monumental mould blown vase, of frosted appearance, 'Palestre', with a continuous frieze of naked Olympian, 'Les Amis', engraved block capital mark 'R. Lalique', 17in (43cm) high.
£10,000–12,000 *Bon*

An amber glass shallow bowl, 'Martigues', marked 'R. Lalique', and wheel cut 'France', 14½in (37cm) high.
£1,500–1,800 *Bon*

A Lalique glass bowl, 'Calypso', decorated with 5 opalescent milky swirling mermaids, marked 'R. Lalique France', 12in (30.5cm) high.
£1,800–2,000 *GC*

A Lalique opalescent glass box and cover, 'Deux Sirènes', engraved 'France No. 43', 10½in (26.5cm) diam.
£1,200–1,600 *Bon*

A Cristal frosted glass vase, 'Bacchantes', engraved mark in script, 'Lalique', c1950, 10in (25.5cm) high.
£700–850 *Bon*

A frosted glass box, 'Paon', with a peacock perched on a bough, heightened with blue, engraved 'R. Lalique', 5in (12.5cm) diam.
£300–400 *Bon*

A Lalique box and cover, 'Libellules', marked, 7in (17.5cm) wide.
£600–750 *Bon*

r. An opalescent 'Volutes' bowl, with beads graduating inside and forming a swirling pattern, with 'R. Lalique' in upper case, 8in (20.5cm) high. **£300–400** *P(M)*

A Lalique frosted glass vase, 'Thibet', moulded with ibex, marked on the base 'R. Lalique, France', 8in (20.5cm) high. **£700–850** *P*

A Lalique blue tinted opalescent glass bowl, moulded with fishes. **£300–400** *GIL*

A frosted desk clock, 'Roitelets', the glass face surrounded by a band of wrens in flight, with Omega timepiece, stencilled 'R. Lalique France', 8in (20.5cm) high. **£3,000–3,500** *Bon*

l. A Lalique opalescent table clock, 'Inseparables No. 765', slight damage, 4⅓in (11.5cm) high. **£1,200–1,600** *Bea*

A Lalique hanging lamp, in the form of a stylized globe artichoke, 'Soustons', with blue enamelled detailing, marked on bottom 'R Lalique France', with metal rosettes, hooks and cords for suspension, 9in (23cm) high. **£500–600** *P*

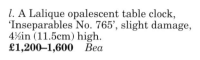

l. A Lalique opalescent bowl, 'Vase Coquilles', 9½in (24cm) diam. **£250–300** *Bea*

A clear and green stained bowl, 'Coupe Filix', moulded with broad leaves, wheel cut mark 'R. Lalique France', 13in (33cm) diam. **£300–400** *Bon*

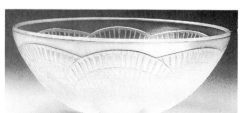

An opalescent and sienna stained dish, 'Anges', moulded in intaglio with angels, wheel cut 'R. Lalique France', 14½in (37cm) diam. **£1,600–2,000** *Bon*

A Cristal Lalique glass vase, 'Meandres', stencilled mark, 6½in (16.5cm) high. **£300–350** *S*

A Lalique opalescent dish, 'Nonnettes', 8in (20.5cm) diam. **£300–400** *ASA*

A frosted glass powder box, 'Degas', engraved mark in script 'R. Lalique, France No. 66', and moulded 'Lalique' on cover, 2½in (6.5cm) diam.
£500–600 *Bon*

A Nemours Lalique blue stained bowl, moulded 'R. Lalique France', 10in (25.5cm) high.
£400–500 *CSK*

A Lalique car mascot, in clear and satin finished glass, moulded signature 'R. Lalique France', c1930, 6in (15cm) wide.
£1,000–1,200 *C*

A glass car mascot, 'Archer', intaglio moulded 'R. Lalique France', 5in (12.5cm) high.
£750–900 *Bon*

A frosted and polished glass car mascot, 'Tête d'Aigle', relief moulded 'R. Lalique', circular base offset polished, 4½in (11.5cm) high.
£1,000–1,200

A glass car mascot, 'Hirondelle', with pale tint, relief moulded mark 'R. Lalique France', rim chip base underside, 6in (15cm) high.
£800–1,000 *Bon*

A Lalique frosted glass car mascot, 'Longchamps', moulded 'R. Lalique France', 5in (12.5cm) high.
£2,000–2,500 *P*

A Lalique frosted glass mascot, 'Vitesse', moulded 'R. Lalique France', original Breves Galleries, Knightsbridge chromed mount with coloured filter, 7in (18cm) high.
£2,500–3,000 *P*

r. A Lalique frosted glass chandelier of 12 sections, 'Hirondelles', with frosted swallows in flight suspended from a chromed rod, the 'nest' marked 'R. Lalique', 24½in (62cm) diam.
£4,000–5,000 *P*

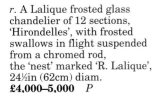

l. A Lalique 'Epis No. 1' stained glass plate, the border moulded and stained in blue with a repeated band of wheatears, with a fluted radiating centre, moulded 'R. Lalique', engraved 'France', c1922, 12½in (32cm) diam.
£100–120 *ASA*

A Lalique frosted glass car mascot, 'Petite Libellule', with moulded veining, moulded 'Lalique France', and engraved 'R. Lalique France', 6½in (16.5cm) high.
£1,800–2,000 *P*

A Lalique blue opalescent glass vase, 'Soucis', in clear and satin finished glass, acid stamped signature 'R. Lalique', 6½in (16.5cm) high.
£1,000–1,200   *C*

A Lalique glass vase, 'Coqs et Plumes', heightened with blue staining, signed 'R. Lalique, France', 6in (15cm) high.
£500–600   *P*

A Lalique vase, 'Gui', the clear satin finished glass with turquoise staining, engraved signature, 'Lalique', rim slightly ground, 7in (18cm) high.
£500–600   *C*

A Lalique frosted glass vase, 'Carmargue', acid stamped 'R. Lalique, France', 11in (28cm) high.
£2,000–2,200   *C*

A Lalique amber glass vase of amost globular form moulded in high relief with spiralling motifs, 'Tourbillon', 8in (20.5cm) high, signed 'R. Lalique, France' and 'No. 973'.
£5,000–6,000

A Lalique blue opalescent cylindrical vase, 'Alicante', satin finished glass, engraved 'R. Lalique, France', 9½in (24.1cm) high.
£3,500–4,000   *C*

A Lalique blue opalescent cylindrical vase, 'Danaides', in clear and blue satin finished glass, engraved 'R. Lalique, France, No. 972', 7in (18cm) high.
£1,800–2,000   *CEd*

A Lalique opalescent vase, 'Six Figurines et Masques', moulded and etched 'R. Lalique, France', with lamp fitting, 10in (25.5cm) high.
£3,500–4,000   *C*

A Lalique opalescent glass ashtray, with beetle design, 'Jamaique', 5½in (14cm) diam.
£250–350   *ASA*

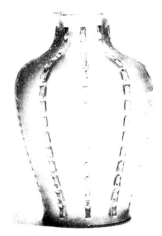

A Lalique baluster vase, 'Bandes de roses', the satin finished glass with blue staining, moulded signature, 'R. Lalique', 9½in (24cm) high.
£700–850   *C*

A clear, frosted and stained lamp, 'Poissons', with 'Pirongue' glass shade, stencilled mark 'R. Lalique France', c1931, 13in (33cm) high.
£7,000–8,500   *Bon*

A clear frosted and blue stained vase, 'Bordures Epines', with everted rim moulded with trailing thorned branches, wheel cut mark 'R. Lalique', 8in (20.5cm) high.
£500–600 *Bon*

A clear, frosted and blue enamelled vase, 'Bornes', wheel cut mark 'R. Lalique, France', 9in (23cm) high.
£2,000–2,500 *Bon*

A Lalique opalescent and frosted glass vase, 'St. François', etched 'R. Lalique', 7in (18cm) high.
£1,000–1,200 *P*

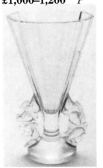

A clear and satin vase, 'Roitelets', stencilled 'R. Lalique, France', 11½in (29cm) high.
£1,000–1,200 *Bon*

A Lalique glass vase of trumpet shape, 'Epis', the sides moulded with ears of barley, with pale brown staining, marked on base 'R Lalique, France', 6½in (16.5cm) high.
£350–450 *P*

A Lalique opalescent glass vase, 'Chardons', heightened with blue staining, marked 'R. Lalique, France' on base, 7½in (19cm) high.
£600–700 *P*

A smoked glass vase, 'Béliers', moulded at the rim with a pair of stylized rams, wheel cut 'R. Lalique', 7in (18cm) high.
£1,500–1,800 *Bon*

A satin opalescent vase, 'Ronsard', the 2 handles moulded as semi-circular garlands of flowers, each enclosing a seated nude female figure, fracture to one arm, stencilled 'R. Lalique', engraved 'France', 8½in (21.5cm) high
£1,500–1,800 *Bon*

A blue stained frosted glass vase, 'Chevreuse', stencilled 'R. Lalique, France', 6½in (16.5cm) high.
£500–600 *Bon*

A clear and frosted glass vase, 'Yvelines', the handles moulded with deer, etched 'R. Lalique, France', 8in (20.5cm) high.
£700–800 *Bon*

A frosted, clear and green stained vase, 'Camées', relief moulded 'R. Lalique', 10in (25.5cm) high.
£3,500–4,500 *Bon*

A Lalique glass vase, 'Fougère', heightened with blue staining, signed on base 'R. Lalique', 9in (23cm) high.
£850–1,000 *P*

A Lalique opalescent glass vase, engraved mark 'R. Lalique France', c1920.
£550–650 *SB*

A Lalique opalescent glass vase, 'Poissons', detailed with green stain, moulded mark 'R. Lalique', c1920, 9½in (24cm) high.
£1,800–2,000 *SB*

A Lalique frosted glass dahlia perfume bottle, c1930, 7in (17.5cm) high.
£200–250 *MT*

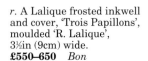

r. A Lalique frosted inkwell and cover, 'Trois Papillons', moulded 'R. Lalique', 3½in (9cm) wide.
£550–650 *Bon*

A drinking set, 'Hespérides', with electroplated carrying basket, the glass with acid-stamped signature 'R. Lalique', jug 8½in (21.5cm) high.
£1,000–1,200 *C*

A set of 6 clear glass footed beakers, moulded with bands of leaping fish stained in blue, stencilled 'R. Lalique', 3½in (9cm) high.
£400–500 *CSK*

l. A clear and sepia-stained claret jug and stopper, 'Satyre', the handle moulded as a satyr mask with horns, etched script mark 'R. Lalique pour Cusenier', 9½in (24cm) high.
£750–850 *Bon*

A 17-piece drinking set, 'Strasbourg', with moulded motif incorporating 2 male nudes, with acid-stamped and engraved signatures 'R. Lalique, France, No. 5084'.
£1,500–1,800 *C*

r. A plafonnier, with gilt-metal mounts and suspension chains, damaged, moulded signature 'R. Lalique', 20½in (52cm) diam.
£2,200–2,400 *C*

A grey-stained frosted glass
vase, 'Esterel', wheel engraved
'R. Lalique, France',
6in (15cm) high.
£250–350 *C*

A frosted and opalescent bowl,
'Dauphins', signed on base
'R. Lalique, France', c1930,
3½in (9cm) diam.
£400–500 *GH*

A grey-stained opalescent vase,
'Oléron', moulded with a shoal of
leaping fish, etched script mark
'R. Lalique, France, No. 1008'.
£450–550 *Bon*

An opalescent and clear vase,
'Boutons d'Or', moulded in relief
beneath the rim with poppy
flowerheads, stencilled mark
'R. Lalique, France',
5½in (14cm) high.
£500–600 *Bon*

A Lalique opalescent vase,
'Ronces', in milky glass
with turquoise staining,
engraved mark 'Lalique',
1920s, 9in (23cm) high.
£500–600 *SB*

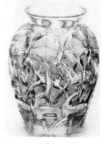

A blue stained clear and frosted
vase, 'Chamois', moulded with
panels of chamois antelope,
stencilled 'R. Lalique, France',
5½in (14cm) high.
£500–600 *Bon*

A blue stained opalescent vase,
'Tournai', moulded with vertical
panels of leafy branches,
stencilled 'R. Lalique, France',
5in (12.5cm) high.
£600–700 *Bon*

A frosted and opalescent vase,
'Pinson', moulded with sparrows
among berried branches, all above
a narrow foot, stencilled mark 'R.
Lalique', 7in (17.8cm) high.
£1,800–2,000 *Bon*

A Lalique table lamp, the clear
satin finished glass with amber
staining, etched and engraved
signature 'R. Lalique',
10in (25.4cm) high.
£5,000–6,000 *C*

l. A frosted, clear and frosted
stained vase, 'Charmille',
moulded with overlapping beech
leaves, intaglio moulded
'R. Lalique', 14in (35.6cm) high.
£1,500–1,800 *Bon*

A red-amber vase, 'Aras',
moulded on the body with crested
parakeets among berried
branches, intaglio moulded
'R. Lalique', 9in (23cm) high.
£2,600–3,000 *Bon*

A Lalique frosted and opalescent glass 'Laurier' vase, c1930, 7in (17.5cm) high.
£400–500 *MT*

A Lalique frosted glass bottle and domed stopper, 'Enfants', base rim ground and polished, 4in (10cm) high.
£250–300 *Bon*

A Lalique frosted clear and black-enamelled box, 'Roger'.
£350–450 *Bon*

A Lalique spherical frosted glass scent bottle and stopper, 'Dans la Nuit', moulded in relief with stars, the reverse stained blue, in original box, moulded 'R. Lalique', 3in (7.5cm) high.
£200–250 *CSK*

l. A Lalique clear scent bottle, 'Imprudence', designed for Worth, formed as a series of graduated discs, marked 'France', paper label 'Fatice', 3in (7.5cm) high.
£200–250 *Bon*

This bottle is sealed and contains its original contents.

r. A Lalique opalescent 'Bruce' scent bottle, 'Papillons', 7½in (19cm) high.
£1,000–1,200 *Bon*

A set of three brown-tinted Lalique scent bottles, made for D'Orsay, moulded 'R. Lalique', paper labels for 'Fleurs de France', 'Charme D'Orsay' and 'La Flambé-D'Orsay', in original fitted case, each bottle 3½in (9cm) high.
£400–500 *P*

A frosted and black-enamelled glass scent bottle, 'Parfuma' (Skyscraper) designed for Lucien Lelong, marked 'No. 10 France', in original chromed and enamelled metal case, marked 'Lucien Lelong' and 'VDSA 11876 1931', 4½in (11.5cm) high.
£2,000–2,500 *Bon*

A Lalique opalescent jade green glass vase, 'Ormeaux', moulded in relief with overlapping leaves, chips to rim and pontil, etched 'R. Lalique', No. 985, 6½in (16.5cm) high.
£1,400–1,800 *CSK*

A Lalique opalescent and frosted glass encrier, 'Quatre Sirènes', with turquoise tint, Mk. No. 6, 6½in (16.5cm) diam.
£1,000–1,200 *Bon*

r. A Lalique perfume bottle and stopper, 'Althea', base moulded, marked 'RL' and 'Brevète', 4in (10cm) high.
£1,200–1,400 *Bon*

A Lalique glass vase, 'Espalion', engraved signature, c1930, 8in (20.5cm) high.
£700–800 *SS*

A Lalique glass bowl and cover, with pink-brown tint, engraved 'R. Lalique France No. 614', c1920, 6in (15cm) high.
£800–1,000 *S*

A Lalique glass vase, 'Sauterelles', moulded with green grasshoppers on a matte blue ground, engraved 'R. Lalique', 11in (28cm) high.
£1,500–1,800 *P*

Three Lalique glass scent bottles, one in green for 'Jasmine' by Coty, moulded 'R. Lalique', c1920, 5½in (14cm) high.
£200–400 each *S*

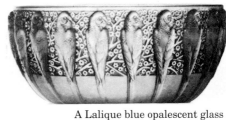

A Lalique blue opalescent glass bowl, 'Peruches', moulded with budgerigars, etched 'R. Lalique France', 9in (23cm) high.
£1,200–1,500 *CSK*

A Lalique frosted and polished glass vase, 'Martin et Pêcheurs', with green and grey staining, damaged, moulded 'R. Lalique', 9½in (24cm) high.
£1,500–1,800 *Bon*

A Lalique opalescent blue-stained vase, 'Tournesol', etched 'R. Lalique France', 4½in (11.5cm) high.
£700–850 *Bon*

A Lalique mascot, 'Coq Houdan', marked, c1920, 8in (20.5cm) high.
£800–1,000 *S*

r. A Lalique car mascot, 'Victoire', moulded mark, minor chips, c1930, 10in (25.5cm) high.
£1,800–2,200 *SS*

A Lalique brown-tinted glass scent bottle, 'Origan', made for D'Héraud, moulded on one side with the face of a girl with goat's horns, with original box, 2½in (6.5cm) high.
£800–950 *P*

A Lalique smoked glass two-handled vase, 'Caudebec', the handles moulded with flowerheads and foliage, moulded mark, 5½in (14cm) diam.
£500–600 *WW*

A Lalique opalescent glass shallow dish, 'Algues', etched mark, 14in (35.5cm) diam.
£400–600 *WW*

A grey-stained glass cendrier, 'Archers', the rim moulded with panels of kneeling archers, moulded 'R. Lalique', 4½in (11.5cm) diam.
£200–300 *Bon*

A Cristal Lalique glass paper-weight, 'Perche', in the form of a fish resting on its dorsal fin, moulded mark 'R. Lalique' and signed base 'Lalique France', 4in (10cm) high.
£180–200 *P*

A sepia stained, clear and frosted presse-papiers, 'Deux Aigles', moulded in intaglio 'R. Lalique', 3in (7.5cm) high.
£500–600 *Bon*

A Lalique glass carafe and stopper, moulded in high relief, heightened with silver grey tint, the stopper moulded with a shell-like spiral, moulded 'Lalique', engraved 'France', 14½in (37cm) high.
£800–950 *P*

A set of 6 Lalique figurines, tinted silver grey, signed 'R. Lalique France', 4in (10cm) high, in original Lalique fitted case.
£1,500–2,800 *P*

r. A Lalique blue tinted scent bottle and stopper, 'Amphitrite', inscribed 'R. Lalique, France', 4in (10cm) high.
£1,200–1,400 *Bea*

A frosted and clear glass scent bottle, 'Claire Fontaine', the stopper moulded as a spray of lily of the valley, etched 'Lalique, France', and labels with 'Made in France' and 'Cristal Lalique', c1950, 4½in (11.5cm) high.
£150–180 *Bon*

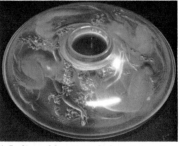

A Lalique blue tinted glass inkwell, 'Sirènes', moulded with 4 mermaids, moulded signature 'Lalique', 6in (15cm) diam.
£1,000–1,200 *P(Re)*

A Lalique amethyst and clear glass scent bottle, 'Flacon Muguet', the stopper moulded as a spray of lily of the valley in frosted and polished glass, 4in (10cm) high.
£1,800–2,200 *Bon*

r. A Lalique clock, 'Sirènes', with Swiss 8-day movement, in a milky blue panel moulded with female figures, within an onyx and malachite frame, marked 'Lalique', 5in (12.5cm) high.
£1,500–2,000 *GSP*

A Lalique glass scent bottle, 'Pan Quatre Têtes de Faunes, moulded 'R. Lalique', 1920s, 5in (12.5cm) high.
£600–700 *SB*

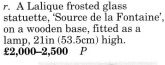

r. A Lalique frosted glass statuette, 'Source de la Fontaine', on a wooden base, fitted as a lamp, 21in (53.5cm) high.
£2,000–2,500 *P*

A Lalique opalescent and frosted glass nude female dancer, 'Thais', right hand slightly reduced, etched mark 'R. Lalique, France', 8½in (21.5cm) high.
£1,800–2,000 *Bea*

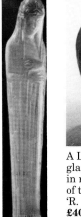

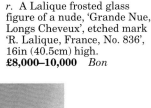

A Lalique mauve-tinted frosted glass vase, 'Nefliers', moulded in relief with leaves and blossom of the medlar tree, signed 'R. Lalique', 5½in (14cm) high.
£400–500 *P*

l. A blue glass vase, 'Epines', intaglio moulded 'R. Lalique', 9½in (24cm) high.
£1,500–1,800 *Bon*

r. A Lalique frosted glass figure of a nude, 'Grande Nue, Longs Cheveux', etched mark 'R. Lalique, France, No. 836', 16in (40.5cm) high.
£8,000–10,000 *Bon*

l. A Lalique 'Alicante' vase, blue tinted with moulded budgerigar heads and wheat ears, etched signature 'R. Lalique, France', with removable fittings for use as a table lamp, 10in (25.5cm) high.
£1,000–1,200
r. A Lalique 'Laurier' vase, in blue opalescent glass, incised mark and 'No. 947', 7in (18cm) high.
£400–500 *DN*

A Lalique frosted glass vase, 'Domrémy', moulded with a thistle design and stained in light blue, signed 'R. Lalique, France, No. 979', 8½in (21.5cm) high.
£600–700 *P*

A Lalique pale brown opaque glass vase, 'Six Figurines et Masques', signed on base, 9½in (24cm) high.
£1,500–1,800 *P(Re)*

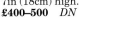

An opalescent vase, 'Dordogne', intaglio moulded and engraved mark 'R. Lalique, France', 7in (18cm) high.
£1,200–1,500 *Bon*

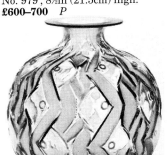

A large Lalique frosted glass vase, 'Penthièvre, signed on base 'R. Lalique France No. 1011', 10½in (26.5cm) high.
£2,500–3,000 *P*

r. A blue opalescent glass vase, 'Coquilles', etched script mark 'R. Lalique, France', 7½in (19cm) high.
£700–800 *Bon*

A Lalique blue frosted and polished glass vase, 'Peruches', moulded with budgerigars and prunus, etched mark 'R. Lalique, France, No. 876', 10in (25.5cm) high.
£6,000–7,500 *Bon*

A Lalique blue-tinted glass vase, moulded with stylised antelope, stencilled mark 'R. Lalique France', 5in (12.5cm) high.
£700–850 *Bon*

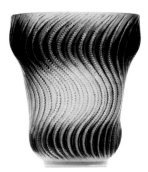

A Lalique opalescent frosted and blue tinted glass vase, stencilled mark 'R. Lalique', 9in (23cm) high.
£600–750 *Bon*

A Lalique frosted, clear and blue-tinted vase, 'Aigrettes', moulded with egrets, chips to footrim, marked 'R. Lalique, France', 10in (25.5cm) high.
£2,500–3,000 *Bon*

A Lalique opalescent glass vase, 'Salmonides', heightened with matte blue staining, impressed 'R. Lalique, France, No. 1015', 11½in (29cm) high.
£3,000–4,000 *P*

A Lalique grey-tinted frosted glass vase, 'Inseparables', moulded with budgerigars, minor damage, 13½in (34.5cm) high.
£3,000–3,500 *Bon*

A Lalique frosted, clear and sepia-tinted surtout, 'Faisan', moulded with 4 panels each with an Oriental pheasant, interspersed by slender panels with candle sconce surmounts, marked 'Lalique, France', 5in (12.5cm) high.
£750–900 *Bon*

A Lalique blue-tinted frosted glass bowl, marked 'R. Lalique, France', 9½in (24cm) diam.
£400–600 *P*

r. A Lalique opalescent glass bowl, 'Coupe Calypso', marked 'R. Lalique France', 12in (30.5cm) diam.
£1,600–2,000 *P*

A Lalique peppermint green and opalescent bowl, 'Muguet', the sides moulded with lily of the valley, stencilled mark 'R. Lalique, France', 9in (23cm) diam.
£1,800–2,000 *Bon*

A Lalique clear and frosted glass clock, 'Pierrots', stencilled 'R. Lalique, France', 5in (12.5cm) high.
£900–1,000 *Bon*

A Lalique clear and satin polished glass mascot, 'Longchamps', damaged, moulded 'R. Lalique, France', 5in (12.5cm) high.
£1,500–1,800 *Bon*

A Lalique opalescent glass statuette, 'Moyenne Voilée', engraved 'R. Lalique, France', 5½in (14cm) high.
£800–1,000 *Bon*

A Lalique clear and satin glass vase, 'Hirondelles', moulded with swallows, moulded mark and engraved 'France', c1939, 9½in (24cm) high.
£800–1,000 *C*

A Lalique glass cockerel mascot, 'Coq Nain', signed, 8in (20.5cm) high.
£400–500 *ASA*

l. A Lalique clear polished glass car mascot, 'Tête d'Eperviers', with chromium-plated base, damaged, moulded 'Lalique, France', 2½in (6.5cm) high.
£800–1,000 *Bon*

A Lalique clear, frosted and sienna tinted glass chalice, 'Vigne', damaged, engraved 'Lalique', 7in (18cm) high.
£1,500–1,800 *Bon*

l. A set of 8 Lalique wine glasses, the stems moulded with grapes, engraved 'R. Lalique, France', 5in (12.5cm) high.
£700–850 *C*

r. An opalescent and frosted glass hanging shade, 'Coquille', marked 'R. Lalique, France, No. 385', 12in (30.5cm) diam.
£400–500 *CSK*

A Lalique lamp base, 'Marisa', the milky-white glass moulded with fish, engraved 'R. Lalique, France', 9in (23cm) high.
£2,000–2,400   *C*

A Lalique plafonnier, moulded and engraved 'R. Lalique', 12½in (32cm) diam.
£600–750   *C*

l. An amber pendant, 'Colombes' with the head of a young woman, etched 'Lalique', 1½in (4cm) high.
£250–350   *Bon*

l. An opalescent pendant, 'Muguet', with a spray of lily of the valley, moulded 'Lalique', 1½in (4cm) long.
£250–350   *Bon*

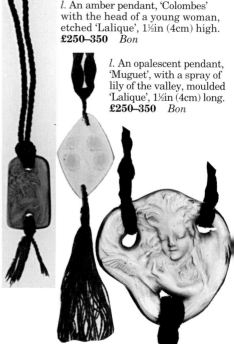

A frosted glass hanging shade, 'Acanthus', inscribed 'R. Lalique, France', 18in (45.5cm) diam.
£800–1,000   *CSK*

r. A glass pendant, moulded with a woman and a dove, engraved signature 'R. Lalique, France'.
£400–500   *C*

l. A clear and frosted scent bottle, 'Tulipes', with traces of sienna staining, moulded 'R. Lalique, France', 3in (7.5cm) high.
£300–350   *Bon*

A blue-stained, frosted and clear decanter, 'Carafe Coquilles', engraved 'R. Lalique, France', with applied retailer's label, 13½in (34.5cm) high.
£600–750   *Bon*

A mirror-pendant, 'Naiade', the white metal mounted glass with a sea-sprite, the reverse with bevelled edged mirror, the frame stamped 'Lalique', 3½in (9cm) long.
£400–500   *C*

l. A frosted pendant, in the form of a perfume amphora, engraved 'R. Lalique, 1½in (4cm) high.
£1,200–1,400   *Bon*

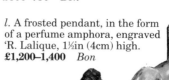

A frosted glass atomizer, with gilt-metal collar and plunger, marked 'Lalique, France', 3½in (9cm) wide.
£200–250   *P*

r. An amber-stained scent bottle and stopper, 'Pan', with moulded signature 'R. Lalique' inscribed 'Lalique', 5in (12.5cm) high.
£700–850   *C*

l. A frosted glass atomiser, enamelled in orange, moulded 'R. Lalique, France', mounts stamped 'Le Parisien', 5½in (14cm) high.
£400–500   *CSK*

An amber glass pendant, 'Guepes', engraved 'R. Lalique', 2½in (6.5cm) high.
£400–500   *Bon*

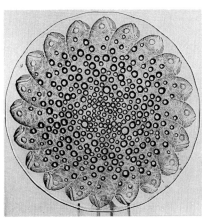

A Lalique clear blue-stained glass dish, 'Roscoff', the underside moulded with radiating fish, the centre with a myriad of bubbles, engraved 'R. Lalique France', 14in (35.5cm) diam.
£700–850 *Bon*

A Lalique glass pendant, 'Narcisse Debout', in a white metal frame, the foil-backed and black-stained glass with relief decoration of a nymph in a landscape, the reverse with mirror, engraved 'R. Lalique France', 3in (7.5cm) high.
£400–500 *C*

A Lalique dark blue frosted glass dish, 'Phalènes', moulded to the underside with a stylized flower, the rim moulded in intaglio with moths, slight reduction to rim, wheel cut 'R. Lalique France', 15in (38cm) diam.
£1,200–1,400 *Bon*

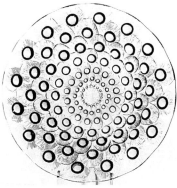

A Lalique opalescent glass dish, 'Plumes de Paon', the underside moulded with a peacock feather, engraved 'R. Lalique France', 12in (30.5cm) long.
£400–500 *Bon*

A Lalique glass pendant in white metal frame, the gold foil-backed and black-stained glass with relief decoration of a maiden's face framed with flowers, the reverse with mirror, the frame stamped 'Lalique', 3in (7.5cm) high.
£600–750 *C*

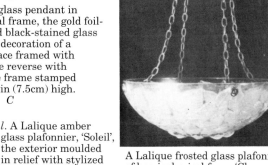

A Lalique green glass brooch, 'Sauterelles et Cabochons', signed 'Lalique', 3in (7.5cm) long.
£1,600–2,000 *CNY*

A Lalique frosted glass plafonnier of hemispherical form, 'Charmes', moulded with overlapping beach leaves, the suspension chain and ceiling rose, moulded 'R. Lalique', 13½in (34.5cm) diam.
£700–850 *CSK*

l. A Lalique amber glass plafonnier, 'Soleil', the exterior moulded in relief with stylized sunburst motifs, small chip to rim, moulded 'R. Lalique', 12in (30.5cm) diam.
£800–1,000 *CSK*

l. A Lalique black opaque glass pendant, moulded with 2 panels of wasps, heads facing inwards and with down-curved bodies, engraved 'R. Lalique', 2in (5cm) long.
£700–800 *Bon*

r. A Lalique frosted glass plaffonier, 'Stalactites', moulded as icicles, minor chips, wheel cut 'R. Lalique', 10½in (26.5cm) diam.
£800–1,000 *CSK*

A Lalique clear and frosted glass chandelier, 'Charmes', moulded 'R. Lalique', 14in (35.5cm) diam.
£900–1,100 *CNY*

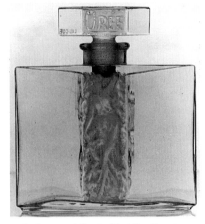

A black glass scent bottle and stopper, moulded at each corner with a woman, moulded mark 'Lalique, Ambre d'Orsay', original box, 5in (12.5cm) high.
£800–1,000 *CSK*

A clear and frosted bottle, the stopper moulded with the words 'Orée, Claire Paris', engraved 'Lalique' on stopper, 3in (7.5cm) high.
£1,200–1,400 *Bon*

A black glass bottle, the central panel moulded with 'Le Parfum NN Forvil', and 'R. Lalique', 3½in (9cm) high.
£3,000–4,000 *Bon*

A clear and frosted glass scent bottle and stopper, 'Amphytrite', traces of brown staining, moulded marks 'Lalique', 4in (10cm) high.
£1,200–1,400 *CSK*

A clear and russet stained bottle, 'La Belle Saison', for Houbigant, moulded 'R. Lalique', 5½in (14cm) high.
£800–1,000 *Bon*

A clear glass scent bottle for Molinard, 'Le Baiser du Faune', outer ring for scent, intaglio moulded 'R. Lalique', 6in (15cm) high.
£1,800–2,000 *Bon*

r. A cologne bottle 'Fleurettes', the stopper decorated with a blue stained flower border, damaged, moulded signature 'Lalique', 8in (20.5cm) high.
£300–400 *C*

A clear glass scent bottle, 'Paquerettes', with tiara stopper for Roger et Gallet, stopper moulded 'Lalique', 4in (10cm) high.
£1,800–2,000 *CSK*

r. A glass perfume bottle, 'Roses' for d'Orsay, the stopper in the form of a maiden, moulded 'Lalique' with extended 'L', 4in (10cm) high.
£800–1,000 *P*

r. A frosted glass seal, 'Souris', damaged, engraved 'R. Lalique, France, No. 185', 4½in (11.5cm) high.
£1,500–1,800 *Bon*

A Lalique hanging light, 'Boule de Gui', composed of 2 hemispherical and 8 rectangular glass panels, linked by metal rings to form a globe, moulded with mistletoe, wired for electricity, 17½in (44.5cm) high.
£5,000–6,000 *C*

A frosted plafonnier, 'Deux Sirènes', moulded with 2 water nymphs, their hair forming streams of bubbles, with matching ceiling rose, moulded 'R. Lalique', 15½in (39.5cm) diam.
£2,000–2,500 *Bon*

An opalescent glass and chromium-plated metal table lamp, 'Coquilles', moulded with 4 clam shells, suspended from a C-shaped mount on stepped circular base, wheel cut 'R. Lalique France', 12in (30.5cm) high.
£400–500 *Bon*

l. A frosted glass vase, 'Druids', moulded with entwined mistletoe and polished clusters of berries in relief, moulded to base, 'R. Lalique', 7in (18cm) high.
£500–600 *P*

A vase, 'Laurier', with raised leaves and berries in blue, etched near the base 'R. Lalique', 7in (18cm) high.
£500–600 *P(M)*

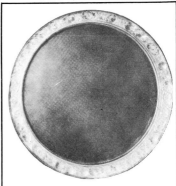

A rare early frosted mirror, 'Anemones', moulded with flowerheads, with metal easel support, impressed 'Lalique', 15in (38cm) diam.
£3,000–3,500 *Bon*

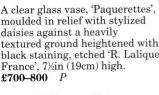

A clear glass vase, 'Paquerettes', moulded in relief with stylized daisies against a heavily textured ground heightened with black staining, etched 'R. Lalique France', 7½in (19cm) high.
£700–800 *P*

A clear and frosted vase, 'Annecy', moulded with alternating waved and serrated horizontal bands, stencilled 'R. Lalique France', 6in (15cm) high.
£400–500 *Bon*

A turquoise stained vase, 'Oursin', the clear and satin finished glass moulded with protruding bubbles, with acid stamped signature 'R. Lalique France', 7½in (19cm) high.
£600–750 *C*

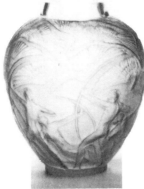

l. A grey stained vase, 'Archers', moulded with archers and eagles, engraved signature 'R. Lalique France', 10½in (26cm) high.
£1,800–2,000 *C*

r. An opalescent, clear and blue stained ashtray, 'Cendrier Statuette', with a miniature 'Source de la Fontaine' figure, etched 'R. Lalique', 4½in (11.5cm) high.
£500–600 *Bon*

A Lalique black glass seal, 'Bleuet', on solid base and moulded with cornflowers, heightened with green staining, with metal base engraved with monogram, signed on edge 'R. Lalique', 2in (5cm) high.
£200–250 *P*

A Lalique opalescent glass plafonnier, 'Deux Sirènes', converted into a table lamp, comprising an oval marble base of 4 chrome bun feet, surmounted by semi-circular shade in chrome metal mount, minor chips, 15½in (39.5cm) high.
£700–850 *CSK*

A Lalique opalescent glass vase, 'Ceylan', moulded in relief with 4 pairs of lovebirds perched amid prunus blossom, heightened with blue staining, etched 'R. Lalique France,' complete with original mica shade of octagonal outline painted with lovebirds amid berried boughs, and with detachable electrical mount, 20in (51cm) high.
£2,000–2,500 *P*

A set of 6 Lalique conical wine glasses, 'Strasbourg', the stems moulded in relief with 2 naked figures gripping hands, stencil etched 'R. Lalique', 6in (15cm) high.
£300–350 *P*

A Lalique clear glass oval fruit dish, 'Saint Gall', with folded over rim, the underside moulded in relief with swags of bubbles, and 4 matching candlesticks with detachable nozzles, acid stamped 'R. Lalique', damaged.
£400–500 *CSK*

A Lalique vase, 'Aigrettes', chipped, 10in (25.5cm) high.
£400–500 *SS*

A Lalique glass vase, 'Ricquewihr', the clear glass decorated with horizontal banding moulded with grapes and vines, heightened with brown staining, marked 'Lalique' in block letters, 5in (12.5cm) high.
£400–500 *P*

l. A Lalique hand mirror, 'Narcisse Couché', moulded with a panel depicting narcissus gazing into a pool, with foliate panels forming the surround later, signed 'R. Lalique', 11½in (29cm) long.
£1,200–1,400 *P*

r. A pair of misty grey opaque vases, 'Aigrettes', with high relief of birds of paradise, inscribed 'R. Lalique France, No. 988', 10in (25.5cm) high.
£1,800–2,000 *BA*

A set of 4 Lalique blue, green, amber and frosted glass menu holders, moulded 'Lalique', hallmarks for Birmingham 1924, 2in (5cm) high.
£400–500 *P*

A pair of silvered bronze table mirrors, produced for Van Cleef & Arpels, c1925, 20in (51cm) high.
£2,000–2,500 *P*

l. A frosted seal, 'Figurine Mains Jointes', etched 'R. Lalique', 3½in (9.5cm) high.
£500–600 *Bon*

A Lalique clear glass scent bottle, for Worth, 'Requête', the stopper moulded with 'W', moulded 'Lalique, France', 3½in (9cm) high.
£300–350 *Bon*

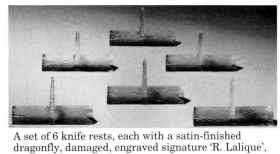

A set of 6 knife rests, each with a satin-finished dragonfly, damaged, engraved signature 'R. Lalique', 4in (10cm) long.
£600–750 *C*

A glass and metal hand mirror, 'Deux Figurines', stamped on metal 'Lalique', 12in (30.5cm) long, in original case.
£1,500–1,800 *P*

A black polished glass seal, 'Tête d'Aigle', engraved 'R. Lalique, France No. 175', 3in (7.5cm) high.
£600–750 *Bon*

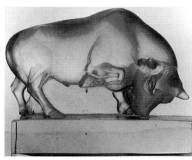

A clear and frosted paperweight, 'Taureau', stenciled 'R. Lalique, France', 3½in (9cm) high.
£300–350 *Bon*

l. A frosted table decoration, 'Perdrix', moulded as a French partridge, stencilled 'R. Lalique, France', 7in (18cm) high.
£400–500 *Bon*

A clear and frosted vase, 'Faune', the stem moulded as the head of Bacchus, 2 exaggerated horns forming curved handles, stencilled 'R. Lalique, France', 12½in (32cm) high.
£800–1,000 *Bon*

A Gallé bottle and stopper, enamelled with small polychrome flowers on gilt stems, repeated on the button stopper, crack to neck, painted mark 'Emile Gallé', c1900, 4in (10cm) high.
£800–1,000 *S(S)*

A Gallé carved, acid etched and enamelled cameo vase, the pale amber glass with polychrome striations, overlaid with dark amber vines, with green enamel decoration, carved signature 'Gallé', 9in (23cm) high.
£1,000–1,200 *C*

l. A Gallé vase, overlaid in green and brown and etched with seed pods and leaves, cameo signature, c1900, 5in (12.5cm) high.
£300–350 *S(S)*

A Gallé cameo glass vase, yellow tinted grey glass body overlaid in shades of sealing wax red, cameo mark 'Gallé', c1900, 9in (23cm) high.
£1,500–1,800 *S*

A pair of Gallé cameo glass vases, with brown foliage on an amber ground, signed, 20½in (52cm) high.
£1,200–1,400 *SWO*

A Gallé cameo vase, overlaid in red on a yellow ground, signed, 7in (18cm) high.
£300–350 *SWO*

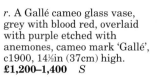

A Gallé cameo glass vase, pink tint overlaid in pale purple and green, cameo mark 'Gallé' with star, c1904, 10½in (26.5cm) high.
£900–1,100 *SB*

r. A Gallé cameo glass vase, grey with blood red, overlaid with purple etched with anemones, cameo mark 'Gallé', c1900, 14½in (37cm) high.
£1,200–1,400 *S*

A Gallé cameo glass vase, in grey glass tinted with pink, dark red-brown and blue, incised mark 'Gallé', c1900, 7½in (19cm) high.
£1,000–1,200 *S*

A Gallé enamelled and etched green glass bottle vase, pink, mauve and white, marked, 10½in (26.5cm) high.
£800–1,000 *CSK*

A Gallé cameo glass oviform vase, signed in cameo 'Gallé', 10in (25.5cm) high.
£1,200–1,400 *P*

A Gallé triple overlay mould-blown glass vase, of flared baluster form, the transluscent yellow ground overlaid in red, chestnut and burgundy etched with lilies, cameo signature 'Gallé', 14½in (36.5cm) high.
£25,000–30,000 *CNY*

A Gallé marine cameo glass vase, the lemon-tinted body with inky blue striations and overlaid with orange glass acid-etched with seaweeds and a snail, signed in cameo 'Gallé', 9½in (24cm) high.
£2,600–3,000 *P*

A Gallé double overlay etched glass vase, the transparent ground overlaid in pink and green etched with umbelliferous plants, intaglio signature 'Gallé', 7½in (19cm) wide.
£1,200–1,400 *CNY*

l. A Gallé cameo glass vase, with pale yellow metal cased in deep blue and carved with bleeding hearts, cameo signature and retailer's label, c1900, 5½in (14cm) high.
£600–750 *SS*

A Gallé cameo vase, green
tinted and overlaid with orange
and brown, signed in cameo
'Gallé', 6in (15cm) high.
£500–600 *P*

A Gallé cameo vase, coral and
green overlaid in green and
brown, etched with trees,
cameo mark, 8in (20.5cm) high.
£700–850 *CSK*

A Gallé double
overlay glass
vase, the grey
ground overlaid
with blue, green
and amethyst,
cameo mark,
8in (20.5cm) high.
£800–1,000 *CSK*

A Gallé cameo glass landscape dish,
the amber tinted grey glass overlaid
with deep blue, cameo mark 'Gallé',
c1900, 5½in (14cm) high.
£1,800–2,000 *S*

A Gallé cameo glass lamp base,
etched with wild grass, cameo mark
'Gallé', c1900, 16½in (42cm) high.
£350–450 *S*

A Gallé fire polished cameo glass vase,
the caramel ground shading to turquoise,
overlaid and etched, cameo mark 'Gallé',
9in (23cm) high.
£1,200–1,400 *CSK*

l. A Gallé cameo glass vase,
the pink body overlaid with
orange, mauve and green
glass acid-etched with
nasturtiums, signed in cameo
'Gallé', 7½in (18.5cm) high.
£700–850 *P*

r. A cameo vase, the milky-amber
glass overlaid with purple-blue
and etched fuchsia, cameo mark
'Gallé', c1900, 5in (12.5cm) high.
£700–800 *S*

A Gallé cameo glass dish, the
body with deep inky turquoise-
blue overlaid in bright pink and
green, cameo mark 'Gallé', with
a star, c1905, 7in (18cm) wide.
£700–800 *S*

A Gallé glass perfume bottle and
stopper, smoky-brown, enamelled
and gilt, marked 'E. Gallé à
Nancy', 1880s, 4in (10cm) high.
£600–800 *S*

A Gallé enamelled glass vase in
twisted and ribbed smoked glass,
decorated in pink, green, red and
black enamel, heightened with
gilding, enamelled 'Emile Gallé à
Nancy', 1890s, 10in (25.5cm) high.
£1,200–1,400 *S*

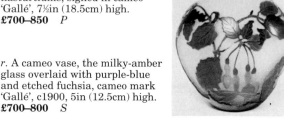

A Gallé cameo glass vase, the grey glass tinted pink, overlaid in white, deep purple and dark green, cameo mark 'Gallé' with a star, after 1904, 10in (25.5cm) high.
£700–850 *SB*

A Gallé cameo glass vase, in pink-tinted grey glass overlaid with purple, cameo mark 'Gallé', c1900, 23½in (59.5cm) high.
£2,000–2,400 *SB*

A Gallé three-colour layered cameo glass vase, c1900, 11¾in (30cm) high.
£800–1,000 *G*

A Gallé overlaid spill vase, on yellow oil ground with mauve rose decoration, 15in (38cm) high.
£1,400–1,600 *Lan*

A Gallé two-colour layered cameo glass vase, c1900, 9½in (24cm) high.
£600–700 *G*

A Gallé cameo glass vase in pinkish-grey glass, overlaid with clear amber-green, incised mark 'Gallé', c1900, 13½in (34.5cm) high.
£1,200–1,400 *SB*

A Gallé cameo landscape glass vase, overlaid with brown and lilac glass and acid etched, signed in cameo 'Gallé', 12in (30.5cm) high.
£700–850 *P*

A Gallé two-colour layered cameo glass vase, c1900, 11½in (29cm) high.
£1,000–1,200 *G*

A Gallé cameo glass vase, the greyish body overlaid with orange and deep ruby glass, acid etched and polished, signed 'E. Gallé', 17½in (44.5cm) high.
£2,000–2,400 *P*

r. A Gallé three-colour layered cameo glass vase, c1900, 10in (25.5cm) high.
£1,200–1,400 *G*

A Gallé carved cameo glass vase, in opaque milky-green glass, underside with impressed mark, 'Gallé modèle et décors déposés', c1900, 7½in (19cm) high.
£800–1,000 *SB*

An early Gallé enamelled glass vase, inscribed in gilt 'Lien d'Amour', signed in relief 'Gallé', 6½in (16.5cm) high.
£1,000–1,200 *P*

A Gallé three-colour
layered cameo glass
vase, 9in (23cm) high.
£1,200–1,500 *G*

A Gallé cameo vase, in
grey glass tinted pink at
the base, overlaid in white
lilac and green, cameo
mark 'Gallé', c1900,
10½in (26.5cm) high.
£700–850 *SB*

A Gallé three-colour
layered cameo glass
vase, c1900,
8½in (21.5cm) high.
£1,000–1,200 *G*

A Gallé three-colour
layered mould blown
'Souffle' vase, 'Clematis',
of Japanese inspiration,
c1900, 9½in (24cm) high.
£7,000–8,000 *G*

l. A Gallé two-handled
bowl, the green tinted
glass with polychrome
enamelled floral spray,
dragonfly and water lily
decoration, with gilt and
enamel borders, signed
'E. Gallé Nancy Déposé',
9½in (24cm) diam.
£900–1,100 *C*

A Gallé cameo glass vase,
in grey glass tinted pink,
overlaid in white and green,
cameo mark 'Gallé', c1900,
12in (30.5cm) high.
£1,000–1,200 *SB*

A Gallé etched and enamelled
vase, in pale green glass
overlaid in milky-green glass,
heightened with gilding,
cameo mark, 'Gallé', c1900,
3½in (9cm) high.
£700–850 *SB*

A cameo glass flask, the greyish
body overlaid with orange and
ruby glass, stopper missing,
signed 'Gallé' on a four-leafed
clover, 5in (12.5cm) high.
£500–600 *P*

A Gallé three-colour layered cameo
glass vase, 5in (12.5cm) high.
£1,200–1,400 *G*

l. A Gallé three-colour cameo
glass vase, designed with
Japanese inspiration, c1900,
10½in (26.5cm) diam.
£2,200–2,400 *G*

r. A Gallé purple glass flask,
streaked internally with yellow/grey
body, with incised signature, 'Gallé',
c1900, 5in (12.5cm) high.
£1,000–1,200 *SB*

Two Gallé cameo glass vases, with signatures, 7in (18cm) high.
£800–1,000 *DSH*

A Gallé triple overlay etched glass vase, of flattened, tapered cylindrical form with peaked rim, the translucent yellow ground overlaid in white, lime green and brown etched with a lake scene and cottages, cameo signature 'Gallé', 14in (35.5cm) high.
£1,200–1,400 *CNY*

A Gallé cameo vase, the slim body overlaid in brown and green and carved with trees in a lakeland setting on a frosted pink tinted ground, signed, 8in (20.5cm) high.
£1,000–1,200 *Bea*

A Gallé cameo glass vase, the greyish body with evidence of slight vertical ribbing, overlaid with ruby glass acid-etched with waterlily blooms, tendrils and leaves, fire-polished, etched on leaf with vertical signature 'Gallé', applied with brass rim to base, repaired, 22½in (57cm) high.
£1,000–1,200 *P*

r. An etched and double overlay glass vase, the light amber ground overlaid in green and brown, etched 'Gallé', 5in (12.5cm) high.
£500–700 *CG*

A Gallé cameo double overlay glass perfume bottle, the frosted white glass overlaid with sapphire blue and puce, cameo signature, the matching stopper etched with a dragonfly, 4in (10cm) high.
£1,000–1,200 *CNY*

r. A Gallé vase, the green and yellow ground etched, enamelled and gilded with a medallion, inscribed 'Cristallerie Emile Gallé à Nancy', 7in (18cm) high.
£4,000–5,000 *CNY*

l. A Gallé vase, the pale amber glass with gold foil inclusions overlaid with white and blue, engraved 'Gallé', 7½in (18.5cm) high.
£2,500–3,000 *C*

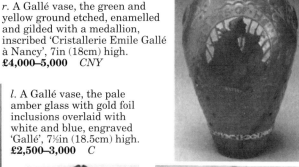

A Gallé plum triple overlay mould-brown glass vase, the translucent yellow ground overlaid with sapphire, purple and chestnut brown, cameo signature, 15½in (39.5cm) high.
£5,000–6,000 *CNY*

r. A Gallé cameo glass vase, with mountain scene in blue and brown overlaid on amber, trefoil shaped rim, signed 'Gallé', 8½in (21.5cm) high.
£1,200–1,400 *PSG*

A Gallé flask-shaped scent bottle, enamelled with stylized flowers, branches and dragonflies in yellow and green against green tinted glass, enamelled signature 'E. Gallé Nancy déposé', rim chip, 5in (12.5cm) high.
£400–500 *C*

A Gallé enamelled glass jug and stopper, chipped, enamelled signature 'E. Gallé à Nancy', 8in (20.5cm) high.
£400–500 *C*

A Gallé baluster-shaped overlay vase, minor chip to base, signed 'Emile Gallé' on a leaf, c1900, 16½in (42cm) high.
£2,600–3,000   C(Am)

A Gallé glass vase, the yellow and white ground overlaid in mauve, signed 'Gallé' in the overlay, 19in (48.5cm) high.
£1,800–2,200   C(Am)

l. A Gallé cameo glass vase, the greyish body overlaid with pale green and brown, signed in cameo 'Gallé' with star, 13½in (34cm) high.
£1,000–1,200   P

A Gallé cameo glass vase, tinted amber and overlaid with blue and amethyst glass acid etched with fir trees and mountains, signed 'Gallé' in cameo, 5½in (14cm) high.
£1,200–1,400   P

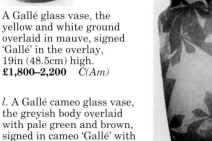

A Gallé triple overlay glass vase, the matte ground overlaid in white, ochre and green, signed 'Gallé' in the overlay, c1900, 16½in (42cm) high.
£1,500–1,800   C(Am)

A Gallé clear glass jug, enamelled in colours, base marked 'Emile Gallé déposé', 9½in (24cm) high.
£700–800   CSK

An Art Nouveau marbled frosted glass vase, signed 'Gallé', 10in (25.5cm) high.
£1,000–1,200   DSH

Above from left. A Gallé bottle vase, cameo signature, c1900, 9in (23cm) high.
£500–600
A Gallé bottle vase, with purple wisteria on yellow ground, cameo signature, c1900, 6in (15cm) high.
£500–600
A Gallé cameo glass vase, acid etched through violet overlay, cameo signature, c1900, 4½in (11.5cm) high.
£500–600
A Gallé bottle vase, yellow metal cased in lavender blue, cameo signature, c1900, 9½in (24cm) high.
£1,400–1,600   SS

A Gallé cameo glass vase, the greyish body tinted amber in places, overlaid with amethyst glass, signed in cameo 'Gallé' with star preceeding, 16in (40.5cm) high.
£1,800–2,200   P

The star preceeding the signature was used for a short time as a tribute to Gallé after his death in 1904.

A Gallé cameo glass vase, cameo mark 'Gallé', c1900, 17½in (45cm) high.
£1,800–2,200   S

A Gallé glass vase, overlaid in pink and green, etched signature in the Chinese manner 'Gallé', 6in (15cm) high.
£700–800 *CNY*

A Gallé glass vase, the white ground overlaid in light brown, signed, 9½in (24cm) high.
£1,600–2,000 *CNY*

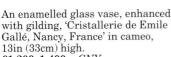

An enamelled glass vase, enhanced with gilding, 'Cristallerie de Emile Gallé, Nancy, France' in cameo, 13in (33cm) high.
£1,200–1,400 *CNY*

A Gallé four-layer cameo glass vase, signed in cameo, 14½in (37cm) high.
£2,000–2,400 *PSG*

A Gallé glass vase, the cream coloured ground overlaid in red, with cameo signature 'Gallé', 5in (12.5cm) high.
£500–600 *CNY*

A Gallé glass lamp base, blue and white overlaid in olive green and brown, cameo signature 'Gallé', 4in (10cm) high.
£700–850 *CNY*

A Gallé vase, the frosted and cream coloured ground overlaid with purple, cameo signature 'Gallé', 5½in (14cm) high.
£1,200–1,400 *CNY*

A Gallé vase, overlaid in deep brown, cameo signature 'Gallé', 5½in (14cm) high.
£700–800 *CNY*

A Gallé four-layer cameo glass vase, decorated with chrysanthemum, signed in cameo, 6in (15cm) high.
£1,500–1,800 *PSG*

A Gallé four-layer cameo glass vase, decorated with flowering clematis, signed in cameo, 6½in (17cm) high. **£1,800–2,200** *PSG*

r. A Gallé cameo glass vase, in shades of purple, brown, blue and cream, 8in (20.5cm) high.
£900–1,100 *Bea*

l. A Gallé two-layer cameo glass solifleur vase, decorated with wild flowers, signed in cameo, 7in (18cm) high.
£500–600 *PSG*

A Gallé four-layer glass vase, decorated with clematis flowers, signed in cameo, 9in (23cm) high.
£1,200–1,400 *PSG*

A Gallé four-layer cameo glass vase, decorated with flowers and leaves, signed in cameo, 9½in (24cm) high.
£2,500–3,000 *PSG*

r. A Gallé acid etched and enamelled vase, in green, amber, red and yellow, carved signature, 10½in (27cm) high.
£1,400–1,600 *C(Am)*

A Gallé cameo vase, decorated with a riverside landscape, in brown and ochre on a peach ground, 3½in (9cm) high.
£400–500   *HCH*

A Gallé plum overlay and mould-blown glass vase, the amber ground with purple pendant branches, cameo signature, 12½in (32cm) high.
£6,000–7,500   *C*

A Légras cameo vase, the milky opaque amber body overlaid in mottled pink/brown with a light iridescent sheen, cameo mark 'Légras', c1910, 20½in (52cm) high.
£700–850   *S*

A Gallé cameo glass 'Acorn' vase, in deep green mottled internally with streaks of blue/brown and bubbling overlaid in clear brown and etched, cameo mark 'Galle', c1900, 9½in (24cm) high.
£1,200–1,500   *S*

A Lalique glass box and cover, 'Meudon', heightened with pale blue staining, impressed on base 'R. Lalique', engraved 'France', 3½in (9cm) diam.
£180–220   *P*

An etched and overlay glass vase, by Charles Schneider, the milky white and pink mottled glass overlaid in claret and orange, etched 'Le Verre Français', 14in (35.5cm) high.
£700–800   *CG*

A Lalique circular glass box and cover, 'Deux Sirènes', of amber colour, moulded on cover 'R. Lalique', 10in (25.5cm) diam.
£1,500–1,800   *P*

A Lalique brooch, frosted glass over blue metallic foil, gilt-metal backing, stamped 'Lalique', c1910, 1in (2.5cm) diam.
£500–600   *S*

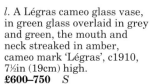

r. A Gallé cameo glass vase, the lemon coloured body overlaid and acid etched with violets on leafy stems, etched 'Gallé', 6½in (16.5cm) high.
£800–1,000   *P*

l. A Légras cameo glass vase, in green glass overlaid in grey and green, the mouth and neck streaked in amber, cameo mark 'Légras', c1910, 7½in (19cm) high.
£600–750   *S*

A Lalique circular glass box and cover, 'Rambouillet', heightened with blue/grey staining, moulded on cover 'R. Lalique', engraved on edge 'R. Lalique No. 60', 3½in (9cm) diam.
£300–350   *P*

l. A Daum glass vase, signed in gilt and with Croix de Lorraine, 4in (10cm) high.
£400–500 *Bon*

A Gallé green glass jug, enamelled in white, blue and red, inscribed 'E. Gallé Nancy', 8½in (21.5cm) high.
£700–800 *CSK*

A d'Argental cameo glass vase, in turquoise overlaid with navy, signed in cameo 'd'Argental', 6in (15cm) high.
£300–450 *Bon*

A Daum cameo glass vase, the matte streaked yellow ground overlaid in shades of purple, cameo signature 'Daum Nancy France', retailer's paper label, 19in (48cm) high.
£1,800–2,000 *C(Am)*

A Légras cameo glass vase, 'Chestnuts', 20in (51cm) high.
£800–1,000 *AA*

A De Latte cameo vase, overlaid in amber with orchids against a mottled ground signed 'De Latte, Nancy', 19½in (50cm) high.
£700–800 *C*

A Gallé enamelled and green glass jardinière, marked on base with acid etched mushroom and signed 'Emile Gallé delt, Serie C, ft', and 'déposé' in fine red script, 13in (33cm) wide.
£1,200–1,400 *P*

A Gallé oviform vase, overlaid and etched in amber, red and green with daffodils among grasses, cameo signature 'Gallé', bearing label, 13in (33cm) high.
£1,500–1,800 *C(Am)*

A Gallé cameo glass vase, tinged with yellow and pink overlaid in deep amber and decorated with acid etched and carved decoration of anemones, cameo signed 'Gallé', c1905, 10in (25.5cm) high.
£1,200–1,400 *C(Am)*

l. A Gallé cameo glass vase, the frosted white and lemon sides overlaid with deep purple, signed in cameo 'Gallé', 7½in (19cm) high.
£700–800 *Bon*

r. A Gallé cameo glass vase, rich brown ochre overlaid on an amber ground with a design of tiger lilies, signed 'Gallé', 8in (20.5cm) high.
£1,800–2,000 *PSG*

An iridescent glass vase, attributed to Loetz, covered with an all-over pulled thread design in a silvery yellow and blue, 7¼in (18.5cm) high.
£800–1,000 *CSK*

A Loetz iridescent glass bowl, designed by Michael Powolny, with ruby tones and internal crackled silver iridescence, with a pale green rim, supported on 3 black glass ball feet, 10½in (26.5cm) diam.
£600–750 *PC*

A Loetz red glass vase, with a black glass rim, the shape designed by Josef Hoffman, 9in (23cm) high.
£500–600 *P*

An iridescent glass vase, attributed to Loetz, the white glass decorated at the base with dappled pink/peacock lustre and pots of bright green with tiny metallic inclusions, the neck in dappled gold lustre, underside with faintly enamelled mark '2/219n787', 17in (43cm) high.
£300–400 *S*

An iridescent glass vase, attributed to Loetz, deep blue decorated with splashed peacock lustre, c1900, 10½in (26.5cm) high.
£300–400 *S*

A Loetz iridescent glass vase, deep ruby and peacock blue, 7in (18cm) high.
£800–1,000 *P*

A Loetz iridescent glass vase, decorated with fine blue meandering bands and random pale peacock blue/violet splashes overall, 8½in (21.5cm) high.
£400–500 *P*

A Loetz cameo glass vase, the pale lemon body overlaid with pale brown, apple green and red, signed in cameo 'Loetz', 6in (15cm) high.
£500–600 *P*

A Loetz iridescent glass shell vase, the shell splashed with a gold/green lustre, mottled surface, 9in (23cm) high.
£400–500 *Bon*

A Loetz iridescent glass vase, pale amber with internal pale peacock lustre, iridescent engraved crossed arrows mark, c1900, 12½in (32cm) high.
£600–750 *S*

A Loetz iridescent glass vase, the aubergine glass decorated with iridescent feather design, signed 'Loetz Austria', c1900, 5½in (14.5cm) high.
£800–1,000 *C(Am)*

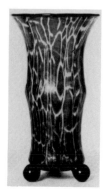

l. A Loetz iridescent vase, designed in the manner of Josef Hoffmann, the body of yellow tone covered with marbled silver blue iridescence, 9¾in (24.5cm) high.
£600–750 *P*

A Gallé etched and enamelled casket, in clear amber glass, detailed in naturalistic enamels and gilding, c1890, 6in (15cm) wide.
£2,800–3,200 *SB*

A Lalique glass powder box and cover, with traces of green staining, moulded mark 'R. Lalique, Made in France', 1920s.
£400–500 *SB*

An Art Deco wall mirror, flanked by 2 Lalique panels 'Oiseaux', each moulded with a jackdaw, 36in (91.5cm) wide.
£2,500–3,000 *P*

A Lalique glass inkwell, 'Mures', moulded on the underside with fruiting brambles, engraved 'R. Lalique France No. 431', 1920s, 6½in (16.5cm) diam.
£700–850 *SB*

A Gallé acid etched table lamp and shade, signed, mounted in bronze, with electric light fittings, 16in (40.5cm) high.
£3,000–4,000 *HSS*

A Lalique smoky grey glass ashtray, 'Souris', centred with a model of a crouching mouse, signed 'R. Lalique France', 3in (7.5cm) high.
£250–300 *P*

l. A French Art Deco table lamp and shade, with landscape decoration, by Légras, 15in (38cm) high.
£1,000–1,200 *Lan*

A Daum etched glass vase, pale blue glass etched with horizontal bands against a frosted ground, faint stencilled mark 'Daum Nancy', c1930, 9in (23cm) high.
£800–1,000 *S*

A Daum green tinted etched glass vase, with stippled banding, incised 'Daum Nancy France', 1930s, 13in (33cm) high.
£500–800 *S*

An Etling opalescent glass figure, moulded 'Etling France 141', 13in (33cm) high.
£500–650 *P*

Above left and right. A pair of green Art glass cylindrical vases, signed 'Daum Nancy', 11in (28cm) high.
£1,000–1,200
centre left. A green Art glass conical shaped vase, signed 'Daum Nancy', 8½in (21.5) wide.
£500–600
centre right. A green Art glass three-tier shaped vase, signed 'Daum Nancy', 13in (33cm) high.
£800–1,000 *DSH*

l. A Gallé cameo glass footed vase, the frosted white and light green sides overlaid with deep purple, signed 'Gallé', 4in (10cm) high.
£400–500 *Bon*

r. A Gallé cameo glass vase, overlaid in deep mauve with sprays of laburnum, cameo mark 'Gallé', c1900, 12½in (32cm) high.
£800–1,000 *L*

l. A Gallé enamelled glass vase, the clear sepia glass enamelled in tones of mustard, pink, turquoise and grey, details highlighted in gilt, etched 'Gallé', c1885, 11½in (29cm) high.
£800–1,000 *Bon*

A Gallé cameo glass vase, the frosted white sides overlaid in lime green, signed in cameo 'Gallé', 3½in (9cm) high.
£250–300 *Bon*

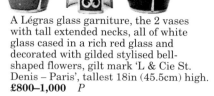

A Légras glass garniture, the 2 vases with tall extended necks, all of white glass cased in a rich red glass and decorated with gilded stylised bell-shaped flowers, gilt mark 'L & Cie St. Denis – Paris', tallest 18in (45.5cm) high.
£800–1,000 *P*

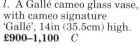

l. A Gallé cameo glass vase, with cameo signature 'Gallé', 14in (35.5cm) high.
£900–1,100 *C*

A Gallé glass vase, with overlaid ruby decoration of flowers, signed, 5in (12.5cm) high.
£300–400 *CW*

A Gallé green ground overlay vase, 'Parlante', with brown floral decoration, with a verse: 'Béni soit le coin combre où s'isolent nos coeurs', by the French Symbolist poet, Marceline Desbordes-Valmore, c1901, 12in (30.5cm) high.
£2,200–2,500 *Wor*

A Gallé cameo glass vase, with amber tinted body overlaid with 2 tones of ruby glass, signed in cameo 'Gallé', 5½in (14cm) high.
£500–600 *P*

A Müller Frères cameo glass landscape vase, pale green overlaid in amber and blue, cameo mark 'Müller Frères, Lunéville', 1900, 8½in (21.5cm) high.
£800–1,200 *S*

A Loetz iridescent pink and gold glass vase, c1900, 6in (15cm) high.
£300–500 *C(Am)*

A Müller Frères cameo glass vase, with mottled orange, ochre and deep violet sides overlaid with turquoise, signed in relief 'Müller Fres/Lunéville', 5in (12.5cm) high.
£800–1,000 *Bon*

Three Clutha glass vases, 2 in green glass with internal bubbling and coppery inclusions with white streaks, the third in opaque amber glass swirling with white, 1880s, largest 5in (12.5cm) high.
£200–400 each *S*

A green glass goblet, probably Clutha, with coppery internal streaks and profuse bubbling, c1880, 11in (28cm) high.
£600–700 *S*

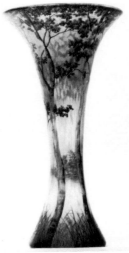

A Daum cameo glass landscape vase, enamelled in green and blue, the base inscribed 'Daum Nancy', 15½in (39.5cm) high.
£2,600–3,000 *WW*

A Daum silver-mounted, etched and enamelled glass bowl, the clear body overlaid in brilliant clear emerald green and etched, stencilled mark 'Daum Nancy', c1900, 10in (25.5cm) diam.
£1,600–2,000 *S*

A cameo amber glass vase, overlaid with red and etched with fuchsias, marked 'd'Argental', c1900, 9½in (24cm) high.
£350–450 *S*

A Daum cameo glass vase, the pale orange and yellow body overlaid with brown and green, signed in cameo 'Daum Nancy', 10in (25.5cm) high.
£1,000–1,500 *P*

A Daum cameo dappled glass vase, overlaid with orange and brown, signed in cameo 'Daum Nancy, France', 10in (25.5cm) high.
£1,200–1,400 *P*

A cameo glass vase, grey overlaid with rich amethyst glass, engraved signature 'Gallé', 8in (20.5cm) high.
£8,000–12,000 *P*

l. A Gallé cameo vase, white, amethyst and green, signed, 23½in (60cm) high.
£1,800–2,200 *P*

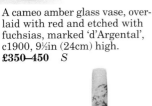

A Gallé cameo glass landscape vase, the greyish body tinted amber at the top, overlaid with apple green and ruby glass, signed 'Gallé', 19½in (49.5cm) high.
£2,800–3,200 *P*

l. A Gallé cameo glass vase, the greyish body amber tinted, overlaid with green and brown glass, signed in cameo 'Gallé', 9in (23cm) high.
£500–600 *P*

A Gallé cameo 'vase parlant', with deep blue and rust-red inclusions, overlaid with brown glass, with a verse by Rollinat, signed in cameo 'Gallé', 14in (35.5cm) high.
£2,500–3,000 *P*

A Gallé cameo glass landscape vase, amber tinted and overlaid with pale blue and amethyst, intaglio signature 'Gallé', 13½in (35cm) high.
£3,500–4,000 *P*

A French cameo glass vase, signed 'Le Verre Français', c1900, 12in (30.5cm) high.
£600–750 *ASA*

A glass vase by Loetz, with all-over silvery iridescence, inscribed 'Loetz Austria', 6in (15cm) high.
£1,000–1,200 *CNY*

r. A Loetz glass vase, with random splashes of golden iridescence shading through pale turquoise and violet, and applied with a silver coloured metal collar, 13in (33cm) high.
£400–500 *P*

A double overlay and carved glass vase, by Eugène Michel, in green and white, and finely carved to depict water lilies in blossom, the interior with iridescence, 5in (12.5cm) high.
£2,500–3,000 *CNY*

An overlaid and carved glass vase, inscribed 'D. Christian Meisenthal', 3½in (9cm) high.
£1,000–1,200 *CNY*

A glass vase, overlaid in green and aubergine, with finely etched leaves, vines and passion flowers, inscribed 'D. Christian Meisenthal Loth', 7in (18cm) high.
£1,000–1,200 *CNY*

A Favrile blue iridescent glass vase, inscribed 'X.182, L. C. Tiffany Favrile', 9in (23cm) high.
£800–1,000 *CNY*

A Favrile glass paperweight vase, with stylized morning glory blossoms amid streamers encased in clear glass, the interior with iridescence, crack to foot, engraved 'U4113 Louis C. Tiffany', c1904, 7½in (19cm) high.
£400–500 *CNY*

A Favrile iridescent glass comport, inscribed 'L. C. Tiffany Inc. Favrile W41N', 3in (7.5cm) high.
£600–700 *CNY*

A Favrile iridescent glass comport, in all-over blue and purple iridescence on a short stem and circular foot, inscribed '1531 2104 L. L. C. T. Tiffany Favrile', 6½in (16.5cm) high.
£600–700 *CNY*

r. A Favrile iridescent gold glass flower bowl, with central detachable flower frog, both incised 'L. C. Tiffany Favrile 5344K', 14½in (36cm) diam.
£700–850 *CNY*

A Favrile glass centrepiece, the ribbed body with all-over blue iridescence, inscribed 'L. C. Tiffany Favrile, 8412K', 10in (25.5cm) diam.
£700–850 *CNY*

A Müller vase, in clear and frosted glass, signed 'Müller Lunéville France', c1930, 8in (20.5cm) high.
£500–600   *C*

An amethyst glass table lamp base, moulded 'A. Hunibelle, Modèle Dep de R. Cogneville, Made in France, 11in (28cm) high.
£300–350   *P*

A French geometric enamel and glass decanter, with black and red decoration, 12in (30.5cm) high.
£150–180   *ASA*

An Art Deco Lalique-style glass decanter and 6 glasses.
£250–300   *CDC*

A glass decanter, black enamelled with geometric and starburst designs, 5 tots ensuite, 10in (25.5cm) high.
£200–250   *CSK*

An Orrefors grey tinted vase, designed by Simon Gate, engraved 'Orrefors S. Gate 234.27 A.D.', c1927, 9½in (24cm) high.
£1,200–1,400   *C*

A moulded glass vase, moulded signature 'A. Verlys, France', c1930, 11½in (29cm) high.
£300–400   *C*

A cut-glass decanter and stopper, with geometric patterns in black and frosted glass, and 6 liqueur glasses, decanter 7½in (19cm) high.
£300–400   *CSK*

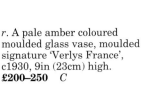

r. A pale amber coloured moulded glass vase, moulded signature 'Verlys France', c1930, 9in (23cm) high.
£200–250   *C*

A set of 6 glass goblets, enamelled with peacocks in green and blue, and female figures, against a black enamelled ground, one chipped, some signed, 8in (20.5cm) high.
£500–600   *GSP*

An Etling opalescent glass figure, moulded 'Etling France 50', 8in (20.5cm) high.
£1,000–1,200　*P*

Seven glass goblets and 8 finger bowls, signed 'Verdar'.
£1,000–1,200　*M*

A decanter and 6 glasses, the clear glass faceted with square panels and alternately flashed with amber, one chipped.
£200–250　*P*

An engraved and clear glass octagonal lamp, on a gilt-metal base, 13½in (34.5cm) high.
£600–750　*CSK*

A glass decanter and 6 glasses, with panels of black enamel and frosted and engraved decoration.
£250–300　*P*

An Austrian blue glass jar and cover, attributed to Moser of Karlsbad, in the style of Josef Hoffman, 6in (15cm) high.
£400–500　*P*

l. A Moser blue glass vase, heightened with gilding, marked 'Moser' and 'L.K.M.', for Ludwig Moser Karlsbad, 13½in (34.5c m) high.
£200–250　*P*

A Décorchement pâte-de-verre bowl, in green and brown marbled glass, with impressed mark, c1940, 10in (25.5cm) wide.
£2,600–3,000　*C*

A Venini patchwork vase, the clear glass internally decorated in red, green and blue, acid stamped 'Venini Murano Italia', 4½in (11.5cm) high.
£1,200–1,400　*C(Am)*

A Sabino opalescent glass lamp, signed 'Sabino France', 13½in (34.5cm) high, on a chromed base incorporating lamp fitments.
£700–950　*P*

A Sabino opalescent glass figure, 'Suzanne', unsigned, 9in (23cm) high, with wooden mount, fitted for electricity.
£1,500–1,800　*P*

Identification checklist for buying Tiffany lamps

- Does the shade or base bear a signature and model number?
- Is the shade made of leaded glass that looks as if it could be around 90 years old?
- Is the base made of bronze, with a century-old patina, and is the socket and cord old?
- Is the condition of the lamp good, with few cracks, and little replaced glass or hardware?
- Is there a good provenance (history) on the lamp?
- Is the lamp expensive, but not exceptionally high in price?
- Is the seller prepared to take the lamp back and provide a full refund if a mutually agreed expert will not authenticate the lamp?

r. A French lamp, 'L'Orchidée', from a model by Louis Chalon, early 20thC, 29in (73.5cm) high.
£4,500–5,500 *CNY*

A 'Cypriot' glass hanging lantern, by Tiffany Studios, 18in (45.5cm) high.
£8,000–10,000 *CNY*

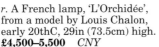

l. A geometric leaded glass and metal chandelier, by Tiffany Studios, the shade suspended from 6 link chains, 14in (35.5cm) high.
£12,000–15,000 *CNY*

A geometric leaded glass and bronze lampshade, by Tiffany Studios, 12½in (32cm) high.
£6,000–7,000 *CNY*

A 'Clematis' leaded glass shade, by Tiffany Studios, 18in (45.5cm) diam.
£25,000–30,000 *CNY*

An 'Iris' leaded glass and bronze chandelier, attributed to Tiffany Studios, 22in (56cm) high.
£5,500–6,500 *CNY*

A stained and leaded glass dome light shade, decorated with grapes and leaves, 28in (71cm) diam.
£600–700 *JL*

An iridescent glass and brass chandelier, attributed to Koloman Moser, c1902, 25in (63.5cm) high.
£6,000–7,500 *CNY*

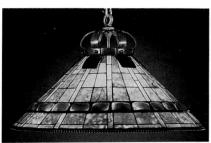

A geometric 'Turtle-back' chandelier, by Tiffany Studios, 22in (56cm) high.
£8,000–10,000 *CNY*

r. A 'Turtle-back' tile and leaded glass hanging lantern, by Tiffany Studios.
£12,000–16,000 *CNY*

A paperweight glass bowl, by Tiffany Studios, inscribed '1333E L. C. Tiffany-Favrile', 8in (20.5cm) diam.
£4,000–5,000   *CNY*

A Le Verre Français cameo glass bowl, signed, 9in (23cm) high.
£900–1,000   *MAG*

A Favrile glass plaque, by Tiffany Studios, inscribed 'L.C.T.', 19in (48.5cm) high.
£5,000–6,000   *CNY*

A mould blown, overlaid and etched glass bowl, signed 'Gallé', 12½in (32cm) diam.
£6,000–7,000   *HFG*

An internally decorated and engraved glass coupe, 'La Vague', engraved 'Daum Nancy', 6½in (16.5cm) high.
£20,000–25,000   *HFG*

A 'Grand Vase de Tristesse', by Gallé, for the Paris Exposition, 1889, base cracked, signed, 14in (35.5cm) high.
£6,000–7,500   *CNY*

A glass vase, decorated with violets, signed 'Daum'.
£4,500–5,500   *CNY*

A triple overlaid and etched glass vase, signed in cameo 'Gallé', 28½in (72.5cm) high.
£5,000–6,000   *CNY*

A double overlay and etched glass vase, cameo signature 'Gallé', 26in (66cm) high.
£5,500–6,500   *CNY*

An overlaid and etched glass vase, cameo signature 'Gallé', rim damaged, 15½in (39.5cm) high.
£5,500–6,500   *CNY*

A cameo glass vase, signed 'Le Verre Français'.
£800–1,000   *MAG*

A cameo glass vase, signed 'Le Verre Français'.
£800–1,000   *MAG*

l. A cameo glass vase, signed 'Le Verre Français', 19in (48.5cm) high.
£10,000–12,000   *MAG*

r. An internally decorated glass vase, marked 'Gallé'.
£15,000–18,000   *HFG*

A Monart blue and ochre vase, with whorls, 9in (23cm) high.
£250–300 *FA*

A Monart vase, the surface decorated in yellow and lustred white stripes, c1925, 8in (20.5cm) high.
£800–1,000 *FA*

A Gallé carved, acid etched and partially fire-polished vase.
£3,500–4,500 *C*

A Gallé carved and acid etched double overlay vase, with carved signature, 12½in (32cm) high.
£2,000–2,500 *C*

A Daum martelé acid textured and carved vase.
£5,000–6,000 *C*

A Daum two-coloured glass vase.
£10,000–12,000 *C*

A frosted glass vase, 'Perruches', by René Lalique et Cie, on a bronze stand, 10½in (26.5cm) high.
£3,000–4,000 *CNY*

An amber glass vase, 'Serpent', by René Lalique et Cie, 10in (25.5cm) high.
£5,500–6,500 *CNY*

l. A frosted amber glass vase, 'Languedoc', by René Lalique et Cie.
£6,000–7,500 *CNY*

r. A Favrile glass paper-weight vase, by Tiffany Studios, 6in (15cm) high.
£9,000–10,000 *CNY*

A Müller glass vase, c1900, 11in (28cm) high.
£1,800–2,200 *ABS*

l. A Daum overlaid and etched glass vase, 15in (38cm) high.
£4,000–5,000 *CNY*

r. A gold Tiffany Favrile 'Jack-in-the-Pulpit' vase, 20in (51cm) high.
£9,500–11,000 *CNY*

A Tiffany Favrile lava glass vase, inscribed 'L.C. Tiffany/Favrile/ Exposition/Special, 6354N', 7in (18cm) high.
£18,500–20,000 *S(NY)*

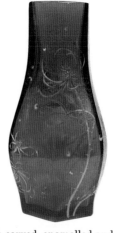

A carved, enamelled and gilt vase, gilt signature 'Emile Gallé', c1890, 8½in (21.5cm) high.
£2,000–2,400 *PSG*

A cameo glass vase, signed 'Daum Nancy', c1900, 13in (33cm) high.
£2,000–2,400 *PSG*

A Gallé marquetrie sur verre wheel carved cameo glass vase, by c1900, 9in (23cm) high.
£10,000–12,000 *S(NY)*

A Daum glass vase, with etched and enamelled winter landscape, c1900, 5in (12.5cm) high.
£1,000–1,200 *PSG*

A Gallé four-layer cameo glass charger, signed c1900, 14½in (37cm) diam.
£6,000–7,000 *PSG*

A cameo glass vase, decorated internally, signed 'Gallé', c1890, 9½in (24cm) high.
£6,000–7,000 *PSG*

Make the Most of Miller's

In Miller's Art Nouveau and Art Deco Buyer's Guide *we do NOT just reprint saleroom estimates. Our consultants work from realized prices and then calculate a price range from similar items, thus avoiding uncharacteristic 'one off' high or low results.*

A cameo glass table lamp, signed on the base and shade 'Gallé', with star, 24in (61cm) high.
£12,000–15,000 *P*

A Daum cameo glass vase, internally decorated, signed, c1900, 10½in (26.5cm) high.
£4,000–5,000 *PSG*

An enamelled cameo glass vase, signed 'Daum/Nancy', c1910, 20in (51cm) high.
£3,500–4,500 *S(NY)*

A Gallé four-layer cameo glass vase, signed, c1900, 7in (18cm) high.
£1,400–1,600 *PSG*

Four Daum glass vases.
£2,000–4,000 each *C*

A Daum internally
decorated glass lamp,
17in (43cm) high.
£3,000–4,000 *CNY*

A Daum cameo
glass and wheel
carved vase, signed
in intaglio, c1900,
7½in (19cm) high.
£1,500–1,800 *PSG*

A Daum
enamelled vase,
marked 'Daum
Nancy', c1900,
13in (33cm) high.
£3,000–5,000 *S*

A Daum overlaid
and etched glass lamp,
18in (45.5cm) high.
£10,000–12,000 *CNY*

Three Daum carved, enamelled
and painted vases, painted
signatures and Cross of Lorraine.
£2,000–4,000 each *C*

A Daum carved
cameo and
marqueterie sur
verre glass vase,
engraved 'Daum
Nancy'; c1900,
8in (20.5cm) high.
£5,000–6,000 *S*

A Daum enamelled
glass lamp, marked
'Daum Nancy', c1900,
24⅓in (62cm) high.
£12,000–16,000 *S*

A Daum etched and
enamelled cameo glass
vase, signed, c1900,
7½in (19cm) high.
£1,500–1,800 *PSG*

An etched, enamelled and
applied 'Snail' vase, Daum
Nancy, 8in (20.5cm) high.
£10,000–12,000 *CNY*

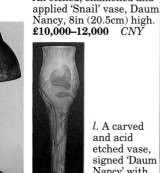

Two carved and acid etched
lamps, carved signatures 'Daum
Nancy', 14in (35.5cm) high.
£3,000–4,000 each *C*

l. A carved
and acid
etched vase,
signed 'Daum
Nancy' with
Cross of
Lorraine,
12½in (32cm)
high.
£2,500–3,000
C

A Daum carved and acid
etched overlay vase,
9in (23cm) high.
£10,000–15,000 *C*

A wrought-iron lamp,
by Edgar Brandt, c1925.
£6,500–7,500 *S*

A double overlay and etched glass vase, signed 'Gallé', 22½in (57cm) high.
£8,000–10,000 *HFG*

A double overlay glass vase, by Emile Gallé, 8in (20.5cm) high.
£10,000–12,000 *HFG*

A Tiffany Favrile glass vase, engraved signature 'L. C. Tiffany Favrile', 12½in (32cm) high.
£2,000–2,500 *C*

A Gallé cameo glass vase, engraved signature, 16in (41cm) high.
£3,000–3,500 *PSG*

A cameo glass vase, amethyst overlaid on amber, signed 'Gallé', 8in (20.5cm) high.
£2,200–2,600 *PSG*

A cameo glass vase, signed 'Gallé', 6½in (16.5cm) high.
£1,500–2,000 *PSG*

A Daum etched and enamelled cameo glass vase, enamelled signature, 9in (23cm) high.
£2,000–2,400 *PSG*

A Daum cameo glass landscape vase, enamelled signature, 5in (12.5cm) high.
£800–1,200 *PSG*

A Monart vase, red, black and gold, 5½in (14cm) high.
£300–400 *FA*

A cameo glass vase, probably by Thomas Webb, 6in (15cm) high.
£700–1,000 *SWO*

r. Two Lalique vases, 'Saphora' and 'Vases Davos', both signed, largest 11½in (29cm) high.
l. **£3,000–3,500**
r. **£2,000–2,500** *C*

A 'Grand Vase Libellules', carved, acid etched and applied, carved signature 'Daum Nancy', 23½in (59.5cm) high.
£12,000–14,000 *C*

r. A Daum vase, 'Anemones', engraved 'Daum Nancy', 9½in (24cm) high.
£5,000–6,000 *C*

r. An acid etched, carved, enamelled and gilt decorated landscape vase, signed 'Daum Nancy', 11in (28cm) high.
£3,000–3,500 *C*

Two Daum cameo glass vases, cameo marked 'Daum Nancy', 16½in (42cm) high.
l. **£1,500–2,000**
r. **£2,600–3,000**   *Bon*

A frosted glass vase, 'Lutteurs', relief moulded 'R. Lalique', engraved 'France', 5in (12.5cm) high.
£1,500–1,800   *CNY*

A cire perdu glass vase, wheel cut 'R. Lalique, France', c1924, 9in (23cm) high.
£30,000–35,000   *CNY*

Use the Index!

Because certain items might fit easily into any number of categories, the quickest and surest method of locating any entry is by reference to the index at the back of the book.

This index has been fully cross-referenced for absolute simplicity.

An etched and enamelled coupe, signed 'Daum Nancy', 9in (23cm) high.
£1,800–2,000   *PSG*

An etched and enamelled vase, signed 'Daum Nancy', 10½in (26.5cm) high.
£2,000–2,500   *PSG*

A Daum vase, with overlaid enamel painted Alpine scene, enamelled signature 'Daum Nancy', with the Cross of Lorraine, 11½in (29cm) high.
£2,600–3,000   *C*

An enamelled glass vase, 'Tourbillons', wheel cut 'R. Lalique, France', engraved 'No. 973', 8in (20.5cm) high.
£14,000–18,000   *CNY*

A double overlay and wheel carved martelé vase, engraved signature 'Daum Nancy' with the Cross of Lorraine, 15½in (39.5cm) high.
£3,000–4,000   *C*

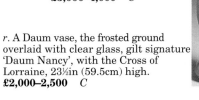

r. A Daum vase, the frosted ground overlaid with clear glass, gilt signature 'Daum Nancy', with the Cross of Lorraine, 23½in (59.5cm) high.
£2,000–2,500   *C*

A Gallé intrecalaire, intaglio carved 'verrerie parlante' vase, signed, 4½in (11.5cm) high.
£8,000–10,000 *C*

A Gallé cameo glass vase, signed, c1900, 8½in (21.5cm) high.
£2,000–3,000 *PSG*

A Gallé 'Soufflé' vase, signed, 6½in (16.5cm) high.
£2,800–3,200 *C*

A Gallé glass vase, the frosted ground overlaid and etched to depict wisteria, cameo signature, 24½in (62cm) high.
£30,000–35,000 *CNY*

A Gallé triple overlaid and etched glass table lamp base, cameo signature, 25in (38cm) high, with metal mount.
£3,000–3,500 *CNY*

A Gallé vase, 'Pine Cone', signed, 12in (30.5cm) high.
£2,000–2,500 *ABS*

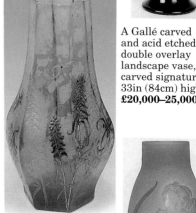

A Gallé martelé enamel vase, 12in (30.5cm) high.
£7,500–8,500 *C*

A Gallé glass vase, c1900, 14in (35.5cm) high.
£3,000–3,500 *S*

A Gallé carved and acid etched double overlay landscape vase, carved signature, 33in (84cm) high.
£20,000–25,000 *C*

A Gallé cameo glass 'Iris' vase, cameo mark, c1900, 20½in (52cm) high.
£7,500–10,000 *S*

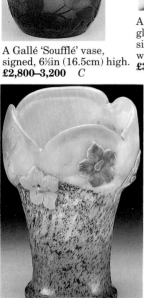

A Gallé internally decorated carved cameo vase, c1900.
£8,000–12,000 *S*

A Gallé vase, signed, 17in (43cm) high.
£4,000–5,000 *CNY*

r. A Gallé carved and acid etched vase, cameo signature, 17½in (44.5cm) high.
£15,000–18,000 *C*

A glass vase, overlaid with a design of spring flowers, signed 'Gallé', c1900, 9in (23cm) diam.
£1,500–1,800 *PSG*

r. A glass vase, 'Les Sept Princesses', by Emile Gallé, inscribed 'Exposit', 1900, 9in (23cm) high.
£18,000–20,000 *CNY*

l. A poppy triple overlay cameo glass vase, by Emile Gallé, with cameo signature, 24in (61cm) high.
£9,000–11,000 *CNY*

A Gallé 'Clematis' vase, signed 13in (33cm) high.
£1,500–1,800 *PSG*

A vase overlaid on amber with a design of chrysanthemums, signed, 'Gallé', 12½in (32cm) high.
£3,000–3,500 *PSG*

A glass vase, with a design of anemones, signed 'Gallé', c1900, 8in (20.5cm) high.
£2,000–2,500 *PSG*

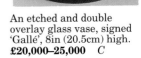

A Gallé overlay glass vase, 'Roses de France', engraved Gallé, 7½in (19cm) high.
£40,000–50,000 *C*

A vase overlaid on apricot with a design of nasturtiums, signed 'Gallé', 9in (23cm) high.
£1,800–2,000 *PSG*

An etched and double overlay glass vase, signed 'Gallé', 8in (20.5cm) high.
£20,000–25,000 *C*

A double overlay and etched glass charger, cameo signature 'Gallé', 15½in (39.5cm) high.
£7,000–9,000 *CNY*

A carved acid etched triple overlay landscape vase, with carved signature 'Gallé', 20in (51cm) high.
£4,000–5,000 *C*

A blue lily triple overlay mould blown glass vase, cameo signature 'Gallé', 14in (35.5cm) high.
£30,000–40,000 *CNY*

A bronze mounted vase, with engraved signature 'Gallé ft. 1891–93', bronze foot signed with 'EG' monogram, 11½in (29cm) high.
£20,000–25,000 *C*

A mould blown vase, carved and acid etched with rhododendrons, carved 'Gallé', 10in (25.5cm) high.
£7,000–8,000 *C*

A Gallé double overlay vase, repaired, 9in (23cm) high.
£1,200–1,500 *EG*

An acid etched and enamelled vase, engraved 'Cristallerie d'Emile Gallé, Nancy', 28in (71cm) high.
£2,500–3,000 *C(Am)*

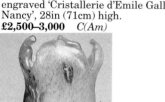

A triple overlay carved and acid etched 'Discus' vase, carved signature 'Gallé', 9in (23cm) diam.
£3,000–4,000 *C*

Make the Most of Miller's

Condition is absolutely vital when assessing the value of an antique. Items in good condition are more likely to appreciate than less perfect examples. Rare, desirable items may command higher prices even when in need of restoration.

l. A triple overlay vase, 'Premier Gel d'Automne', carved signature 'Gallé', 13in (33cm) high.
£15,000–18,000 *C*

r. A pâte-de-verre vase, 'Gazelles et des Fleurs' c1928, moulded signature 'G. Argy-Rousseau' and 'France', 3½in (9cm) wide.
£4,000–5,000 *C*

A bronze and ivory figure, 'Danseuse de Thebes', inscribed 'Cl. J. R. Colinet', 10in (25.5cm) high.
£9,000–11,000   *C*

A bronze and ivory figure, 'Towards the Unknown', signed 'Cl. J. R. Colinet', 18½in (47cm) high.
£9,000–11,000   *C*

A Belgian cold-painted, gilt-bronze and white marble group of a snake charmer, 'Dance of Carthage', inscribed 'Cl. J. R. Colinet', early 20thC, 22in (56cm) high.
£18,000–21,500   *CNY*

l. A bronze and ivory figure, 'Mandolin Player', signed 'F. Preiss' in marble, 23½in (59.5cm) high.
£12,000–15,000
r. A bronze and ivory figure, 'Flute Player', from a model by F. Preiss, 19in (48.5cm) high.
£9,000–11,000   *C*

A French cold-painted, damascened and silvered-bronze and ivory group of a cabaret act, 'Two Girls', inscribed 'Laurent Hely' and 'Bronze', early 20thC, 21in (53.5cm) high.
£12,000–14,000   *CNY*

r. A bronze and ivory figure, 'Girl Dancer', the bronze base decorated with 3 masks, signed in the bronze 'O. Hoffmann', foundry mark, on a twelve-sided striated marble base, 14in (35.5cm) high.
£8,500–10,000   *C*

A patinated bronze and ivory figure, 'Ankara Dancer', by C. J. R. Colinet, c1925, 25in (63.5cm) high.
£40,000–50,000 *S(NY)*

A patinated bronze and ivory figural group, 'The Girls', by Demêtre H. Chiparus, mounted on an onyx base, minor losses, inscribed, 20½in (52cm) high.
£90,000–110,000 *S(NY)*

A bronze and ivory figure, 'Hindu Dancer', by Demêtre H. Chiparus, c1925.
£12,000–15,000 *S(NY)*

A painted bronze and ivory figural group, 'The Sisters', by Demêtre H. Chiparus, c1925, mounted on a brown onyx base, 29in (73.5cm) high.
£45,000–55,000 *S(NY)*

A carved bronze and ivory figure, 'Cleopatra', by Bruno Zach, 14in (35.5cm) high.
£5,000–6,000 *ASA*

Three bronze and ivory figures of female athletes, by Ferdinand Preiss, c1925:
l. 'Oars Woman'
c. 'Javelin Thrower'
r. Skater', 12½in (32cm) high.
£9,000–11,000 each *S(NY)*

A cold-painted bronze and ivory figural group, 'Finale', by Demêtre H. Chiparus, c1925, 16½in (42cm) high.
£30,000–36,000 *S(NY)*

Demêtre H. Chiparus (Romanian)

Although born in Romania, Chiparus worked in Paris. He was the chief exponent of chryselephantine, a combination of bronze and ivory, and specialized in depicting exotic women, many inspired by the Ballet Russes. He nearly always signed his work on the base.

A gilt and silvered-bronze and ivory figure, 'Semiramis', by Demêtre H. Chiparus, c1925, 26½in (67cm) high.
£60,000–75,000 *S(NY)*

A bronze and ivory figure, 'The Archer', on a green onyx base, signed 'F. Preiss', 8½in (21.5cm) high.
£12,000–14,000   *C*

A bronze and ivory figure, 'Autumn Dancer', signed with F. Preiss monogram, 14½in (37cm) high.
£20,000–25,000   *C*

Two silver-patinated bronze figures, 'Ball Player' and 'Stella', by M. Guiraud Rivière and Etling, Paris, largest 25½in (65cm) high.
£3,500–4,500   *C*

A bronze and ivory figure, 'Starlight', signed 'D. H. Chiparus', on a marble base, 23½in (59.5cm) high.
£12,000–14,000   *C*

A bronze and ivory figure, 'Charm of the Orient', signed 'A. Godard', on a marble base, 19½in (49.5cm) high.
£8,000–10,000   *C*

A bronze and ivory group, 'High Priestess', on a white marble plinth, signed on the base 'A. Bouraine', 24½in (62cm) high.
£7,000–9,000   *C*

A gold-patinated bronze and ivory figure, 'Exotic Dancer', signed 'Gerdago', on an onyx base, 12in (30.5cm) high.
£12,000–15,000   *C*

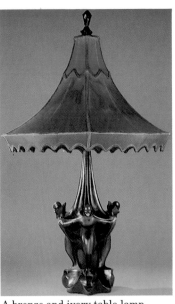

A bronze and ivory table lamp, 'Batwoman', with a waxed cotton shade, signed in the bronze 'Roland Paris', 37in 994cm) high.
£8,000–10,000   *C*

A gilt bronze and silver patinated figure, the bronze base signed 'E. Barrias', 17in (43cm) high.
£7,000–8,500   *C*

r. A bronze statuette of the 'Spirit of Ecstasy', by Charles Sykes, 23½in (59.5cm) high.
£6,000–7,500   *C*

A bronze and ivory figure, marked 'Bruno Zach', 15in (38cm) high. **£4,000–4,500** *S*

A bronze figure, by Bruno Zach. **£3,000–3,500** *CNY*

A gold and enamel buckle, now fitted with a watch, stamped 'Vever Paris', c1900, 3in (6.5cm) high. **£10,000–12,000** *S*

A parcel-gilt cold-painted bronze figure, 23½in (59.5cm) high. **£6,500–7,500** *CNY*

A gilt and enamelled bronze figure of a snake dancer, by Otto Poertzel, c1930, 20⅜in (52cm) high. **£13,000–15,000** *ASA*

A bronze and ivory group, by Otto Poertzel, 16½in (42cm) high. **£8,500–10,000** *C*

A bronze and ivory figure, by Philippe, 14in (35.5cm) high. **£12,000–14,000** *ASA*

A parcel-silvered bronze and ivory figure of an archer, by Pierre le Faguays, early 20thC, 17in (43cm) wide. **£3,000–3,500** *CNY*

A bronze and ivory figure of a dancer, 'Alméria', by D. Chiparus, c1925, 25in (63.5cm) wide. **£40,000–50,000** *S*

A cold-painted bronze and ivory female figure, by Ferdinand Preiss, early 20thC, 9in (23cm) wide. **£7,500–9,000** *CNY*

An ivory figure, 'Ecstasy', by Ferdinand Preiss, 17in (43cm) high. **£7,000–8,500** *CNY*

l. A bronze and enamel clock, on a marble base, marked 'Maple & Cie, Paris', c1920, 10½in (26.5cm) wide. **£7,000–8,500** *S*

An Art Deco bronze and ivory figure, by Demêtre H. Chiparus, 21in (53.5cm) wide. **£50,000–60,000** *P*

A silvered, cold-painted bronze, ivory, marble and onyx figure, 'Antinea', by Chiparus, c1925.
£50,000–60,000   *S*

A cold-painted bronze, tinted ivory, marble and onyx figure, 'Ecstasy', by F. Preiss, c1930, 22in (56cm) high.
£12,000–14,000   *S*

A cold-painted bronze and marble figure, 'Dancer with Thyrsus', by Pierre Le Faguays, 1920s, 22in (56cm) high.
£4,500–5,500   *S*

A cold-painted bronze, ivory and onyx figure, by Ferdinand Preiss, 1930s.
£4,000–5,000   *S*

A bronze and ivory figure, 'Pierrot', by D. Chiparus, 1920s.
£5,500–6,500   *S(S)*

A bronze figure of a dancer, by Morante, 16in (40.5cm) high.
£1,500–1,800   *ASA*

A cold-painted bronze, ivory and onyx figure, 'Dancer', c1925, 10in (25.5cm) high.
£1,000–1,200   *S*

A bronze and ivory figure, 'Daphne', silvered bronze and marble, by Fredy Stoll, c1925.
£12,000–15,000   *S*

A bronze and ivory figure, by Joe Descamp, 15in (38cm) high.
£10,000–12,000   *ASA*

A bronze figure, 'Bacchante', by Pierre Le Faguarys.
£7,500–9,000   *C*

r. A bronze and ivory figure, 'Autumn Dancer', by Ferdinand Preiss.
£15,000–18,000   *C*

r. A cold-painted bronze and ivory figure, 'Grecian with Torch', by Ferdinand Preiss.
£2,500–3,000   *S*

BRONZE & IVORY FIGURES

A freedom of expression hitherto unknown was demanded by the sculptors of the 1890s. Previously, the route to artistic acclaim required that they follow a rigid classical tradition. Young artists, desperately needing government patronage, had continued to interpret the Old Masters in a classical idiom, because only by so doing could they hope to have work accepted for public display at the prestigious annual Salon exhibitions, where large institutions made purchases and placed commissions.

Gradually, demand from the public for private ownership of sculpture for the home was increasing, thus affording an alternative outlet for the energies of the emerging artists. This was recognized by the bronze founders who exploited this new market by making use of a new invention called a Pantograph – a type of tracing machine, use of which enabled them to reproduce accurately scaled down models of large marble sculpture to domestic proportions. The model, cut from a soft plaster blank, could then be cast in bronze.

The Barbedienne founders made substantial profits by reproducing limited editions of bronzes cast from classical marble statuary. Thankfully they also recognized and catered to the growing demand for Romantic sculpture, thus providing a forum for those artists whose work had previously been eschewed by the Salons. The artists in turn could depend less on commissions for unique pieces, and rely more on the royalties accruing from the multiple production of their work.

The beginning of the 20th century saw the burgeoning of Art Nouveau design. One of the more obvious images was the portrayal of 'woman'. Freed from the constraints of a 19th century literary tradition which portrayed her as stiflingly respectable, and liberated physically from her rigid corsets, she now danced with gay abandon. The fluid, sensual sculptures of Agathon Leonard, the mysterious 'Le Secret', by Maurice Bouval, and the oft-repeated image of the American dancer Loïe Fuller most notably portrayed by Raoul Larche, are amongst the more typical and desirable of Art Nouveau sculpture.

The electric light bulb was still a novelty and many artists engaged its properties. It was to be found concealed within the scarf held above the head of Loïe Fuller as she danced, illuminating 'The Milky Way' – a blue and opal glass globe clutched by the pensive female sculpted by Leo Laporte Blairsy, secreted into nautilus shells held aloft by a mermaid, or often replacing stamens in the flowerheads of a myriad of lamps which combined the images of women and plant forms.

By the 1920s, life had changed markedly. The rigours of war, the birth of the machine age, and the discovery of Tutenkhamun's tomb in 1921, were amongst the influences reflected in the work of Art Deco artists and sculptors. The woman they portrayed was bolder, stylish, more self-assured.

Bruno Zach's ladies were often erotic, scantily clad and provocative. They were modelled in their underwear, holding whips, dressed in trousers or smoking cigarettes. 'Airwoman' by Ferdinand Preiss was almost certainly modelled on Amy Johnson, and was undoubtedly a celebration of her achievements. The image, cast in bronze, her hands plunged deep into the pockets of her cold-painted red flying suit, and her neat facial features captured in carved ivory, indicate the changing status of women.

While never portrayed covered in the mud of the trenches, artists such as Pierre le Faguays and Marcel Bouraine did cast some females symbolically in the role of noble warriors. Although still scantily clad, they could be seen throwing spears or dancing in victory while waving daggers and shields. Lorenzl, meanwhile, was busy modelling females in a highly stylized and elongated fashion. His ladies were long and lithe, young and flawless. They danced, largely naked, but often waving scarves or balancing hoops on their exaggerated outstretched limbs.

Theatrical images inspired by the birth of Hollywood pervaded the sculpture of the period. 'Lighter than Air', by Preiss, was modelled on Miss Ada May, who appeared in the C. B. Cochran review of 1930. Much of the later work of Demêtre H. Chiparus was based on the theatre and ballet. The Ballet Russe inspired many of his works, in particular 'Russian Dancers', which depicted Nijinsky and Ida Rubinstein in their roles in 'Scheherazade'.

The opening of the Pharoah's tomb in the early 1920s was a terrific source of inspiration for Chiparus. He modelled Egyptian dancers in bronze, and also bronze and ivory, embellishing the bronze of their costumes and headdresses with beaded and jewelled decorative detail, which was then highlighted in the cold-painting process with appropriately vivid colours.

Casting in bronze has always been expensive, whether the process of lost wax or sand-casting is employed. Extensive highly skilled and labour intensive techniques are required to ensure a fine quality end result. The stages of production begin once the sculptor has made a model of the subject, usually in clay or terracotta, which he takes along to a founder. In the 1920s those founders known to produce the highest quality work allied themselves to the leading sculptors of the day. On Art Deco figures particularly, a founder's seal, together with an artist's signature, usually denotes work of a high standard.

When casting figures it was not unusual for separate moulds to be made for the limbs, head and torso. A more complicated model required more pieces to be cast separately and assembled later. The bronze that is removed from the moulds has quite a rough surface and lacks much of the fine detail of the original model. Following preparatory retouching, it is the task of the chaser, using an engraving tool called a Burin, to pains-takingly recreate that lost detail. This process is one that the sculptor may choose to oversee.

Finally, the required finish, or patina, is applied. On many Art Nouveau sculptures this finish was achieved by painting a solution of mineral salts and acids on to the surface and applying heat with a torch to accelerate the chemical reaction. Most were applied with colours ranging from verdigris to rich chocolate, although it is not unusual to see gilding. The sculptors of the Art Deco period experimented much more with their finishes. Electroplating, cold-painting, gilding and enamelling were used in various combinations to create exciting and colourful images.

Ivory was used for the head and exposed limbs of a figure which, of course, had to be carved and fitted to the bronze. Much of this was individually carved by hand. Even when the preliminary carving was done by machine, the fine detailing of the final stages would be hand-crafted.

Sadly, relatively few artists today work in bronze. Given the procedures outlined above, it is not difficult to see that the costs of the processes involved are now prohibitive.

Bronze sculpture from the first half of the 20th century has a unique flavour. It is dramatic and totally evocative of the age. The charm and spirit it exudes, together with the exquisite quality and craftsmanship it often displays, have ensured increasing attention from a growing body of discerning collectors. Despite the high prices commanded by the most desirable pieces, in terms relevant to the cost of current production many are still affordable. However, the supply is finite. The short-lived Art Nouveau movement managed only to span two decades at the turn of the century. Its romantic languid images could hardly survive once the nation's thoughts had turned to war.

The Art Deco movement emerged after WWI. A considerable amount of the artistic output, and records relating to it, were lost or destroyed during the devastation of European cities in WWII. Art Deco style has grown so much in popularity over the last couple of decades that today the immense appeal of its instantly recognizable forms can be seen reproduced on a mass scale. The market for original pieces is stronger than ever, and the escalation in price is correspondingly impressive. Apart from a short time at the end of 1987, and during 1988, when prices surged wildly and then fell back, growth has been constant.

In 1983 it was possible to buy medium sized Art Deco bronze figures by one of the more popular and prolific artists such as Lorenzl, for between £100 and £200. In 1995 collectors could expect to pay in the region of £800–1,200 for a similar piece. Today that price would be more like £1,200–1,800. Fine and highly stylized examples of bronze and ivory figures by Colinet, Philippe, Chiparus, Preiss, Descomps, Zach and others, have seen percentage increases in their market value that are equally impressive.

Those Art Deco figures made in the 1930s from less expensive materials such as spelter (a metal containing zinc and lead, plated to resemble bronze and silver) and manufactured using simpler and cheaper processes, have seen some increase in price, but these have been less marked. A pair of spelter figure bookends which sold in 1983 for £60–90 and would have cost £150–175 in 1995, can still be found for sums in the low hundreds. Large spelter groups, depicting women and birds or women and small animals, mounted on marble bases, were made in abundance in the 1930s to satiate the demand for the style at all social levels. The market value of such pieces in 1983 would have been in the order of £125–250. The most shining examples (and many are not!) could still be found for around £400–500 in 1995. There has been little change in the price of such pieces over the past five years.

Collectors should always endeavour to buy bronzes that display the talent of the artist and the skill of the founder. Discerning buyers will always seek out the finer pieces. As seen above, time does not improve the quality or desirability of poor examples.

It has never been my policy to market bronzes based purely on their investment potential, but it is comforting, and not at all surprising, to see that long term they have proved to be more than competitive and a whole lot more attractive to look at than a bank book.   **Audrey Sternshine**

A bronze bust, 'Dalila', cast from a model by E. Villanis, signed in the bronze and with 'Société des Bronzes de Paris' foundry mark, 17½in (44.5cm) high.
£1,500–1,800 *C*

A bronze figure of a pierrot, by L. Alliott, 13½in (34.5cm) high.
£2,500–3,000 *ASA*

A bronze figure, cast from a model by Marius Vallet, on a marble base, signed 'Mars Vallet, Siot Decauville Fondeur Paris', 12in (30.5cm) high.
£3,000–3,500 *P*

A gilt-bronze figure of a dancer, cast from a model by Agathon Leonard, inscribed 'A. Leonard Sclp' and stamped with founder's seal, 'Susse Frères Editeurs, Paris, M', 19½in (49.5cm) high.
£9,000–11,000 *C*

A Lorenzl bronze figure of a dancer, signed, on an onyx base, 9in (23cm) high.
£1,000–1,200 *ASA*

A silvered bronze group, 'Carthage', cast after a model by Théodore Rivière, signed, marks for 'Susse Frères Editeurs, Paris', 22in (56cm) high.
£3,000–3,500 *P*

A French bronze figure of the Pied Piper playing a flute, with ivory face and hands, signed 'E. Barillot', on a slate socle, 10in (25.5cm) high.
£800–1,000 *GSP*

A bronze and ivory figure, cast and carved from a model by A. Brandel, on a shaped repainted base, indistinctly signed 'A. Brandel', 10½in (26.5cm) high.
£1,000–1,200 *C*

A bronze bust, 'La Sibylle', cast from a model by E. Villanis, signed 'E. Villanis' and with 'Société des Bronzes de Paris' foundry mark, 28½in (72.5cm) high.
£3,000–4,000 *C*

A bronze figure,
'Dagger Dancer',
by Marquet, c1930,
19in (48.5cm) high.
£2,000–2,500 *ASA*

A bronze seated figure, by
Lorenzl, 4in (10cm) high.
£450–500 *ASA*

A bronze and ivory figure,
cold-painted in rose pink,
marked on base 'F. Preiss',
1930s, 8in (20.5cm) high.
£800–1,000 *SB*

A bronze figure of a mummy
and sarcophagos, by
Bergman, 6in (15cm) high.
£800–900 *ASA*

A bronze and ivory
figure, 'Innocence',
by D. Chiparus, c1930,
9½in (24cm) high.
£5,000–6,000 *ASA*

A pair of spelter figures,
by Auguste Moreau,
c1900, 30in (76cm) high.
£2,000–2,500 *ASA*

A French spelter figure,
'L'Inspiration', after T. H. Somme,
early 20thC, 22½in (57cm) high,
on a marble base.
£350–450 *GAK*

A bronze figure, by
Fesler Felix, signed,
14½in (37cm) high.
£750–900 *P*

A green patinated bronze figure, etched on
base 'D. H. Chiparus', 29in (73.5cm) wide.
£350–450 *CSK*

l. A carved ivory
figure of a dancer,
by F. Preiss, signed,
7in (18cm) high,
on an onyx base.
£3,000–3,500 *P*

A bronze bust, signed in
the maquette 'H. Müller'
c1900, 5in (12.5cm) high.
£1,000–1,200 *SB*

A painted bronze and ivory figure
of a young girl in a pleated dress
with a ruff collar and a red conical
hat, cast and carved from a model
by Ferdinand Preiss, signed, on
a marble base, 6in (15cm) high.
£1,000–1,200 *P*

A gilt-bronze and ivory figure of a dancing girl, signed 'Joe Descamps', on a marble socle, 1920s, 16½in (42cm) high.
£2,000–2,500 *SB*

A painted bronze and ivory figure, modelled as an Oriental maiden wearing a pale green kimono, signed 'Harders R.u.M.', 16½in (42cm) high.
£3,000–3,500 *P*

An Art Deco ivory and bronze figure, by Lorenzl, c1920, 11in (28cm) high.
£1,000–1,200 *LEX*

A painted bronze and ivory figure of a girl, wearing a silvered brown dress, on an onyx base, inscribed 'Lorenzl', 13½in (34.5cm) high.
£1,200–1,400 *P*

A painted bronze and ivory figure of a lady, wearing a green skirt with a gilt tunic, on an onyx base, inscribed 'Lorenzl', 13½in (34.5cm) high.
£3,000–3,500 *P*

A bronze group, on a mottled grey marble base, engraved mark 'Kelety', 1920s, 15½in (39.4cm) high.
£3,500–4,500 *SB*

A painted bronze and ivory figure, modelled as a girl wearing a pink tinted tunic, signed 'P. Philippe R.u.M.'
£3,500–4,000 *P*

A pair of silvered and gilt painted bronze figures, by Lorenzl, on a green onyx base, signed, 10½in (26.5cm) high.
£2,500–3,000 *CSK*

A painted bronze and ivory figure, 'The Hoop Girl', by F. Preiss, on a brown onyx base, 8½in (21.5cm) high.
£3,000–3,500 *P*

A bronze and ivory figure of a girl in a gilt and green dress, inscribed 'F. Preiss', 7in (17.5cm) high.
£2,000–2,500 *P*

A pair of bronze and ivory
figures, 6in (15cm) high.
£4,000–4,500   *ASA*

A bronze and ivory figure of a
dancer, by Lorenzl, 15in (38cm) high.
£2,200–2,600   *ASA*

A bronze and ivory figure of
a dancer, on an onyx dish,
8in (20.5cm) high.
£1,300–1,500   *ASA*

l. A carved ivory figure of a
young girl with a skipping
rope, on an onyx base, signed
'F. Preiss', 6in (15cm) high.
£800–950   *P*

A gilded bronze and ivory figure
of a dancing girl, on a green
onyx pedestal, signed in the
bronze 'H. Fugière', the base
plate stamped 'Fabrication
Français Paris – G.M.',
damaged, 19in (48.5cm) high.
£1,300–1,500   *MAT*

A cold-painted bronze and ivory
figure, 'The Respectful Splits',
from a model by Paul Philippe,
signed 'P. Philippe', 7in (18cm)
high, on a green onyx base.
£3,000–3,500   *Bon*

A bronze and ivory figure,
by Claire J. Colinet,
12in (30.5cm) high.
£6,000–7,000   *ASA*

A bronze figure of a
girl, by S. Molselsio,
signed and dated
'S. Molselsio, 1919',
12½in (32cm) high.
£700–850   *P*

A bronze and ivory figure
of Henry Fielding playing
Dante, by Montini, slight
damage, 1930s,
16in (40.5cm) high overall.
£1,300–1,500   *HCH*

An ivory figure,
by F. Preiss, signed,
on an onyx base,
7in (17.5cm) high.
£850–1,000   *SS*

A gilt-bronze and ivory
figure, 'Priestess', cast
and carved from a model
by Demêtre Chiparus,
with enamelled blue and
green simulated jewellery,
inscribed 'Chiparus',
17in (43cm) high.
£6,000–7,000   *C*

A bronze figure of a winged female, cast from a model by Charles Sykes, inscribed 'Chas. Sykes', 14in (35.5cm) high.
£900–1,100 *CSK*

A green patinated bronze figure, 'Boy with Frog', by William Reid-Dick, signed and dated 'Reid Dick 1931', 26½in (67.5cm) high.
£4,500–5,500 *P*

There is a similar figure in the Queen's Garden, Regent's Park, London, resulting from Queen Mary having seen this piece. The owner, instead of giving it to the Queen, gave her the name and address of the sculptor.

A French polychrome bronze statuette of a woman dancer, cast from a model by A. Gory, surface rubbed in some areas, on a mottled marble base, 20in (51cm) high.
£2,000–2,500 *C*

A green painted bronze figure, from a model by Fayral, inscribed, 20⅓in (52cm) high. **£1,200–1,400** *CSK*

A pair of cast bronze bookends, inscribed 'Raoul Benard', early 20th C, 9⅓in (24cm) high.
£800–950 *LBP*

A gilt-bronze figure, 'Juggler', cast from a model by Claire J. R. Colinet, on a buff onyx base, inscribed 'Cl. J. R. Colinet', 7in (18cm) high.
£700–900 *CSK*

A gold cold-painted bronze figure, the flowers and bowl in painted plastic, on a mottled stepped brown marble base, engraved 'Duverand', 1930s, 12in (30.5cm) high.
£1,000–1,500 *S*

A bronze group of 2 dancing Bacchantes, marble engraved 'Cl. J. R. Colinet', 1930s, 22in (56cm) high.
£3,000–3,500 *S*

l. An Art Deco bronze figure, by Lorenzl, c1920.
£2,000–2,500 *ASA*

A patinated bronze figure of a dancer with a hoop, by A. Bouraine, on a marble socle, 18in (45.5cm) high.
£1,500–1,800 *EH*

A French cold-painted silvered bronze and marble bust of a lady in a turban, cast and carved from a model by A. Gory, inscribed 'A. Gory', early 20thC, 15in (38cm) high, on a white alabaster base.
£2,500–3,000 *CNY*

A bronze and ivory figure, 'Beach Ball Girl', inscribed 'F. Preiss', 15in (38cm) high.
£1,000–1,200 *CSK*

A gilded bronze and ivory figure of a girl on stepping stones, by F. H. Monginot, signed, 8in (20.5cm) high.
£900–1,100 *M*

A figure of a naked boy seated on a tree stump, removing a splinter from his foot, raised on a tapered onyx base with malachite edge, inscribed 'F. Preiss', 4½in (11.5cm) high.
£750–850 *HSS*

An Austrian bronze draped female, by J. Benk, 1907, 11in (28cm) high.
£1,500–1,800 *ASA*

l. An Austrian gilt bronze and ivory figure, signed 'Brandel Wien', 19in (48.5cm) high.
£3,000–3,500 *P*

A bronze and ivory figure of a young lady, cast after the model by Quenard, signed 'Quenard', on a marble base, 13in (33cm) high.
£1,000–1,200 *CSK*

A French part gilded bronze and ivory figure of a lady playing a harp, signed 'Gregoire', fitted for electric light, original shade, 13½in (34.5cm) high.
£1,000–1,200 *PWC*

l. An ivory figure of a naked girl, slight damage, 20thC, 6in (15cm) high.
£900–1,100 *SC*

r. A bronze and ivory figure, 'Girl with a Cigarette', cast and carved after a model by Bruno Zach, slight damage, signed in the bronze 'Bruno Zach', and monogram within a square, c1925, 29in (73.5cm) high.
£13,000–15,000 *C*

A bronze and ivory figure, by Gerdago, with coloured enamel decoration, c1920. **£4,000–5,000** *ASA*

A bronze figure of a girl, by Bruno Zach, with rich light brown patination, on a marble column, 18in (45.5cm) high overall. **£2,500–3,000** *S*

An Art Deco electroplated figure, by G. H. Gantchell, on a black marble base, 11in (28cm) high. **£300–350** *CDC*

A bronze figure, cast from a model by Lorenzl, inscribed, on a green onyx pedestal. **£1,300–1,600** *CSK*

A cold-painted metal figure of a kneeling huntress, by D. H. Chiparus, 1930s, 23½in (59.5cm) wide. **£900–1,100** *S*

A bronze bust of a man's head, 'Energie', signed 'Kélety', bronze stamped '255', rubbed green patination, on a marble base wih presentation plaque, early 20thC, 14½in (37cm) high. **£1,500–1,800** *SS*

r. A silvered bronze figure, 'Goat Charmer', signed by H. Fugère, 19½in (49.5cm) high. **£1,500–1,800** *ASA*

l. A bronze and ivory figure of a young concertina player, singed 'D. H. Chiparus', early 20thC, 10in (25.5cm) high. **£1,200–1,400** *SC*

A bronze and ivory figure, 'Oriental Water Carrier', from a model by Dominique Alonzo, inscribed 'D. Alonzo, Etling Paris', 13½in (34.5cm) high. **£1,200–1,400** *CSK*

r. A bronze group of a woman and 2 greyhounds, signed in the maquette 'Cl.J. R. Colinet', 1920s, 17½in (44.5cm) wide. **£1,500–1,800** *S*

A gilt-bronze and ivory group of 2 children as flower and fruit sellers, by Joseph d'Aste, signed, 9in (23cm) high. **£600–750** *M*

A patinated bronze and
ivory figure, 'Pierrot',
inscribed 'D. H. Chiparus',
12in (30.5cm) high.
£4,000–4,500   *CSK*

An Art Deco bronzed spelter and
simulated ivory figure, by Menneville,
of a seated girl reclining on an onyx
veneered vase, 13in (33cm) wide.
£1,000–1,200   *S(S)*

A bronze bust, inscribed
'Raoul Larche', founder's seal
'Silot Decauville Paris', serial
No. 973K, 17½in (44.5cm) high.
£2,000–2,500   *C*

l. A bronze and ivory figure,
by A Gory, signed on bronze
'A. Gory', 11½in (29cm) high.
£2,600–3,000   *P*

A bronze and ivory figure,
'Dancing Girl', carved and
cast from a model by Bruno
Zach, signed, mounted on
a black marble base,
15in (38cm) high.
£4,000–4,500   *C*

A bronze and ivory figure, 'Little
Chilly One', cast and carved from
a model by D. H. Chiparus, signed
on marble base, 9in (23cm) high.
£1,000–1,200   *P*

An Art Deco bronze and ivory
figure of a Dutch boy, by
J. Bertrand, in the style of
L. Sosson, 5½in (14cm) high, on
a plinth, with incised signature.
£350–450   *HSS*

A gilded bronze and ivory figure
of a girl feeding poultry, by
D. Alonzo, signed, 9½in (24cm) high.
£1,000–1,200   *M*

r. A gilt-bronze and ivory group,
by D. H. Chiparus, signed, on
an onyx plinth, 6in (15cm) high.
£2,000–2,500   *L*

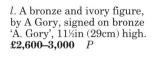

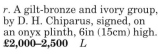

A parcel-gilt-bronze and ivory group, 'Morning Walk', cast and carved after a model by A. Becquerel, cold-painted in red, on a marble base, inscribed 'Becquerel', 10½in (26.5cm) high.
£2,000–2,500   C

A damascened, silvered and gilt-bronze figure of a scarf dancer, cast from a model by Raymond Guerbe, inscribed '42, Raymond Guerbe', early 20thC, 30½in (77.5cm) high.
£3,500–4,500   CNY

A gilt-bronze figure, entitled 'Nenette', by Juan Clara, signed, 8½in (21.5cm) high.
£900–1,100   M

A German bronze group by Jaeger, signed 'Jaeger', 13½in (34.5cm) high.
£750–850   P

A bronze and alabaster lamp, cast after a model by A. Kélety, signed in the bronze, c1925, 22in (56cm) high.
£2,000–2,500   C

A bronze and gilt-bronze figure, cast from a model by A. Gory, signed 'A. Gory', c1920, 21in (53.5cm) high.
£1,300–1,500   C

A bronze group of 2 men, by Nepa, on a marble base, 27½in (70cm) wide.
£900–1,100   CSK

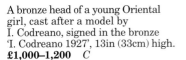

A painted bronze and ivory figure, by Lorenzl, signed on reverse 'Lorenzl', 13in (33cm) high, on a green onyx base.
£1,800–2,200   P

A bronze head of a young Oriental girl, cast after a model by I. Codreano, signed in the bronze 'I. Codreano 1927', 13in (33cm) high.
£1,000–1,200   C

r. A bronze figure, by Prof. Poertzel, 13in (33cm) high.
£3,000–4,000   JJIL

A Preiss bronze and
ivory figure of 'Vanity',
8½in (21.5cm) high.
£5,500–6,000   *ASA*

A painted bronze and ivory
lamp, 'Oriental Waiter', cast
and carved from a model by
Ferdinand Preiss, signed on
base, 19in (48.5cm) high.
£3,000–3,500   *P*

A bronze figure of a reclining
greyhound, cast from a model by
Daniel Bartelletti, base inscribed
'Bartelletti', 20in (51cm) wide.
£450–550   *CSK*

A bronze and ivory figure of
a girl, cast and carved from
a model by Ferdinand Preiss,
unsigned, 6½in (16.5cm).
£4,500–5,500   *P*

*This model is known as 'The Necklace'.
In this example the necklace that the
girl should be holding is missing.*

A figure group, 'Friends',
by Demêtre Chiparus, on
a shaped brown onyx base,
signed, 16½in (42cm) high.
£7,500–9,000   *HSS*

l. A painted bronze and
ivory lamp, unmarked
but possibly by F. Preiss,
23in (58.5cm) high.
£1,500–1,800   *P*

l. A gilt-bronze and ivory figure,
'Old Style Dancer', cast and
carved from a model by Demêtre
Chiparus, cold painted in dark
olive green on brown, black and
green marble base, inscribed
'Chiparus', 16in (40.5cm) high.
£6,000–7,000   *C*

r. A painted bronze and
ivory figure, 'Little
Cricketer', modelled
as a young boy wearing
pale brown short trousers,
signed 'F. Preiss' on base,
7in (18cm) high.
£2,000–2,500   *P*

A bronze figure, 'A Lioness', cast after a
model by Demêtre Chiparus, signed in the
marble 'D. Chiparus', 22½in (57cm) long.
£2,500–3,000   *C*

l. A French cold-painted, gilt-bronze and ivory
figure of an exotic dancer, cast and carved
from a model by Demêtre Chiparus, the white
alabaster base signed 'D. Chiparus',
early 20thC, 14in (35.5cm) high.
£8,000–9,500   *CNY*

A cold-painted bronze and ivory dancing
girl, restored, signed 'Lorenzl', 15in
(38cm) high. **£1,800–2,200**   *DSH*

A bronze and ivory figure, on a marble base, 12in (30.5cm) high.
£8,000–10,000 *BWe*

A gilt-bronze figure, on a stepped marble base, 27in (68.5cm) high.
£2,000–2,500 *CSK*

An ivory figure on an onyx base, c1930, 10in (25.5cm) diam.
£500–600 *JAD*

l. A bronze and ivory figure, 'Flamenco Dancer', from a model by Prof. Poertzel, on a marble base, signed, 23in (58.5cm) high.
£4,000–4,500 *C*

A bronze figure, 'Scarf Dancer', cast from a model by Demêtre Chiparus, the marble base incised 'D. H. Chiparus', 27in (68.5cm) high.
£8,000–9,500 *C*

r. A gilded and painted bronze figure, 'Venus', cast from a model by Edouard Drouot, on a mound base cast with waves and a rising sun, inscribed 'E. Drouot', 34in (86.5cm) high.
£3,000–3,500 *Bon*

l. A bronze figure, cast from a model by Lorenzl, patinated in green, on an onyx base, signed Lorenzl, 17½in (44.5cm) high.
£2,000–2,500 *P*

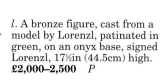

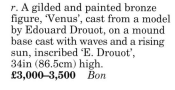

A bronze and ivory figure, 'Clown', cast and carved from a model by Jaeger, signed in the metal 'Jaeger R.v.M.', 10in (25.5cm) high.
£2,000–2,500 *C*

A bronze and ivory figure, 'The Courtier', cast and carved from a model by Lorenzl, signed in the bronze 'Lorenzl', 7in (17.5cm) high.
£1,000–1,200 *C*

An ivory figure, carved
in the style of Ferdinand
Preiss, 2½in (6.5cm) high.
£800–950 *CSK*

l. A bronze figure, by Philippe,
signed, 8½in (21.5cm) high.
£3,000–3,500 *ASA*

A green-patinated bronze and ivory
figure, 'Juggler', cast and carved from
a model by Jaeger, signed in the
bronze Jaeger and stamped 'Vrai
Bronze Déposé', 36½in (91.5cm) high.
£2,000–2,500 *C*

l. A bronze and ivory figure, signed
'Philippe', 16in (40.5cm) high.
£8,500–10,000 *ASA*

A bronze and ivory figure,
by Tereszczuk.
£1,100–1,300 *ASA*

A bronze and ivory figure,
'Page Boy', cast and carved from
a model by Prof. Otto Poertzel,
cold-painted green cape, bronze
foot and striated marble base,
signed in the bronze 'Prof. O.
Poertzel', 11½in (29cm) high.
£3,000–3,500 *C*

A bronze figure, 'Radha',
by Philippe, 22in (56cm) high.
£5,000–6,000 *ASA*

l. An ivory figure, 'Girl with
Skipping Rope', carved from
a model by Ferdinand Preiss,
signed 'F. Preiss', 6in (15cm) high.
£900–1,100 *P*

r. A bronze figure,
by Philippe, 9in (23cm) high.
£1,400–1,600 *ASA*

An ivory figure,
carved from a model
by P. Philippe, on a
brown onyx striated
pedestal base,
the base inscribed
'P. Philippe',
9in (23cm) high.
£2,000–2,500 *C*

A gilt-bronze and
ivory figure, cast
and carved from a
model by H. Keck,
on an onyx base,
signed in the
bronze 'H. Keck',
with foundry mark,
12in (30.5cm) high.
£900–1,100 *CSK*

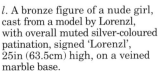

l. A bronze figure of a nude girl,
cast from a model by Lorenzl,
with overall muted silver-coloured
patination, signed 'Lorenzl',
25in (63.5cm) high, on a veined
marble base.
£3,500–4,500 *P*

An Art Deco bronze group signed 'H. Fugère', c1920, 18in (45.5cm) wide. £1,500–1,800 *IHA*

A painted bronze and ivory figure, with gilt, red and green costume, signed 'Gerdago', 'AR' founder's mark, 15½in (39.5cm) high. £2,000–2,500 *P*

A silvered and gilt-bronze figure, on a red-green marble base, signed 'Guiraud Rivière', 1920s, 20½in (52cm) high. £5,500–6,500 *S*

A silvered and gilt-bronze and ivory figure of a young woman, in a pyjama suit, silvered and oxidized, with gilt design, base marked 'G. Gori', 1920s, 14in (35.5cm) high. £2,000–2,500 *S*

A Lavroff patinated bronze figure of a woman, on a stepped marble base, signed in the maquette, 1920s, 17in (43cm) high. £1,400–1,700 *S*

A bronze lamp, marked 'Guillemard', fitted for electricity, 1920s, 15½in (39.5cm) high. £1,500–1,800 *S*

A bronze and ivory bust, by Agathon Leonard, on a green onyx base, signed 'A. Leonard', 6in (15cm) high. £900–1,000 *P*

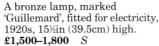

A Keck bronze and ivory figure, cold-painted with metallic bronze-green, brown detailed hair, bronze base plate marked 'H. Keck fec', c1920, 13in (33cm) high. £2,000–2,500 *S*

A polished bronze nude dancer, marked 'Lorenzl', 1930s, 16in (40.5cm) high. £1,800–2,200 *S*

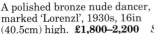

A dark bronze nude female figure, cast from a model, inscribed 'Lorenzl', 17½in (44.5cm) high. £1,800–2,200 *CSK*

A cold-painted bronze and ivory figure of a temple dancer, by Lorenzl, silvered patina, inscribed, 14in (35.5cm) high. £2,000–2,500 *C*

l. A green patinated bronze group of a pair of dancers, signed 'Lorenzl', 10½in (26.5cm) high. £1,200–1,400 *P*

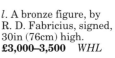

l. A bronze figure, by R. D. Fabricius, signed, 30in (76cm) high. £3,000–3,500 *WHL*

r. A bronze figure, 'The Kicking Dancer', cast from a model by Bruno Zach, on a green onyx base, bronze inscribed 'B. Zach', 12½in (32cm) high.
£1,000–1,200 *C*

A bronze figure, 'Con Brio', cast after a model by Ferdinand Preiss, on a black and green marble base, signed on the base 'F. Preiss', 13½in (34.5cm) high.
£3,000–3,500 *C*

A bronze figure, 'Girl Skipping', from a model by Bruno Zach, signed in the bronze 'Zach', 14½in (37cm) high.
£2,500–3,000 *C*

A bronze group, signed in the bronze 'JB', 15½in (63.5cm) wide.
£2,500–3,000 *C*

A gilt-bronze figure of a girl with a dog, 12in (30.5cm).
£2,500–3,000 *C*

A large cold-painted bronze figure of a young woman, by Bruno Zach, on a grey veined black marble plinth, signed, 36½in (92.5cm) high.
£12,000–14,000 *HSS*

A bronze study of Lucifer, 20thC, 8in (20.5cm) high.
£800–1,000 *CSK*

A bronze model of a panther, cast from a model by M. Prost, inscribed 'M. Prost,' and 'Susse Fres. Editrs. Paris', 7½in (19cm) high.
£1,000–1,200 *C*

A green and gilt patinated bronze figure of a female archer, unsigned, 15in (38cm) high.
£1,000–1,200 *GC*

r. A French bronze model, 'A Seated Monkey', cast from a model by Edouard Marcel Sandox, formed as a finial, inscribed 'Ed M Sandoz', early 20thC, 4½in (11.5cm) high.
£1,000–1,200 *GC*

l. A bronze and ivory figure, by Marcel Bouraine, on a marble base, 12½in (32cm) high.
£1,800–2,200 *ASA*

A gilt-bronze and ivory figure of a clown, signed 'C. Mimo', c1920, 9in (23cm) high.
£1,000–1,200   *S*

A bronze figure, 'Pert', on a bronze base, signed 'Roland Paris', 12in (30.5cm) high.
£1,200–1,400   *P*

A bronze figure of a nude dancer with a hoop, on a marble plinth engraved 'Aurore Onu', 1930s, 19in (48.5cm) high.
£1,200–1,600   *S*

A bronze and alabaster bust, 'The Jester', signed 'Roland Paris', 10in (25.5cm) high.
£900–1,100   *P*

A cold-painted bronze and ivory figure, on stepped onyx base, signed 'M. Munk, Vienna', 14in (35.5cm) high.
£1,400–1,800   *SS*

A bronze and ivory group of a woman and 2 hounds, cold-painted in red gold, marked 'Prof. Poertzel', with foundry mark 'PK', 1920s, 19½in (49.5cm) high.
£6,000–7,000   *S*

A gilt-bronze nude figure, attributed to Philippe, 1920s, 22½in (57cm) high.
£2,000–2,500   *S*

A bronze and ivory figure of a pierette, signed in the maquette 'A. Gilbert', 1920s, 9in (23cm) high.
£3,000–3,500   *S*

An amber and gold painted bronze and ivory figure, on green onyx base, signed 'F. Preiss', 14½in (37cm) high.
£9,000–11,000   *P*

A pair of ivory figures, 'Greek Maidens', 7in (17.5cm) high.
£1,200–1,600   *CSK*

A painted bronze and ivory figure, 'Sun Worshipper', signed on onyx 'F. Preiss', 7½in (19cm) high.
£7,000–8,500   *P*

r. An Art Deco figure, 'The Tennis Player', by F. Preiss, with gold and bronze costume, ivory head, limbs and tennis racket, on a signed onyx base.
£12,000–14,500   *GSP*

A cold-painted gilt bronze figure, in the style of Bruno Zach, on a green onyx base, 12in (30.5cm) high.
£1,000–1,200 *Bon*

l. A bronze figure, 'Nocturne', cast after a model by Edward-Louis Collet, inscribed in the bronze 'Collet Scpt', stamped foundry mark 'E Colin & Co Paris', 18in (45.5cm) high.
£900–1,100 *C*

r. A bronze figure cast after a model by Hugo Lederer, dark brown patina, on a stepped circular speckled grey marble base, signed in the bronze 'Hugo Lederer', c1925, 17in (43cm) high.
£1,500–1,800 *C*

r. A bronze figure, 'Stella', Giraud Rivière inscribed on star 'Giraud Rivière, Etling Paris', and 'Bronze, France', 11½in (29cm) high.
£4,000–4,500 *P*

l. A German gilt-bronze figure, inscribed 'Schmidt-Hofer', 16in (40.5cm) high.
£500–600 *P*

A silvered bronze figure, signed 'Pierre Laurel', stamped 'Marcel Guillemard 14', 17½in (44.5cm) high.
£3,000–3,500 *P*

l. A silvered bronze figure, 'Vestal', by Le Faguays, each hand holding an onyx cup, inscribed 'Le Faguays', 14½in (37cm) high.
£2,000–2,500 *CSK*

A pair of cold-painted bronze figural bookends, 'Chinese Students', on marble bases, signed 'H. M. White', 8½in (21.5cm) high.
£450–500 *P*

A bronze figure, 'Dancer of Olynthus', by D. Chiparus, signed on base 'Chiparus', 15in (38cm) high.
£1,500–1,800 *P*

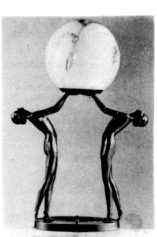

A bronzed electric table lamp, with mottled globular glass shade, the oval base with an onyx stand, 20in (51cm) high.
£850–1,000 *AG*

A green patinated
bronze figure of a nude
femal dancer, on
a circular marble base,
signed 'A. Bouraine',
17½in (44.5cm) high.
£1,300–1,500   *P*

A bronze and ivory figure of
a dancing girl, on a pale green
marble base, marked 'Gerdago',
with founder's stamp, 1920s,
13in (33cm) high.
£2,000–2,500   *SB*

A bronze and ivory figure
of a girl in Easter costume,
the carved ivory head-
dress set with red stones,
some damage, marked
'B. Grundmann fec'.
£1,300–1,500   *SBe*

A cold-painted simulated bronze, ivory and marble
group, inscribed 'Limousin', 14⅝in (37cm) high.
£400–500   *C*

A polished bronze figure,
on a marble base, signed
in the maquette 'G.
Lavroff', 1920s,
18in (45.5cm) high.
£1,300–1,500   *SB*

r. A bronze figure, cold-painted
silver, pink and green, marked
'Lorenzl', 1930s, 12in (30.5cm) high.
£1,200–1,400   *SB*

A bronze and ivory
figure, dressed in
carnival costume, base
marked 'Lorenzl', 1920s,
13in (33cm) high.
£2,000–2,500   *SB*

l. A bronze and ivory figure,
'The Champagne Girl', by F.
Preiss, red cold-painted, base
marked 'F. Preiss', damaged,
16in (40.5cm) high.
£5,000–6,000   *SBe*

A cold-painted bronze figure of
a dancing girl, marked 'Lorenzl',
1920s, 16in (40.5cm) high.
£3,000–3,500   *SB*

A cold-painted bronze figure
of a dancing girl, by Lorenzl,
9½in (24cm) high.
£800–950   *SBe*

A bronze and ivory figure of
a girl, engraved mark 'Le
Faguays', 16½in (42cm) high.
£1,500–1,800   *SB*

A gilt-bronze figure, cast from a model by Lorenzl, on a green onyx base, inscribed 'Lorenzl', 10in (25.5cm) high.
£1,200–1,400 *CSK*

A cold-painted bronze and ivory figure, by Lorenzl, enamelled in colours, on an onyx base, damaged, signed 'Crejo', 10in (25.5cm) high.
£1,000–1,200 *CEd*

A bronze and ivory figure of Harlequin, by Lorenzl.
£2,400–2,800 *ASA*

A bronze and ivory figure, by Lorenzl, c1930.
£1,200–1,500 *ASA*

r. A cold-painted bronze figure, 'Sword Dancer', cast from a model by Nan Greb, inscribed, 21in (53.5cm) high.
£2,000–2,500 *CSK*

A bronze figure, cast from a model by Le Faguays, signed on base, 25in (63.5cm) high.
£2,500–3,000 *CSK*

l. A cold-painted bronze figure, cast from a model by Nan Greb, inscribed, 11in (28cm) high.
£1,000–1,200 *CSK*

A bronze and ivory figure, 'Gamine', after a model by Ferdinand Preiss, cold-painted in green, on a green marble base, some hairline cracks, inscribed, 13½in (34.5cm) high.
£6,500–8,000 *CEd*

A bronze figure, 'Hoop Girl', by D. H. Chiparus, 11in (28cm) high.
£3,000–3,500 *ASA*

A bronze figure of a dancer, by Ferdinand Preiss, c1930.
£3,000–3,500 *ASA*

A bronze and ivory figure, in the manner of F. Preiss, on a black marble plinth, 11in 928cm) high.
£6,500–8,000 *BWe*

l. A bronze figure of a motor-cyclist, unsigned but attributed to Bruno Zach, the marble base applied with metal tag stamped 'B. Zach Sculp. Argentor Vienna', 8in (20.5cm) high.
£3,000–3,500 *P*

Locate the Source

The source of each illustration in *Miller's Art Nouveau & Art Deco Buyer's Guide* can be found by checking the code letters below each caption with the Key to Illustrations.

A bronze group, cast from a model by C. Kauba, dark gilt patina, signed in the bronze 'C. Kauba', on a marble base, 5½in (14cm) high.
£800–950   *C*

A figure lamp, by Le Verrier, c1930, 19in (48.5cm) high.
£1,500–1,800   *ASA*

A bronze figure, cast from a model by Jaeger, signed 'Jaeger', stamped 'Vrais-Bronze Déposé K', foundry marks, 26in (66cm) high.
£450–500   *P*

l. A bronze figure, 'The Racing Driver', cast from a model by Saalmann, inscribed, stamped 'Echte Bronze', 11in (29cm) high.
£2,500–3,000   *C*

A cold-painted gilt-bronze and ivory figure, c1930, 17in (43cm) high.
£800–950   *S*

A bronze figure, 'A Torch Dancer', after a model by Ferdinand Preiss, with dull golden bronze patina, on a black and green marble base, signed on base 'F. Preiss', 13½in (34.5cm) high.
£3,000–3,500   *C*

A silvered bronze figure, 'A Huntress', cast from a model by G. None, signed in the bronze 'G. None Gorini Fres Editeurs, Paris', 13½in (34.5cm) high.
£2,500–3,000   *C*

l. A bronze figure, cast from a model by Ferdinand Liebermann, in various cold coloured patinas, including gilt, dark gold and red, signed in the bronze 'F. Liebermann', 15½in (39.5cm) high.
£3,000–3,500   *C*

A bronze figure of a hunter, cast from a model by Pierre Le Faguays, bronze inscribed 'P. Le Faguays', 14in (35.5cm) high, and another similar bronze cast from a model by Le Faguays.
£1,200–1,400   *CSK*

A silvered bronze 'Messenger of Love', by Pierre Le Faguays, c1930, 30½in (77.5cm) high.
£6,500–8,000   *ASA*

A bronze group, cast from a model by A. Boucher, dark patina, signed in the bronze 'A. Boucher' and with Siot-Paris foundry stamp, 19½in (49.5cm) high.
£5,000–6,000 *C*

A bronze and ivory figure, by F. Preiss, on a stepped green and black onyx base, lacking hands, signed in the maquette, c1930, 5in (12.5cm) high.
£450–500 *S(S)*

A bronze inkwell, by P. Tereszczuk, with a young girl crossing a stream, a basket in each hand, signed, c1920, 12⅝in (32cm) wide.
£400–500 *S(S)*

l. A silvered bronze figure, by Hélène Grünne, indistinct foundry mark, 1920s, 11½in (29cm) high.
£1,200–1,400 *S(S)*

A bronze and ivory figure, 'Dancer', cast and carved from a model by Gerdago, her costume with gold patination and cold-painted geometric decoration in red and shades of blue, on an oval green onyx base, decoration rubbed, signed in the bronze 'A. R. Gerdago', 13in (33cm) high.
£5,000–6,000 *C*

An enamelled bronze and ivory dancer, in red and black shoes, her dress decorated in orange, red, blue, green, black and gilt flowerheads, a wide-brimmed hat similarly painted, raised on a stepped oval green onyx base, incised 'Austria' on the base, 1920s, 12⅝in (32cm) high.
£5,000–6,000 *S(S)*

A chrome plated sculpture of a reclining figure, worn, stamped 'A Reimann, Ges Gesch, Made in Germany', 5½in (14cm) long.
£900–1,100 *S(S)*

A Dutch brass model of a dancer, signed 'Th. A. Vos' and 'Kunst-Bronsgieterij, De Kroon, Haarlem', 19in (48.5cm) high.
£800–950 *C(S)*

Thomas Vos was born in Groningen in the Netherlands in 1887. Having learned to sculpt in Brussels, he worked principally on figures of women, animals and children until his death in Haarlem in 1948.

An ashtray, with a figure of a boy, 6in (15cm) high.
£1,000–1,200 *ASA*

A silvered bronze and ivory figure of a dancing girl, painted with bell-formed blue flowers and green foliage, raised on a green onyx base, damaged, moulded mark 'Lorenzl', painted 'Crejo', 1920s, 14½in (37cm) high.
£3,000–3,500 *S(S)*

l. A bronze and polychrome marble figure, 'Reading', cast and carved from a model by Schumacher, signed in the bronze 'Henry', 10in (25.5cm) high.
£1,500–1,800 *C*

A bronze and ivory figure, 'Dancing Girl', signed 'Lorenzl', 9in (23cm) high.
£1,200–1,400 *C*

l. A gilt-bronze and ivory figure, 'Mystery', cast and carved from a model by V. Seifert, signed in the bronze 'V. Seifert', 11½in (29cm) high.
£1,400–1,700 *C*

A bronze figure, 'Spanish Flamenco Dancer', cast from a model by Sonher, inscribed 'Sonher', 13½in (34.5cm) high.
£1,300–1,500 *C*

A bronze figure, 'The Fencer', cast from a model by H. Müller, signed in the bronze 'H. Müller', 17½in (44.5cm) high.
£1,000–1,200 *C*

r. A bronze figure, 'Athlete', cast from a model by H. Henjes, signed in the bronze 'H. Henjes fec. 10', 14in (35.5cm) high.
£900–1,100 *C*

A bronze and ivory figure, 'Feeding the Birds', cast and carved from a model by L. Barthelémy, signed in the bronze, 12in (30.5cm) high.
£3,000–3,500 *C*

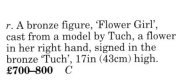

A spelter and ivorine group, 'Pierrot and Columbine', cast from a model by Demêtre Chiparus, on a striated marble plinth, 30in (76cm) high.
£1,500–1,800 *C*

r. A bronze figure, 'Flower Girl', cast from a model by Tuch, a flower in her right hand, signed in the bronze 'Tuch', 17in (43cm) high.
£700–800 *C*

A silver patinated bronze figure, 'Amazon', by Marcel Bouraine, the stylized nude female warrior kneeling on a dark patinated base, signed in the bronze 'Bouraine', 7in (17.5cm) high.
£2,000–2,500 *C*

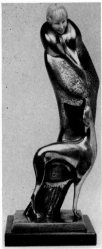

A pair of bronze figures, by
Pierre Laurel, 11½in (29cm) high.
£3,500–4,000 *ASA*

l. A marble and bronze figure,
by Lothar, signed.
£2,500–3,000 *ASA*

A bronze figure, 'Speedskater', cast
from a model by Carl Fagerberg,
signed on the bronze plinth 'Carl
Fagerberg, Stockholm' and dated
'April 1932', 20½in (52cm) high.
£3,000–3,500 *C*

*This piece was commissioned for
a competition and exhibition
commemorating the 1932 Los
Angeles Olympic Games, and bears
its original exhibition label on the
underside of the base.*

A gold patinated bronze and
ivory group, 'Elegant', from
a model by S. Bertrand,
on a bronze plinth and black
marble base, slightly chipped,
signed, 12in (30.5cm) high.
£3,000–3,500 *C*

l. A bronze and ivory figure, cast and
carved from a model by Lorenzl, on
green onyx base, stamped 'Lorenzl,
Made in Austria', 13½in (34.5cm) high.
£2,500–3,000 *P*

A bronze and ivory figure of the
poet Dante, signed in the bronze
'D. H. Chiparus', 28in (71cm) high.
£3,000–3,500 *C*

A bronze and ivory figure,
wearing a green patinated dress
with puff sleeves, cast and carved
from a model by Boulard, signed
in the bronze, on green onyx
base, 14in (35.5cm) high.
£900–1,100 *CSK*

A bronze and ivory
figure by Lorenzl,
12½in (32cm) high.
£2,000–2,500 *ASA*

A cold-painted bronze figure,
poised on one leg with a green
serpent around her ankle,
attributed as a model by
Colinet, 20in (51cm) high.
£2,000–2,500 *P*

A cold-painted bronze and
ivory figure, cast and carved
from a model by Lorenzl, on
a geometric green and black
onyx base, signed 'Lorenzl',
10in (25.5cm) high.
£1,500–1,800 *P*

A gilt-bronze figure, 'Beside the
Missouri', cast from a model by
Claire Jeanne Roberte Colinet,
inscribed in the marble 'Cl. J. R.
Colinet', 19½in (49.5cm) high.
£2,000–2,500 *CSK*

l. A bronze figure, 'Cleopatra',
cast from a model by D. H.
Chiparus, signed in the bronze
'Chiparus', 19in (48.5cm) wide.
£4,500–5,500 *C*

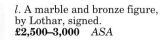

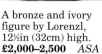

SILVER & METALWARE

The collector of silver and metalware from the Art Nouveau and Art Deco periods has an enormous range from which to choose, as the items illustrated on the following pages indicate. A vast array of forms, materials, makers and designers are available and, regardless of the depth of one's pockets, there is something for everyone.

Towards the end of the 19th century, forms and styles in silver and metalware began to move away from the elaborate medieval, baroque or rococo designs favoured during the mid-19th century. Christopher Dresser, a prominent designer for Elkington's from 1875 to 1888, was inspired by a visit to Japan in 1876. His work shows a cleanness of line that anticipated the styles of the 1920s and 1930s – the Machine Age – and are now highly sought after. A plated teapot made in 1879 sold for £40,000 in 1986, and another from the same group fetched almost £70,000 in 1994. A teapot made £120,000 in America in 1999.

Other British designers/makers of note working in silver and representing the Arts & Crafts Movement were Charles Robert Ashbee (1863–1942) at the Guild of Handicraft Ltd, Omar Ramsden, Alwyn Carr and Gilbert Marks. They worked according to two principles: the rejection of mass-market machine-made items, and appreciation of the forms and styles of decorative pieces produced during the Middle Ages.

Liberty & Co combined innovative design and a craft 'look' with mass production. Founded by Arthur Lasenby Liberty in 1875, the company launched its Cymric range of silverware in 1899, and in 1901 Liberty & Co (Cymric) Ltd was formed, in conjunction with the Birmingham-based silver firm of W. H. Haseler. Archibald Knox was one of Liberty's most important designers, producing designs for Cymric silver ware and for the Tudric pewter range introduced in 1903. Together with Rex Silver and Oliver Baker, Knox established the 'Liberty Style' in the early years of the 20th century, and his designs have shown huge increases over the last five years.

The use of combinations of different metals became popular during this period. A. E. Jones used silver and copper together and produced pleasing jewellery caskets, and W. A. S. Benson designed lamps using copper and brass that were retailed through William Morris & Co, as were embossed copper pieces by John Pearson who had spent time at Ashbee's Guild of Handicraft.

In Germany, the firm of WMF (Württembergische Metallwarenfabrik) created a range of metalwares which epitomize the popular conception of Art Nouveau. They produced machine-made, mass-produced vessels, cutlery and mirrors embellished with maidens, sinuous forms and motifs from nature, providing for a large clientele, and consistently sought by collectors today. The huge number of WMF reproductions has adversely affected the value of some of the WMF items.

A constant reminder of the past pre-eminence of Art Nouveau in France are Hector Guimard's Metro entrances, made from green-patinated bronze, emblematic of the power of growth exhibited everywhere in nature. Louis Majorelle of Nancy produced stunning ormolu mounts for his furniture, and there are examples of his collaboration with the glass factory, Daum Frères. Daum Frères and Emile Gallé also chose leading silversmiths of the day to fashion quality mounts for their glassware.

The Exposition des Arts Decoratif of 1925 in Paris showed what was considered the best of the period, and later the name 'Art Deco' was used to categorize such pieces. In 1935, France launched the luxury liner SS *Normandie*, making her maiden voyage to New York. Her interior was a showcase of Art Deco, with the very best of French design, fittings, cuisine and crew: tableware by Puiforcat and Christofle, glassware by Lalique, Daum and St Antoine, and furniture by Ruhlmann.

Technological advances in transportation and communications had considerable influence on architecture and design: steamlining became a prominent design feature, combining the principles of aerodynamic engineering and geometry. In addition, discoveries such as the tomb of Tutankhamun in 1922 encouraged the development of an Egyptian style.

The Art Deco metalwares of Swiss designer/maker Jean Dunand (1877–1942) deserve a mention. He produced extraordinary patinated copper vases using a technique called dinanderie, often featuring strong angular lines and with a geometric bias.

Also working in this style was Claudius Linossier (1893–1955) who was noted for the elegant design and textured surfaces of his vases, bowls and plates. Pieces by these two designers are particularly sought after. Finely executed and designed silver cigarette cases and compacts with geometric motifs, were produced by Gerard Sandoz (b1902) and Raymond Templier (1891–1968), reflecting the opulence of the very rich in the 1920s and 1930s.

When buying Art Nouveau and Art Deco silver, always buy what you find pleasing and can most afford. Never buy something which you have reservations about, however reasonable the price. Always ask advice from reputable sources if you are not sure.

Whatever your taste or collecting criteria, there will surely be something for the discerning collector from these most colourful, exotic and dynamic periods in the Decorative Arts. **Keith Baker**

A Liberty & Co Tudric pewter flower vase, possibly designed by Archibald Knox, stamped marks, 'Tudric 0441', 4in (10cm) high.
£1,500–1,800   P

A bronze vase, signed 'J. Ofner', 13in (33cm) high.
£1,200–1,400   CSK

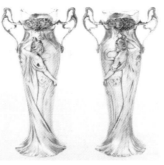

A pair of WMF figural metal vases, with glass liners, stamped marks on base, 14½in (37cm) high.
£2,000–2,500   P

A silver vase, maker's marks 'G & Co Ld', Birmingham 1963, 10½in (26.5cm) high.
£400–450   P

A Hagenauer plated mirror, with linear decoration on one side, stamped on reverse 'WHW' in circle, 9½in (24cm) high.
£800–950   P

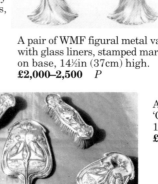

A silver backed brush set, embossed with kingfishers and waterlilies, Chester 1909, cased by Oldfields, Liverpool.
£400–450   P(CW)

A hammered-copper framed mirror, 21 x 15in (53.5 x 38cm).
£350–400   ST

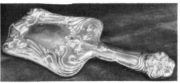

A silver-backed hand mirror, 1907.
£150–180   PC

An Arts and Crafts mirror, with a moth enamelled in relief, 19 x 15in (48.5 x 38cm).
£600–700   ST

A silver and enamelled picture frame, marked 'H & A', Birmingham 1904, 6½in (16.5cm) square.
800–950   P

A brass flower, the petals remove to make individual ashtrays, c1900, 9½in (24cm) wide.
£120–150   GAL

A pair of Liberty & Co silver and enamelled picture frames, marked 'L & Co', Birmingham 1913, 5½in (14cm) diam, in original Liberty box.
£1,200–1,400   P

A pewter garniture, by Margaret Gilmore, comprising oval mirror and a pair of double candle sconces, each embossed with a Celtic interlaced design and stamped 'M.G.', mirror 30in (76cm) wide.
£2,000–2,500   CEd

A Hukin & Heath 'Japanesque' teapot and sugar bowl, with silver colour on a copper ground, inscribed 'Designed by Dr. C. Dresser', teapot 4in (10cm) high.
£1,500–1,800   *P*

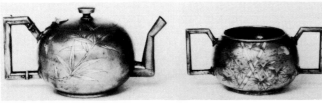

A beaten pewter and ebonized wood rectangular wall mirror, designed and executed by Margaret and Frances Macdonald, impressed 'Margaret Macdonald, Frances Macdonald, 1897', 27in (69cm) high.
£12,000–14,000   *C*

On graduation from the Glasgow School in 1894, the Misses Macdonald opened a studio at 128 Hope Street, Glasgow where they devoted themselves to the applied arts. The metal items produced by the two sisters were, apart from a very few examples, not only designed but worked entirely by themselves and although closely collaborating, few examples of their metalwork now exist bearing both signatures. The studio closed when Frances Macdonald married Herbert MacNair in 1899.

A silver punch bowl, by F. Fattorini & Son Ltd, Birmingham 1905, 12½in (32cm) wide, 37oz.
£1,200–1,500   *L*

A silver and enamel flared cylindrical vase, probably designed by Archibald Knox, indistinct stamped marks, 'Rd 467167', damaged, 7in (17.5cm) high.
£1,000–1,200   *C*

A silver comport, chased with roses and foliage on a hammered ground, by W. Walker & B. Tolhurst, signed 'L. Movio 1904', 13⅝in (34.5cm) high, 50oz.
£2,500–3,000   *GSP*

A Goldsmiths & Silversmiths Co silver and enamel presentation cup and cover, London 1902, 12in (30.5cm) high, 25½oz.
£2,500–3,000   *C*

A Guild of Handicrafts Ltd silver toast rack, probably to a design by Charles Robert Ashbee, maker's mark for London 1906, 5in (12.5cm) wide, 7oz.
£1,500–1,800   *P*

A Walker & Hall silver-mounted jug, inspired by a design by Christopher Dresser, maker's mark, Sheffield 1906, 9in (23cm) high.
£300–350   *S*

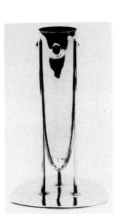

r. A William Hutton & Sons silver dressing set, designed by Kate Harris, maker's marks, '1900/03/04', mirror 11in (28cm) high, 7oz.
£800–950   *S*

l. A Liberty & Co silver vase, designed by Archibald Knox, the rim set with turquoises, maker's mark, stamped 'Cymric, Birmingham 1903', 6in (15cm) high.
£1,800–2,000   *S*

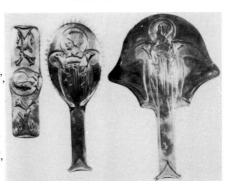

A Goldsmiths & Silversmiths Co silver box, by Kate Harris, maker's marks for London 1901, 4in (10cm) high, 22oz.
£1,200–1,400   P

An Edwardian rose bowl, by Hamilton & Inches, Edinburgh 1902, 9in (23cm) diam, 38oz.
£1,200–1,400   CDC

A claret jug, Birmingham 1905, 10½in (26.5cm) high.
£800–950   CDC

A silver teaset, marked 'GD. DF', London 1901, teapot 5½in (14cm) high, 35.5oz.
£280–340   P

A Hukin & Heath plated metal and glass biscuit barrel, marked 'H & H' and '1894', 5½in (14cm) high.
£250–300   P

A Hukin & Heath plated toast rack, H & H mark, lozenge mark for 9th October 1878, 'Designed by Dr. C. Dresser', and No. '1987', 7in (17.5cm) wide.
£2,000–2,400   P

A silver-plated five-piece tea service, with green ball feet on stepped bases, 1930s, 23in (58.5cm) wide. £500–600   S

An Aesthetic Movement silver-plated kettle, the design attributed to Christopher Dresser, maker's marks for R. & R. Hodd & Sons, and a design lozenge for 16th May 1878, 7½in (19cm) high.
£350–400   P

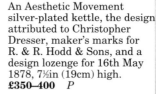

A Hukin & Heath silver-plated sweetmeat bowl, stamped 'H & H No. 2047' 'Designed by Dr. C. Dresser', 7in (17.5cm) wide.
£550–650   P

A Keswick School of Industrial Arts silver buckle, each half stamped 'KSIA', 3in (7.5cm) wide.
£700–800   DWB

A Dixon & Sons silver-plated teapot, designed by Christopher Dresser, maker's marks, facsimile signature and No. '2277', 5in (12.5cm) high.
£50,000–60,000   P

A William Hutton & Sons silver-plated cruet set, after a design by Christopher Dresser, maker's mark, c1900, 2½in (6.5cm) high.
£100–120   P

A Hukin & Heath silver-plated sweetmeat dish, designed by Christopher Dresser, stamped 'H & H No. 2593', 7in (17.5cm) wide.
£200–250   P

A Georg Jensen hammered silver teapot, with ebony handle, stamped '456', 'GS, and import marks for London 1929, 6in (15cm) high, 16oz.
£800–950   *CEd*

A Hukin & Heath silver teaset, designed by Christopher Dresser, the teapot with wicker handle, the domed cover with button finial, with milk jug and sugar bowl, both contained within the pot, maker's marks for Birmingham 1880, registration lozenge for 18th October 1879, teapot 4½in (11.5cm) high.
£1,500–1,800   *P*

A pewter ale jug and cover, in the style of C. F. A. Voysey, probably made for Liberty & Co, 14½in (37cm) high.
£1,000–1,200   *P*

An Orfevrerie Gallia silver-plated tea and coffee set, stamped factory marks, No. '4643' and '4644', tray 20½in (52cm) wide.
£1,200–1,400   *P*

r. A silver goblet, Chester 1905, 8in (20.5cm) high.
£700–800   *TVA*

A Mappin & Webb silver coffee set, comprising hot milk jug, sugar bowl and coffee pot, marked for Sheffield 1938, coffee pot 7in (17.5cm) high.
£1,000–1,200   *P*

A Modernist silver-coloured metal teaset, stamped '800' and '210ff', teapot 5in (12.5cm) high.
£1,200–1,400   *P*

l. A pair of pewter four-branch candlesticks, by Just Anderson, c1920, 9in (23cm) high.
£600–700   *GAL*

r. A pair of Liberty Tudric pewter candlesticks, with detachable driptrays, No. 01769, 8in (20.5cm) high.
£200–300   *HCH*

A WMF pewter dish with a figure, 9in (23cm) high.
£650–750 *GAL*

A German pewter bowl, by Osiris, 5½in (14cm) high.
£300–350 *GAL*

A Guild of Handicraft plated copper tazza, to a design by Charles Robert Ashbee, 10½in (26.5cm) high.
£2,000–2,500 *P*

A Jean Després silver-plated bowl, with hammered finish, signed on base and 'JD' poinçon on rim, 4in (10cm) high.
£900–1,100 *P*

l. An Arts and Crafts stemmed bowl, attributed to John Paul Cooper, inscribed 'In memory of a Labour of Love, Ascension Day 1914', 6in (15cm) high.
£2,000–2,500 *P*

A silver-coloured metal bowl, stamped 'David Anderson 830S' and numbered '5485', 16½in (42cm) wide.
£650–750 *P*

A Liberty & Co pewter and Clutha glass stemmed bowl, the mount marked 'English Pewter' and '0276', 6½in (16.5cm) high.
£2,000–2,500 *P*

A WMF silvered pewter covered two-handled punch bowl, and ladle, stamped, 21½in (54.5cm) high.
£2,000–2,500 *CAm*

An Omar Ramsden silver soup ladle, stamped 'OR', marked for London 1924, 10½in (26.5cm) high.
£650–750 *P*

A Georg Jensen Continental pattern silver table service, comprising 57 pieces, stamped marks, import marks for London 1934, 68oz.
£2,000–2,500 *CEd*

A Georg Jensen Scroll pattern silver table service, comprising 79 pieces, designed by Johan Rohde, stamped 'Georg Jensen' and 'Sterling Denmark', 136oz.
£2,500–3,000 *P*

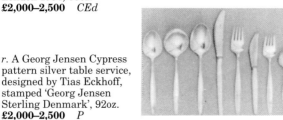

r. A Georg Jensen Cypress pattern silver table service, designed by Tias Eckhoff, stamped 'Georg Jensen Sterling Denmark', 92oz.
£2,000–2,500 *P*

A Georg Jensen cased set of 6 silver coffee spoons, stamped 'G. S.', import mark for London 1925.
£200–250 *CEd*

A Liberty & Co pewter and enamel clock, c1903, 11in (28cm) high.
£1,800–2,000 *ZEI*

l. An Art Nouveau pewter mirror, 22in (56cm) high.
£1,200–1,500 *ZEI*

A WMF plated pewter mirror, the surround cast in relief with the figure of a maiden in long flowing drapery, her hair adorned with flowers, stamped factory marks, 14½in (37cm) high.
£1,000–1,200 *P*

l. A Liberty & Co pewter teaset and tray, c1910, tray 17in (43cm) wide.
£600–700 *ASA*

A Guild of Handicraft silver jam spoon, designed by C. R. Ashbee, set with turquoise, engraved 'Lorna', stamped 'G of H Ltd', London hallmarks for 1904.
£300–350 *C*

An A. E. Jones hammered silver rose bowl, decorated with a repoussé frieze of Tudor roses amid foliage, mounted on a wood plinth, stamped maker's marks 'A.E.J.', Birmingham hallmarks for 1909, 9in (23cm) diam, 31oz.
£2,000–2,500 *C*

A Liberty & Co silver and enamel christening set, comprising: a teaspoon and matching napkin ring, in original box, both with moulded floral design, heightened with blue and green enamel, maker's mark for Birmingham 1908, 4in (11cm) high.
£500–600 *P*

A WMF silver-plated dessert service, with unusual box, 13in (33cm) wide.
£800–950 *ARE*

l. A pair of Liberty & Co Cymric silver candlesticks, design attributed to Archibald Knox, maker's mark for Birmingham 1909, one repaired.
£12,000–14,000 *P*

A WMF silver-plated pewter champagne bucket, signed and dated '1906'.
£1,200–1,500 *ASA*

A WMF silvered-pewter bowl, with swing handle, and green glass liner, stamped marks, 10in (25.5cm) wide.
£500–600 *CSK*

A WMF silver-plated box, 5in (12.5cm) diam.
£200–250 *ASA*

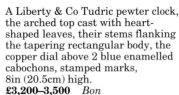

A pewter bowl, moulded with female heads and swirling draperies, with a cut-glass liner.
£750–900 *LRG*

A Liberty & Co pewter and enamel clock, c1900, 7½in (19cm) high.
£1,700–2,000 *ASA*

A Liberty & Co Tudric pewter clock, the arched top cast with heart-shaped leaves, their stems flanking the tapering rectangular body, the copper dial above 2 blue enamelled cabochons, stamped marks, 8in (20.5cm) high.
£3,200–3,500 *Bon*

r. A pair of Liberty & Co Tudric candlesticks, attributed to Archibald Knox, 5½in (14cm) high.
£600–700 *NCA*

A Liberty & Co pewter and enamel clock, 4½in (11.5cm) high.
£600–700 *ASA*

A Tudric pewter picture frame, with stylised honesty decoration, 10in (25.5cm) high.
£1,200–1,500 *C*

A Liberty & Co pewter and enamel clock, 8in (20.5cm) high.
£2,500–3,000 *ASA*

Two Liberty & Co silver and enamel cigarette cases, detailed in turquoise enamel, one stamped 'Cymric', Birmingham, 1902, 3½in by 3in (9cm by 7.5cm).
£1,000–1,200 *S*

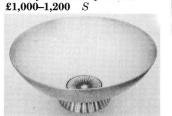

A silver-coloured metal shallow bowl by Georg Jensen, maker's mark, Denmark, stamped Sterling, 6½in (16cm) diam, 8½oz. **£400–500** *L*

A WMF electroplated dish, marked, c1900, 8½in (21cm) high.
£800–1,000 *S*

A WMF teaset, with teapot, hot water jug, milk jug and sugar bowl, all on a tray.
£2,500–3,000 *S*

l. & r. A pair of German Art Nouveau wine coasters, stamped mark of Württembergische Metallwarenfabrik (WMF), 3½in (9cm) high.
£300–350
c. A German Art Nouveau jewel casket, stamped mark of Württembergische Metallwarenfabrik (WMF), 7¼in (18.5cm) overall length.
£200–250 *L*

A set of 6 William Hutton & Sons silver salts, with spoons, maker's mark and hallmarks for London 1901, also Austrian importation marks, fitted case, 1½in (3.5cm) high, 5oz.
£700–850 *P*

A silver and enamelled christening set, each piece embellished with a blue enamelled plant form, maker's marks 'E.J.& S.', Birmingham 1905, cup 3in (7.5cm) high, in a fitted case.
£300–350 *P*

An Irish silver plated copper tazza, c1900, 8½in (21.5cm) high.
£350–400 *S*

A WMF standish, c1900, 13½in (34cm) high.
£200–250 *TA*

An Elkington Art Nouveau bowl, of pierced oval outline, with curved handles supported on 2 C-shaped stems above an oval domes base, stamped 'E. & Co.', with Birmingham hallmarks for 1910, 7in (17.5cm) high.
£400–450   *P*

A C. R. Ashbee hammered-silver bowl, with pierced design of stylized fruit laden branches, stamped 'CRA' with London hallmarks for 1899, 8in (20.5cm) diam.
£1,200–1,500   *C*

A Liberty & Co, silver rose bowl, designed by Bernard Cuzner, engraved with Golden Wedding dedication on one side, marked 'L & Co.', Birmingham 1916, separate grille top for flower display, 6½in (16.5cm) diam.
£3,500–4,000   *P*

A Tiffany & Co silver child's mug, the body decorated in low relief, with etched detailing, with a scene of children preparing a number of small dogs to jump through a hoop, stamped 'Tiffany & Co. 410SE', Sterling Silver 925-1000 M, 3in (7.5cm) high.
£350–400   *P*

An Art Nouveau preserve jar and spoon, by George Lawrence Connell, with plain glass jar, hammered openwork trefoil frame and tripod handle to cover, Birmingham 1909, the spoon with heart shaped bowl and enamelled interlace motif terminal, spoon 1912, 5in (12.5cm) high.
£1,000–1,200   *S(S)*

A Georg Jensen silver vase and cover, of baluster form, on a small circular foot, the lip moulded with leaves, the overhanging cover with moulded piecrust edge, set with 4 cabochon amethysts in flower buds, impressed marks for Georg Jensen and import marks for 1924, 8½in (21.5cm) high.
£7,000–8,000   *P*

An Art Nouveau silver photograph frame, stamped in relief with entrelac scrolls, with enamelled hearts and ovals in mottled blue and green, on later wood mount and easel support, Birmingham 1904, 8in (20.5cm) high.
£650–800   *CSK*

A Guild of Handicraft hammered-silver beaker, designed by C. R. Ashbee, with repoussé and engraved decoration of stylized flowers and leaves, stamped 'G of H Ltd' with London, hallmarks for 1904, 4in (10cm) high.
£800–950   *C*

r. A silver-plated tureen and cover, designed by Christopher Dresser, with ivory handles and raised on triple spike feet.
£1,700–2,000   *AAV*

This piece has been well used and is missing a ladle, which would have increased the value considerably.

Pricing Pointers

A popular maker or designer can affect price: a piece designed for Liberty & Co, for example, will have a relatively high value because there is a strong body of collectors for items by Liberty.

A Liberty & Co hammered pewter rose bowl, the design attributed to Oliver Baker, set with 5 green glass studs, on 5 curved legs and trefoil feet, stamped 'English Pewter made by Liberty & Co, 01130', 6½in (16.5cm) high.
£600–700 *C*

A pewter jug, 12in (30.5cm) high.
£250–300 *ASA*

A German claret jug, with a pewter top, 11½in (29cm) high.
£450–500 *ASA*

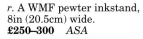

A WMF pewter dressing table mirror, 12½in (32cm) high.
£450–500 *APO*

r. A WMF pewter inkstand, 8in (20.5cm) wide.
£250–300 *ASA*

r. A Liberty Tudric pewter four-piece tea set, different tray, 18½in (47cm) wide.
£600–700 *APO*

l. A German green glass and pewter claret jug, 14in (35.5cm) high.
£250–300 *ASA*

A Continental pewter plaque, with central dished panel chased with the head of a Pre-Raphaelite maiden, flanked by curved uprights with pendant husks and stepped cresting, the reverse initialled 'EP' and stamped '279', 8½in (21.5cm) wide.
£250–300 *HSS*

A WMF electroplated pewter tazza, 12½in (32cm) high.
£550–650 *HEW*

A Liberty Tudric pewter vase, cast in relief with sprays of honesty and inscription 'For Old Times Sake', stamped marks, 8in (20.5cm) high.
£400–450 *CSK*

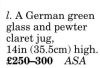

An Art Nouveau pewter desk
blotter, 6in (15cm) wide.
£250–300 *ZEI*

A Liberty & Co pewter biscuit
barrel and cover, embellished
with stylised buds and tendrils,
having swing handle and
domed cover, stamped marks
and numbered '01167',
5in (12.5cm) high.
£300–350 *P*

Liberty

Liberty & Co was the principal
outlet for Art Nouveau
designed in England. Arthur
Lasenby Liberty (1843–1917)
founded his furniture and
drapery shop in 1875. Later
he commissioned designs
exclusive to his store, including
Cymric silver and Tudric
pewter, which gave rise to a
distinctive Liberty style.

A pair of Liberty Art
Nouveau pewter vases,
10in (25.5cm) high.
£800–900 *ASA*

A Liberty & Co Tudric jardinière,
with pink enamelled insects.
£600–700 *ZEI*

A Liberty & Co Tudric pewter
clock, with embossed copper face
above a blue and green enamelled
plaque, flanked and mounted
by stylized scrollwork, impressed
'Tudric 0367', with key,
6½in (16.5cm) high.
£1,000–1,200 *I*

A Liberty & Co pewter salad
bowl, designed by Rex Silver,
with an openwork design of
interwoven entrelacs extending
to form 2 small handles, marked
'English Pewter Made by
Liberty & Co', numbered '0318',
with original green glass liner,
probably by Whitefriars,
10½in (26.5cm) diam.
£1,200–1,500 *P*

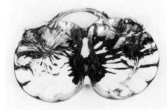

A Kayserzinn pewter dish,
11in (28cm) wide.
£275–325 *ZEI*

A Glasgow School pewter wall
mirror, attributed to Margaret
Gilmour, mounted in a wooden
frame faced in pewter and
embossed with a peacock at
either end, united by branches
with stylized leaves, enamelled
with a blue/green panel, reserved
against a textured ground,
12 x 24½in (30.5 x 62cm).
£3,000–3,500 *P*

*Similar use of enamelling can
be seen on a wall clock by
Margaret Gilmour, illustrated
in* Glasgow Girls – Women in Art
and Design 1880–1920, *and
similar style leaves are shown
in* The Glasgow Style, *by Gerald
and Celia Larner, No. 182.*

A Kayserzinn lidded pewter jug,
9in (23cm) high.
£350–400 *ZEI*

l. An Art Nouveau pewter lamp,
c1900, 14in (35.5cm) high.
£1,200–1,300

A Hukin & Heath plated spoon warmer, probably designed by Christopher Dresser, stamped 'H & H 2693', 5in (12.5cm) high.
£1,500–1,800 *P*

A Hukin & Heath electroplated soup tureen, designed by Christopher Dresser, with ivory finial and twin ivory handles, maker's marks and registration mark for 1875, 8in (20.5cm) high.
£1,500–1,800 *P*

A William Hutton silver faced oak photograph frame, the upper corners inlaid with blue/green enamel, London 1904, stamped mark, 7in (17.5cm) high.
£1,000–1,200 *CSK*

An Art Nouveau ladle, 6in (15.2cm) long. **£30–35** *ASA*

A James Dixon & Sons electroplated teapot and cover, designed by Christopher Dresser, stamped 'J.D.& S 2272', registration mark for 25 November 1880, 7in (17.5cm) wide.
£1,000–1,200 *C*

A Ramsden & Carr silver inkwell and cover, with glass liner, engraved 'Omar Ramsden et Alwyn Carr me Fecerunt', maker's mark, London 1912, 3in (7.5cm) high.
£1,000–1,200 *SB*

A Liberty & Co silver stopper, the design attributed to Archibald Knox, maker's mark, stamped '2226', Birmingham 1906, 2½in (6.5cm) high.
£500–600 *SB*

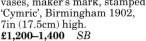

r. A Guild of Handicraft Ltd tea tray, London 1901, 21½in (54.5cm) wide.
£2,000–2,500 *SBe*

A set of 6 Liberty & Co silver coffee spoons, maker's mark, dates between 1926–32, in original fitted box, 4½in (11cm) long.
£550–650 *SB*

A pair of Liberty & Co silver vases, maker's mark, stamped 'Cymric', Birmingham 1902, 7in (17.5cm) high.
£1,200–1,400 *SB*

A Mappin & Webb fruit tazza, Sheffield, 1903, 12in (30.5cm) high.
£700–800 *SB*

A WMF electroplated vase, maker's mark, 16in (40.5cm) high.
£500–600 *SBe*

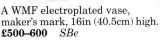

r. An Art Nouveau silvered metal sweetmeat dish, stamped 'AK & Cie', 9½in (24cm) high.
£300–350 *CSK*

l. A spelter figure of a young girl, cast from a model by L. Alliot, inscribed, 30in (76cm) high.
£1,000–1,200 *C*

A WMF green glass claret jug, with pewter mounts, stamped marks, 16in (40.5cm) high.
£700–800   P

A Jean Dunand wrought-metal vase, inlaid in contrasting metals, marked 'Jean Dunand 1913', 7in (17.5cm) high.
£700–800   SB

A Ramsden & Carr silver ciborium, maker's mark, engraved 'Omar Ramsden et Alwyn Carr me Fecerunt', London 1905, 7in (17.5cm) high.
£1,500–1,800   SB

A pair of pewter two-branch candelabra, designed by Albert Reimann and manufactured by Gerhardi & Cie, 15in (38cm) high.
£1,200–1,500   C

An Art Nouveau pewter mirror, stamped '120', c1905, 21½in (54.5cm) high.
£850–1,000   SB

A Guild of Handicraft Ltd. silver and enamel box and cover, maker's mark 'London 1901', 4½in (11.5cm) diam.
£1,700–2,000   SBe

A Guild of Handicraft Ltd silver loop-handled stemmed cups, after a design by C. R. Ashbee, each with maker's mark, London 1904, 4in (10cm) high.
£3,500–4,000   SB

An Art Nouveau pewter sweetmeat centrepiece, 8½in (21.5cm) high.
£250–300   LEX

A pair of silvered pewter wall plates, stamped mark 'as', 9½in (24cm) diam.
£250–300   SBe

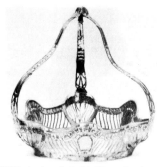

A WMF electroplated triform basket, with clear glass liner, WMF monogram, 11in (28cm) high.
£250–300   SBe

A Guild of Handicraft Ltd silver tea caddy, maker's mark London, 1906, 3in (7.5cm) high.
£500–600   SB

A Guild of Handicraft Ltd silver and enamel two-handled dish and cover, the design attributed to C. R. Ashbee, maker's mark, London 1902, 10½in (26.5cm) wide.
£5,000–6,000   SB

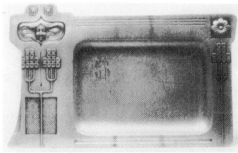

A Heath & Middleton silver pepper pot, design attributed to Christoper Dresser, maker's marks 'JTH. JHM', Birmingham 1892, 3½in (8.9cm) high, 1½oz.
£600–700   P

A Russian Art Nouveau pen tray, by O. Korlyukov, Moscow 1899–1908, 10½in (26.5cm) wide.
£700–800   C

An Arts & Crafts metal and enamelled triptych, by Nelson and Edith Dawson, with 'D' and 2 dated '1901', 10½in (26.5cm) high.
£7,000–8,000   P

An enamelled cigaretee case, after a design by Eugène Grasset, maker's mark 'MZ', French poincons, c1900, 3in (7.6cm) wide. **£700–800   S**

Pewter

Pewter is an alloy consisting mainly of tin, and has been used in Britain since Roman times. When no lead is used in the alloy, pewter tends to remain bright and almost like silver; the higher the proportion of lead, the darker the colour.

Largely ousted during the 19thC, pewter was revived as a material by exponents of the Arts & Crafts Movement, and their contemporaries and successors, followers of the Art Nouveau.

In Britain and Germany particularly, Art Nouveau pewter work achieved great popularity and high standards of craftsmanship. Liberty's Tudric range of pewter wares, decorated with motifs taken from the Celtic, included tea and coffee services as well as clocks, tableware, bowls and vases. The chief German exponent was Engelbert Kayser (1840–1911), whose range was as extensive as Liberty's, but fashioned in the 'high' Art Nouveau style.

A William Hutton & Sons silver faced frame, enamelled blue and green panels, stamped maker's mark, London 1903, 8in (20.5cm) high.
£1,000–1,200   CSK

A polished pewter photograph frame, the design attributed to Archibald Knox, 7in (17.5cm) high.
£1,000–1,200   CSK

A Jugendstil electroplated pewter mirror frame, by Kayserzinn, c1900, 18in (45.5cm) high.
£700–800   S

An Art Nouveau silver faced mirror, stamped maker's mark 'W.N.', Chester 1903, 12in (30.5cm) high.
£200–250   CSK

An Art Nouveau WMF white metal mirror, stamped marks, 20in (51cm) high.
£1,200–1,400   CSK

Silver & Metalware

*What does 'white metal' mean
when it looks like silver?*

The British Hallmarking
Council, which has jurisdiction
over the selling of silver in
Britain, does not recognize
foreign marks indicating a
standard below Sterling
(925 parts per thousand),
and as such they cannot be
considered as approved
standard marks. Consequently,
such items cannot be called
silver legally, or sold as such,
hence the rather ambiguous
term 'white metal'. A piece that
has been assayed in Britain and
found to be of the necessary
standard will have the relevant
marks stamped and will then
be saleable legally, and referred
to as silver.

A Ledru bronze pitcher, cast
with grotesque fish, the handle
in the form of a naked nymph,
signed in the maquette 'Ledru',
c1900, 13½in (34.5cm) high.
£1,300–1,500   *SB*

An Art Nouveau copper tray,
22in (55.5cm) wide.
£130–150   *HM*

A bronze hand
mirror, from a
model by
A. Bartholomé, gilt
patina, inscribed,
stamped 'P.39 Siot,
Paris', 14in
(35.5cm) high.
£1,700–2,000   *C*

A silver and copper tea caddy and
cover, by Albert Edward Jones,
stamped maker's initials, Birmingham
1913, 5in (12.5cm) high.
£500–600   *CSK*

A St Lerche gilt-bronze
vase, signed in the
maquette 'St Lerche',
stamped 'Louchet', c1900,
5in (12.5cm) high.
£500–600   *SB*

An Art Nouveau copper
inkstand, 8in (20.5cm) wide.
£70–80   *ASA*

An Art Nouveau oval copper
dish, 12in (30.5cm) wide.
£85–100   *HM*

A pair of Art Nouveau
hand hammered
copper candlesticks,
10in (25.5cm) high.
£130–150   *ASA*

l. An Art Nouveau
hand hammered
copper candlestick,
6½in (16.5cm) high.
£50–60   *ASA*

r. An Art Nouveau hand-
hammered copper vase,
5in (12.5cm) high.
£60–70   *ASA*

A Liberty Tudric pewter box
and cover, designed by
Archibald Knox, underside
stamped '9 Tudric 0194',
c1905, 4½in (11.5cm) wide.
£500–600   *SB*

A WMF pewter matchbox cover.
£60–70   *ASA*

A set of silver buttons.
£100–130   *ASA*

An Arts & Crafts copper
candlestick, with 3 garnets
inset on the stem.
£170–200   *ST*

A pair of Edwardian Arts &
Crafts candlesticks, by James
Dixon, Sheffield 1907,
8½in (21.5cm) high.
£1,200–1,400   *HCC*

A Coberg wrought-iron and copper
candlestick, c1910, 13½in
(34.5cm) high.   **£170–200**   *ST*

A pair of copper candlesticks, c1910.
£170–200   *ST*

A pair of WMF pewter
candelabra, decorated with
nymphs entwined around
tendrils forming the sconces,
on spreading bases,
10in (25.5cm) high.
£2,000–2,500   *P(M)*

A Liberty & Co silver bowl, stamped
'L & Co', London hallmarks,
2½in (6.5cm) high, 8oz.
£600–650   *C*

A pair of pewter candlesticks,
8½in (21.5cm) high.
£500–600   *ASA*

A copper bowl, by Keswick School of
Industrial Arts, 16in (40.5cm) wide.
£250–300   *ST*

An Arts & Crafts copper bowl,
possibly by the Birmingham
Guild of Handicraft,
7½in (19cm) high.
£325–375   *ST*

l. A German silver-
plated fruit comport,
with glass liner,
marked, 12½in
(32cm) wide.
£350–400   *ASA*

A Guild of Handicraft
electroplated muffin dish and
cover, designed by C. R. Ashbee,
8in (20.5cm) diam.
£600–750   *C*

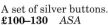

A pair of Gallia silvered-metal candlesticks, unmarked, 9⅖in (24cm) high.
£450–500   *P*

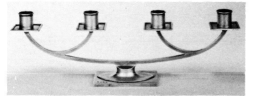

A pair of Hawksworth Eyre & Co silver four-light candelabra, stamped maker's marks, Birmingham 1913, 15in (38cm) wide, 35oz.
£1,000–1,200   *C*

An Art Nouveau silver-faced photograph frame, stamped 'W.A', 'Rd 40047', Birmingham 1902, 4½in (11.5cm) wide.
£350–400   *C*

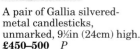

An Art Nouveau William Hutton & Sons silver and enamelled picture frame, embossed and hammer-textured with green and violet enamelling, maker's mark for London, 1902, 8in (20.5cm) high.
£1,200–1,400   *P*

A pair of Art Nouveau silver frames, maker's mark 'W.N', Chester 1907, 12in (30.5cm) high.
£1,000–1,200   *C*

An Arts & Crafts silver-faced double photograph frame, glazed, mounted on a blue plush covered wood, stamped 'W.J.H.', Birmingham 1904, 4½in (11.5cm) wide.
£450–550   *C*

A Georg Jensen 64-piece part table service, designed by Gundorph Albertus in the cactus pattern, all with firm's stamped marks, weight without knives and salad servers, 84oz.
£3,000–3,500   *C*

r. An Art Nouveau silver-faced photograph frame, enamelled in turquoise and violet, maker's mark 'G.A.D.W.D.', Chester 1905, 6¼in (16cm) high.
£450–500   *CSK*

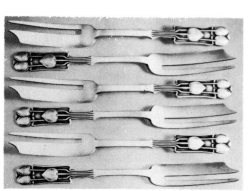

A set of 6 pastry forks, by Liberty & Co, Birmingham 1930, in original case.
£350–400   *L*

A Georg Jensen 50-piece Acorn pattern part table service, designed by Johan Rohde, all with firm's stamped marks, weight without knives 52oz.
£3,000–3,500   *C*

A Hutton & Sons silver and enamelled picture frame, heightened with blue and green enamelling, maker's marks and hallmarks for London 1904, 8in (20.5cm) high.
£1,200–1,400 *P*

A pair of Leuchare silver and shagreen candlesticks, stamped maker's mark 'WL' and 'Leuchare, London and Paris', London 1887, 8in (20.5cm) high.
£1,000–1,200 *CSK*

An Art Nouveau electroplated mirror, stamped 'V.S.', 19½in (49.5cm) high. **£800–950** *CSK*

An Art Nouveau WMF electroplated and glass jardinière, stamped marks, 18in (45.5cm) wide.
£600–700 *CSK*

A WMF silver on pewter bowl, 21in (53.5cm) wide.
£500–600 *CDC*

A brass, wood and glass punch set, comprising: 12 brass cups with glass liners, and a twin-handled tray, stamped with crossed swords and 'C.D.E.' in shield, 30in (76.5cm) high.
£600–700 *P*

An Arts & Crafts wrought-iron and copper hearth set, possibly made by the Birmingham Guild of Handicrafts.
£500–600 *P*

A spun brass-mounted glass punch bowl and ladle, with brass-tipped glass stem, c1910, 14½in (37cm) wide.
£350–400 *S*

An Art Nouveau pewter and green tinted glass claret jug, mounted on a pewter pedestal foot and overlaid with trailing leaves and flowers, 12in (30.5cm) high.
£400–500 *CSK*

A Wiener Werkstätte silver-coloured metal dish mount, designed by Josef Hoffmann, maker's and designer's monograms, Austrian poinçons, c1905.
£1,500–1,800 *S*

l. An Art Nouveau WMF claret jug, the green glass with pewter mounts, stamped 'WMF EP 1/10' and small 'as', 16½in (42cm) high.
£700–800 *WHL*

A WMF electroplated pewter three-piece mixed set, on trestle feet, stamped, teapot 8in (20.5cm) high.
£200–250   *C*

A mixed metal sugar bowl and cream jug, applied with copper castings of foliage, birds and insects, the bronze handles each cast in the form of a stylized elephant's head, with traces of gilding on the interiors, by Gorham, Providence, both marked, '1882', sugar bowl 4in (10cm) diam, 11.5oz gross.
£2,500–3,000   *CNY*

A Martelé inkstand, with removable glass liner, the stand repoussé and chased with serpentine ribs and flowers, on ball feet, by Gorham, Providence, marked 'Martelé 9584', c1905, 10in (25.5cm) wide, 9½oz.
£1,200–1,400   *CNY*

A Liberty muffin dish, designed by Archibald Knox, 11½in (29cm) diam.
£700–800   *ABS*

An Art Nouveau silver photo frame, Birmingham, 1902.
£275–300   *DSA*

A Tiffany fruit bowl, of fluted circular form on spreading base with lightly hammered surface, mid-20thC, 10½in (26.5cm) diam.
£2,000–2,500   *CNY*

A Mappin & Webb silver and enamelled frame, on easel support, cast in relief with shamrocks, stamped 'M & W, Sheffield', 1904, 8in (20.5cm) high.
£700–800   *CSK*

A silver and copper box, by Birmingham Guild of Handicraft, signed 'B.G.H.', c1900, 8⅛in (20.5cm) wide.
£1,200–1,300   *DID*

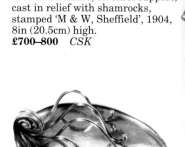

A silver toast rack, by Georg Jensen, c1930, 6in (15cm) wide.
£1,200–1,300   *DID*

An Art Nouveau style malacca walking stick, the white metal handle modelled with a figure of a young woman kneeling amid reeds.
£350–400   *CSK*

A hammered silver raised bowl, by A. E. Jones, the frieze cast with foxes chasing geese, on a raised foot, Birmingham 1915, 4in (10cm) diam.
£300–350   *P(M)*

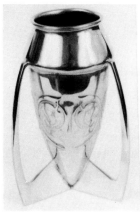

A Tudric vase, the design attributed to Archibald Knox, 7½in (19cm) high.
£350–400 *BLO*

A Guild of Handicraft toast rack, designed by C. R. Ashbee, the end panels with repoussé decoration of stylized trees, stamped 'G of H Ltd', with London hallmarks for 1906, 5in (12.5cm) wide, 7oz.
£2,000–2,500 *C*

An ormolu and hand-cut coloured glass lantern, 16in (40.5cm) high.
£500–600 *HAE*

A laminated copper frame, c1900.
£60–70 *BLO*

A WMF dish, with a female figure, 10½in (26.5cm) diam.
£350–400 *ASA*

A silver hand mirror, with embossed cherubs, London 1896.
£200–250 *PCh*

A Liberty pewter muffin dish and cover, stamped 'Tudric C293', 9½in (24cm) diam.
£500–600 *P*

A peal gong, as illustrated in Liberty's 1898 Yuletide catalogue.
£250–300 *CEd*

A silver repoussé picture frame, decorated in relief with kingfishers and water plants, stamped maker's marks 'W.N.' and Chester hallmarks for 1904, Patent 9616, on a wood back panel, 12½in (32cm) high.
£400–500 *C*

A WMF pewter dish, 14in (35.5cm) wide.
£250–300 *ASA*

l. A pair of Tudric pewter candlesticks, the design attributed to Archibald Knox, 9in (23cm) high.
£1,300–1,500 *BLO*

A chrome four-piece tea service.
£60–70   *CIR*

A chrome picture frame,
10½ x 7½in (26.5 x 48.5cm).
£50–60   *DEC*

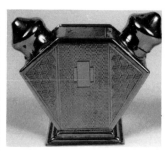

A chromium-plated cruet,
2½in (6.5cm) high.
£35–40   *CIR*

A chromium-plated cake stand,
8in (20.5cm) high.
£25–30   *CIR*

A chrome novelty aeroplane
cruet, c1950, 4½in (11.5cm) high.
£85–100   *DEC*

A Dunhill shagreen
cigarette lighter,
c1930, 2in (5cm) high.
£100–120   *ASA*

A pair of chrome candlesticks,
trimmed with green Bakelite,
5in (12.5cm) high.
£85–100   *DEC*

A clock garniture.
£300–350   *SH*

A chrome desk lamp, 18in (45.5cm).
£100–120   *DEC*

A chrome cruet set, 8in (20.5cm) wide.
£50–60   *DEC*

A chrome cake basket, with etched
glass, 11½in (29cm) wide.
£50–60   *DEC*

A pair of American bronze book ends, by Chase, 6in (15cm) high.
£200–250 *GAL*

A chrome and enamel cigarette box, 9½in (24cm) wide.
£85–100 *GAL*

A set of 6 Liberty & Co silver and enamel-handled cake forks, Birmingham 1931.
£300–350 *HCH*

A French electroplated tea and coffee service, with rosewood handles and finials, stamped 'GM', tray 21in (53.5cm) wide.
£700–800 *C*

A four-piece tea service, by Edward Barnard & Sons Ltd, London 1934, 54oz.
£1,200–1,400 *DN*

l. A Hukin & Heath electroplated toast rack, designed by Christopher Dresser, stamped with maker's mark, 5in (12.5cm) high.
£2,500–3,000 *CSK*

A pewter candlestick, c1955, 8½in (21.5cm) high. **£100–120** *GAL*

A pair of candlesticks, with carved oak barley-twist stems, hammered silver square bases and circular nozzles, by A. E. Jones, Chester, 1922, 9in (23cm) high.
£600–700 *Bea*

A Art Deco-style Walker & Hall four-piece tea set, Sheffield 1944, 50oz.
£500–600 *WIL*

A silver tea and coffee service, by Mappin & Webb, with ivory handles, 1937 and 1939.
£2,500–3,000 *SWO*

A Guild of Handicraft silver chalice, lightly hammered, stamped marks 'G of H Ltd', London hallmarks for 1902. 8½in (21.5cm) high.
£3,000–3,500 *C*

r. A pair of Art Deco-style chrome uplighters, 75in (190.5cm) high.
£300–350 *RG*

A pair of chrome posy holders, 6in (15cm) long. **£35–40** *CIR*

A WMF silver-plated punchbowl
and ladle, on a stepped base, each
side with a figure of Minerva in
high relief, dedicated to Rev Joseph
Larzan, bowl and ladle impressed
with firm's marks, 20in (51cm) high.
£2,000–2,500   *CNY*

A WMF pewter jug, c1900,
15in (38cm) high.
£700–800   *ASA*

A pewter mirror,
probably Osiris, c1900.
£1,000–1,200   *DID*

An Art Deco lamp, with a silver
and gold plaster figure of a lady.
£150–180   *LRG*

A Danish three-piece demitasse
service, by Georg Jensen,
comprising: coffee pot, sugar bowl
and cream jug, with bone handles
and knop finials with beaded
joins, c1945, 18½oz gross.
£2,000–2,500   *CNY*

A Hagenauer shallow hammered bowl,
on a tapering foot with openwork
decoration of horses, stamped mark
'wHw Hagenauer Wien Made in
Austria', 12½in (32cm) diam.
£800–950   *C*

l. A pair of Asprey chromium
plated cocktail shakers, each
dumb-bell shaped, with strainer,
one end forming the lid, one
dented, stamped mark 'A & Co.
Asprey London 6333 Made in
England', 10½in (26.5cm) high.
£600–700   *C*

An Art Deco-style silver
three-piece tea service,
Birmingham 1935,
20oz gross.
£600–700   *GAK*

r. A Hagenauer brass sculpture
of a bird and a golfer, stamped
'Hagenauer wHw Made in Austria'
golfer 15in (38cm) high.
Bird   **£700–800**
Golfer   **£1,200–1,500**   *C*

An internally decorated vase, with applied vertical grips, engraved 'G. Dumoulin', c1930.
£1,800–2,400 *C*

An enamelled glass vase by G. Argy-Rousseau, gilded mark, 1920s, 6in (15cm) high.
£3,000–3,500 *S*

A Venini bottle vase, designed by Fulvio Bianconi, acid stamped mark, 9in (23cm) high.
£7,000–8,000 *C*

A set of 6 Liberty & Co silver and turquoise enamel buttons, with entrelac Celtic design, stamped 'L&Co, Cymric', Birmingham 1907, in original fitted case. **£500–600** *C*

An Art Deco Cartier brooch, set with calibre cut black onyx and round diamonds, mounted in platinum.
£25,000–30,000 *CNY*

A Pforzheim plique-à-jour pendant, c1910, 2½in (6.5cm) high.
£1,000–1,200 *DID*

An Art Deco jade, rock crystal, diamond and enamel desk clock, signed 'Cartier' c1930.
£28,000–32,000 *CNY*

Three Liberty & Co silver pendants.
£400–500 each *DID*

r. An Art Deco Cartier carved emerald, diamond and enamel bracelet.
£45,000–50,000 *CNY*

Two Liberty & Co pendants, and one by Murrle Bennet & Co.
£400–500 each *DID*

A Georg Jensen silver coloured metal necklace, monogrammed 'GJ', c1920, 9in (23cm) long.
£1,000–1,200 *S*

A Guild of Handicraft white and yellow metal brooch, designed by C. R. Ashbee, set with blister pearls, pearls, sapphires, 2 paste replacements, tourmalines and moonstones.
£10,000–12,000   *C*

A white metal brooch, by Henry Wilson, the domed seven-sided form of cast stemwork with a central flowerhead and pale turquoise enamel detail.
£1,000–1,200   *C*

An Arts & Crafts circular clip brooch, attributed to Sibyl Dunlop, with gold leaves, tourmalines and mother-of-pearl.
£900–1,100   *P*

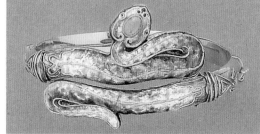

A yellow metal and enamelled bracelet, designed by James Cromer Watt, formed as a snake, blue and green enamel set with opals, stamped monogram 'JCW'.
£4,000–5,000   *C*

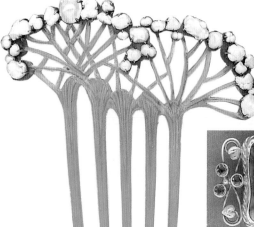

A horn hair comb, by Fred T. Partridge, set with baroque pearls in white metal, formed as an umbellifer, slight damage, signed.
£1,000–1,200   *C*

A white metal and enamel brooch, set with citrines, stamped 'G. Hunt 1922', and another set with amazonite.
£1,000–1,200   *C*

A yellow metal, enamel and rock crystal brooch, by Henry Wilson or Henry G. Murphy, set with opals and a central cabochon amethyst.
£1,800–2,000   *C*

A green and mottled white enamel pendant, designed by Sir Frank Brangwyn for La Maison de l'Art Nouveau, Paris, with monograms 'F.B., W.B.'
£3,500–4,000   *C*

A yellow metal, ivory and enamel brooch, by George Hunt, set with opals and pearls, stamped 'Medusa, G.H.'
£2,500–3,000   *C*

A Liberty & Co yellow metal and enamel ring, by Archibald Knox.
£2,500–3,000   *C*

A yellow metal and sapphire ring, by Henry Wilson, with pierced decoration.
£2,000–2,500   *C*

A Guild of Handicraft silver peacock brooch, designed by C. R. Ashbee, set with enamel, abalone and a ruby, stamped, maker's marks, London hallmarks for 1907.
£2,500–3,000   *C*

A Liberty gold and opal ring, designed by Archibald Knox, marked.
£1,300–1,500 *DID*

An Art Nouveau Liberty opal pendant, possibly designed by Oliver Baker.
£1,000–1,200 *DID*

An Art Nouveau 15ct gold, turquoise and pearl brooch, by Murrle Bennet & Co, c1910.
£500–600 *DID*

A Liberty gold, mother-of-pearl and pearl necklace, designed by Archibald Knox.
£3,500–4,000 *DID*

A Liberty gold, opal and pearl pendant, by Archibald Knox.
£3,000–3,500 *DID*

r. A Liberty gold and turquoise pendant, by Archibald Knox.
£3,500–4,000 *DID*

A gold, opal and pearl necklace, designed by Archibald Knox.
£2,500–3,000 *DID*

A gold and turquoise pendant, designed by Archibald Knox.
£3,000–3,500 *DID*

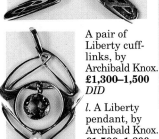

A pair of Liberty cuff-links, by Archibald Knox.
£1,300–1,500 *DID*

l. A Liberty pendant, by Archibald Knox.
£1,500–1,800 *DID*

A Liberty platinum and diamond pendant, by Archibald Knox.
£3,500–4,000 *DID*

A Liberty gold and mother-of-pearl bracelet, by Archibald Knox.
£2,000–2,500 *DID*

r. A Liberty gold and turquoise brooch, by Archibald Knox.
£1,300–1,500 *DID*

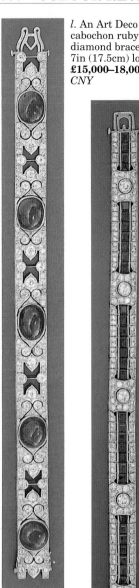

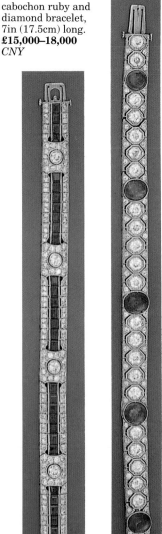

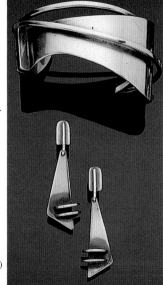

l. An Art Deco cabochon ruby and diamond bracelet, 7in (17.5cm) long. **£15,000–18,000** *CNY*

l. An Art Deco diamond and emerald bracelet. **£10,000–11,000** *CNY*

An Art Deco diamond and platinum bracelet, 7in (17.5cm) long. **£12,000–14,000** *CNY*

l. An Art Deco emerald and diamond bracelet, mount in platinum, signed 'Tiffany & Co', 7in (17.5cm) long. **£14,000–15,500** *CNY*

r. An Art Deco ruby, diamond and platinum bracelet, 7in (17.5cm) long. **£12,000–14,000** *CNY*

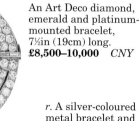

An Art Deco diamond, emerald and platinum-mounted bracelet, 7½in (19cm) long. **£8,500–10,000** *CNY*

A silver-coloured metal abstract brooch, stamped 'Ed Wiener', c1955, 3in (7.5cm) high. **£650–800** *S*

An Art Deco diamond dress clip, mounted in platinum, signed by Van Cleef & Arpels, No. 37.383. **£8,500–9,500** *CNY*

r. A silver-coloured metal bracelet and earrings, the bracelet and one earring stamped 'Ed Wiener', c1947, bracelet 3in (7.5cm) maximum width. **£900–1,100** *S*

An Art Deco diamond, ruby, emerald and cultured pearl clip, mounted in platinum.
£13,000–15,000   *CNY*

A pair of Art Deco platinum-mounted diamond clips, set with square, baguette, bullet and old European cut diamonds.
£5,500–7,000   *CNY*

A Liberty & Co pendant, designed by Archibald Knox, c1902.
£3,000–3,500   *S*

An Art Deco diamond double clip brooch, set with pavé and round diamonds, enhanced by an old European cut diamond, mounted in platinum.
£10,500–12,000   *CNY*

A silver-coloured metal brooch, by Harry Bertoia, c1945.
£2,500–3,000   *S*

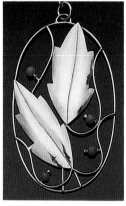

A silver-coloured metal and coral pendant, stamped 'Stüber', c1908.
£900–1,100   *S*

An Art Deco emerald and diamond set platinum ring, 2⅓ct.
£4,500–5,500   *MJB*

A silver-coloured metal and enamel buckle, by Albrecht Holbein, c1900.
£1,000–1,200   *S*

An Art Deco diamond and gem-set double clip brooch, mounted in platinum.
£5,500–6,500   *CNY*

A rose quartz and gold pendant, c1905.
£800–950   *S*

A silver, enamel and chalcedony pin, decorated with a stylized bird, by Theodor Fahrner for Murrle Bennet & Co, c1900.
£1,000–1,200   *S*

An Art Deco diamond, emerald and black onyx bracelet, mounted in platinum, 7in (17.5cm) long.
£10,000–12,000   *CNY*

An Omar Ramsden silver punch bowl, with everted
rim, inscription and stamped marks 'Omar Ramsden
me fecit', London hallmarks for 1931, 9in (23cm) wide,
65oz 14dwt.
£8,000–9,500
A Ramsden & Carr silver tea caddy and spoon, 1931,
4in (10cm) wide, 13oz 7dwt.
£3,000–3,500   *C*

A silver, amber and chrysolite cloak
brooch, designed and made by Georg
Jensen, impressed 'G1830S I', c1905,
2oz gross.
£3,500–4,000   *CNY*

A Liberty silver and enamel picture
frame, designed by Archibald Knox,
with Celtic stylized turquoise and
green enamelling, 2 pins set with
turquoise cabochons, stamped 'L. &
Co. Cymric', Birmingham hallmarks
for 1904, 8½in (21.5cm) wide.
£10,000–12,000   *C*

A six-piece tea service and tray, by Gorham
Manufacturing Co, Providence, each with stylized
monogram 'PEM', tray 31in (78.5cm) wide, 374oz.
£12,000–14,000   *CNY*

A centrepiece, with lightly hammered oval bowl
on a pierced stem with foliage and tendrils, stamped
'Georg Jensen 925S 306', with 'Master C. F. Heise'
assay mark, c1928, 15in (38cm) diam, 58oz 5dwt.
£4,000–4,500   *C*

A pair of candelabra, each with 5 cup-shaped
candle nozzles and circular drip pans, stamped
marks 'Georg Jensen 383A', 10½in (26.5cm) high.
£20,000–25,000   *C*

A silver centrepiece, the hammered bowl with peaked
and scrolled corners with clusters of grapes, engraved
'Joseph Ambrose and Elizabeth Genevieve Braun,
June 9th 1926', impressed 'Georg Jensen Sterling 380
Denmark GI 925S, 16in (40.5cm) diam, 102oz.
£12,000–14,000   *CNY*

A gilt-bronze lamp, marked 'G. Flamand', c1900, 33in (84cm) high. **£4,000–4,500** *S*

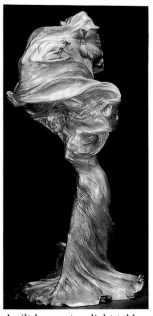

A gilt-bronze two-light table lamp, 'Loïe Fuller', by Raoul Larche, early 20thC. **£8,000–9,500** *CNY*

A Gurschner bronze and nautilus shell lamp, marked, c1900, 21in (53.5cm) high. **£15,000–18,000** *S*

A silver and lapis lazuli humidor, by Cartier, 1928, 9½in (24cm) wide. **£7,000–8,000** *S*

A pair of Art Nouveau gilt-bronze lamps, marked 'M. Bouval', with foundry mark 'Thiébaut Fréres', c1900, 20in (51cm) high. **£10,000–12,000** *S*

A WMF-style electroplated metal tazza, c1900, 18in (45.5cm) high. **£1,500–1,800** *S*

An alabaster and metal lamp, by Roland Paris, c1925. **£6,000–7,000** *S*

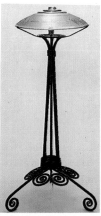

l. A wrought-iron lamp, with an etched glass shade, by Müller Frères, c1925, 41in (104cm) high. **£2,000–2,500** *S*

A pair of Georg Jensen silver tureens and covers, 1928. **£7,000–8,000** *S*

A pair of silver five-light candelabra, by Georg Jensen, marked, c1930, 10½in (26.5cm) wide, 185¼oz. **£20,000–25,000** *CNY*

A napkin ring, by Henri Husson, c1905, 2½in (6.5cm) diam. **£800–950** *S*

An agate, gold and enamel plate, by E. Tourrette and Georges Fouquet, the enamel signed 'E. Tourrette'. **£12,000–14,000**   *CG*

A Martin Bros. stoneware grotesque bird, signed, dated '11-1899', 16½in (42cm) high. **£12,000–14,000**   *P*

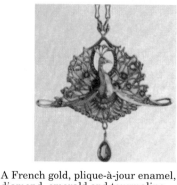

An Arts & Crafts pendant and chain, designed by Edgar Simpson. **£3,000–3,500**   *C*

A gold, plique-à-jour enamel, diamond and pearl pendant, by Georges Fouquet. **£70,000–80,000**   *CG*

A Favrile mosaic glass fireplace surround, by Tiffany Studios, 60in (152.5cm) wide, with a wooden mantel. **£20,000–25,000**   *CNY*

l. A blonde horn, opal and diamond plaque of a collier de chien, by Lucien Gaillard. **£9,000–11,000**   *CG*

A French gold, plique-à-jour enamel, diamond, emerald and tourmaline pendant. **£5,000–6,000**   *Bea*

A Favrile mosaic glass fireplace surround, by Tiffany Studios, 89in (226cm) wide. **£10,000–12,000**   *CNY*

A gold, opal, ruby, emerald and diamond dragonfly brooch, by Georges Fouquet. **£20,000–25,000**   *CG*

An E. Bingham & Co electroplated 42-piece table service, designed by Charles Rennie Mackintosh.
£10,000–12,000   *C*

A silver and rosewood powder box, bowl and circular box, by Puiforcat, marked, 1927, 21½oz gross. **£5,000–6,000**   *CNY*

A silver two-handled tea tray, by Georg Jensen, 830 standard, inscribed and dated '1925', marked, 34in (86.5cm) wide.
£6,000–7,000   *CNY*

A set of 12 silver plates, designed by Johan Rohde in 1930, made by Georg Jensen, marked, post-1945, 11in (28cm) diam.
£6,000–7,000   *CNY*

A nickel-plated metal smoker's companion, 1930s, 10⅖in (26.5cm) wide.
£1,200–1,400   *S*

A WMF electroplated metal photograph frame, marked, c1900, 14½in (37cm) high. **£1,000–1,200**   *S*

A Liberty & Co silver and enamel ceremonial spoon, by Archibald Knox, Birmingham 1900.
£1,500–1,800   *C*

A parcel-gilt silver jug, by Georges Lecomte, Paris, marked, c1945, 18in (45.5cm) high, 133½oz.
£9,000–10,000   *CNY*

A Georg Jensen 77-piece canteen of cutlery, various Jensen marks.
£4,000–4,500   *S*

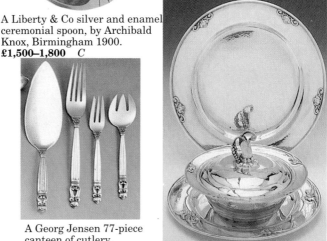

A Georg Jensen muffin dish, cover and stand, various marks, c1920 and c1940. **£3,000–4,000**   *S*

A patinated silvered
bronze vase, stamped
'Christofle B63G', c1925.
£600–700 *S*

A gilt rosewood mirror, for the
Wiener Werkstätte, c1925.
£12,000–14,000 *S*

A patinated and silvered bronze fish, marked
'E. M. Sandoz', and initialled 'E.R.', c1920.
£6,000–7,000 *S*

A silver-coloured metal box and cover, with
'WW' monograms and trademark, c1904.
£15,000–18,000 *S*

A brass jar and cover,
by Dagobert Pêche for the
Wiener Werkstätte, c1920.
£7,000–8,000 *S*

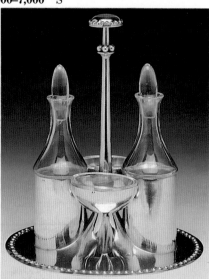

A silver-coloured metal, coral
and glass cruet set, marked,
'WW' monogram, c1905.
£18,000–20,000 *S*

A parcel-gilt silver vase, maker's
mark 'Tiffany & Co, New York',
c1885, 6½in (16.5cm) high, 16oz.
£20,000–25,000 *CNY*

Two Christofle electroplated
champagne buckets, c1935.
£1,200–1,400 *S*

A silver-coloured metal dish
and cover, by Josef Hoffmann
for the Wiener Werkstätte,
marked, 1927.
£4,000–4,500 *S*

A pair of Art Nouveau WMF decanters, and
a visiting card tray, with factory marks, c1905.
Decanters: **£1,800–2,000**
Tray: **£900–1,100** *S*

A Georg Jensen
silver vase, signed
'Arno Malinowski',
7in (17.5cm) high.
£1,500–1,800
S(NY)

A Georg Jensen silver-
coloured metal inkwell,
with glass liner, 1919.
£1,200–1,400 *S*

A Maurice Dufrène silver-plated tea and coffee service and tray, by Gallia, retailed by La Maitrise, c1925.
£2,000–2,500   *S(NY)*

A Tiffany Studios bronze candlestick, 'Saxifrage', c1910.
£8,500–10,000   *C(NY)*

A bronze figure, 'The Mushroom Fairy', by Gilbert Bayes.
£3,000–3,500   *C(NY)*

A floor lamp, by Edouard-Wilfrid Buquet, c1925, 67in (170cm) high.
£10,000–11,000   *S(NY)*

A pewter timepiece, the copper dial enamelled, impressed '0760', made by Liberty & Co, 4⅛in (11.5cm) wide.
£600–700   *P*

A William Hutton silver picture frame, maker's mark, London 1904.
£1,000–1,200   *C*

A William Hutton silver and enamel photograph frame, 1903.
£1,500–1,800   *C*

A Danish silver three-piece coffee set and tray, by Georg Jensen Silversmithy, designed by Johan Rohde, 1930.
£4,000–4,500   *S(NY)*

l. A Dutch bronze antelope clock, c1920, 11in (28cm) high.
£1,100–1,300   *S(NY)*

r. A Cornelius van der Hoef silver-plated tea service.
£1,400–1,600   *S(NY)*

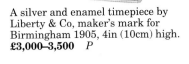

A silver and enamel timepiece by Liberty & Co, maker's mark for Birmingham 1905, 4in (10cm) high.
£3,000–3,500   *P*

A Tudric pewter mantel timepiece, for Liberty & Co, c1930.
£500–600   *HCH*

A Danish silver seven-piece tea and coffee set and matching tray, by Georg Jensen Silversmithy, numbered '2, 2B, 2D', 'Blossom' pattern, all except tongs, engraved with names and date '1924', all marked, 188oz 10dwt.
£20,000–25,000   *S(NY)*

A silver, lapis lazuli and glass cigarette box, stamped 'Cartier', importer's mark 'J.C.', 1930, 7in (17.5cm) wide. **£2,000–2,500** *S*

A Georg Jensen silver four-piece tea and coffee set, Nos. '71' and '181A', marked on bases, c1930. **£5,000–6,000** *S(NY)*

A Georg Jensen silver four-piece tea and coffee set, c1940. **£5,000–6,000** *S(NY)*

An Otto Prutscher tea and coffee service, executed by Edouard Friedmann, each piece with maker's mark, c1913. **£60,000–70,000** *S*

An Art Nouveau vase, by Frans Zwollo Snr, signed and engraved, 1899. **£6,000–7,000** *S(Am)*

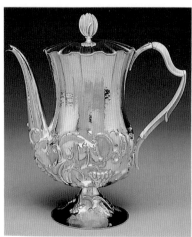

A Dagobert Pêche silver-coloured metal and ivory coffee pot, for the Wiener Werkstätte, 1922. **£10,000–12,000** *S*

A pair of Georg Jensen silver two-light candelabra, each marked '324', c1938, 9in (23cm) high, 73½oz. **£8,500–10,000** *CNY*

A Josef Hoffmann silver-coloured metal and ivory teapot, for the Wiener Werkstätte, c1924. **£5,000–6,000** *S*

An Aesthetic Movement electroplated sugar basin, and 7 cruet sets, designed by Christopher Dresser for Hukin & Heath, c1880. Sugar basin: **£800–1,000**   Cruet sets: **£1,200–1,500 each** *S*

A pair of Art Nouveau Limoges decorated enamelled copper vases, restored, c1900, 12in (30.5cm) high. **£3,000–3,500** *S(NY)*

An aluminium, Bakelite and brass lamp. **£2,000–2,500** *S(NY)*

A silver-plated brass tea infuser, by Hans Pryzrembel, c1930.
£600–700
S(NY)

A silver tea infuser, by Christian Dell, c1925, 6in (15cm) long.
£600–700
S(NY)

A Danish silver four-piece tea and coffee set and matching tray, designed by Henning Koppel, by Georg Jensen Silversmithy, marked on bases, numbered '1017', 20in (51cm) wide, 151oz 10dwt.
£12,000–14,000 *S(NY)*

A Peter Behrens brass electric tea kettle by A. E. G., Berlin, c1909, underside stamped '3592/14'.
£400–450 *S(NY)*

A Peter Behrens brass tea kettle, impressed maker's mark, c1908.
£600–650 *S(NY)*

Cleaning Silver and Metalware

Beware of over cleaning. Keep your treasures presentable, use a soft impregnated cloth, but not a cleaner that is too abrasive. Fine detail on a piece of metalware can be gradually removed over a period of time, and silver is surprisingly soft. Smokey environments with sulphur in the air, and gas fires, can cause tarnish. Some pieces may have had inscriptions removed, and the result is that the piece remains a little thin – check this, or ask the vendor to advise you.

A Charles Rennie Mackintosh electroplated spoon, designed for Miss Cranston's Willow Tea Rooms, Glasgow, impressed mark, c1904.
£300–350 *S(NY)*

A Peter Behrens chromium-plated electric tea kettle, element missing, impressed 'A. E. G., Berlin', c1909.
£400–450 *S(NY)*

A WMF silver-plated metal, painted wood and glass punch set, stamped factory mark, c1930.
£1,000–1,500 *S(NY)*

Six pieces of Joseph Maria Olbrich silver-plated tableware, by Christofle, 1903.
£600–700 *S(NY)*

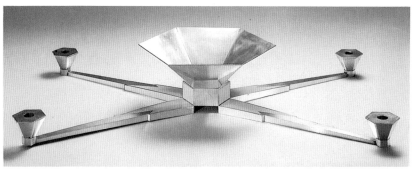

An enamelled silver centrepiece, the satellites fitted with optional candle holders, the central dish with optional silvered-bronze floral arranger, inscribed 'Jean Goulden/CXXII/1930', stamped maker's mark, 45in (114.5cm) wide.
£28,000–30,000 *S(NY)*

A 142-piece flatware service, by Tiffany & Co, with Japanese-style cast applied decoration of silver, gold and copper, c1880.
£30,000–35,000   *CNY*

A Martelé centrepiece bowl, decorated with scenes of the seasons, by Gorham Manufacturing Co, Providence 1906, import marks of Birmingham 1908, 27in (68.5cm) wide. 178oz 10dwt.
£22,000–25,000   *CNY*

A 'Navajo' vase, by Tiffany & Co, for the Exposition Universelle, Paris, and the Pan-American Exposition, Buffalo, NY, damaged, c1900, 8½in (21.5cm) high, 89oz.
£30,000–35,000   *CNY*

A vase-shaped ewer, by Tiffany & Co, with applied sea motifs surrounded by seaweed, marked on base, c1895, 14in (35.5cm) high, 86oz 10dwt.
£15,000–18,000   *CNY*

A 242-piece parcel-gilt Persian pattern service, each engraved with a crest, by Tiffany & Co, New York, 1978–91, 332oz 10dwt.
£10,000–12,000   *CNY*

A silvered-bronze mantel clock, the drum body with Arabic chapters, on a marble base, stamped 'E. Brandt, France', 12in (30.5cm) high.
£5,000–6,000   *C*

A vase, the body formed of 5 rows of owls' heads and talons, by Tiffany & Co, New York, Chicago Exposition 1893, 10½in (26.5cm) high, 26oz.
£25,000–30,000   *CNY*

An Imperial cake box and cover, with mother-of-pearl inlay, the black ink cakes moulded with floral sprays and inscriptions, minor chips, Qianlong period, 12in (30.5cm) wide.
£8,500–10,000   *CHK*

A pair of Liberty Cymric silver candlesticks, attributed to Archibald Knox, stamped 'L & Co', Cymric and Birmingham hallmarks for 1902, 8½in (21.5cm) high, 22oz.
£12,000–14,000   *C*

An 'Edelzinn' pewter and mahogany tray, designed by Joseph Maria Olbrich, c1904, unmarked, 22½in (57cm) wide.
£2,000–2,500   *P*

r. A silver-gilt and carved ivory tusk flagon, set with stones, by Tiffany & Co, New York, 1910, marked, 23in (58.5cm) high.
£25,000–30,000   *CNY*

An ashtray, executed at the Bauhaus metal workshop, stamped 'Bauhaus', c1924, 2½in (6.5cm) high.
£8,000–9,000 *C(Am)*

A silver and ebony Bauhaus teapot, 'Tee Extraktkannchen', fitted with a tea strainer, by Marianne Brandt, c1924, 3in (7.5cm) high.
£120,000–125,000 *C(Am)*

A hand-wrought hammered silver and ebony Bauhaus coffee pot, Sterling and '925' silver mark, 8½in (21.5cm) high.
£9,000–11,000 *C(Am)*

A silver-mounted iron cylindrical vase, by Tiffany & Co, New York, c1880, 9in (23cm) high.
£7,000–8,000 *CNY*

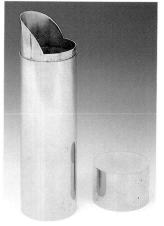

A metal plated brass tea caddy, stamped 'Bauhaus', c1925, 8½in (21.5cm) high.
£12,000–14,000 *C(Am)*

An ivory and hand-wrought hammered silver and wine jug, maker's monogram 'CD', with '800' silver mark, 11½in (29cm) high.
£23,000–25,000 *C(Am)*

A hand-wrought hammered silver and ebony Bauhaus coffee pot, stamped 'CD' and '900' silver mark, 9in (23cm) high.
£30,000–35,000 *C(Am)*

A silver and ivory espresso service, and 8 demi-tasse spoons, for Georg Jensen, c1935, 22oz.
£4,000–4,500 *CNY*

r. A WMF silver-plated tea and coffee service.
£1,200–1,400 *CNY*

A silver espresso service, designed by Johan Rohde for Georg Jensen Silversmithy, comprising: a coffee pot, cream jug, sugar bowl and tray, maker's marks, coffee pot 7in (17.5cm) high.
£5,500–6,500 *CNY*

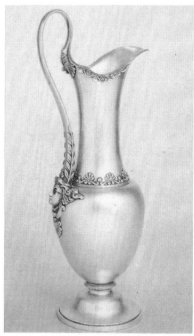

A baluster ewer, stamped 'Tiffany & Co
Makers', and 'Sterling Silver,
925-1000', Pattern No. 14106, c1899,
19in (48.5cm) high.
£3,000–3,500   *P*

A liqueur set, comprising: a decanter and 6 cups, stamped with
'935' German silver mark, and 'PH', for Patriz Huber, c1900,
decanter 7in (17.5cm) high.
£7,000–8,000   *C*

A bronze group of a mermaid and a
fisherman, signed 'Ed. Lanteri', dated
'1898', 24in (61cm) high.
£4,500–5,000   *P*

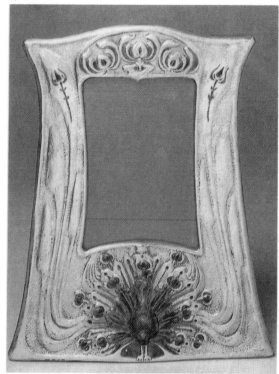

A silver and enamelled picture frame, stamped 'W.H.H.',
for W. H. Haseler, Birmingham 1899, 11in (28cm) wide.
£2,500–3,000   *P*

l. A two-division frame, Birmingham 1901,
3in (7.5cm) high.
r. An Edward VII Art Nouveau photograph frame,
by F. J. Hall, decorated with stylized foliate motifs
and whiplash on a textured ground, Birmingham
1903, 12in (30.5cm) high.
c. A plain photograph frame, Birmingham 1914,
7½in (19cm) high.
£850–1,000   *Bea*

A Georg Jensen Acorn pattern 155-piece table
service, with stamped marks.
£5,000–6,000   *CSK*

A Hukin & Heath electroplated toast
rack, designed by Christopher Dresser,
convex base on bun feet, wire frame
with 7 supports joined by small spheres,
the central support raised to a handle,
stamped 'H & H 2556', with date
lozenge for May 1881, 5in (12.5cm) wide.
£450–550   *C*

A Hukin & Heath plated
spoon warmer, designed by
Christopher Dresser, with
open top, sealed hot water
reservoir, straight ebonized
handle and 4 spiked feet,
maker's mark and '2693',
6in (15cm) wide.
£1,800–2,200   *P*

A WMF silver-plated
centrepiece, c1905,
33in (84cm) high.
£1,300–1,500   *ZEI*

A silver and enamel
rouge pot, c1930.
£70–80   *ASA*

An Art Nouveau brass
and copper vase, by
Fisher, 6in (15cm) high.
£120–150   *KNG*

A tortoiseshell and silver powder
compact, 2in (5cm) diam.
£85–100   *HOW*

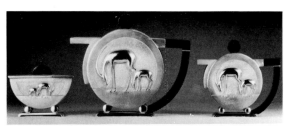

A silver teaset, with Bakelite handles, made in India.
£850–950   *JJIL*

A Liberty Cymric bowl, designed by
Oliver Baker, set with Connemara
marble discs, Birmingham 1901,
8½in (21.5cm) diam.
£3,000–3,500 *DID*

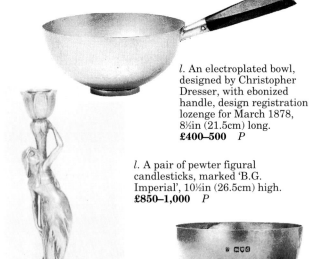

l. An electroplated bowl,
designed by Christopher
Dresser, with ebonized
handle, design registration
lozenge for March 1878,
8½in (21.5cm) long.
£400–500 *P*

l. A pair of pewter figural
candlesticks, marked 'B.G.
Imperial', 10½in (26.5cm) high.
£850–1,000 *P*

A Mappin & Webb vase, the handles
with heart-shaped terminals, the base
with inverted hearts in relief with
inscription, maker's mark, London
1903, 5in (12.5cm) high.
£250–300 *P*

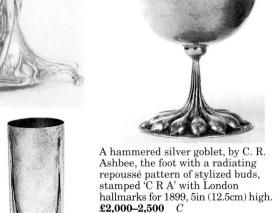

A hammered silver goblet, by C. R.
Ashbee, the foot with a radiating
repoussé pattern of stylized buds,
stamped 'C R A' with London
hallmarks for 1899, 5in (12.5cm) high.
£2,000–2,500 *C*

l. A Liberty Cymric silver vase,
designed by Archibald Knox,
the base with 3 turquoise
cabochons and 3 wire supports,
maker's marks, Birmingham
1903, stamped 'Cymric 2126',
4½in (11.5cm) high.
£1,800–2,100 *P*

A plated pewter pen and inkstand,
8½in (21.5cm) high.
£200–250 *P*

A WMF silvered-metal teaset, comprising:
a teapot, coffee pot, covered sugar bowl and
creamer, with two-handled lobed tray, all cast
with curvilinear foliage, tray 24½in (62cm) diam.
£2,000–2,500 *CNY*

A Liberty & Co silver pen tray, each end decorated
with a cabochon turquoise, with owner's initials
'A.M.W.', stamped marks 'L & Co.' and
Birmingham hallmarks for 1912, 7in (17.5cm) long.
£250–300 *C*

WMF

An abbreviation of Württembergische
Metallwarenfabrik, one of the principal
German producers of Art Nouveau
silver and silver-plated items during
the early 20th C.

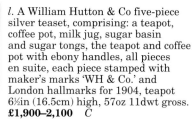

l. A William Hutton & Co five-piece silver teaset, comprising: a teapot, coffee pot, milk jug, sugar basin and sugar tongs, the teapot and coffee pot with ebony handles, all pieces en suite, each piece stamped with maker's marks 'WH & Co.' and London hallmarks for 1904, teapot 6½in (16.5cm) high, 57oz 11dwt gross.
£1,900–2,100   *C*

r. A Liberty Cymric silver vase, attributed to Archibald Knox, marked 'L & Co', Cymric Birmingham hallmarks for 1903, numbered '2020', 5½in (14cm) high.
£1,500–1,800   *P*

l. A Tiffany & Co cup and saucer, embellished against a copper ground, marked 'Tiffany & Co', Sterling silver and other metals, pattern Nos 5623, c1879–80, cup 2½in (6.5cm) high.
£700–800   *P*

A Liberty & Co silver biscuit box, marked 'Cymric' and 'L & Co', with Birmingham hallmarks for 1902, 5½in (14cm) wide, 20oz 14dwt.
£1,200–1,400   *C*

A Tiffany & Co hammered white metal and parcel-gilt three-piece teaset, comprising: a teapot, milk jug and sugar bowl, engraved maker's mark, Sterling silver and other metals and various numbers, c1890, teapot 6½in (16.5cm) high.
£3,700–4,200   *C*

l. A Tiffany & Co Japanesque jug, applied with copper and brass against a 'martelé-textured ground, stamped 'Tiffany & Co', Sterling silver and other metals, pattern No. 5051, c1878, 8½in (21.5cm) high.
£25,000–30,000   *P*

An Art Nouveau silver overlay decanter.
£350–400   *Vin*

An Art Nouveau dressing table tray, maker's mark 'R.P.', Birmingham 1902, 14in (35.5cm) wide, 13½oz.
£400–450   *Bea*

An Art Nouveau silver condiment set, all with green liners.
£400–450   *Bon*

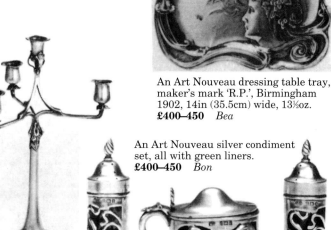

A silver box, with inserted miniature on ivory, signed, hallmarked 1904.
£150–180   *PJ*

r. A German four-light candelabra, stamped with crown, crescent and '800', maker's marks for probably Bruckmann and retail mark for M. Stumpf & Sohn, 17½in (44.5cm) high.
£1,500–1,800   *P*

An Edwardian rose bowl,
H. E. Ltd, Sheffield 1901,
9in (23cm) high, 17¾oz.
£400–450   *CSK*

A set of WMF pewter and glass
tea holders, each with scrolling
handle and pierced entrelac and
ivy decoration, stamped with
WMF marks, 3in (7.5cm) high.
£130–150   *CA*

A Danish silver dish-on-stand,
marked, 5½in (14cm) high.
£250–300   *ASA*

r. Two copper vases, by
Keswick School of Industrial
Art, 7½in (19cm) high.
£275–300   *ST*

A set of Liberty & Co
silver teaspoons, marked,
Birmingham 1908,
in a silk-lined wooden box.
£500–600   *OBJ*

A pewter photograph frame,
8in (20.5cm) high.
£130–150   *ASA*

An electroplated mirror-on-
stand, the cartouche form
decorated with maidens and
trumpets amid scrolling
foliage, 16½in (42cm) high.
£300–350   *C*

l. A Georg Jensen silver
tazza, 7½in (19cm) high.
£1,000–1,200   *ASA*

A Georg Jensen Acorn pattern
131-piece table service, designed
by Johan Rohde, stamped marks,
225oz gross, in original fitted case.
£4,000–4,500   *C*

A German pewter mirror,
18in (45.5cm) high.
£600–700   *ASA*

A Liberty & Co silver and
enamel inkwell, with design
by Archibald Knox, marked
'Liberty & Co', hallmarked
Birmingham c1906,
2in (5cm) high.
£250–300   *OBJ*

A pair of silver picture frames, Chester hallmark, 12in (30.5cm) high.
£850–1,100 *ASA*

A bronze inkwell, 8½in (21.5cm) high.
£700–800 *ASA*

An Arts & Crafts footed tobacco jar, c1900.
£225–275 *ST*

A pewter wall plaque, 5in (12.5cm) diam.
£40–50 *ASA*

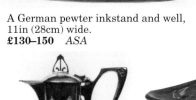

A German pewter inkstand and well, 11in (28cm) wide.
£130–150 *ASA*

A spelter figure on a tray, 6½in (16.5cm) wide.
£130–150 *ASA*

A WMF jug with lid, 13½in (34.5cm) high.
£350–400 *ASA*

A WMF wall plaque, 12½in (32cm) diam.
£500–600 *ASA*

A Newlyn School coper plate, stamped 'Newlyn', c1900, 10in (25.5cm) diam.
£250–300 *OBJ*

A pewter wall plaque, 5in (12.5cm) diam.
£40–50 *ASA*

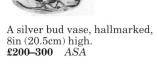

A tray with figure in relief, 15½in (39.5cm) wide.
£400–450 *ASA*

A silver bud vase, hallmarked, 8in (20.5cm) high.
£200–300 *ASA*

A Tiffany & Co Japanesque hip flask, stamped 'Tiffany & Co,' '325M8903', Sterling silver and other metals, 5½in (14cm) high.
£1,500–1,800 *HSS*

A Scottish pewter teapot stand, 7in (17.5cm) square.
£70–80 *ASA*

A Wiener Werkstätte plated fish
knife, designed by Josef Hoffmann,
stamped with trademark,
'WW', Hoffmann's monogram and
'JF' in circle, 7½in (19cm) long.
£200–250   *P*

A bronze eight-light chandelier,
cast after a design by Carlo
Bugatti, c1910, 65in (165cm) high.
£2,500–3,000   *C*

A pair of pewter candlesticks,
stamped 'Kayserzinn 4521',
c1900, 12in (30.5cm) high.
£850–1,000   *C*

A pair of pewter candelabra,
with geometric decoration, and a
central holder, probably Dutch,
c1900, 18in (45.5cm) high.
£1,000–1,200   *C*

A German 48-piece part canteen
of cutlery, comprising: 12 forks,
spoons and fish knives and forks,
silver-coloured metal stamped
with '800' and maker's mark for
A. C. Frank of Hamburg.
£700–800   *P*

An Arts & Crafts brass hanging
chandelier, glass shades missing,
25in (63.5cm) wide.
£250–300   *P*

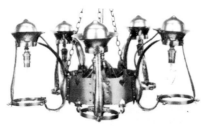

A silver caddy spoon, marked
'RS' for Robert Stebbings,
London 1903, 4½in (11.5cm) long.
£100–120   *P*

A lignum vitae dressing table
set, by Omar Ramsden, with Art
Nouveau silver mounts and the
initials 'MH' with red enamelled
background, 1926–27.
£1,500–1,800   *P*

A set of 6 Liberty & Co silver
and enamelled coffee spoons,
with shaded blue/green enamels,
marked 'L & Co' with Birmingham
marks for 1937, in original fitted
case, 4½in (11.5cm) long.
£500–600   *P*

An Art Nouveau silver-mounted
dressing table set, maker's mark,
'CD', PODR No. 374815/7, dated
'1903', '1904' and '1905'.
£850–1,000   *L*

l. A bronze figure of Circe, by
Bertram Mackennal, incised on
the base with artist's signature and
foundry mark of Gruet Jeune,
verdigris patches, 23in (58.5cm) high.
£14,000–16,000   *Bon*

A bronze figure of Daphne, signed
'Raoul Larche', 37½in (95.5cm) high.
£6,000–7,000   *Bon*

An Art Nouveau-style pewter and coloured enamel dressing mirror, attributed to the March Brothers, 20in (51cm) high.
£850–1,000   *L*

A WMF silver-plated pewter-mounted green glass decanter, stamped 'WMF' and other usual marks, c1900, 15½in (39.5cm) high.
£600–700   *C*

An Art Nouveau green glass wine jug, with pewter swirling mounts and handles and feather pattern stopper, 11in (28cm) high.
£300–350   *CDC*

A Walker & Hall silver-mounted claret jug, after a design by Christopher Dresser, maker's marks for Sheffield 1904, 9½in (24cm) high.
£500–600   *L*

A Liberty & Co silver Coronation spoon.
£250–300   *JJIL*

A WMF pewter centrepiece, in the form of an Art Nouveau maiden, her dress flowing outwards to form 4 dishes, stamped marks, 10in (25.5cm) high.
£600–700   *P*

A brass standing table mirror, impressed 'WMF', c1900, 16in (40.5cm) high.
£600–700   *C*

Silver and Metalware

By law, all British silver must be hallmarked. The date, maker and provenance of a piece can be checked by referring to a catalogue of marks. The letter F added to a British hallmark indicates that the piece is a foreign import which has met the British silver standard.

A set of 4 Hukin & Heath silver salts with salt spoons, decorated in silver, copper and silver-gilt, marked 'H & H', Birmingham hallmarks for 1879, 1½in (4cm) high, 6oz.
£850–950   *C*

A silver photo frame, Birmingham 1902.
£250–300   *PC*

l. A WMF silvered centrepiece, 14in (35.5cm) high.
£850–1,000   *Re*

A Liberty pewter and Clutha glass bowl on stand, designed by Archibald Knox, the green glass bowl with milky and aventurine streaks, stamped 'Tudric 0276', c1900, 6½in (16.5cm) high.
£2,500–3,000   C

A Liberty Tudric-Moorcroft cake tray, stamped 'Tudric Pewter 0357', 12in (30.5cm) wide.
£850–1,000   P

A WMF electroplated pewter tea and coffee set, all pieces with usual impressed marks, c1900, 25in (63.5cm) wide.
£1,200–1,400   C

A Georg Jensen silver tazza, stamped marks, 7½in (19cm) high.
£750–850   CSK

A Barnard Aesthetic Movement silver-gilt christening set, comprising: a tankard, a knife, fork and spoon, all engraved and gilded, stamped 'W.B.J.', maker's marks for London 1879, tankard 3½in (9cm) high, 9oz, in original Goldsmith & Silversmith Company box.
£600–700   P

A Hukin & Heath silver-mounted claret jug, designed by Christopher Dresser, with ebony handle, stamped with maker's monogram 'JWH & JTH', London hallmarks for 1884, 9in (23cm) high.
£1,200–1,400   C

A Heath & Middleton silver and glass claret jug, in the manner of Christopher Dresser, maker's marks 'JTH/JHM' and Birmingham 1892, 15in (38cm) high.
£500–600   P

An Art Nouveau bronze model, 'Seagull and Sail', by Guy Edouard, on a marble base.
£600–700   Ksh

l. An Art Nouveau silver and enamelled garniture of 3 vases by Hutton & Sons, with blue/green enamelled motif, London 1902/3.
£850–1,000   TW

A William Hutton & Sons silver and enamelled picture frame, heightened with blue and green enamelling, fabric-backed, maker's marks for London 1905, 5½in (14cm) high.
£850–1,000   P

A Guild of Handicraft silver beaker base, designed by Charles Robert Ashbee, set with 7 oval garnet cabochons, marked 'CRA' in shield and London hallmarks for 1900, 4½in (11.5cm) high, 6½oz.
£2,000–2,500 *P*

An Art Nouveau silver frame.
£400–450 *JJIL*

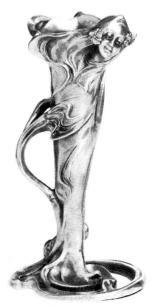

A pair of French Art Nouveau pewter vases, inscribed 'H. Sibeud', 12in (30.5cm) high.
£600–700 *P*

A William Hutton & Sons silver and enamelled double picture frame, maker's marks for London 1903, 8in (20.5cm) high.
£1,200–1,400 *P*

An H. Meinhardt silver-coloured metal vase, 25½in (65cm) high.
£1,500–1,800 *Re*

An Arts & Crafts toast rack, by the Guild of Handicraft, set with turquoise stones, one end split, London 1904, 5in (12.5cm) wide, 7½oz.
£2,000–2,500 *DWB*

A Hukin & Heath plated letter rack, designed by Christopher Dresser, marked 'H & H', numbered '2555' and registration mark for 9th May 1881, 5in (12.5cm) wide.
£350–400 *P*

l. A hammer textured silver-coloured metal four-piece tea service, by Tiffany & Co, the tray inlaid in green, yellow and red coloured metals, maker's marks and '5176M1781, 5291/2633', c1890, tray 15in (38cm) wide, 70oz gross.
£4,000–4,500 *N*

l. A Victorian Aesthetic Movement three-piece teaset, inscribed by Messrs Barnard, 1877, teapot 8in (20.5cm) high, 39½oz.
£850–1,000 *P*

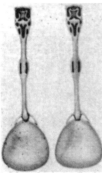

A pair of silver and enamelled spoons, marks for George Lawrence Connell, London 1904, 7in (17.5cm) long.
£300–350   *P*

A set of 6 Liberty silver and turquoise enamel coffee spoons, stamped 'L & Co', Birmingham 1930, in a fitted case.
£500–600   *C*

An ivy-chased jug, by Tiffany & Co, later inscribed 'Corrie Cup won by Burnswark, nos. by David Bell Irving Esq. 1886', c1870, 9in (23cm) high, 27½oz.
£4,000–4,500   *P*

A copper and brass kettle on stand, by W. A. S. Benson, stamped, 34in (86.5cm) high.
£700–800   *C*

A Hukin & Heath silver condiment set, designed by Christopher Dresser, stamped, London hallmarks for 1881, 5½in (14cm) wide.
£1,200–1,400   *C*

A pair of WMF pewter-mounted green glass vases, 19in (48.5cm) high.
£2,500–3,000   *ASA*

A white metal hors d'oeuvre dish, 14½in (37cm) wide.
£1,000–1,200   *CSK*

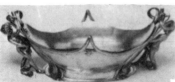

A silver-coloured metal centrepiece, with liner, possibly Austrian or German, unmarked, 22½in (57cm) wide.
£1,500–1,800   *P*

A WMF pewter dish, 9in (23cm) wide.
£200–250   *JJIL*

A French white metal vase, with 2 scantily clad females draping the body, with various marks, signed and dated '1902', Marcelle Devuit foundry seal, 26½in (67.5cm) high.
£1,700–2,000   *ASA*

A William Hutton & Sons silver toast rack, maker's marks and Sheffield hallmarks for 1902, 5in (12.5cm) wide, 11oz 5dwt.
£450–500   *C*

A Hukin & Heath electroplated picnic teapot, designed by Dr Christopher Dresser, stamped maker's mark, 'H & H, 2109 Designed by Dr C. Dresser' with registration lozenge for 18th October 1879, 3½in (9cm) high.
£650–800   *C*

A pair of copper and brass vacuum flasks, attributed to W. A. S. Benson, with pewter liners, brass strap hinges, wooden lids and brass handles, 19in (48.5cm) high.
£300–350   *C*

A WMF electroplated pewter drinking set, comprising: a lidded decanter, 6 goblets and a tray, all with usual impressed marks, c1900, tray 19in (48.5cm) wide.
£1,000–1,200 *C*

A silver cup and cover, by John Paul Cooper, stamped with beetle mark, dated '1903', 6½in (15.5cm) high.
£1,000–1,200 *P*

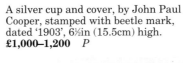

A set of 6 Art Nouveau silver teaspoons, Birmingham 1900, in a fitted case.
£500–600 *FHF*

A Tiffany Studios bronze and iridescent glass candlestick, with separate pendant snuffer, with overall greeny-brown patination, stamped 'Tiffany Studios New York 1212', 10in (25.5cm) high.
£1,000–1,200 *P*

A seven-branch brass candlestick, the design attributed to Bruno Paul, with a raised circular base and central column on which the arms pivot, with case decoration of concentric rings, 12in (30.5cm) high.
£3,000–3,500 *C*

An Art Nouveau silver caddy spoon, by Liberty & Co, Birmingham 1911.
£250–300 *SBe*

l. An Art Deco cocktail shaker, and a tray with glasses.
£170–200 *LEX*

An Arts & Crafts plated metal cross, in the manner of Omar Ramsden, engraved with a memorial to 'Frederic Wilkins, Priest', dated '10th January 1937', 22in (56cm) high.
£1,000–1,200 *P*

A pair of bronze firedogs, 24in (61cm) high.
£300–350 *C*

A Benham & Froud copper and brass kettle, on a wrought-iron and copper stand, designed by Christopher Dresser, stamped 'Benham & Froud' mark, 26in (66cm) high.
£500–600 *C*

JEWELLERY

At the end of the 19th century, the design and construction of jewellery was to undergo a dramatic change from the styles of the previous 100 years. The fantastic creations of French masters such as René Lalique, Lucien Gaillard, the Vever Brothers and Georges Fouquet raised the craft to a level of originality and excellence of execution that has probably not been superseded. The intrinsic value of the jewellery lay in the originality and workmanship of the piece, rather than the amount of valuable gemstones used. Lalique, for example, used semi-precious stones that were sometimes carved. These he complemented with often translucent enamels, in a decorative technique known as *plique-à-jour*. He also used moulded glass in his creations, which eventually led him to a career in glass production for which he is better known.

Like Lalique, British designers and manufacturers of the Arts and Crafts period often used natural or organic forms as a source for inspiration. They were also inspired by the work of the medieval Guilds – groups of skilled workers who believed in the principles of trueness to materials, the integrity of manufacture, and the direct involvement of the artist in the craft.

William Morris's and John Ruskin's teachings and ideologies inspired a whole group of artists and craftsmen in Britain, the rest of Europe, the United States and Australia. One important figure was Charles Robert Ashbee, who founded the Guild of Handicraft in Britain in 1887. His workshops produced foliate brooches and pendants, with wirework embellishment set with chrysoprase (a green stone) or mother-of-pearl, amethysts or enamel. A favourite subject was the peacock, which appeared in many forms, with the body and the tail feathers set with stones. The sailing boat was also popular, a motif that amusingly came to be knows as the 'craft' of the Guild. Tiffany in the United States produced exquisite work in enamels and gemstones, as did Marcus and Co. Simple but effective embossed silver brooches of girls' faces were made by the Unger Brothers and William B. Kerr.

In Europe we see the bold and curvilinear designs of Henri van de Velde in Germany and Belgium, and the formal but striking pieces by Bert Nienhuis in Holland. Theodor Fahrner and Murrle Bennet in Pforzheim, Germany, mass-produced good quality and well-designed jewellery. The high degree of stylization in the designs of Josef Hoffmann and Koloman Moser of the Wiener Werkstätte (Vienna Workshops) in Austria (and to some extent the designs of Charles Rennie Mackintosh in Glasgow), influenced jewellery design in an exciting way. Geometry played a greater part, with the use of materials with contrasting shapes and colours anticipating the styles to come in the 1920s and 1930s.

After the harsh realities of World War I, jewellery design took on a whole new look: the somewhat frothy styles of the Belle Epoque and Art Nouveau periods must have seemed overly sentimental to post-War emancipated women. There were simpler variations of natural forms, which finally became completely abstracted and geometric. The 1925 Exposition des Arts Decoratifs in Paris was the showcase of the new style and gave it the name we now recognize – Art Deco.

The 'Roaring Twenties' saw the first mass-produced motorcars and air travel, the radio and the 'movies', all influencing everyday design. Jewellery complemented other products of this 'machine age' with the sweeping lines of aeroplanes and railway carriages, and shapes reminiscent of cogwheels or other mechanical components.

The use of newly-created materials in everyday life was also reflected in jewellery manufacture, with recently-developed plastics set with stones, and silver cufflinks plated in 'genuine chromium plate'. It seems hard to believe that many of these materials are now commonplace, and regarded as inappropriate for jewellery.

There was room for fun with amusing costume jewellery – playful Scotty dog brooches with paste-set bodies, Chinamen, deer leaping through foliage, and enamelled tennis players. Of course there was also the superb quality of design and workmanship of major jewellers such as Cartier, Van Cleef & Arpels, Boucheron and their contemporaries, available for the very wealthy.

The most useful advice for the contemporary buyer must surely be to choose the best quality at a price one can afford. Never buy something that you are indifferent about just because the price is right. Look out for good design: a well-designed piece in an inexpensive material is often more pleasing than an ill-conceived piece made from precious stones or metals. If you are unsure when buying a piece of jewellery, do not be afraid to ask about condition and authenticity. Many items of jewellery the collector may encounter will have a maker's mark, monogram or signature, but beware – this is not a foolproof means of identification as marks on fakes are known. There is no shortcut to knowledge, but perseverance will show results – learning is a very gradual process, and experienced collectors and dealers will usually be pleased to advise you.

Keith Baker

A gold and opal brooch, shaped with an arc of gold beading above, set with central opal, marked 'IX', c1905, 1in (2.5cm) wide.
£150–180 *SB*

A silver and enamel brooch, after a design by G. Slatin, with large dragonfly wings detailed in blue, turquoise and green enamels, indistinct maker's mark, French poinçons, with box for Lefèbvre, Paris, 3½in (9cm) long.
£300–350 *SB*

A part-oxidised silver-coloured metal buckle, with a lily between French poinçons, maker's mark 'E(?) F', c1900, 3¼in (8.5cm) wide.
£125–150 *SB*

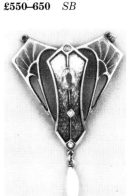

A Theodor Fahrner silver and stone buckle, maker's mark of Murrle Bennet & Co, London, 1902, 2½in (6.5cm) wide.
£550–650 *SB*

A Vever parcel-gilt and oxidised silver-coloured metal buckle, marked 'FE', c1900, 5in (12.5cm) wide.
£350–400 *SB*

A German Jugendstil brooch, in the style of Patriz Hubert, silver coloured metal set with lapis cabochon and hung with triangular lapis cabochon, c1900, 1½in (4cm) wide.
£300–350 *SB*

A Charles Horner pendant, enamelled green, turquoise and yellow, stamped 'C.H.' and Chester marks for 1909, 1½in (4cm) wide.
£150–180 *P*

An Art Nouveau plique-à-jour pendant, enamelled in mauve and yellow green and amethyst plique-à-jour enamels, with freshwater pearl drop, 2¼in (5.5cm) wide.
£350–400 *P*

An Art Nouveau silver-coloured metal belt.
£50–60 *ASA*

An Art Nouveau hair comb, with embossed openwork scrolling foliage set with blue stained chalcedony cabochons and blue enamelling, probably Scandinavian, 5½in (14cm) wide.
£350–400 *P*

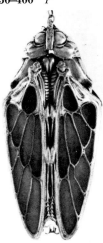

An electroplated metal and plique-à-jour enamel scent phial, the cicadas heads forming the removable cap, c1900, 2in (5cm) high.
£350–400 *SB*

A navette-shaped gold wirework brooch, by Murrle Bennet, with turquoise matrix and 3 seed pearls, stamped 'MB' monogram, and '15ct' on pin, c1900, 1½in (4cm) wide.
£250–300 *C*

An Art Nouveau silver and enamelled pendant, picked out in coloured enamels, stamped 'M & B', Birmingham 1909.
£250–300 *P*

An Art Nouveau pendant brooch, with central circular plaque of mother-of-pearl flanked by enamelled leaves of shaded blue and white, 5cm across, sold with Liberty & Co fabric-covered oval box and cover.
£500–600

A necklace, set with 3 plaques of Tiffany iridescent 'cypriote' glass, flanking a rose-cut diamond, with glass drop below and suspended on chains spaced with further mounted segments of Tiffany glass, the catch also set with glass, 17in (43cm) long.
£1,800–2,000   *P*

A Danish Art Nouveau hammered silver brooch, set with lapis lazuli, Continental silver marks, c1910, 4½in (11.5cm) high.
£300–350   *C*

A silver, enamel and paste brooch/clip, c1920.
£170–200   *ABS*

A Mexican silver and inlaid semi-precious stone necklace, designed by Ladesma, c1945.
£170–200   *ABS*

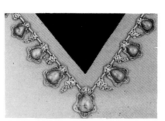

An American gold and turquoise necklace, with teardrop-shaped cabochons of turquoise matrix, stamped 'Im' and '14k', 16in (40.5cm) long.
£450–500   *P*

An Arts & Crafts chalcedony, amethyst and mother-of-pearl openwork pendant with matching drop and neck chain; and a chalcedony, chrysoprase and marcasite articulated, drop brooch/pendant.
£400–450   *CSK*

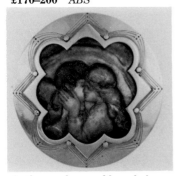

A silver and enamel brooch, by Phoebe Anna Ramsay Traquair, the central enamel panel with 2 lovers in medieval costume, coloured in blue, green, pink, brown and yellow with touches of gold, in a silver mount with single bar pin, the enamel inscribed to the reverse 'The Kiss' and with P.R.T. monogram, the silver Edinburgh 1935, 2in (5cm) diam.
£5,000–6,000   *C(S)*

l. A citrine single stone and diamond pendant/brooch, with frosted crystal and diamond surround to a diamond and gemset suspension, with detachable fittings for conversion to a clasp.
£600–700   *CSK*

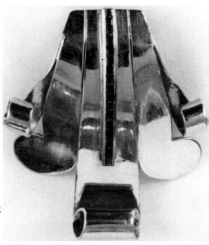

r. An 18ct gold clip, set with rubies, c1940.
£700–800   *ABS*

An Arts & Crafts pendant, in the medieval style, with rubies, sapphires, emeralds and pearls and picked out in enamels, 6in (15cm) long overall.
£700–800 *P*

A silver and turquoise pendant, with baroque pearl drops and diamonds.
£350–400 *ASA*

A silver and enamel pendant, c1900.
£200–250 *ASA*

A pendant with amethysts.
£350–400 *ASA*

A silver and green enamel brooch, signed and dated, c1900.
£200–250 *ASA*

A green paste and tourmaline brooch, by Arthur Gaskin, c1900.
£1,200–1,400 *DID*

A Liberty Cymric enamelled silver belt buckle, decorated with pendant honesty against a blue/green enamel background, with stamped mark 'L. & Co. Cymric', and Birmingham hallmarks for 1903.
£500–600 *C*

l. An Austrian silver and plique-à-jour enamel brooch, stamped '800 Silver', c1905, 1½in (4cm) wide, and a silver and plique-à-jour enamel bar brooch in the form of a scarab, turquoise enamel and plique-à-jour details, maker's mark, 'G.K.', stamped 'Real Silver', c1910, 2in (5cm) wide.
£250–300 each *S*

A Liberty & Co gold, enamel and mother-of-pearl pendant necklace, maker's mark, stamped '15ct', c1910, 3in (7.5cm) long.
£1,000–1,200 *S*

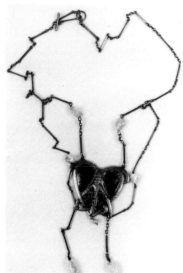

An Art Nouveau necklace,
by Murrle Bennet, in enamel
and silver, c1900.
£550–600 *DID*

A German Art Nouveau 15ct
pendant, with ruby, diamond
and pearl, Pforzheim in the
style of Kleeman.
£550–600 *DID*

An Art Nouveau silver, enamel and
pearl necklace, by Murrle Bennet & Co.
£450–500 *DID*

A silver, gold and enamel
pendant necklace, c1910,
2in (5cm) long.
£350–400 *S*

An Art Nouveau carved horn
pendant of a butterfly, on a woven
silk cord with 2 blue glass beads
between wooden spacers,
3in (7.5cm) long.
£400–450 *CSK*

A 15ct gold pendant, set with
turquoise, by Murrle Bennet.
£750–800 *DID*

A horn and
turquoise necklace,
signed 'Bonté'.
£500–600 *OBJ*

A pair of costume jewellery clips,
by Boucher, c1940.
£250–300 *ABS*

An Art Nouveau
tortoiseshell comb,
in silver and olivine,
by Wm. Soper,
5½in (14cm) high.
£450–500 *DID*

A Guild of Handicraft white metal
cloak clasp, designed by C. R.
Ashbee, each piece with repoussé
decoration of pinks.
£1,700–2,000 *C*

A Guild of Handicraft white
metal and enamel waist clasp,
designed by C. R. Ashbee,
each piece with pierced floral
decoration and set with
turquoises, the centre with
green/blue enamel.
£1,800–2,200 *C*

r. An Argentinian bracelet, stamped 'Axel Giorno? – Buenos Aires', 8in (20.5cm) long.
£200–250 *P*

l. An Art Nouveau plique-à-jour brooch, stamped 'Déposé' and '900', 1½in (4cm) wide.
£700–800 *P*

r. A powder compact and 2 lipstick holders, the compact marked 'Boucheron, London, No. 875012, Made in France', one lipstick holder marked, 'Boucheron Paris', the other 'Boucheron, London 875012', compact 3in (7.5cm) high.
£850–1,000 *C*

l. An Unger Brothers Art Nouveau brooch, stamped with maker's monogram, 'Sterling', and '925 fine', 2¼in (5.5cm) wide.
£400–450 *P*

A silver and enamel circular brooch, signed 'Omar Ramsden Me Fecit', London silver marks, 2¼in (5.5cm) diam.
£600–700 *P*

r. An Arts & Crafts pendant brooch, 2½in (6.5cm) long.
£500–600 *P*

r. An Art Nouveau enamelled pendant, the sliding front revealing a mirror, stamped '900', 'Déposé', and dragonfly maker's mark, probably Austrian, 1½in (4cm) wide.
£250–300 *P*

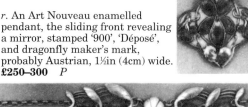

An Art Nouveau necklace, 21½in (54.5cm) long.
£300–350 *P*

An Arts & Crafts enamelled pendant, painted in naturalistic enamelled colours, signed on reverse 'Pegram', 2¼in (5.5cm) wide.
£250–300 *P*

l. A Liberty & Co pendant, designed by Bernard Cuzner, the ship's hull set with a pale blue tourmaline cabochon, unmarked, 2in (5cm) wide.
£1,000–1,200 *P*

r. A Liberty & Co enamelled silver pendant, designed by Jessie M. king, marks for W. H. Haseler and 'Silver', 2in (5cm) wide.
£600–700 *P*

l. A German Art Nouveau pendant of red and green paste, stamped with '900', a wolf's head and 'W' maker's mark, 2¼in (5.5cm) wide.
£300–350 *P*

r. A Murrle Bennet & Co gold and mother-of-pearl pendant, designed in the manner of Knox, stamped 'MB&Co', monogram and '15ct', 2¼in (5.5cm) wide.
£400–450 *P*

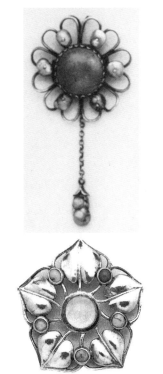

A Guild of Handicraft white metal brooch, designed by C. R. Ashbee, in the form of winged insect with an articulated body formed by an opal, in original case.
£1,500–1,800 *C*

Two Guild of Handicraft white metal brooches, one designed by C.R. Ashbee with openwork repoussé decoration of stylized foliage, set with moonstone and turquoise, stamped marks 'G of H Ltd', and one with wirework design in the form of a flower set with baroque pearls and turquoise enamel and a pear-shaped drop.
£1,500–1,800 each *C*

Three white metal brooches, by Bernard Cuzner, one with a pierced and chased design of birds amid foliage, one with pierced decoration of leaves and berries, set with a central amazonite, and another with wirework heart shaped design set with a central Ruskin Pottery circular plaque, all with maker's mark.
£1,000–1,200 each *C*

Two Guild of Handicraft brooches, one designed by C. R. Ashbee, with openwork design in the form of a tree, with repoussé details set with turquoise enamel and baroque pear-shaped drops, in its original fitted case, engraved 'LC', and another with a wirework scrolled design, set with turquoises and turquoise enamel.
£1,400–1,600 *C*

A Liberty & Co silver and enamel waist clasp, designed by Jessie M. King, with circular openwork decoration of stylized flowers and birds with blue/green enamel details, stamped 'L & Co', Birmingham hallmarks for 1906.
£1,200–1,400 *C*

A white metal and cloisonné enamel buckle, and 2 white metal brooches, all by Nelson and Edith Dawson.
£1,000–1,200 *C*

Two sets of 6 Guild of Handicraft white metal buttons, each of stylized foliage motif, set with agate and chrysoprase, one set in original fitted case.
£1,000–1,200 *C*

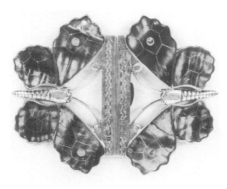

A silver buckle, each piece in the form of a butterfly with shaded mother-of-pearl wings, marked 'R.P.', Birmingham 1910, 3½in (9cm) wide.
£300–350   *P*

A plique-à-jour and diamanté pendant, the ivory and mother-of-pearl bust mounted in a gilt white metal setting, the wings and fan tail with shades of green and turquoise plique-à-jour enamel, set with white and pink gems, in fitted leather case, 13in (33cm) high.
£5,000–6,000   *C*

A French 18ct gold brooch, the sculpture effect hand finished, c1900.
£700–800   *DID*

A 9ct gold pendant, by Murrle Bennet & Co, set with an opal flanked by 2 pale aquamarines and 2 citrines, c1900.
£700–800   *DID*

A Liberty & Co silver belt buckle, in the style of Archibald Knox, with stylised spade-shaped flowers, supported on entwined entrelacs, the surface beaten, stamped marks 'L & Co' Cymric, Birmingham 1901, 2in (5cm) wide.
£400–450   *S(C)*

A hammered silver, turquoise and blue enamel belt, by William Hutton & Son, each plaque with hallmarks, buckle with full hallmarks for 1904, maker's monogram 'W.H. & S. Ld.' within shaped surround, 28in (71cm) wide.
£850–1,000   *C*

A rose diamond plique-à-jour enamel butterfly brooch, with baroque pearl, untested, rose diamond and gem body.
£2,500–3,000   *CSK*

A diamond and rose diamond cluster brooch, the pierced and chased floral scrollwork shoulders each set with 2 rose diamonds.
£400–450   *CSK*

l. A Liberty & Co silver and enamel belt buckle, attributed to Archibald Knox, enamelled in mottled blue and green, some enamel replaced, stamp marks 'L & Co' Cymric, Birmingham 1901, 3in (7.5cm) wide.
£450–500   *S(C)*

r. An 18ct gold lady's cocktail watch, with synthetic rubies and diamonds, c1940.
£850–1,000   *ABS*

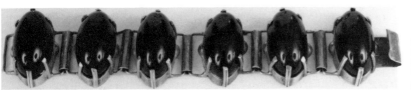

l. A Mexican silver and semi-precious stone bracelet, c1945, 7in (17.5cm) long.
£250–300   *ABS*

A Liberty & Co Cymric silver and enamel waist clasp, designed by Archibald Knox, stamped maker's mark, Birmingham 1905.
£600–700 *CSK*

A Liberty & Co Arts & Crafts necklace, chain 2½in (6.5cm) long.
£600–700 *P*

An Art Nouveau German-style pendant, probably by Murrle Bennett.
£300–350 *P*

A Liberty & Co pendant, enamelled in blue and green with wirework stamens and mother-of-pearl centre, 1½in (4cm) long.
£400–450 *P*

A George Hunt cruciform pendant, marked 'GH', 4in (10cm) long.
£600–700 *P*

An Art Nouveau brooch, pierced and set with an amethyst plaque flanked by 2 ovals of mother-of-pearl with a faceted amethyst drop, stamped '900', monogram for Carl Hermann of Pforzheim, 1½in (4cm) wide.
£350–400 *P*

A brass 'posy' brooch, fashioned as a butterfly, stamped with design lozenge for 1868 and 'Perry & Co. London', 2in (5cm) wide.
£300–350 *P*

A gold, turquoise and pearl necklace, stamped 'Reg 422909', 16in (40.5cm) long.
£300–350 *P*

An Arts & Crafts gold and lapis lazuli ring, showing affinities to the work of John Paul Cooper or Henry Wilson.
£300–350
An Arts & Crafts ring, characteristic of the Birmingham School under the influence of Gaskin.
£200–250
A Theodor Fahrner opal ring, stamped '925 Fahrner' and 'TF'.
£350–400
A George Hunt ring, marked 'GH'.
£200–250
An Arts & Crafts ring, with lapis lazuli cabochon, stamped 'Sterling'.
£300–350 *P*

l. An Arts & Crafts pendant, set with amandine garnet cabochons, and another drop, 1½in (4cm) long.
£600–700 *P*

The leaf motifs show the characteristics of the work of Sibyl Dunlop.

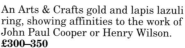

l. An Arts & Crafts pendant, with turquoise cabochon and drop, 1½in (4cm) long.
£350–400 *P*

An Arts & Crafts pendant with oval plaque of lapis lazuli, set with a blister pearl, freshwater pearl drop, 1½in (4cm) wide.
£150–180
An Arts & Crafts necklace, characteristic of the Birmingham School under the influence of Gaskin, 2in (5cm) long.
£850–1,000
A Liberty & Co gold, amethyst and pearl necklace, by Archibald Knox, 15in (38cm) long.
£2,500–3,000
A Liberty & Co Arts & Crafts necklace, 16in (41cm) long.
£1,200–1,500 *P*

l. An Arts & Crafts gold, silver, plique-à-jour and opal hair ornament, attributed to Henry Wilson, 6½in (16.5cm) long.
£1,400–1,700 *P*

A Charles Horner silver, opal and turquoise enamel brooch, maker's mark, Chester 1907, 1in (2.5cm) wide.
£90–110 *S*

A Georg Jensen silver bracelet, designed by Henning Koppel, formed by 5 amoebic-like openwork plaques linked together, Danish maker's marks and London import marks, 8½in (21.5cm) long.
£600–700   *P*

A Liberty & Co silver cloak clasp, with foliate design set with seed pearls, stamped 'L & Co', Birmingham hallmarks for 1905.
£300–350   *C*

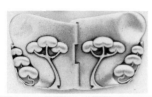

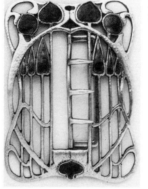

Two Liberty & Co silver waist clasps, one from a design for a bell push by Arthur Penny, each section of stylised honesty decorated with a central turquoise, marked 'LCCUD Cymric' with Birmingham hallmarks for 1903, and another stamped 'L & Co', with Birmingham hallmarks for 1899.
£600–700   *C*

A Liberty & Co Glasgow-style silver and enamel waist buckle, with openwork decoration of stylized foliage with enamel details, stamped 'L & Co', Birmingham hallmarks for 1902.
£900–1,100   *C*

A white metal and enamel brooch, by Ernestine Mills, with polychrome foil enamel decoration of a bird on a branch of flowering prunus, 'EM' monograms; and a set of 6 enamel buttons, by Beatrice Cameron, in green, turquoise and purple scrolling foliate cloisonné enamel decoration, in original fitted case, damage to enamel.
£1,200–1,400   *C*

Three white metal brooches, by Mary Thew, one brooch with blister pearl and chrysoprase, one with abalone shell with wirework decoration set with blister pearl, another with openwork decoration of a sailing vessel, set with baroque pearls, citrine and amethyst, and the hatpin set with agate.
£300–350 each   *C*

l. An Artificers Guild yellow and white metal pendant, by J. H. M. Bonnoir, of a Viking ship in full sail, with wirework details and decoration of sea creatures, suspended from a loop with the North Star, set with enamel, opals and garnet, with monogram 'J.H.M.B.'
£1,500–1,800   *C*

An Art Nouveau hair comb, the gilt floral openwork head set with 3 opals within curvilinear frame to the blonde tortoiseshell comb, the reverse with stamped signature, in maker's case stamped 'Ch. Dubret, 83 rue de la Liberté, Dijon'.
£1,000–1,200   *CSK*

r. A yellow and silver pendant on a chain, by Joseph A. Hodel, the wirework foliate design set with a black opal, baroque pearls and 2 modelled and cast yellow metal maidens, stamped 'Hodel'.
£1,500–1,800   *C*

A white metal and enamel pendant, by Nelson and Edith Dawson, the central floral enamelled medallion mounted in an octagonal frames, suspended from an earlier wirework bow set with crystal, and crystal drop, inscribed 'ND'.
£2,000–2,500   *C*

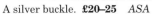

A silver buckle. **£20–25** *ASA*

A silver-coloured linked bracelet. **£70–80** *ASA*

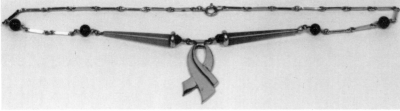

A chrome necklace, with red beads. **£70–80** *ASA*

l. A silver necklace, set with green stones. **£40–50** *ASA*

l. A chrome necklace, with green beads. **£70–80** *ASA*

l. A chrome and red beaded necklace. **£70–80** *ASA*

GLOSSARY

Acid-cutting A method of decorating glass by which an object is coated with wax or another acid-resistant substance, then incised with a fine steel point and dipped in acid.

Aesthetic Movement An artistic movement prevalent in Britain c1860–80, which advocated a return to a harmony of form and function in design and decoration.

Appliqué The decorative application of a second fabric to the main fabric ground.

Arts & Crafts A late 19thC artistic movement led by William Morris, which advocated a return to medieval standards of craftsmanship and simplicity of design.

Bauhaus A German school of architecture and applied arts founded in 1919 by Walter Gropius.

Bentwood Solid or laminated wood, steamed and bent into a curvilinear shape. First used in 18thC, it was favoured by Wiener Werkstätte craftsmen.

Britannia metal A 19thC pewter substitute, which was an alloy of tin, antimony and a trace of copper.

Cameo glass Decorative glass formed by laminating together two or more layers of glass, often of varying colours, which are wheel-carved or etched to make a design in relief.

Cased glass (overlay) Similar to cameo glass, but with the design on the outer layer cut away rather than in relief.

Chasing A method of embossing or engraving metal, especially silver.

Chryselephantine An expensive combination of ivory and a metal, usually bronze.

Cire perdue ('lost wax') The French term for a process of casting sculpture that results in unique casts.

Cold painting A technique for decorating bronze whereby coloured enamels are annealed or painted on to the metal.

Crackled glaze A deliberate cracked effect achieved by firing ceramics to a precise temperature.

Dinanderie The application of patinated enamel to non-precious metals such as copper and steel.

Electroplating The process whereby silver is electronically deposited on a copper, nickel silver or Britannia metal base.

Entrelac A type of interlaced decoration used on jewellery. Of Celtic origin, its use was revived by Arts & Crafts designers.

Favrile From the Old English word meaning hand-made.

Federal style A chronological rather than stylistic term applied to American arts of the period from the the establishment of the Federal Government in 1789 to c1830.

Hallmarks The marks stamped on silver or gold pieces when passed at assay (the test of quality).

Impressed Indented, as opposed to incised.

Incised Decoration or maker's mark cut or scratched into the surface, rather than impressed.

Intaglio carving A type of carving whereby forms are sunken into , as opposed to moulded on to, a surface.

Jardinière A plant container made from a variety of materials, including glass or pottery.

Jugendstil The term for German and Austrian design in the Art Nouveau style. Named after the Munich-based publication, *Jugend.*

Lustreware Pottery with a polished surface produced using metallic pigments, usually silver or copper.

Macassar A rare form of ebony.

Maquette A rough wax or clay model for a sculpture.

Marquetrie-de-verre A glass making process whereby pieces of coloured glass are pressed into the warm, soft body of a piece and rolled in. The insertions are wheel-carved.

Marquetry Furniture decoration in which shapes are cut into a sheet of wood veneer and inlaid with other woods or materials.

Martelé The French for 'hammered'; the term for silverware with a fine hammered surface produced first in France and revived by the American Gorham Corporation during the Art Nouveau period.

Millefiori A glass-making technique whereby canes of coloured glass are arranged in bundles so that the cross section creates a pattern. Slices of millefiori canes can be used as decoration or fused together to form hollow wares.

Modernism/Functionalism
International movement in 1930s
furniture design. Clean lines and the
cube shape were emphasised.

Opalescence A translucent white
quality in glass; a reddish core is visible
when held up to the light.

Pap-boat A small boat-shaped vessel,
usually of silver or pottery, used for
feeding infants.

Pâte-de-cristal Near transparent glass
made of powdered glass paste which has
been fused in a mould.

Pâte-de-verre Translucent glass
similar to pâte-de-cristal but with a
lower proportion of lead.

Pâte-sur-pâte A form of ceramic
decoration developed at Sèvres whereby
white slip is applied and fired in layers,
building up a cameo effect.

Patina The fine layer or surface sheen
on metal or furniture that results with
time, use or chemical corrosion.

Plique-à-jour An enamelling method
whereby a backed, many-celled mould is
filled with translucent enamel of
different colours. When the backing is
removed, the finished piece resembles
stained glass.

Pontil mark The mark left by the iron
rod upon which some glass is supported
for final shaping after blowing.

Pressed glass Glass items produced in
a mechanical press mould.

Repoussé The term describing relief
metalwork decoration created by
hammering on the reverse side.

Rock crystal A form of engraved lead
glass cut and polished to simulate the
natural facets of actual rock crystal.

Sand-cast A method of casting bronze
in a mould made from pounded quartz
and sand.

Secessionist The term for the
movement formed in opposition to
established artistic taste which surfaced
in Munich, Berlin and Vienna toward
the end of the 19thC, and which
initiated the Art Nouveau movement.

Sgraffito A form of earthenware
decoration incised through slip,
revealing the ground beneath.

Shagreen A type of untanned leather,
originally made from the skin of the
shagri, a Turkish wild ass, soaked in
lime water and dyed. By the 19thC it
was made mainly of sharkskin.

'Silvered' glass Items produced by
injecting silver between two layers
of glass.

Slip A smooth dilution of clay and
water used in the making and decoration
of pottery.

Slip-trailed decoration A form of
ceramic decoration involving thin trails
of slip trailed across the body of a piece.

Slipware Earthenware decorated with
designs trailed in or incised through slip.

Stilt mark The mark left on the base
of some pottery by supports used
during firing.

Stipple engraving A technique of
decorating glass with designs made up of
incised dots of varying density, giving an
appearance of light and shade, and a
much richer effect than line engraving.

Stoneware Non-porous pottery, a
hybrid of earthenware and porcelain,
made of clay and a fusible substance.

Studio glass One-off pieces made by
designers and glass makers in
collaboration.

Triple soufflé (blow-out) glass
A variation of mould blowing, this
method involves the overlaying of glass
in the mould and then pumping in air at
very high pressure, pressing the glass
into the recesses of the mould.

Tube-lining A form of ceramic
decoration whereby thin trails of slip
are applied as outlines to areas of
coloured glaze.

Underglaze The coloured decorative
layer applied under the main glaze.

Vase parlante A form of vase produced
by Emile Gallé, the decoration of which
includes an engraved quote from a
literary work.

Vaseline glass A cloudy, yellow and
oily-looking glass, similar in appearance
to vaseline, developed during the 19thC.

Vitro porcelain British art glass, made
from slag, crysolite and glass metal,
giving a streaked opaque green effect,
with purple veining.

Verdigris The green or bluish patina
formed on copper, brass, or bronze.

Ziggurat Stepped pyramid-shaped
pedestal of marble or onyx for small
bronze figures.

Zinc or Spelter A hard, brittle bluish
white metal, alloyed with copper to
make brass.

DIRECTORY OF SPECIALISTS

If you would like to contact any of the following dealers, we would advise readers to telephone before a visit, therefore avoiding a wasted journey.

Arts & Crafts
Suffolk
Puritan Values at
the Dome,
St Edmund's
Business Park,
St Edmund's Road,
Southwold, Suffolk,
IP18 6BZ
Tel: 01502 722211

Zarins,
12 Victoria Street,
Southwold, IP18 6JF
Tel: 01502 724569

Bronze & Ivory Figures
Greater Manchester
A. S. Antiques,
26 Broad Street,
Pendleton, Salford,
M6 5BY
Tel: 0161 737 5938

Ceramics
Rick Hubbard Art Deco
Tel: 023 8074 0368

Clarice Cliff
Dorset
Paddy Cliff's Clarice,
77 Coombe Valley
Road, Preston,
Weymouth, DT3 6NL
Tel: 01305 834945

Hampshire
Bona Art Deco Store,
Hart Shopping Centre,
Fleet, GU13 8AZ
Tel: 01252 616666

London
Beverley,
30 Church Street,
Marylebone, NW8 8EP
Tel: 020 7262 1576

Worcestershire
Rich Designs,
Unit 1, Grove Farm,
Bromyard Road,
Worcester, WR2 5UG
Tel: 01905 748214

Yorkshire
Muir Hewitt,
Halifax Antiques
Centre, Queens Road,
Gibbet Street,
Halifax, HX1 4LR
Tel: 01422 347377

Decorative Arts
Hampshire
Bona Art Deco Store,
Hart Shopping Centre,
Fleet, GU13 8AZ
Tel: 01252 372188/
616666

Lincolnshire
Art Nouveau
Originals,
Stamford Antiques
Centre,
The Exchange Hall,
Broad Street,
Stamford, PE9 1PX
Tel: 01780 762605

London
Abstract,
58–60 Kensington
Church Street,
W8 4DB
Tel: 020 7376 2652

Artemis Decorative
Arts Ltd
36 Kensington
Church Street,
W8 4BX
Tel: 020 7937 9900

Beverley,
30 Church Street,
Marylebone, NW8 8EP
Tel: 020 7262 1576

The Collector,
Tom Power, 4 Queens
Parade Close, Friern
Barnet, N11 3FY
Tel: 020 8361
7787/020 8361 6111

John Jesse,
160 Kensington
Church Street,
W8 4BN
Tel: 020 7229 0312

Sylvia Powell
Decorative Arts,
18 The Mall,
Camden Passage,
N1 0PD
Tel: 020 7354 2977

Shapiro & Co,
Stand 380, Gray's
Antiques Market,
58 Davies Street,
W1Y 1LB
Tel: 020 7491 2710

Titus Omega,
Shop 18,
Georgian Village,
Camden Passage,
N1 8DU
Tel: 020 7226 1571

Zeitgeist Antiques,
58 Kensington
Church St, W8 4DB
Tel: 020 7938 4817

Merseyside
Circa 1900,
11–13 Holts Arcade,
India Buildings,
Water Street,
Liverpool, L2 0RR
Tel: 0151 236 1282

Northamptonshire
Aspidistra Antiques,
51 High Street,
Finedon,
Wellingborough,
NN9 9JN
Tel: 01933 680196

Shropshire
Decorative Antiques,
47 Church Street,
Bishop's Castle,
SY9 5AD
Tel: 01588 638851

Surrey
Church Street
Antiques,
10 Church Street,
Godalming, GU7 1EL
Tel: 01483 860894

Wales
Paul Gibbs Antiques,
25 Castle Street,
Conwy, Gwynedd,
LL32 8AY
Tel: 01492 593429

Yorkshire
Briar's C20th
Decorative Arts,
Skipton Antiques &
Collectors Centre,
The Old Foundry,
Cavendish Street,
Skipton,
BD23 2AB
Tel: 01756 798641

Country Collector,
11–12 Birdgate,
Pickering, YO18 7AL
Tel: 01751 477481

Muir Hewitt,
Halifax Antiques
Centre, Queens Road,
Gibbet Street,
Halifax, HX1 4LR
Tel: 01422 347377

Doulton
London
The Collector,
Tom Power,
4 Queens Parade
Close, Friern Barnet,
N11 3FY
Tel: 020 8361
7787/020 8361 6111

Surrey
Julian Eade
Tel: 020 8394 1515

Dutch Ceramics
London
Pieter Oosthuizen,
Unit 4,
Bourbon Hanby
Antiques Centre,
151 Sydney Street,
SW3 6NT
Tel: 020 7460 3078

Furniture
London
Art Furniture,
158 Camden Street,
NW1 9PA
Tel: 020 7267 4324

Glass
London
Patrick & Susan Gould
Tel: 020 8993 5879

Jewellery
London
Didier Antiques,
58–60 Kensington
Church St, W8 4DB
Tel: 020 7938 2537

Moorcroft
Kent
Peter Hearnden,
Appointment only
Tel: 01634 374132

London
Rumours,
4 The Mall,
Upper Street,
Camden Passage,
Islington, N1 0PD
Tel: 020 7704 6549